BUTTERFLY
GARDENING
FOR THE SOUTH

Theona Checkerspot

BUTTERFLY GARDENING
FOR THE SOUTH

GEYATA AJILVSGI

Foreword by Chess Ezzell McKinney

Chairman, Preservation of Butterflies
The National Council of State Garden Clubs

Taylor Publishing Company
Dallas, Texas

All photographs for this book were taken by the author, using 35mm single-lens reflex (SLR) Nikon FA and Nikon 8008 camera bodies and Fujichrome 100 or Ektachrome 100 Professional film. Lenses were 35mm, 50mm, 55mm macro, and 200mm macro with various close-up rings. Supplementary flash was often used to stop wind motion or the frustrating flutter of a butterfly's wing.

Published by Taylor Publishing Company
        1550 West Mockingbird Lane
        Dallas, Texas 75235

Designed by Whitehead & Whitehead

Library of Congress Cataloging-in-Publication Data

Ajilvsgi, Geyata, 1933-
    Butterfly gardening for the South / Geyata Ajilvsgi.
        p.   cm.
    Includes bibliographical references and index.
    ISBN 0-87833-738-5: $34.95
    1. Butterflies—Southern States.   2. Butterfly attracting--Southern States.   3. Gardening to attract wildlife—Southern States.   4. n-usu.   I. Title.
    QL551.S85A35   1991
    595.78'9'0975—dc20   90-20565
                                                     CIP

Printed in the United States of America

10 9 8 7 6 5 4

CONTENTS

Janais Patch

Foreword

I am very pleased to introduce you to *Butterfly Gardening for the South*. At last, here is a remarkable, beautiful, yet practical book that fills a longstanding need for Southern gardeners. As a person with a strong commitment to butterflies and butterfly gardening, and who from childhood has had deep respect, appreciation, and love of nature, I welcome this celebration of the butterfly.

Delightfully written, *Butterfly Gardening for the South* covers the life cycle and needs of the butterfly, how to design your garden, descriptions of the butterflies you'll discover in the South, lists of larval and nectar plants, and much, much more. Geyata Ajilvsgi, through her valuable research and firsthand experience, has created a treasury of vital information that is a must for all gardening libraries—especially those that appreciate butterflies and gardens of fragrance as they relate to our rich Southern heritage. Our "flowers of the air" have never had a better champion.

Butterfly Gardening for the South is a book that you will read again and again. With its stunning color photography, this beautiful, intriguing, and brilliantly written book is destined to become a beloved and favorite addition to every Southern gardener's library—it has a very important place in mine.

Chess Ezzell McKinney
Chairman, Preservation of Butterflies
The National Council of State Garden Clubs

Giant Swallowtail

Acknowledgments

During the preparation of the text, I consulted many books, magazine articles, and other sources on several subjects dealing with butterflies as well as wildflowers, flower gardens, and gardening in general. Bibliographies of many of these sources appear in the Appendix.

This book would never have become reality without the help, advice, and enthusiastic support of outstanding experts in the fields of lepidopterology, botany, and gardening. Some of these were good friends from the beginning; some have become good friends in the making of this book. It has been a privilege to meet and exchange information with many others.

In the butterfly world I must give special heartfelt thanks to Roy and Connie Kendall and Dr. Timothy Friedlander for their friendship, hospitality, sharing of field trips, and inestimable sources of information. Appreciation also goes to Dr. Christopher J. Durden for much helpful advice and to Samuel A. Johnson, Kevin MacDonnel, and Gregory S. Forbes (Las Cruces) for sharing scrupulously compiled field notes on both the butterflies and their nectar sources.

I also wish to thank Roger Peace for sharing his firsthand experiences in the growing of various *Aristolochias*, Tim Friedlander for help with the regional map and for reviewing the butterfly descriptions, and Herbert K. Durand, Burr Williams, Benny Simpson, John Fairey, and Carl M. Schoenfeld for critiquing portions of the plant descriptions. Dr. Mike Rose was most helpful with the extreme closeup shots of wing scales. Stephen Myers and Paul Montgomery were of tremendous help in reviewing the photography section and generously shared suggestions, techniques, and their own experiences. I am especially grateful to Dr. Raymond W. Neck for a most thorough review of the entire manuscript as well as much help with ranges, scientific names, and answers to a multitude of questions. Thanks also to my friend Martha Bell for reviewing the manuscript and, as always, a most wonderful job on the landscape drawings.

Dr. William F. Mahler and Barney Lipscomb at the Southern Methodist University Herbarium were most gracious and generous, as always, with help in plant indentification.

For help in locating gardens and needed information, I extend my appreciation to Burr Williams, Sheryl McLaughlin, Martha Henshen, and Sally Wasowski, and to Patty Leslie and Paul Cox at the San Antonio Botanical Center, Doug Williams at the Houston Arboretum, and John Koros at the Mercer Arboretum. And thanks to John Thomas of Wildseed, Inc., for enough wildflower seed to

Palamedes Swallowtail

cover my entire twenty acres in Robertson County—even though it was mostly wooded.

To my friend John Meeks a special thanks for the vanloads of plants he gave me to try in the butterfly garden, for gardening advice, and for the spiritual connection to keep me grounded to Mother Earth—and to my desk—during the early writing of this book.

John Kartesz was invaluable with his research on plants for the South.

I am deeply grateful to James H. Yantis who was a constant source of advice and support during the major writing of this book.

To those of you, too numerous to mention by name, who opened your gardens to me for photographing and took the time to answer lengthy and probing correspondence and telephone calls, I offer my deepest gratitude. With your contributions and sharing, this book is surely more worthwhile than anything I ever could have accomplished alone.

Introduction

For Native Americans, the circle of life is singularly the most important symbol of our culture. For us it represents all of life with no beginning and no end, portraying the roundness of the all. Within our world, everything is of equal importance—animals, rocks, plants, the waters, the sky above, and the earth below. Within this circle of life, each being has its place and its importance. And so, as with a tree or a man, butterflies have their importance in the whole, the roundness of things, and their place to be on the Earth Mother. With this book, I share with you a small portion of the fascinating world of the butterflies, which forms one link in the roundness. I have tried to show their beauty and a few facets of their life through photographs. And I have offered suggestions on how you can bring them closer by filling their simple needs.

This book, then, is my gift to all of you who, in attracting butterflies to your gardens, come to know more of their ways and, in the knowing, recognize their place, along with our own, in the circle of life. And it is a gift to my people the Cherokee, who honor the butterfly, *kamama*, in their daily lives as they honor and respect all things in the natural world.

Butterflies are complicated creatures, and with certain species it is sheer folly to make flat, irrevocable statements about their lives. Little is known about many species, and much study must be done before any hypotheses can be ventured as to their life cycles or habitats. Even their distribution within the South is often determined by such climatic factors as unusually heavy rains, extreme droughts, uncommonly cold or mild winters, and hurricanes. Any one of those things can determine whether and where a butterfly may wander or establish a temporary colony far outside its normal breeding range. Such unpredictability only makes searching for, watching, and attracting butterflies more enjoyable.

This book is written in a nontechnical style and especially for gardeners living in Alabama, Florida, Georgia, North Carolina, South Carolina, Virginia, Tennessee, Louisiana, Mississippi, Arkansas, Oklahoma, and Texas. Texas, where in its wide expanse of almost 270,000 square miles come together many climatic zones, geologic provinces, and botanical realms, has no equal in North America in the

Left. Giant Swallowtail
Above. Butterfly larvae consume food at an amazing rate, increasing their initial weight by as much as one thousand times.

number of butterflies, leading all other states in the United States with more than 450 species and subspecies. Consequently, I have broken Texas into five regions in order to adequately cover the state: High and Rolling Plains (region 1), East Texas (region 2), Chaparral and Rio Grande Valley (region 3), Hill Country (region 4), and West Texas (region 5). (See Appendix for map.)

So often a how-to work is so general that it is of little help or even proves worthless for a particular purpose or area. All butterflies and plants discussed in this text can be found in the South—identified by states and the five regions of Texas. To attract butterflies into gardens, the more knowledge you can glean of the life cycles of the insects, their habits, and their eccentricities, the more beneficial it will be. Also, becoming better acquainted with the butterfly itself can only deepen your interest and appreciation for this insect as the beautiful and complex organism it is. It is my hope that you will enjoy what you find here and that it will be useful in creating your personal garden for butterflies. Above all, it is my wish that butterflies will bring some small measure of beauty and wonder and a sense of oneness into your life.

BUTTERFLY GARDENING
FOR THE SOUTH

American Painted Lady

CHAPTER ONE

Understanding the Butterfly

Butterflies, along with moths, are easily differentiated from all other insects. They belong to the order *Lepidoptera*, a name made by two Greek words combined to mean "scale winged," which aptly describes their most obvious feature. The wings, as well as the body, are almost always entirely covered with flattened scales. In some instances the scales covering the body are long and silky and appear almost hairlike.

In most respects butterflies and moths are quite similar, but there are four characteristics which usually separate them. In almost all species of butterflies, their antennae end in a club or swelling at the tip, while the antennae of moths are slender or feathery, but rarely clubbed. Also, butterflies generally fly during the day, while moths fly primarily at night. However, with the moths there are numerous exceptions to the generality, with many flying about during the day. Another telltale characteristic is that butterflies usually rest with their wings closed and held vertically over the back. Exceptions to this are when they are basking, when they may spread their wings flat, and the skippers, which frequently rest with their wings half spread. On the other hand, most moths rest with their wings outstretched and held flat against the surface on which they are resting, or drawn back tightly along the sides of the body. Last, as a general rule, moths form a tough, silken cocoon in which to pupate. Butterflies more often form an unprotected chrysalis in the open.

3

Life Cycle

In their life cycle, butterflies go through four distinct stages, together known as the complete metamorphosis. These stages of growth are the embryo stage (egg or ovum), the wormlike growing stage (caterpillar or larva), the mummy-like transition state (chrysalis or pupa), and the winged reproductive stage (adult or imago).

Normally the eggs are laid by the adult on or near the food plant which will sustain the larvae upon hatching. The eggs are almost always left unattended and will usually hatch in a few days. In some species the eggs are left to overwinter, and in some rare cases they will not hatch for two years or more.

The egg is very soft when first laid and is attached firmly to the food source with a sticky, gluelike substance. Slowly, the egg takes on its particular form and color as the shell dries and hardens. The shape is usually characteristic for the species, and under magnification each egg manifests its own beautiful markings and coloring. It may be round, domed, flattened, elongated, or shaped like a minute barrel, urn, pincushion, spindle, or sea urchin. The surfaces of the egg may be pearly smooth or elaborately sculptured with raised or sunken ribbing, horizontal furrows, pits, grooves, knots, spikes, or other ornamentations. Eggs of the Cabbage White (*Artogeia rapae*) are fat yellow cones with intricate lengthwise striations. The Pipevine Swallowtail (*Battus philenor*) lays large, reddish-brown, almost perfectly spherical eggs, while the eggs of the Guava Skipper (*Phocides palemon*) resemble beautifully ribbed and flattened turbans.

The female of each species instinctively chooses the exact food plant on which to deposit her eggs, using an intricate detection system which involves sight, feel, taste, and smell. Many butterflies lay their eggs singly, but others attach several in a single layer or in clusters of up to five hundred to the underside of a leaf. Depending on the species, a female may lay between one hundred and two thousand eggs during her lifetime.

Immediately upon hatching, the young caterpillar eats all or a portion of the eggshell as its first meal, thus gaining vital nutrients which have been passed on from the mother. Evidently this is extremely important to larvae, for many will not survive if they do not do so. The caterpillar then begins feeding on the leaf or flower it is on. In this nutritive stage of the larva's life, its entire purpose is to eat—and eat it does. As it grows it ravenously consumes food at an astonishing rate. By the time the larva has finally become satiated, it may have increased its weight by as much as one thousand times.

Some larvae, such as the Common Sulphur (*Colias philodice*), are carnivorous in the sense that they consume eggs or already formed chrysalids along with foliage if they happen to be attached where the caterpillar is feeding. The larva of another butterfly, the Harvester (*Feniseca tarquinius*), eats only aphids for its food.

Above. Eggs of the Pipevine Swallowtail

Above right. The eggs of the Guave Skipper resemble turbans.

Right. Some butterflies may lay hundreds of eggs in one cluster on the undersides of foliage.

Variegated Fritillary

Zebra Longwing

The skin, or exoskeleton, of a caterpillar is incapable of stretching, so to grow any larger, a caterpillar must shed the old, too-tight skin for a new one. Through a complicated process, the skin splits and the larva emerges with a totally new skin. At first the new skin is much too large, but as the larva continues to eat, the skin eventually becomes stuffed to bursting again and repeats the process of splitting down the back; the larva emerges with yet another loose skin to fill up. Changing skins is called molting. After each molt the old skin may be abandoned, but it is more commonly eaten by the caterpillar.

A larva will go through this process several times, the number of molts varying with the species. Most Hairstreaks and Blues (*Lycaenidae*) molt only four times, while many of the Metalmarks (*Riodinidae*) change skins from six to nine times. The period of a larva's life between each molt is called a stage or an instar, and the new skin of each instar is often colored and patterned differently from the last one.

At the end of the last instar, the larvae of many butterflies spin a small pad of silk on a stem or a branch and attach themselves to it. Others pupate in silk-lined

Above. Cloudless Giant Sulphur

Right. Cloudless Giant Sulphur

leaf-nests made from their respective food plants. During this transformational phase, sometimes requiring several hours, the caterpillar slowly undergoes a complete change inside the skin and eventually sheds the skin to emerge in a totally different shape—as the chrysalis or pupa. In this form it will remain, immobile and helpless, for several days or months. During this period of its life, the butterfly is open to attack by all sorts of enemies, such as ants, parasitic wasps, birds, and lizards. It is only natural, then, for the caterpillar to seek a protected place when the time comes to pupate.

When the appropriate, species-specific time is completed, yet another change takes place within the pupal case. The cells multiply, change, and rearrange themselves into the various parts of the soon-to-be adult butterfly. The pupa changes color, with its outer skin becoming almost translucent and the wing colors of the butterfly being visible inside. After finally splitting the pupal shell and freeing its head, the butterfly uses its legs and contortions of its body to free itself. It slowly pumps fluids into the veins of its crumpled wings until they are completely expanded; then the wings dry into their beautiful colorings and patterns.

7

The Body of the Butterfly

The body of a butterfly is separated into three main divisions: the head, the thorax, and the abdomen. The head bears the principal sense organs. Two of the most obvious are the pair of antennae projecting from the top of the head. Each antenna is composed of short joints or segments, with the segments near the tip being larger and causing the antennae to appear knobbed or clubbed. The antenna is quite moveable and is used for balancing, touching, hearing, and tasting. It also has most of the main detection sites of smell situated in the tip. At the base of the antenna is an organ used for orientation, especially while flying.

Enormous, almost hemispherical compound eyes are just below the antennae. They are among the most complex and intricately designed mechanisms used by animals for seeing. The shape, structure, and position of the butterfly's eyes enable it to see in all directions except directly beneath its body. They are called compound eyes because they are actually made up of thousands of honeycomblike facets—between two thousand and twenty thousand facets, depending on the species. Instead of seeing a single light image or object, the butterfly sees a separate image with each tiny facet, making thousands of images. These images are then integrated by its brain into a mosaic picture.

The butterfly does not have long-distance vision and depends on the sense of smell for detecting odors beyond its immediate vicinity. Its eyes are well suited for detecting any type of nearby movement, however—butterflies of the opposite sex as well as their numerous predators. The eyes are fixed and cannot move, rendering the insect unable to keep objects approaching it in focus. Instead, as the butterfly nears an object (or the object nears it), images move toward the inner part of each eye, with the visual angle decreasing.

The spectral or color range visible to the butterfly extends from ultraviolet through yellow-orange and red, fully covering the visual spectrum of humans as well as that of other insects. This gives the butterfly the broadest spectrum of color vision known to exist in the animal kingdom.

Recognizing more colors gives the butterfly advantages for communication, feeding, and protection. Besides the colors visible to us, a butterfly's wing may reflect a little or a lot of ultraviolet to another butterfly. This ultraviolet coloring plays an important role in courtship and mating. Also, since vegetation generally absorbs ultraviolet light, reflection from the flowers and foliage serves to maximize color contrast, aiding the butterfly in plant identification.

Also on the head, situated below and extending upward to the side of the eyes, are two soft, furry or scaly palps. These palps are sensitive receptors which test the suitability of the food source and also protect the mouth and the tongue-like proboscis. The proboscis is divided into two grooved parts or half-tubes which are separated when the butterfly first emerges from the pupal shell. The butterfly must spend several minutes twisting and writhing the parts to securely fasten them together by the interlocking spines along the edges of each half. This

The courtship of the Buckeye

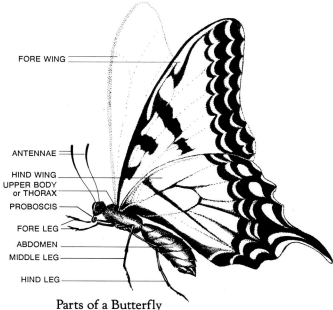

FORE WING

ANTENNAE
HIND WING
UPPER BODY
or THORAX
PROBOSCIS
FORE LEG
ABDOMEN
MIDDLE LEG
HIND LEG

Parts of a Butterfly

tongue, which now forms a long, hollow tube much like a drinking straw, can be rolled up tightly or unrolled at will and is used to suck up liquid food. Some species of butterflies also have, near the top of the proboscis, thick, tubular organs for tasting.

Behind the head is the thick, muscular thorax, divided into three segments and bearing six legs and four wings. Each segment of the thorax has two jointed legs, one on each side of the body. In some, species, however such as the brush-footed butterflies, the legs on the first segment are undeveloped, held close to the body, and rarely used, causing the butterfly to appear to have only four legs. The last portion of each leg consists of five tiny segments which form the foot, and one of the segments ends in a pair of claws. These feet possess organs which enable the butterfly to taste its food. This tasting with the feet triggers an automatic reflex action which causes the proboscis to uncoil. In some instances, the female uses the clawed feet to scratch the surface of plant leaves and stems, testing the chemical content to determine if it is the proper plant for depositing her eggs.

Above the last two pairs of legs on the thorax are the four wings. Each butterfly wing consists of two delicate membranous sheets with an inner framework of veins between the layers. This venation helps strengthen the wings and is in a distinct pattern for each species. This makes for an important tool in identification. The membrane of the wings is usually transparent, but in most butterflies it is completely covered with thousands of tiny, flat or hairlike scales of various shapes and colors. These scales, shingled in overlapping rows, provide insulation from the cold, protection from rain or dew, and help in flying. They are extremely fragile; if you touch the scales, they will readily adhere to your fingers, appearing as colored dust.

9

The third portion of the butterfly's body is the abdomen, which consists of eleven segments, although only seven or eight can readily be seen. The abdomen is very soft and contains the digestive and reproductive organs. At the tip of the abdomen of the male is a pair of grasping organs used to clasp the female during mating. The abdomen of the female is usually much larger than the male's due to the large mass of unlaid eggs.

The Butterfly's Courtship

The butterfly searches for a mate by either perching or patrolling, and almost always it is the male who does the courting. In perching behavior, at a specific time of day the male chooses a certain place—such as a rock, a patch of ground, a post, or a particular tree branch—which offers him a visual observation point. There he waits until some moving object comes into view. Since his sight is limited to close-up vision, he must inspect everything which comes into his range of sight, be it a wasp, bird, dog, cat, squirrel, human, or a butterfly of a different species. The female of each species is naturally drawn to likely spots which the male of that species ordinarily chooses, so finding a mate is not normally a problem. If the object turns out not to be an acceptable female, the male returns to his perch to wait for the next passerby. If a male encounters another male of the same species, great exhibitions of "fighting" occur, where the two fly in close association, often spiralling upward until almost out of sight, before breaking apart and going their separate ways.

The second method used in the search for a mate is called patrolling. A patrolling male flies from one end of a selected site to the other almost continuously until a female flies into the territory. Here again, the female is genetically keyed to locate areas typically selected by the male.

The male butterfly uses a variety of ways to recognize and attract a female of the same species. One way is by color and its placement on their wings. Since butterflies see the colors humans see as well as a large range within the ultraviolet spectrum, the male butterfly sees the colors of a female butterfly's wings entirely differently from how we see them.

Scale coloration is wondrously complicated. Basically, it is of two types, pigmented and structural. Pigmented colors are actual colors, produced by a pigment within the insect itself or derived from the food plant of the caterpillar. The majority of such colors as blacks, grays, tans, browns, brownish-reds, and some yellows are forms of the chemical melanin, the same pigment which produces freckles and suntans in humans. Ivory to deep yellow colors are usually from organic dyes called flavones, which are retained from the larva's food plant. The yellow coloring of the Sulphurs and Yellows (*Pieridae*) is produced by pterines, which are derived from an excretory uric acid. While some white coloring is made from pigment, others are the result of bubbles of air. The scattering of light by transparent particles produces a white effect in the same way that snow

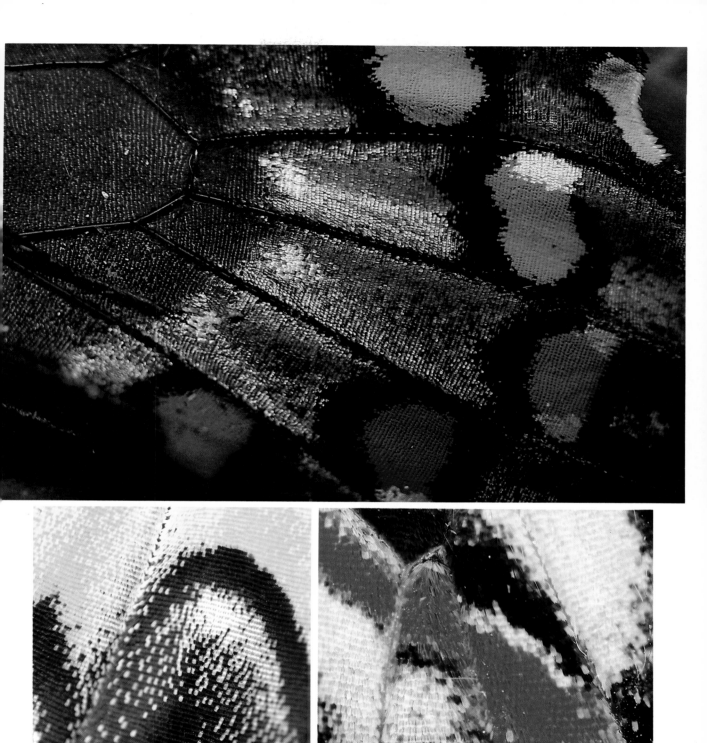

Top. The wing scales of the Pipevine
Swallowtail display a stunning iridescence.

Above. Wing scales of the Palamedes Swallowtail

Right. Wing scales of the Zebra Swallowtail

11

Left. A male Julia Skipper brushes the female
with his scent scales as part of a courtship ritual.
Above. Mating of the Great Southern White

appears white. White hair in humans is similarly produced, being created by tiny air bubbles within the strand of hair which replace the natural color, not by a white coloring substance.

Some of the most striking and beautiful colors, such as most of the blues, greens, golds, and silvers, are the iridescent colors which are due not to pigmentation but to structural features of the scales or hairs. Each scale may be ridged or grooved with microscopic striations. The colors are the result of light being reflected from these physical features, much in the same manner as light refracting off a film of oil on water produces glittering, changing colors. While each scale is of only one color, as a general rule there is a mixture of pigmented and structurally colored scales on almost every species of butterfly. On some, such as the Sulphurs, iridescence can hardly be noticed, but on the Buckeye (*Junonia coenia*) or Pipevine Swallowtail the glow and shimmer is spectacular.

Scent or fragrance also plays an important role in the selection and seduction of a mate. Male butterflies possess special scales which act as dispensers for scents called pheromones. Some of these scents gain the interest of the female, while others calm the female prior to and during the actual mating. Such scent scales are called androconia, from the Greek meaning "male dust." Some courtships involve the male performing an elaborate and prolonged dance in front of or above the female, bathing her in his perfume until she becomes settled and receptive for the actual mating.

12

Many species of freshly emerged male butterflies have a strong, noticeable fragrance, frequently comparable to flowers. The male Monarch (*Danaus plexippus*) has a rather musky, exotic scent somewhat resembling the fragrance of a wild Rose (*Rosa* spp.). The scents of other butterflies have been likened to Violets (*Viola* spp.), Verbena (*Verbena* spp.), Meadowsweet (*Spiraea* spp.), Heliotrope (*Helitropium* spp.), and even chocolate. It is quite understandable that a female would be attracted to a flower fragrance in a male, since this is a scent which also entices her to nectar.

Temperature Control

Butterflies are not as cold-blooded as once believed and described. They are able, under many circumstances, to regulate their body temperatures by an assortment of behavioral acts. They do, however, require some heat to begin operations. They are completely immobile at 40° and cannot fly well until they bring their body temperatures to at least 82°. In order to raise the temperature of the muscles which control their wings and legs, they must absorb radiation from the sun or their surroundings.

Butterflies exhibit five basic positions to obtain and regulate this heat to their body: dorsal, lateral, body, conduction, and dorsally closed. In early mornings and during cool periods, butterflies can often be seen basking in the sunlight with wings spread wide. This dorsal basking is the most common position used by most species. A butterfly basking with wings outspread in this manner snaps them together quickly if a cloud or other shadow passes over its body. This conserves heat while making the insect less conspicuous.

Lateral basking is used by some butterflies, such as the Large Wood Nymph (*Cercyonis pegala*), the Hackberry Butterfly (*Asterocampa celtis*), the Goatweed Butterfly (*Anaea andria*), and the Sulphurs. They keep their wings closed and practically lie down on their sides, exposing the undersurface of the folded wings to the full rays of the sun. This tactic also helps eliminate a shadow, which might be a giveaway to a predator.

Other butterflies are primarily body baskers, opening their wings only wide enough for their bodies to receive some of the sun's rays. In conduction basking, the butterfly chooses a rock, a large leaf, the ground, or a dark-colored twig near the ground for perching, not only to absorb the heat from the sun but also to take advantage of the heat rising from the object on which is it resting.

Butterflies are just as sensitive to excessive heat as they are to cold. On summer days when the temperature reaches over 100°, they attempt to prevent overheating by closing their wings dorsally over the back. They may also turn the head and abdomen directly toward the sun; this edge effect keeps the sun from striking on the larger wing surface and so keeps the insect cooler. If this isn't enough, butterflies take cover in a shaded area.

13

Roosting

As late evening approaches and the air begins to turn cooler, butterflies seek a resting place for the night. Apparently, the major environmental factor which initiates roosting behavior is decreasing radiation from the setting sun, for when clouds pass over the sun before an approaching storm even on a hot summer day, butterflies seek shelter and assume the roosting position.

For many species the selection of a roosting site is preceded by a short period of extremely active and erratic flight. During this period the butterfly spirals several feet above the vegetation, then dips down to a leaf or a grass blade, testing it for suitability. It usually samples several sites before finally settling on one, most often choosing a fairly stable site with no other vegetation close by which would knock the insect from its perch if blown about by high winds. Often the perch is the dead and leafless stem of an herb, perhaps chosen because such a site is not ordinarily visited by ants, one of the butterfly's worst enemies during periods of immobility.

Several different roosting positions are used; again, each species of butterfly habitually uses a certain type. Some butterflies, such as the Eastern Black Swallowtail (*Papilio polyxenes*), roost on westward-facing slopes or the outermost leaves of westward-facing plants in order to benefit from the last rays of the sun. Other butterflies, such as the Gemmed Satyr (*Cyllopsis gemma*) and some of the Wood Nymphs, choose roosting sites which are shaded from the setting sun and will therefore be illuminated by the rising sun; such sites offer earlier warming the following morning and enable the butterfly to begin feeding sooner. However, where the accumulation of dew is great, even butterflies with east-facing roosting sites have a long wait. Until the sun reaches their wings, dispelling the moisture, the insects remain immobile, unable to fly.

Some species of butterflies use sites of one type for a few nights and then switch to a different type of site. During cool spring and autumn nights, undersides of large-leaved trees such as Oak or Hickory are favorite sleeping spots for the Pipevine and Spicebush Swallowtails (*Pterourus troilus*), especially if the tree branches overhang a little-used road. Heat is trapped beneath the trees, with the temperature commonly several degrees higher beneath the branches. This extra heat provides a much warmer bed for the insects. On hot nights during the summer months, though, they seek the cooler outside tips of the upper branches.

Overwintering

Different species of butterflies have evolved their own special devices for surviving the cold of winter. In the very warmest parts of the South, many resident butterflies do not have a diapause, or winter form, so they continue to fly and breed throughout the year. On the other hand, if a butterfly of the same species lives in a colder part of the South, the adults may die and the species will pass the winter in another life stage, as either egg, larva, or pupa.

Some butterflies, such as the Mourning Cloak (*Nymphalis antiopa*), the Hackberry Butterfly, the Red Admiral (*Vanessa atalanta*), the Painted Lady (*Vanessa cardui*), and the American Painted Lady (*Vanessa virginiensis*) pass the winter as adults, tucked away behind loose bark, in narrow cracks of buildings, or in hollows of posts or trees. They are able to survive the freezing cold of winter by thickening the blood (haemolymph) with certain natural substances (glycerol, sorbitol, or alcohol) which act in a manner similar to antifreeze in car radiators. During this time of severe cold, a butterfly's metabolic rate becomes noticeably slowed; instead of continually eating, the insect is sustained mainly from stored body fats. Any period of warmth and sun, however, will see the butterfly out partaking of oozing sap, partially thawed fruit, or any substance containing amino acids.

The Monarch is an exception to all of the above methods, not being able to endure freezing in any stage of its life cycle. For its survival it migrates to the warmer climates of Southern California and Mexico, where it lives out the winter resting on certain roosting trees in areas which have been used for hundreds of years.

Long Distance Flights

Other species of butterflies migrate as well, both northward and southward and at different times of the year. The Painted Lady, Cloudless Giant Sulphur (*Phoebis sennae*), Little Yellow (*Pyrisitia lisa*), Dwarf Yellow (*Nathalis iole*), Buckeye, Gulf Fritillary (*Agraulis vanillae*), and Great Southern White (*Ascia monuste*) all migrate northward each spring, rearing many broods along the way. With the shortening of the day, some of the existing generation heads back southward, often into areas of nonfreezing temperatures; the majority of the insects do not make a return flight and are killed by advancing freezes. The ones that do return as far as the semitropical climate continue to reproduce with no winter diapause. By spring the population will have again built to such numbers that it is necessary to disperse in search of available food plants, so a portion of the population once again heads northward.

Other butterflies, such as the Checkered White (*Pontia protodice*), are notorious for long range dispersal. Dispersal movements differ from migration in being random and erratic in nature, whereas migration follows a habitual and predictable pattern. Checkered Whites show a prime example of uncertain behavior, for they may be encountered almost anywhere in the United States during one breeding season and then not seen in the same area again for several years. Also, Snout Butterflies (*Libytheana bachmanii*) may become extraordinarily abundant after drought-breaking rains and disperse hundreds of miles.

15

Dangers to Caterpillars and Chrysalids

Butterflies, as do all other living creatures, have their enemies. In the larval, plant-eating stage, one of the worst and most common pests is fire ants (*Solenopsis* spp.). This was not always so, but fire ants have spread to the extent that rare is the yard which does not have its bed or two of them. Often the ants form their mound in an out-of-the-way place, and a lot of damage can be done to larvae and chrysalids before the ants are finally noticed. Once they find a larva or chrysalis, it takes only a few minutes for a group to congregate and entirely consume the "future" butterfly. It is time well spent to walk about the yard at least once a week to check for ants. Especially look along the branches and leaves of the food plant.

First-brood larvae are especially susceptible to funguses during the early spring months, when there are many cloudy days, an abundance of rain, and sudden drops in temperature. About the only thing you can do to ensure the survival of larvae during this time is to provide an abundance of the food plant in an area protected from the late spring cold spells.

Spring rains sometimes cause plants to die due to an overabundance of moisture. In the wild this is a normal occurrence and something the larvae can cope with. Normally, they simply move to nearby areas to plants which survived the added moisture. In the garden, you may have to replant, perhaps placing the plants in a location with better drainage. Later in the year, one of the major hazards to the larvae is the dying of food plants due to lack of moisture.

Parasitization of the larvae (as well as the eggs and the pupae) by various species of tiny flies and wasps is a common occurrence. The gardener has little control in this situation. If a plentiful source of the food plant is available, there are normally enough larvae left unparasitized to continue the breeding cycle. The amount of parasitization varies from brood to brood and season to season, so don't become discouraged when it happens.

Perhaps the most often noted predation of butterfly larvae is by birds. Caterpillars are the staple food of young birds in the nest and are eaten quite readily by adult birds as well. Larvae have evolved various methods of protection from birds, the most common being camouflaged coloration, spines, and un-palatability.

Dangers to Adult Butterfly

Even after butterflies have emerged and are on the wing, their lives are still fraught with many dangers. The first broods to emerge in the spring are suscepti-ble to late freezes and sudden thunderstorms. The insects can sometimes survive by finding a crack beneath tree bark or by snuggling low to the ground among dried grasses in order to escape freezing temperatures.

They are not so lucky during really windy rainstorms. During turbulent weather, adult butterflies most commonly seek shelter beneath large leaves. If

An Assassin Bug threatens a Northern Hairstreak.

high winds accompany the rain, the leaves are turned over, exposing the butter-flies to the driving rain. Also, the wind often loosens the butterfly from its hold on the leaf, forcing it to the ground, where it is either drowned or beaten to death.

During the summer months the single most common disaster to butterflies is the loss of their nectar food plants. Nectar sources frequently die due to drought, mowing, or herbicides. Also, a poorly planned garden which leaves a gap when no plants are in flower usually results in either the butterflies dying or their seeking food elsewhere.

Praying mantids, various spiders, carabid beetles, tiger beetles, assassin bugs, stink bugs, robber flies, dragonflies, lizards, green snakes, and birds all readily feed on butterflies. Birds frequently catch butterflies on the wing; other preda-tors lie in wait or stalk the nectaring insects. The large webs of the orb-weaving spiders are another great hazard to butterflies on the wing. Nighttime predation by such animals as mice, raccoons, opossums, and flying squirrels is a major cause of mortality in some species. During the roosting period the butterflies are quiescent and totally defenseless against any kind of disturbance.

Early freezes in the fall take a toll on the adult butterfly population. Some manage to survive the cold by hiding in well-protected spots and will be seen on

17

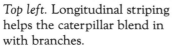

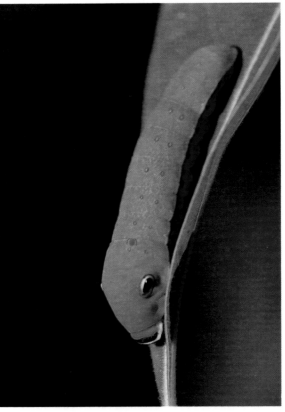

Top left. Longitudinal striping helps the caterpillar blend in with branches.

Top right. The vivid green coloring of this Cloudless Giant Sulphur larva enables it to match foliage.

Above. This Swallowtail larva actually resembles a snake's head.

Right. Swallowtail larva

the wing for several weeks after the first frost or two. With the exception of the species which migrate or diapause, extremely cold weather eventually kills both the nectar plants and the butterflies. And it is not uncommon for larval food plants to be killed before the feeding larvae reach a stage in which they can overwinter successfully.

The Butterfly's Methods of Protection

Eggs, once they are laid, are at the mercy of the weather, parasitic wasps, and predators ranging from beetles to birds. The best the mother butterfly can do to protect her future young is to conceal the eggs as well as possible and to choose a well-protected place on or near a healthy food source. Commonly, eggs are of a light color, either whitish, greenish, or pale yellow, and are generally deposited on the foliage. Eggs laid at the base of a leaf or along stems often become much darker in color after a day or so, blending more readily with their surroundings and becoming less conspicuous to predaceous eyes. Some butterflies use the tactic of wide dispersal of the eggs as a measure of safety, laying only one egg per plant on widely separated plants. Other butterflies use the tactic of overabundance, laying a hundred or more eggs in one cluster.

The most vulnerable period of a butterfly's life is during the larval or caterpillar stage, and it is then that greatest mortality occurs. The extent of their built-in defenses against diseases is not known, but their obvious weapons against predator attack are numerous.

As with eggs, concealment is one of the major visual defenses for caterpillars. They are often pale green, as in the case of the Cabbage White and the Lyside (*Kricogonia lyside*), and remain immobile and hidden beneath a leaf except when feeding. They may be spotted, blotched, or striped to blend with the stems and branches of their food plants. The longitudinal pinkish and reddish-brown striping of the Buckeye makes it practically indistinguishable from the brownish striations of the branches of Gerardia (*Agalinis* spp.), one of its food sources.

The art of appearing as something else is one of the most fascinating strategies evolved by larvae. The first instar larvae of some of the Swallowtails (*Papilionidae*), the Viceroy (*Basilarchia archippus*), and the Red-spotted Purple (*Basilarchia astyanax*) appear as nothing more than fresh bird droppings and are overlooked by all but the most observing eye. The instar larvae of some of the Swallowtails such as the Spicebush, Tiger (*Pterourus glaucus*), Two-tailed Tiger (*P. multicaudatus*), and Palamedes (*P. palamedes*), have large, conspicuous eyespots on the humped thorax which give the frightening impression of a snake's head.

The Red Admiral, Painted Lady, and Variegated Fritillary (*Euptoieta claudia*) use silk to form a leaf or flower nest in which to hide. They eat, rest, and occasionally even form the chrysalis within these nests. Caterpillars of the Theona Checkerspot (*Thessalia theona*), Janais Patch (*Chlosyne janais*), Bordered

19

Patch (*Chlosyne lacinia*), and Mourning Cloak are gregarious in the first instars. By remaining clustered together, they are offered some protection by sheer numbers. If disturbed, they initiate a fright aspect by twitching, jerking, or rearing their heads in unison.

Larvae of the Gulf Fritillary, Zebra Longwing (*Heliconius charitonius*), Mourning Cloak, and Buckeye, among others, are covered with branched spines that, although completely harmless, appear fearsome enough to cause would-be predators to have second thoughts. The egg-laying tubes of some parasitic wasps are not long enough to reach the body of the larva because of the spines, so parasitism is not possible. The larvae of the Monarch, Queen (*Danaus gilippus*), and Pipevine Swallowtail have long, floppy tentacles which wave about menacingly when they are crawling or feeding. Swallowtail larvae possess a most formidable chemical defense—a scent gun. Molest this critter and a two-pronged apparatus suddenly springs up out of the thorax, releasing a strong, almost overpoweringly obnoxious scent. These fleshy horns, called osmeteria, are usually bright orange or reddish. To the predator attacking one of these larvae it is a double whammy: the shock of a large, bright object suddenly appearing and a totally unexpected spraying with a horrible scent.

And of course, some larvae are just plain bad tasting. Having eaten plants which contain poisonous chemicals, the larvae retain the poisons, making themselves unpalatable to predators. Such terrible-tasting caterpillars do not bother to hide. They are usually brightly or strikingly colored and remain in the open, conspicuously and confidently munching away. Birds which feed on a bad-tasting caterpillar usually do not make a second mistake.

Once the site for pupation is selected by the caterpillars and the change from larvae to pupae has been completed, the pupae are unable to move from the site. They have practically no means of defense against predation and must rely principally on shape and coloration for concealment and protection. The pupae of some species are incredibly beautiful, but, as in all other stages in their lives, their colorings and shapes are for protection. Because they are so vulnerable, butterfly pupae have evolved extremely variable shapes and colors which help them to hide from their many enemies. The pale green shell of the Monarch is decorated with a partial band of black and gold with occasional golden flecks, which blends perfectly with its leaf support. Pupae of the Gulf Fritillary and the Question Mark (*Polygonia interrogationis*) have light-reflecting silver or gold spots or splashes, which help them blend into the sunlight-and-shadow areas of the foliage. Pupae of the Janais Patch are a lovely bright yellow speckled with black. This bright coloring would be very conspicuous if placed against green foliage, but when the pupae are attached among the pale stalks of its larval food plant, they are less noticeable to predators. Pupae of the Swallowtails resemble jagged bits of wood or bark or an extension of a leaf rachis or a broken branch.

As adult butterflies are also food for a number of predators, they too have evolved many different protective devices to survive. While we view the intricate

The larva of the Giant Swallowtail appears to be bird droppings.

Fierce, branching spines frighten many predators.

colors, shapes, and patterns on a butterfly's wing with awe and wonder, they have been perfected by that particular insect through a long process of natural selection for a protective rather than aesthetic purpose. One of the most dramatic protection methods is cryptic or camouflage coloration and patterning, which allow the butterfly to blend into its surroundings. Frequently, the wings have the shape or pattern of objects such as broken pieces of bark, the mottling of pebbled ground, or the ribbing and coloration of dead leaves. One of the more common butterflies exhibiting this protective resemblance is the Goatweed Butterfly. When not feeding, the Goatweed Butterfly's usual resting place is on the ground or the trunk of a tree. The tannish or light brown coloring and venation of the closed wings so resembles a dead leaf or a patch of bare ground that the butterfly seems to disappear the moment it comes to rest.

The wing edges of the group of butterflies known as the Anglewings (*Polygonia* spp.) are conspicuously angled, cut, or scalloped. The irregular wing shapes, dull brownish or grayish color, and contrasting markings obliterate their outline, helping them escape detection.

A disruptive pattern is commonly used by species such as the Zebra Swallowtail (*Eurytides marcellus*) and Zebra Longwing. When viewed alone, the sharply and distinctively striped wing pattern is readily visible, but when one of these butterflies comes to rest in dappled shade, it becomes lost among the sunshine and shadows. Large contrasting borders and bands on the Bordered Patch and the

21

Branchlike pupa of the Giant Swallowtail

Red Admiral and the broad yellow bands on the upper surface of the Giant Swallowtail (*Heraclides cresphontes*) break up the overall color and shape. With this type of disruptive coloration, the insect may be seen but is not easily recognized for what it is. Tiger Swallowtails are dramatically visible when gathered around a mud puddle or nectaring at a clump of roadside flowers, but when they glide among tree branches or shrubbery, the yellow and black striping enables them to disappear in the filtered sunlight.

Butterflies which exhibit dull or cryptic coloration on the undersurface of their wings often have a contrastingly bright upper surface. Some have prominent, eyelike spots to frighten prospective predators. Such coloring is used by the Buckeye, whose prominent eyespots are concealed by the brownish, camouflaging pattern of the undersides. When disturbed, the Buckeye suddenly opens its wings and takes off in nervous, erratic flight, startling the would-be predator with brilliant colors and large "eyes" suddenly flashed in its face.

Some butterflies have brightly colored spots or body parts which draw the attention of predators away from the vital parts of the body. The red spots on the lower wings of most of the Swallowtails and the orange-tipped upper wings of the California Sister (*Adelpha bredowii*) and the Falcate Orangetip (*Falcapica midea*) serve this purpose. Collected specimens of these butterflies often have portions of the wings missing near these false eyes, as if a bird or another predator had aimed for what it took to be the head and was left with a mouthful of wing instead.

Such butterflies as the Monarch, Queen, Gulf Fritillary, Julia (*Dryas iulia*), and Pipevine Swallowtail rely on their showy appearances to attract the attention of predators by "thumbing their noses." This warning, or aposematic, coloration is found in butterflies genuinely dangerous or unpalatable to would-be predators. These insects retain poisonous alkaloids or toxins from the larval food plants on through the pupal stage and are quite indigestible. The toxins usually cause a bird or lizard to vomit, become disoriented, and otherwise feel quite ill. Usually one taste is enough. Monarchs and Queens, for instance, feed on members of the Milkweed Family (*Asclepiadaceae*) which contain cardiac glycosides, or heart poisons. The Milkweed plants produce these chemicals as protection against herbivores, but larvae of Monarchs and Queens have developed the ability to tolerate and store these poisonous chemicals, making both the larvae and the adults poisonous to predators.

Some quite harmless and palatable butterfly species have evolved colors and patterns which mimic the unpalatable ones, thereby deriving protection because would-be predators mistake them for the bad guys and leave them alone. The perfectly tasty Viceroy has developed coloration and wing venation much like the Monarch and is hardly ever molested.

The osmeteria of the
Eastern Black Swallowtail

CHAPTER TWO

Create Your Own Butterfly Garden

As the natural habitat of butterflies is being drastically altered and in many instances destroyed entirely, there is much that the home gardener can do to take up the slack by providing these creatures with new areas where they can breed, find food, and lay eggs for future generations. In providing for the needs of butterflies, the gardener has not only the satisfaction of contributing to the continuation of the butterfly population but also the truly phenomenal pleasure of having these beautiful insects around. Also, watching the butterflies around us and trying to give them what they want sharpens our own senses of observation and awareness, so we cannot help learning something new. In such gardening, there is a constant seeking of new ideas, of new ways of doing things, and of offering new plants for the butterflies to try. It is a wonderful opportunity to keep in touch with Mother Earth and with the natural cycles of life.

Butterfly gardening can be as simple or as complex as you want to make it. For the first time you will be compelled to look at your garden through the eyes of others—the butterflies—and to consider their wants and needs along with your own. In many instances, you will let their choices be first. To truly garden for butterflies, you must ask what they would prefer and, to the best of your ability, try to provide it. Usually the butterflies' preferences can be blended in quite nicely with your own garden plans, so that the final effect is satisfactory to both.

Butterfly gardening, like any other gardening, is simply understanding and working with the land. The plants selected for your garden depend upon your ability to interpret the land as well as other environmental factors of your locale. Choose plants that not only do well in that area but also are useful to the butterflies. The purpose of butterfly gardening is to attract the most species in the greatest numbers in a given space. This has been referred to as butterfly production management and is surely descriptive of what we are trying to accomplish here. Such a management program, if carried out with care and thoughtful planning, should be most successful.

To accomplish such intensive site management, it will be necessary to know the species of butterflies that can be attracted to your garden, their larval food plants, and which nectar plants grow best in your area. From a good field guide learn everything possible concerning the local species of butterflies, their habits, and their microhabitats. No matter how intensely you want to garden for butterflies, it is better to start with the most common species which use the most easily provided food plants; then gradually work toward attracting the rarer and more exotic insects. And no matter how hard you try, you cannot attract butterflies which do not already exist in your area. It will do no good to bring in larvae or chrysalids of an exotic species, even if you also introduce their food plant, for both will only die in a matter of time. It is far better to concentrate on attracting the species already existing in your area. But don't be discouraged, for all areas of the South have several species of butterflies that are big, beautiful, and easily enticed to the garden.

Methods of Attracting

As with almost all forms of wildlife, food is by far the most significant influence in a butterfly's life. Here we are talking about two stages of life, which require two different types of food: the larval stage, where as caterpillars they eat only vegetative growth, and the adult life, where nectar is their primary food source.

In addition, we need to consider two types of plants, the "natives" and the cultivated sorts generally planted in gardens. In searching for the proper plants for a butterfly garden, you are frequently going to find plants and seeds advertised and sold as "wild, native plants and/or seeds." This is misleading, for there is a definite difference between a plant's being wild and its being native. A wild plant is any plant which has not been domesticated, meaning not having been developed from a wild plant by genetic manipulation.

The problem comes with using the term *native*. A native plant is a wild plant growing within its natural distribution. The term *native* is no longer accurate when a plant has been taken from the area where it grows naturally and is placed outside its natural range. For instance, a plant with a natural range in one state which has been moved to another is no longer a native. When moved, it then

26

A butterfly garden can be planted in the front of your house.

becomes an exotic, no different than a plant from China or Australia sold by the nursery trade and planted in the U.S. An exotic is simply a wild or domesticated plant growing outside the natural distribution of that species.

The bottom line is, if you want truly wild and native plants, then choose undomesticated plants growing in your own area. There is surely nothing wrong in having plants from anywhere in the world, but it is important to understand a plant's natural range and the correct terminology to describe it.

Two other terms frequently encountered are *escaped* and *naturalized*. An escaped plant is generally a cultivated plant found growing as though wild, not generally reproducing well or expanding in range, but found near introduced sites or along corridors. A naturalized plant is one of foreign origin which has become established and reproduces over a broad area as though a native.

In dealing with domesticated stock, the relatively new term *cultivar* is often encountered. It is derived from the words *cultivated* and *variety* and in its truest sense means that a natural variation (variety) of a native plant has been "improved." With a variation coming from an already domesticated plant, as is common, the terms *cultivar* and *variety* are equivalent.

27

You can plant your butterfly garden along a walkway.

Larval Food Plants

Plants used by the female butterfly for egg deposition and later eaten by the larvae are usually different species from the plants used as nectar sources by the adults. During the larval stage, the butterfly eats mostly vegetation. The flowers which will be so important to it for nectar later are totally useless to it now, unless of course it eats the flowers, which some species do.

The female butterfly finds plants on which to lay her eggs by rather complicated and sophisticated chemical detection. She usually flies slowly from plant to plant, hovering around the leaves or stems, "smelling" and "tasting." Often she scratches the surface of a leaf to get a better smell or taste to determine the chemical content. The odors of some plants, such as Cabbage (*Brassica oleraceae* var. *capitata*), Dill (*Anethum graveolens*), Parsley (*Petroselium crispum*), or Cherry (*Prunus* spp.), are so strong the butterflies can detect them from a great distance and have no problem finding them. Other plants, such as the thin, grasslike Swan-flower (*Aristolochia erecta*), must be diligently searched for among the tangled stems of grasses and other plants.

Some butterflies are very specialized in their larval food choices and use only one genera within a plant family as a larval food source. In other instances, only plants within a few closely related families are used. Specialization goes even further in that there are many situations where the young larvae eat only buds or young fruit; if these are not available, the young hatchlings starve to death. Other species are not so particular: More than seventy-five kinds of plants have been reportedly used by the Spring Azure (*Celastrina ladon*), and more than ninety species are supposedly used by the Gray Hairstreak (*Strymon melinus*).

Some butterflies, such as the Blues and the Hairstreaks, even though they use a wide assortment of plants, are real stay-at-homes, living and breeding within a few hundred yards from where they were born. They use only the plants available to them in that area. Not straying from their original breeding places, they form small local colonies; sometimes there is a distance of several miles to the next populated area of the same species.

For egg laying, almost all species of butterflies more readily use native plants, but occasionally the cultivated sorts are chosen—especially if the wild species are not as abundant or in as good condition. Fortunately for the gardener, many of these wild plants are attractive and add much to the overall scheme of the garden. Wild cherry, the food of the Red-spotted Purple, and Willow (*Salix* spp.) and Elm (*Ulmus* spp.), used by the Viceroy, are all popular landscaping trees. Many shrubs and vines—such as Spicebush (*Lindera benzoin*) for the Spicebush Swallowtail (*Pterourus troilus*), Flame Acanthus (*Aniscanthus quadrifidus*) for the Janais Patch, and the various Passionflower Vines (*Passiflora* spp.) used by the Gulf Fritillary, Julia, and Zebra Longwing—are attractive in the garden. Plantings of either larval or nectar food plants should be in groupings instead of spaced out singly.

Some larval food plants are seasonal, flourishing only briefly in the spring. Others may not be available until the summer or fall. Or perhaps the most commonly used or most preferred plant was killed by an early frost or is not available due to other climatic conditions such as drought or flooding. Both the season and the availability of young, tender growth greatly influence the choice of the female toward egg-laying sites. Thus, eggs may be laid on one species of plant in early spring, then eggs of the second brood may be laid on an entirely different plant as it comes into season. The Buckeye, for instance, uses Toadflax (*Linaria* spp.) and Indian Paintbrush (*Castilleja* spp.) for the first spring egg laying, Plantain (*Plantago* spp.) for the summer broods, and Gerardia for the fall broods. Not only are such diverse choices of food plants to be expected within a particular region, but some species of butterflies use different food plants in different regions. For instance, in East Texas the Mourning Cloak commonly uses Elm, but in West Texas it is more often found on the leaves of Willow, although both trees occur throughout the state. Don't be discouraged if a species which has previously used a food plant in your garden is conspicuously absent one year. This does not mean this particular species is gone from the area. Just give it time and another year—it may be back in even greater numbers. This unpredictable fluc-

A butterfly garden requires only a corner of your yard.

tuation is one of the things that makes butterfly gardening exciting. It may even be that after a while you will begin to refer to time in your garden as "the year we had so many Buckeyes" or "the year the Eastern Black Swallowtails ate all the Parsley—and the Fennel and the Dill" or "the year the Amymones were here."

Adopt a Weed

Many food plants used by larvae are the plants which can only be referred to as downright "weeds": those plants either having undesirable characteristics or with no desirable characteristics to speak of. And it is true that some of these weeds might stretch the patience of a gardener having only a little space, but there are numerous others that maybe could be given a little space in the garden "just for the butterflies." A patch of Nettles (*Urtica* spp.) may not be what you want growing up front among the Zinnias (*Zinnia* spp.), but a healthy stand of it at the back of the border and out of harm's way will ensure you of many generations of Red Admirals. Just cultivate the attitude of mind that Nettles are not really weeds but future butterflies. There will never be a bright show of flower color from

30

The lush, cottage-border approach in this garden allows the gardener to "hide" less attractive food plants at the back of the border. Antique Rose Emporium.

Evax (*Evax* spp.) or Cudweed (*Gnaphalium* spp.) either, but their nondescript leaves and flower heads form a fluffy nest for the American Painted Lady.

Conversely, some weeds, such as Woolly Croton (*Croton capitatus*), the food plant of the Goatweed Butterfly, are very attractive. The Woolly Croton can be used in a mixed border, where its silvery foliage blends beautifully with the brighter green of other plants. The ferny-leaved Partridge Pea (*Chamaecrista fasciculata*), eaten by the Cloudless Giant Sulphur, makes an interesting contrast to coarser leaved cultivated species. Many of the clump-forming native grasses become lovely accents in the flower border and are the main food source of many species of Skippers (*Hesperiidae*).

Check the list of larval food plants given later in the book and choose three or four of the weedy sort which already grow in your area. Then give some thought to adopting one or more of these waifs into your garden. If you do not want them in any of your beds or borders, then consider such areas as along and on the outside of a fence or a building. Allow them their space by not mowing them down. No special care is needed for these wildings, for they are generally extra tough, having developed under such adversities as always being unloved and unwanted.

31

Keep Them Growing

In order for the entire life cycle of butterflies to progress normally in the garden, the caterpillars must have good-quality food and plenty of it at all times. So it goes almost without saying that while it is possible to have an abundance of larval food plants and still not have butterflies, there is surely a greater possibility of attracting them to the garden if the food plants are present. This can be easily accomplished by planning ahead. Besides the trees, shrubs, and perennials which you select, seeds or potted plants of some species can be kept on hand for continual use. Parsley and Dill for Eastern Black Swallowtails can be planted every two to six weeks during the breeding or flight season by scattering the seeds in small, open areas throughout the flower beds.

Fill planters or pots with young plants and place them about the porch or patio, rotating the containers as the foliage is eaten down. After the larvae have eaten a large portion of the potted plants, the hungry little creatures can be moved to larger plants, leaving the eaten plants to form new growth. During the summer months there are practically no native plants available which Eastern Black Swallowtails can eat, so their summer broods depend almost entirely on cultivated members of the Parsley Family (*Apiaceae*). For other species of butterflies, Hollyhocks (*Alcea* spp.), Nasturtiums (*Tropaeolum majus*), and even Cabbage can be planted at regular intervals.

Occasionally pinch or trim back portions of perennials and small shrubs to ensure continual new growth. If you have several well-established plants of the same kind, trim one or two to about four inches above the ground in late summer for lots of tender fall foliage. Do not do this with a plant less than three years old, for its root system may not be able to tolerate it. Keep Dutchman's Pipe (*Aristolochia* spp.), Snapdragon Vine (*Maurandya antirrhiniflora*), Common Balloon-vine (*Cardiospermum halicacabum*), and Passionflower Vine well-watered and growing, especially during the summer months.

Become a Caterpillar Lover

A "worm" to most folks is an ugly, repulsive creature and something to be squashed immediately upon sight. This is a most unfortunate attitude, for none of the caterpillars of North American butterflies bite, sting, or spit in your eye. Not only are they perfectly harmless, but when examined closely they are among the most beautifully and intricately colored of all wild creatures. Many of them rival their final winged stage in patterning and coloration.

To develop an appreciation of caterpillars, you need to become familiar with them and be able to recognize them. If you are providing plants for the larvae in your garden, it will certainly be important to distinguish the "good guys" from the "bad guys." Unfortunately, there is not space in this book to thoroughly cover the caterpillar stage of butterflies, and at this time none of the available field guides have many photographs to help. Most guides do give descriptions of the caterpillars, but again there is a drawback. As discussed earlier, butterfly larvae go through several molts, or skin changes, and often come out with a totally new look, their dress during that particular instar. Most field guides usually describe the way the larvae look only in the last instar, which is often completely different from the earlier stages.

The best thing you can do (which is actually a fun thing to do) is to keep a small notebook with descriptions of the caterpillars you find. You could take pictures of them. Also, it is very important to know what plant a caterpillar is feeding on. Then go to the field guides and look in their indexes; nearly always there will be an additional index of plants. See which butterfly larvae feed on the plant where you found the caterpillar. Check the description of the butterfly to see if its range includes your area. If so, then you most likely have something to get excited about.

A number of butterfly larvae are easily identified as the desired ones since they feed only on very specific plants. These plants, such as the Milkweeds, Passionflowers, and Dutchman's Pipe, contain volatile oils or poisons which are usually totally unacceptable to most other insects. If you find caterpillars eating any of these plants, they are almost certain to be butterfly larvae.

Some literature would have you believe that all larvae of butterflies are a serious problem of garden ornamentals or forage crops. As a general rule it is not true. Taken as a group, neither the adult butterflies nor their larval stage could be considered pests, and they have become innocent casualties of humankind's indiscriminate use of pesticides and herbicides in its war against a few noxious insects and unwanted plant growth. In North America only the imported Cabbage White and the native Checkered White whose caterpillars feed on Cabbage, Cauliflower (*Brassica oleraceae* var. *botrytis*), Broccoli (*Brassica oleraceae* var. *italica*), Brussels Sprouts (*Brassica oleraceae* var. *gemnifera*), and other members of the Mustard Family (*Brassicaceae*), the native Orange Sulphur (*Coliza eurytheme*) which feeds on Alfalfa (*Medicago sativa*), and the Gray Hairstreak which feeds on Cotton (*Gossypium hirsutum*) could be considered real offenders.

If nothing seems to match from all the comparisons and if the larva is not doing extensive damage, you might leave it alone. If not a butterfly larva, it could possibly be the larva of some big, beautiful moth. Keep checking to see what is happening, then one day perhaps it will be in its last instar and recognizable as a really special butterfly you have been trying to attract.

Nectar Plants

Nectar plants, which attract adult butterflies, are found in both the native and domesticated (or cultivated) categories. To attract the greatest number of butterflies to your yard, do not hesitate to mix the natives with the nursery-obtained plants; in almost all instances they grow happily side by side. Be sure their moisture, sun, and drainage needs are similar.

Fortunately, cultivated plants have been genetically worked on until they have tolerance for wide differences in soils, amounts of moisture and heat, and the like. They have also built up resistance to pests and diseases which usually mean death to a wild plant planted out of its native range. You can usually use this nursery-grown stock with confidence that it will generally perform well in your garden.

There are some situations, however, where plants bred for largeness of flowers, hardiness, and so on have in the process lost their former ability to produce copious nectar. Petunias (*Petunia* spp.) are a good example. Most Petunias available at nurseries today are stocky, variously colored, early flowering, and full of blossoms—but they have practically no nectar. The Petunias of fifty years ago were rangy and mostly bluish, pinkish, or white in color, but they bore an abundance of sweet nectar butterflies would fight for.

Flower Visitation

In working out his monumental system of classification, the eighteenth-century Swedish botanist Carl von Linne (Linnaeus) found it necessary to name every plant part in order to describe plants properly and consistently. In so describing and naming, he discovered that many flowers were endowed with structures not directly associated with the reproductive aspects of the plant, yet the structures were often situated very near the reproductive parts. These structures either produced or contained a wet, sweet fluid. As Linnaeus could determine no earthly purpose for their existence, he gave the fluid the name *nectar*—the drink of the Greek gods—and the parts of the flowers producing or containing the fluid he called *nectaries*.

The original purpose of nectar production by plants is still not clearly understood, but nectar did not arise in connection with pollination. There is evidence that a nectarlike substance was produced by plants previous to the evolution of pollination and usually occurred on parts of the plant totally independent of the floral region. The type of nectar we are most familiar with today—the sweet stuff produced by the flowers themselves—is, in evolutionary time, relatively new. Flowers seemingly refined its use and placement, along with the development of pollen, as an added attraction to insects to aid in the pollination process.

Regardless of what nectar is to a plant, for butterflies it is, in most cases, their only means of nourishment. The amount available determines whether they will remain in a certain area-namely, your garden. The one thing which will draw the most butterflies to your garden and keep them there day after day is this celestial beverage, nectar. And nectar means flowers. So, for the gardener wanting to attract butterflies, it can be put in quite simple terms: flowers equals nectar equals butterflies.

So, what is nectar? Basically, it is sugar water, generally containing from twenty-five percent to forty percent sugar and sixty percent to seventy percent water. Some nectar, however, may contain as little as eight percent sugar and

Pink and purple
are the colors that
anchor these borders
of low-growing
perennials like the
vivid fuschia Verbena,
a nectaring favorite.

This sunny garden is protected from wind by a charming picket fence. Antique Rose Emporium.

some as much as seventy-six percent. Along with the sugars (the three primary ones are glucose, fructose, and sucrose or saccharose) are trace amounts of amino acids, proteins, organic acids, phosphates, vitamins, enzymes, and flavonoids. It is the flavonoids which produce the various scents of nectar.

Nectar is generally colorless but may occasionally have a slight yellowish, amber, or greenish coloring. Often it is noticeably scented or possesses a definite taste. Anyone who has broken the end from a Honeysuckle (*Lonicera* spp.) flower or a cluster of wild Verbena (*Verbena* spp.) and licked the sweet juice from along the stamens and pistil and out of the "tube" can attest to the sweetness and distinct taste of their nectar.

Nectar is such a powerful attractant that in some plants it has replaced visual attractants. Flowers yielding abundant nectar are frequently less showy or conspicuous than flowers with less nectar. For instance, the gaudy-colored, dinner-plate-sized flowers of some Hibiscus (*Hibiscus* spp.) yield less nectar than a one-inch, pale-pink Cherry blossom.

Various environmental factors, such as temperature, humidity, wind, day length, sunlight, and soil, and the health of the plant greatly affect production or secretion of nectar. These factors vary in importance for different plants and at different times of the year, making it difficult to determine optimum conditions for good nectar flow for a particular plant at any given time.

Some plants produce nectar at quite low temperatures, while others do not begin secretion until the temperature is fairly high. Many plants flowering in very early spring produce nectar when the temperature is too cold for butterflies to fly. Other plants do not open bloom until the temperature is well into the eighties or nineties. If all other factors are favorable, a general rule is a cool night followed by a clear, hot day brings the most abundant nectar flow.

Wind plays an important role in nectar production, depending upon the circumstances. Strong, cold winds are almost always detrimental, but mild, warm, drying winds after periods of rain are usually quite beneficial.

The length of daylight always affects the amount of nectar secretion, since this is an integral factor of the plant's reproduction cycle. The period of flowering and seed-set are intricately timed with day length, so the production of nectar as an extra pollination attraction during this time is very important.

In most instances, the amount of sunlight received by plants has a direct bearing on the amount of flower nectar produced. This book stresses that in order to attract the optimal number of butterflies to your garden, plants should be placed in full sun. One of the major reasons butterflies prefer the open, sunny places is that the warmth of the sun promotes greater nectar production in the flowers. Therefore, the more sun and warmth received by the plants, the more nectar produced, providing more food for the butterflies. It has been proved that in almost all situations where the same species of plants known to be readily used by butterflies are placed only a few feet apart but with some in sun and some in shade, the plants in the sun will be actively worked by the butterflies while the shaded plants will be virtually ignored. The butterflies may use the shaded plants to some extent when they are the number-one choice for nectar preference and when the plant species in the sun are not to the butterflies' liking. However, the amount of nectar obtained is not nearly as great as if the shaded plants were in the sun. Often the butterflies do not find them worth the effort of exploration.

The type and condition of the soil has a direct bearing on the amount of nectar produced and its sugar content. Such soil conditions as fertility, moisture, and pH may affect not only the growth of the plant, especially if it is a transplanted wilding, but also the secretion of nectar and its quality. A well-grown plant with lush foliage or even adequate blooming does not necessarily mean that maximum nectar secretion is taking place, nor that the nectar is of the best quality. In many instances, when a wild, ordinarily heavy-producing nectar plant is transplanted from one region to another, the nectar production is drastically lowered and the plant is hardly used by butterflies. Very little research has been done on the relation of soils to maximum nectar production and quality, so the best thing the gardener can do is to use native plants which are from as similar environments as possible, supplemented with cultivated stock such as Butterfly Bush (*Buddleia* spp.), Abelia (*Abelia* spp.), Lantana (*Lantana* spp.), and Verbena that are known to produce abundant and high-quality nectar under almost any conditions. But if you should transplant native stock, take a sample of soil and try to duplicate it as closely as possible in the garden.

The general health of a plant is important for nectar secretion. If a plant becomes stressed from lack of moisture to the point of even the slightest sign of wilting, nectar production stops immediately. With perennials, shrubs, and trees, the amount of moisture received months before has a direct bearing on nectar production. Often it is the late fall and winter rains that ensure abundant spring and early summer nectar. Naturally, a good gardening policy is to keep the plants in the best growing condition by proper fertilizing and adequate moisture at all times, even during dry winter months.

Different plants secrete optimal amounts of nectar at different times of the day, and sugar content can also fluctuate considerably. Concentration of nectar in the early morning is often very low in some plants. As the day advances, though, the intensity of sunshine, rising temperatures, or reduction of humidity may cause the sugar percentage to increase up to four times. In some cases, the nectar is the sweetest at the same time it is most abundant. With other plants, the sugar quality remains constant throughout the day, with variations in the amount of nectar produced. In still other situations, the amount of nectar produced is constant, while the amount of sugar varies. Usually the best nectar is produced at midday and is the sweetest when the sun is shining, the temperature increasing, and the humidity decreasing.

At any rate, the variability of the nectar produced and its sugar content is one of the reasons you will notice butterflies using certain plants in one part of the day, then switching to other plants at other periods. Studies have shown that in general, butterflies seem to prefer nectar with somewhat low sugar concentra-

Opposite. Antique Rose Emporium.

tions but high in nitrogen-rich amino acids. A butterfly may prefer the more diluted nectar to prevent water loss to the body; also, the thicker nectar may clog the proboscis and make the gathering difficult.

Nectaries

Nectar is produced by an area of special cells in a plant called a nectary. In most species of plants, the nectaries are located within the flower and are known as floral nectaries or nuptial nectaries since they aid in pollination. It is these floral nectaries which the butterflies are most attracted to. When these cells are situated on parts of the plant other than the flowers, such as on stems, leaves, or bracts, they are called extrafloral nectaries or extranuptial nectaries.

The floral nectaries vary widely in their appearance, sometimes being very striking in shape and color and also very conspicuous in their placement on the flower. They can be found on all parts of the flower—the pistil, the stamen, or along any part of the petals or sepals. Some nectaries are very simple in structure, others more elaborate and in the form of raised or enlarged rings or ridges of tissue, usually at or near the base of the petals.

The nectaries in short-tubed flowers, such as Lantana, Verbena, and Butterfly Bush, are situated at the base of the tube with the nectar readily available. The shorter spurred Violets also allow usage by a great number of butterflies. Here the nectar is produced by nectaries on the stamens with the stamens extending into the spur and allowing the sweet juice to flow into the spur, which acts as a storage tank or storage jug. On the other hand, flowers such as Columbine (*Aquilegia* spp.) and Larkspur (*Delphinium* spp.) have nectaries formed in long conical petals which sometimes taper to a hooked point. Only a butterfly with a very long proboscis can extract the nectar in these longer nectaries.

Although there are some instances of openly exposed nectaries, many flowers have evolved protection for the nectar. Some of the more common methods include drooping flowers, narrow tubes, and passages where water cannot enter; nectaries hidden deep within the flower; and the nectary being covered with thin flaps of tissue or a fringe of hairs. Such arrangements protect the nectar against evaporation, ensuring that it does not rapidly thicken or crystallize. They also prevent the nectar from being diluted by dew or washed away by rain. As an added measure of protection, some plants close the petals during cloudy or rainy weather and at night.

Color

As described earlier, butterflies can see in the full color spectrum. Yet, with observation it is quite obvious that some butterflies fly readily to flowers of one color while passing by an entire bed of flowers of another color. Definitely, some species of butterflies have their favorite colors. Butterflies in general find little

Above. Anemones and Dill

Right. Butterflies fly most often to flowers in purple, yellow, and pink ranges. Red flowers are also popular.

attraction in flowers of greenish-blue to blue-green color. Many butterflies use orange flowers, and others fly most often to red flowers, but by far the most favored flower colors to most species of butterflies occur in the purple, white, yellow, and pink ranges, with true blues next best.

Still, there are factors other than the colors we see which may influence a butterfly's choice of where it will dine. Many flowers possess visual guide marks or lines called nectar guides, which show insect visitors the direct route to the food. In looking over a patch of flowers, the butterfly naturally chooses the ones most clearly marked. It's much the same as if we had a choice of two places to go with the same objective at the end, but with a map drawn to one location and the other with just an address. If our reward was to be exactly the same upon arrival at either location, we would most likely choose the one with the easy-to-follow map. Butterflies are no different, and many flowers have developed such maps. Sometimes these routes are very conspicuous to our own eyes, but in other cases they are marked in the ultraviolet range of colors and are visible only to the butterfly.

41

The guide marks used by some flowers are in the form of a ring of a lighter or darker color at the base of the petals, such as seen in the Morning Glory (*Ipomoea* spp.), Frog-fruit (*Phyla* spp.), Blue-eyed Grass (*Sisyrinchium* spp.), Phlox (*Phlox* spp.), and Verbena. Other flowers, especially the tubular ones like Gerardia, Desert Willow (*Chilopsis linearis*), Lemon-mint (*Monarda citriodora*), most Salvias (*Salvia* spp.), and Penstemons (*Penstemon* spp.), have developed elaborate patterns of dots, splashes, and straight lines on the lower portion of the corollas that point to the nectar source. Still others are conspicuously marked with contrasting lines, as in the Spring Beauties (*Claytonia virginica*) and Violets.

In many instances, flowers which appear solidly colored to us are distinctively patterned to a butterfly. Again, as in the patterns on a butterfly's wing, ultraviolet plays a role. These ultraviolet patterns are more common on the flowers than the patterns we can see. A number of flowers have a combination of nectar guides, both ultraviolet absorbing and visible to us.

The large blotches at the base of petals and on the flower portion or lip of some tubular flowers also act as a visible landing platform for the butterfly. For the insect, this mark is an attraction, but it must be investigated a little further. With the scent-sensitive tips of the antennaes the butterfly probes, and with the feet it taps the petals, until all senses tell it, "I am standing near sugar." Out rolls the proboscis, and the butterfly begins to imbibe the sweet juices.

Fragrance

In locating nectar, butterflies use the fragrance of flowers as much as or more than the visual markings. In fact, tests have shown that scent marks on flowers are more common than visual marks. The ultraviolet and the other visual marks are specially scented, and even flowers which bear no visual nectar guides at all usually have the approach to the nectar marked by an odor guide. Often these scent marks smell quite different from the other parts of the flower. Even the food source itself, nectar (and in some instances pollen), as well as the nectaries are also usually distinguished by a stronger or entirely different scent. This is the reason you can smell a flower once, but with the next whiff it smells a little different. After a few intakes of the fragrances, your brain combines them all. From then on, the combination of these scents is what the flower smells like to you.

After pollination, both the fragrance and the color of the nectar guide change. This can be easily observed by comparing a freshly opened Bluebonnet (*Lupinus* spp.) or Red Buckeye (*Aesculus pavia*) flower with one which has been open long enough to be pollinated. The formerly white, pleasant smelling nectar guide of the Bluebonnet loses much of its fragrance and becomes reddish. The once strongly aromatic guide of the Red Buckeye becomes almost scentless and changes from a striking yellow to a dullish red. These scent and color changes act almost as warnings to insects that the flower has been pollinated and does not want to be bothered anymore. It is now busy making fruit—not nectar.

A flower's shape affects
nectar gathering.
Unicorn-plant
(*Proboscidea parviflora*)

Flower Shape

One important factor to a butterfly selecting flowers on which to feed is the flower shape. Some flowers may be abundant nectar producers, but, because the nectar is situated at the bottom of long tubes or covered by stiff flaps or hairs, the nectar remains unavailable to all except butterflies possessing very long tongues. This inaccessibility definitely limits the number of species which can make use of such flowers.

The actual size of the flower, in most instances, is also important, as is its formation on the stem. The large trumpets of Morning Glories are usually worked by the larger, longer-tongued Swallowtails and Fritillaries. However, because the flower throat is widely spreading, some of the longer-tongued Skippers alight on the rim, then crawl deep within the blossom until the proboscis can reach the nectar. Long-tubed flowers of Salvias and Penstemons, which are arranged vertically along the plant stem, make nectar gathering difficult and are mostly used by the larger butterflies which do not alight but feed while continually beating their wings.

The size of the flower clump is also significant in a butterfly's nectaring choice. A few solitary flowers, no matter how rich in nectar, are rarely as attractive as a cluster of numerous smaller flowers. While butterflies are forced to take nectar where they can get it, their preference is toward a large supply easily obtained. Small, short-tubed flowers with wide, flat rims, with the flowers grouped in clusters, and with many clusters on the plant are ideal. Flowers in the *Phlox* and *Verbena* Families are good examples, and almost any species from either group never fails to attract the butterflies. Many members of the Sunflower Family (*Asteraceae*) are excellent, as are most plants of the Parsley Family. Such a flower arrangement provides a good perch for the insects while taking nectar, and the close clustering of the flowers saves much-needed energy which would otherwise be spent in flying from one solitary flower to another.

Other Attractants

Not all butterflies are attracted solely to flower nectar, readily partaking of the liquid from such things as tree sap, honeydew, overripe or rotting fruit, dung, carrion, and mud. Natural nectar, sap, and overripe fruit contribute much-needed protein to their diets, while dung and carrion provide amino acids. Salts, especially necessary to the males of some species, are normally received from mud puddles or the edges of streams, bogs, or seeps.

In order to get the species more attracted to these types of fluids into a chosen location, it is necessary to garden a little differently. Fortunately, it is not costly and can be quite easy. Since a tree which exudes sap is generally an injured or diseased tree, I do not recommend trying to furnish this particular substance as an attractant. The butterflies which feed on tree sap readily take other liquids which can be more easily provided by the gardener.

In place of natural tree sap, try the process called sugaring. Make an elixir irresistible to butterflies by combining in a blender one can of beer, one pound of brown sugar, approximately one-half cup of dark, strong molasses, and some very old fruit of some sort. Overripe bananas—the mushy kind with black skins—and very soft, squashy peaches are wonderful. Instead of (or in addition to) the beer, some rum can be added; if neither of these is available, add a dash of artificial rum, banana, or peach flavoring. Leave this mixture thick enough to spread but with as much liquid as possible—remember, it's the liquid the butterflies are after. Let the concoction ferment for half a day (or overnight) in an uncovered container, then brush it onto tree trunks or posts, placing it from ground level to shoulder height. Even better, pour it out into a large, shallow dish and place it on the ground. The Goatweed Butterflies, Hackberry Butterflies, Buckeyes, Question Marks, Red-spotted Purples, and Satyrs (*Satyridae*) generally go crazy over the stuff. If there is a wooded area near or adjacent to the flower garden, spread some of the bait on a log or stump in an opening with dappled shade. Then watch some of the less common species, such as Wood Nymphs and Satyrs, gather in mixed groups to sample the feast.

Cherries attract this Goatweed Butterfly.

For the fruit-drink lovers who prefer the "real thing," it is a simple matter of choosing a spot in the sun or a semishaded area of the garden and placing fruit on the ground. Overripe or damaged fruit can often be obtained quite cheaply or for free from grocery stores or fruit stands. Peaches, bananas, pears, and both wild and cultivated plums and persimmons will be considered quite tasty. Tawny Emperors (*Asterocampa clyton clyton*), Hackberry Butterflies, and the Goatweed Butterflies especially love pears and persimmons and often congregate by the dozens to feed on the fruit. Occasionally, Monarchs and Gulf Fritillaries can even be found enjoying the juice. Watermelon rinds with their juices are well liked by several species. Place thick sections or halves in dishes, or bore holes in the sides and hang the fruit by wires or strings from low limbs of trees.

Crushed grapes or berries mixed with a small amount of honey or old molasses and allowed to begin fermentation are very well liked. A bit of added beer or rum draws an even larger crowd. The sippers apparently cannot get enough of this tasty brew and will crawl around the fruit, fluttering their wings erratically.

An excessively juicy mixture is best piled in a shallow, earth-colored pottery dish and placed at the open edge of a flower border. Have several dishes scattered about the garden for best results. If you notice that some of the dishes are not being used, move them to other locations until the butterflies find them.

Place fruit bowls at the open edge of a flower border.

If the fruit is to be placed in the flower border, be sure the area is sufficiently large for the butterflies to feed. Since they are eating on the ground, the feeding space needs to be large enough and clear enough to allow them a quick takeoff in case of danger. Provide an area completely free of plants no smaller than three feet by five feet. If you have provided a basking area, one end of this will do quite nicely as a feeding area.

Some butterflies do not regularly use the true nectar produced by flowers yet commonly feed on a substance which greatly resembles nectar in appearance. This is honeydew or leaf honey, the sweet, sticky substance often found covering the surfaces of tree leaves, your car, and lawn furniture during summer months. It is a tree sap by-product extracted by aphids, scale insects, and leafhoppers. Butterflies such as the Hackberry Butterfly, the Emperors, Mourning Cloak, Snout, and Painted Lady all feed on this "false nectar."

Manure to be used in your flower beds can be piled in a sunny, out-of-the-way corner of the garden for the nourishment of certain species. Try to put the pile where it can be watered frequently, as it is only the liquid the insects seek. The amino acids provided by manure sometimes draw butterflies by the dozens. You can even use raw meat that has gotten too old for table use.

Zebra Swallowtails puddling

Groups of butterflies are often seen feeding at the margins of small puddles or excessively moist areas. Sometimes they congregate in large numbers; sometimes there will be only two or three. The grouping may be of only one species or of a mixture of several species. In almost all instances, the group contains only males. Occasionally, a female will join the group but usually neither stays as long nor appears as interested in the available liquid.

The communal gathering of butterflies at such areas is aptly referred to as a drinking club or a puddling club. Once a butterfly discovers an especially attractive site, others passing by notice the action and stop to join. Once the insects begin their drinking, they become so absorbed in the process they can be easily approached.

The habit of feeding at puddle margins is not necessarily related to water requirements: the insects are seeking salts or amino acids. Frequently, the puddles or moist areas are from water contaminated or polluted by dung, urine, or dead animals, which provide the nutrients needed by the insects. The importance of these salts to butterflies is evident in their continuing to probe certain puddles long after the soil has become almost dry, instead of visiting areas of fresh, uncontaminated water.

47

To provide these salts which the butterflies seem to love so much, you can construct a simple salt and sand area. Begin, as with placing fruit, by choosing an open area of your flower border or an area close by. Be sure to position the area where it can be kept moist. If you plan for the puddling area to be in a border, provide an area large enough and open enough. The next step is to construct a form of short 1- × 2-inch boards in whatever shape you desire to form a corral-type area approximately 2 × 2 feet. The boards may be laid on top of the ground, or the earth may be scooped out and the top of the boards placed flush with the ground. The boards do not have to be nailed together if placed in the ground.

Line the form with heavy plastic, cutting to fit the top of the frame. White plastic is less unsightly in case rain should expose the edges. The plastic helps keep the sand moist as well as keep the salt out of the soil around nearby plants. Fill the form with sand, the kind sold at lumberyards or concrete-mixing places. After placing the sand in the form, water it down; add more sand if needed after settling. Next, sprinkle table salt over the top of the sand, mixing it in well, then barely wet it down again. Rock salt may be sprinkled on the sand before you completely fill the form with another inch of sand sprinkled over the salt. Do not make the area overly salty: a ratio of approximately one-half to three-fourths cup of salt to one gallon of sand should be about right. A bit of manure sprinkled over the top will make it even more attractive.

For the salt to be used by the butterflies, it must be available in the form of liquid. Therefore, the sand bed must be kept moist at all times. If you have a drip system in your garden, the ideal placement of the sand bed is with the bed near one of the drip emitters. Instead of the usual emitter, insert a length of small tubing which reaches the center of the sand bed. Attach the emitter to the free end of the tubing and place near the center of the sand. Cover the tubing and emitter with sand, if desired. Also, the sand bed can be built under or around a faucet (if the faucet is in a sunny location) left barely dripping.

If there comes a time when your yard suddenly seems to be without flowers for one reason or another, butterflies often come to artificial feeders. An easy way of making flowerlike feeders is to wire a long, slender medicine vial to a strong stick or a stiff wire. Fill the vial with a solution of one-half teaspoon of honey, one-half teaspoon of sugar, and a heavy dash of salt in one cup of water. Plug the vial with a cotton stopper, making sure the cotton touches the solution yet protrudes slightly beyond the rim of the vial. A collar of paper or stiff material wired just below the cotton makes a nice landing place for the insect, with the added attraction of color. The colors purple, yellow, pink, and blue are probably the most effective in attracting butterflies to the feeder, since these are the colors they seem to prefer in natural flowers.

Push the stake or wire into the ground, ideally among the foliage of plants just finished blooming; butterflies, being creatures of habit, are more likely to come back to a place where they have been gathering food than to go to an entirely new and unfamiliar place. Artificial food sources are also more successful if placed in a group than if scattered about.

For added enticement, stopper one vial with only the cotton ball; do not add the petal material around the rim. Instead, of the regular feeding liquid, add a drop or two of a flower fragrance such as Honeysuckle, Jessamine, Violet, or Orange Blossom on the cotton stopper. If possible, use a natural-fragrance oil. The fragrance will be a lure in addition to the liquid in the other vials. A warning here: *Never* under any circumstances, should this fragrance be added to the feeding mixture, as it could do irreparable damage to a butterfly's digestive system.

This same honey and sugar water mixture can be placed in a small plastic carton with an orange or yellow plastic scrubber stuffed in the top. Push the scrubber down firmly and far enough that the butterflies have a steady place to perch and also have no trouble reaching the liquid with the proboscis. Place the cartons about the garden in groups, preferably near flowering or previously flowering plants. One of the fragrance vials just described is useful as an attraction here, also. If ants become a problem, place the carton in a round plastic pan (generally like that used beneath potted plants) filled with water, or set several cartons in a large, shallow container filled with water.

Basking

Butterflies spend a lot of time basking in the sun, and they bask more often in early spring and fall. Often, especially in the morning, butterflies can be seen resting with wings outspread, soaking in the warmth. The smaller butterflies and the skippers frequently sit perfectly still with wings outspread on the flowers from which they are feeding. Larger butterflies usually choose an exposed area in the sun for basking, such as a leaf, stick, log, or open ground.

To provide basking areas in your garden, place a decorative log or rock in a more open area of the border among the plants. A sack of pine needles or other freshly fallen leaves spread thickly over a 3- × 5-foot area, with a rock or log added, also works quite well. The dark-colored leaves readily soak up the sun's rays, providing warmth to the butterfly from below as the sunlight does from above. In placing the basking material, whether leaves, rocks, or logs, be sure that it fully catches the early morning sun. Another basking area facing the west will be welcomed by butterflies flying late in the day, especially during the cooler fall months. A convenient place for warming up will allow them a few more minutes for feeding—much needed to see them through the lengthening, cooler nights.

Hibernation

Some species of butterflies, such as the Red Admiral, Mourning Cloak, and Goatweed Butterfly, pass the winter in hibernation as adults. Cracks in logs,

Cracks in fence posts provide hibernation areas for butterflies.

fence posts, loose boards, or tree bark are all potential hibernating sites. Remember the use of such places by insects when tidying up the garden in the fall; leave them in place if not too unsightly.

If your garden doesn't have such sites, construct special boxes for overwintering butterflies. Simply tack rough cedar boards or large slabs of bark in protected places on fences or on the side of the house or garage. Place the boards or slabs vertically, leaving one side not completely nailed down, with a crack where the butterfly can wedge itself inside.

CHAPTER THREE

Your Planting Plan

The one factor that most consistently and permanently will attract butterflies to your garden is the right plant selection. To adequately and attractively provide the larval and nectar plants necessary, you must start with a plan, as you would with any other important project.

One of the bonuses of having a garden with plants that specifically attract butterflies is that, once established, the garden is easy to maintain. A gardener should enjoy the butterflies in the garden and derive pleasure from the efforts to attract them, not be bogged down with so much constant work that the efforts become discouraging and depressing. With this thought in mind, I urge you to plan your garden properly in the beginning, choosing plants specifically used by butterflies. The following pages are intended to help you plan and maintain the garden with a minimum of effort.

Know Your Area

Before ever picking up a shovel or visiting a nursery, there are a few things you should do. First, give some thought to the area in which you live. (Texans should refer to the Regions of Texas map in the Appendix.) Make notes in a sturdy notebook as to the amount of rainfall, general soil type, and first and last freeze dates for your area (a local nursery or state extension office can help). Also study

51

the Zone Map for North America in the Appendix and note the zone in which you live. Such ecological factors are going to determine to a great extent the general species of flowers you will be able to grow in your garden.

After jotting down the general physiographic features of your locality, the next step is to describe what your immediate habitat is—rural, suburban, or urban. Scaling down even further, what kind of minihabitat is your existing garden or property? Is it an open yard or lawn with practically no trees or shrubs, an open area with straight borders along the property lines, a large and formally landscaped garden with shrubs, or an area of well-landscaped but informal beds? Briefly describe your present garden in your notebook. This information will give you an understanding of where you already stand as to the possibilities of attracting butterflies, and it will be a great help in formulating future plans.

To begin the actual plans for planting, take a fairly large sheet of graph paper and draw in your property boundaries. Make the outside boundaries as large on the paper as possible but in as nearly correct proportions as you can make them. The easiest and most accurate way of doing this is to refer to your land plat and original house plans. Make a note on the graph sheet of the scale you are using. This drawing will be referred to frequently, and knowing the scale is important. Sketch in the house, including porches, patios, garage, or any other attached structures. All you need here is an outline of the outside dimensions. Make heavier lines in the house outline to indicate placement of all doors and windows.

The next step is to take your sheet of graph paper, a couple of pencils, a good eraser, a long tape measure, and a buddy to hold one end of the tape and go out into the yard to continue this base model. An on-site drawing of these features is most important, for it is amazing how much you can forget when sitting inside the house. Walking about the yard, and using the tape measure at all times in order to keep things to scale, begin sketching in any existing structures such as the tool shed, swimming pool, fountain, gazebo, benches, birdbath, play equipment, walkways, walls, fences, and hedges. Sketch in all outside water faucets or outlets and include overhead (or underground) power poles, lines, or other utility structures. Continue to draw in all flower beds or borders, vegetable garden, areas of groundcover, and the like. If there are objects on neighboring properties affecting your property—buildings, trees, or water runoff—locate them on the drawing, also.

Now make a second tour of the yard and draw in all specimen trees or shrubs. On an extra sheet of paper or in the notebook, make notes about these plants. Such notes will be important when planning for the addition of butterfly-attracting plants. If some plants are not performing well where planted, perhaps they can be moved to a more desirable location or given to a neighbor, to be replaced with special butterfly plants; mark any such plants.

As you walk about making notes on the existing vegetation, also note which areas receive full sun all day long, sun only part of the day, or full shade during the growing season. The amount and areas of sun and shade are very important when planning new flower beds. Jot down notes about the soils, whether they are sand,

A butterfly garden can be landscaped in any number of attractive ways.

clay, or loam. Pay special attention to the drainage of the garden area and note any problems of erosion or water standing for long periods after rains. Make notes of excessive wind tunnels and whether windbreaks would be helpful. Locate areas of the yard which are viewed from inside the house or from much-used areas, such as a porch or patio. Mark the sight lines of objects which would be better screened or completely hidden from view, whether on your property or your neighbor's. Using dash marks, sketch in areas where new beds can be put in or already existing beds can be enlarged or extended.

If you basically like your yard and feel that you are not going to be able to add many plants to your established borders, then make as many notes as possible on problem areas about the yard. Small patches of lawn that are not doing well, small areas between the house and walkways that are hard to keep, a problem area between garage and street—all of these are potentially new areas for butterfly plants. Other such areas include those outside your fence (perhaps there is a vacant lot there), in rarely used alcoves, behind small buildings such as storage or tool sheds, or around woodpiles or compost bins. The area between the sidewalk in front of your house and the street is a possibility, but only if you live in a low-traffic area; you certainly do not want to entice the butterflies to an area, only for them to wind up in the grilles of speeding vehicles.

53

A butterfly garden can fill problem spaces in your yard.

Last, define the area presently in lawn on your map. In the notebook describe its status as to health, looks, and workability.

Before you can plan the addition of any new beds or any new plants to already existing beds, you need to know exactly what plants you have already growing and where they are. Draw a diagram of each bed on a separate sheet of graph paper, placing all the perennials in the proper spots and drawing in areas where annuals are normally used. Use the tape measure and draw all of these to scale as nearly as possible, but use a larger scale since you have only one bed per sheet and are going to need all the room you can get. This should complete the base map and give you a good guide from which to do any future planning.

Now, spend some time studying both your overall yard sketch and each individual bed with its existing plants. It is vitally important that you know where all present plantings and possible new sites are located, as this information will form the basis for decisions about the type and quantity of any new plantings.

Regardless of how much or how little you eventually decide to do in the garden, well laid-out plans, of both present and future plantings, will save much time and expense later. Such plans, while seemingly frustrating and time-consuming at first, will ensure much greater success in attracting butterflies into the area you plan to provide for them. By knowing your yard thoroughly, you will be able to place future plants in the locations best suited to their needs, guaranteeing thriving, healthy plants, which in turn means less work for you.

Later, if you should decide you need advice in further rearranging your garden or if help is needed with a serious landscaping or building problem, your scale drawing will save much time and cost in landscaping consulting fees. You might want to make several copies of your maps. Covered with a sheet of acetate or clear plastic to prevent dirty fingerprints or smudging of the drawings, they may be easier to work from if taped to a stiff cardboard backing. If you want to combine the various phases of the base plan with drawings of the beds, make each drawing directly onto a sheet of acetate. Use a different colored pen or pencil for each phase so, when you put the sheets together, you can see each phase clearly.

Decision Time

Now that you have a map of what already exists in your garden and notes and sketches of all possible places for new plants or beds, it is time to take a long, hard look at the situation and make some decisions. It is important not to get carried away in your enthusiasm here, for gardening to attract butterflies is meant to be a leisurely and enjoyable experience, not an added chore. In these preliminary stages, consider who will be maintaining the garden and how much time and effort will be spent in the maintenance. Neglected plants are not healthy plants, and it is better to have one small, glorious bed of Verbenas or Zinnias than to have two or three long borders of sickly or scanty-flowering plants which are too much trouble to take care of. Such a planting will be of little attraction or use to butterflies.

Give serious thought to the amount of money you want to spend on the garden. You will need to purchase not only plants from time to time but also watering hose, fertilizer, and perhaps mulching material and the like.

You also need to decide whether you want to plant only larval food plants, only nectar plants, or both. Studies have shown that female butterflies choose to lay their eggs in areas with abundant nectar sources, so a combination of plants will attract the most species of butterflies.

After you have made your decision as to the time and money you are willing to spend and the type of attracting program you would like, it is time to begin formulating future plans.

New Plans

As you begin redesigning your garden, try to see the finished product through the eyes of a butterfly. It is important always to keep in mind that to attract and retain the interest of butterflies, you will basically need to keep the plantings uncomplicated, uncluttered, and in masses of individual species and color.

Now, referring back to the sketches of your yard and flower beds, begin drawing on new sheets, doing as you did before, except this time drawing in the

55

actual work to be done. Again, draw to scale. First, you need to note all structures and plants to take out. Locate on your map the places for additional trees or shrubs you plan to install. If a windscreen is needed, draw it in if it is to be provided by fencing or a living hedge. Draw in any future trellises, walkways, decorative edgings, or retaining walls. If rocks or driftwood for focal interest are to be added, these should be shown on the plans, and all these to scale.

Go to the yard often while making your new plans and keep measuring. Try to visualize the final results of what you are planning to do. Use a water hose to outline new beds so you can take actual measurements to get a more realistic idea of the size needed.

Also, look at the proposed changes from inside the house to be sure you are not making irreparable mistakes. It would be most unfortunate to place a trellis in front of a window or a glass door, blocking your view of the future garden full of beautiful flowers and butterflies.

First-choice areas for any new plantings should of course be designed for maximum sunlight. The sun is the major factor around which the entire life cycles of most butterflies revolve. They choose the sunniest beds of flowers from which to gather nectar and the sunny sides of trees and shrubs on which to lay their eggs. They seek sunny areas in which to mate, and they bask in the sun to control the warmth of their bodies. They also use the sun for orientation during flight. With the major needs of the butterflies in mind, make full use of all areas of the garden where the most sun is available.

Don't expect to completely finish the plans for the garden in one try. You will want to start with a general scheme or drawings, then continue to refine them until you feel that you have the best choices and largest number of butterfly plants possible for your area and your garden.

No matter how many new beds and borders you would like to add to the garden, it is equally important to provide the butterflies with space. Butterflies like to sail and glide, to sample and soar, and must have enough room to escape their enemies. So do not fill your entire yard with tall shrubs or your beds with tall, herbaceous plants. Rather, through careful selection, create plenty of openings and an overall sense of spaciousness.

Do not be discouraged if your gardening area is small, for even the tiniest city lot has the potential for attracting and rearing butterflies. Even though the limited space means limited possibilities, if carefully planned it can still attract many species of butterflies. A look of largeness and naturalness can be obtained even in the small garden by curving the outlines of the beds and staggering the heights of the plants in an undulating fashion, rather than having perfectly straight and flat beds, which give a feeling of stiffness and formality. If you have only a small garden surrounded with a high fence, keep the beds along the fence line and leave the center of the garden open. Or perhaps add only one small, irregularly shaped bed containing low-growing flowers such as Dwarf Zinnias or Petunias bordered with Pansies (*Viola* spp.) or Sweet Alyssum (*Lobularia maritima*) toward the center of

Above. Weeping Lantana (*Lantana montevidensis*) works well in small spaces as a solid planting. *Above right.* Staggering plants for height is one option for gardens on sloping ground.

the open area. A solid bed of low, reclining Lantana or Verbena would be a real butterfly feast table yet would not interfere with their flight from one border to another.

It is worthwhile early on in the planning to visit local nurseries and garden centers to see the materials available for terracing, paths, edgings, fencing, patios, containers, and the like. Not only will this give you an idea of what you have to work with in the garden, but nurseries often will have displays with the products in use, giving you ideas for your own yard.

Should your sunniest areas for new beds be on sloping ground, you are a good step ahead, for staggering plants for height is much easier. By using plants of approximately the same height, you can create a solid, slanting sheet of color. Otherwise, the plants can still be broken up in various heights for even more interest. Any kind of boulder or piece of driftwood usually appears its loveliest when viewed from a sloping angle and blends in with this type of planting more naturally.

Slopes so steep as to cause drainage or erosion problems can be terraced. This is more trouble in the beginning, but if done properly it will be as self-sustaining after a year or so as any other type of planting. Terracing can be done with railroad ties, bricks, treated half-log edging, or stones. Use the material best suited to your house and the time and money you care to invest. The shapes of the beds should offer ease of maintenance and the best possible plant exposure to the butterflies.

57

This walled garden and the trees in it protect butterflies from strong winds.

In planning new beds or enlarging already existing ones, the question of width is important. In some instances, with a small yard you have no choice but to have somewhat narrow beds. If plenty of space is available, however, two factors should be considered. First, the beds should be wide enough to provide plenty of spreading space for both perennials and annuals. Second, the beds should be kept narrow enough for easy maintenance. Usually a bed of six to eight feet is about right. Any narrower than this, and you will have to forget about having flowering shrubs fronted with lower growing plants. Any wider, it will be almost impossible to do the necessary clipping, bug inspecting, plant division, or fertilizing that will be needed from time to time.

An alternative is to have two or more smaller beds with a very narrow walkway between them. This is an excellent idea if you are planning an extensive attracting program using a lot of beds or intend to photograph the butterflies. Make a narrow walkway by placing a simple, narrow strip of flat stones on top of the mulching material, or simply leave a walkway by spacing the plants apart.

You might want to construct paths and walkways from one part of the garden to another either for utility or aesthetics. In making the drawings, perhaps it would be better to note that paths are wanted and draw in a sketch of possible sites. Do not make any plans for actual construction of paths or walks until at least after the first season, and after the second season would probably be even better. This will give you the time and opportunity to see where the "lines of least resistance" are, which routes you naturally take in moving about in the garden. It will also give you time to see where underground water lines are needed and get them permanently installed. When installing paths, keep them simple, with thought as to durability and low maintenance.

If you have a low spot or sink area in the yard or lawn which has been a real eyesore or problem area, consider it now a blessing. Instead of trying to get grass to grow there, plan to keep the grass pulled or cut back and to keep the area deliberately wet. A flat stone or two can be placed around the edge of the area, with beer, sugar water, or honey poured on the area from time to time. This may very well become the favorite gathering place for members of the local butterfly puddle club. It may never be as alluring as the ruts of a county road after a rain or ordinary barnyard muck, but if such places are not readily available to the butterflies of your neighborhood, then your little spot may prove a much-needed substitute.

Look around your garden and note the route the butterflies will most likely take in leaving the garden. If it will be directly out into street traffic, a fence or a hedge may be required. Such a structure will force the butterflies to fly up, putting them above the traffic. Good temporary solutions are inexpensive yet attractive cane fencing, lattice panels, or tall-growing perennials or annuals. Another pretty solution is to attach chicken wire to lattice panels and then plant vines such as Passionflower, Morning Glory, or Coral Vine (*Antigon leptopus*) to cover the wire. Ideally, a combination of fencing and plants would be better, for some plants might not reach a workable height until late in the season, whereas the fencing would give immediate benefit.

Butterflies need protection from strong winds while feeding. If there is a constant strong flow across your property channeled by open fields or heavy street traffic, consider the possibility of minimizing or breaking up this flow. Use the house or another building as partial screening, extending it with lattice panels, wooden fencing, or by planting trees and shrubs. By using larval food plants or good nectar producers as the extensions, you would be serving a dual purpose here.

In redesigning your garden, give some thought to your own enjoyment of the plants you intend to grow as well as their use by the butterflies. Place some of the really fragrant plants such as Butterfly Bush, Mimosa (*Albizia julibrissin*), Bee-brush (*Aloysia gratissima*), Lilac (*Syringa* spp.), Summer Phlox (*Phlox panaculata*), and old-fashioned Petunias close to a bedroom window, a porch or patio, or the driveway. If there are particular portions of the house where you spend large portions of your at-home time, try to make the scenes from the windows or glass doors of these rooms colorful and arresting. When you have a butterfly-attracting border beneath a kitchen window but not visible from inside, hang some baskets from the roof overhang to be viewed from the window. Butterflies will fly to these as well as visit the flowers in the bed below.

If you have a large acreage with a portion naturally wooded, perhaps on the edge of town or in the country, you will be able to attract species of butterflies which rarely come to the open, sunny areas. These butterflies, while seen less often, are very beautiful, and their shyness gives them a special beauty. If the wooded area is close enough to be included in the garden planting, you are very fortunate. Even if it extends somewhat away from your already existing beds, this area can be brought closer by planting the space between the woods and the beds with choice trees, shrubs, and native flowering plants used by butterflies.

For instance, extend your woodlands with Flowering Dogwood (*Cornus florida*), Hercules-club (*Zanthoxylum clava-herules*), Sassafras (*Sassafras albidum*), Spicebush, and Red Bay (*Persea borbonia*)—all important larval food plants. In front of the trees, plant shrubs such as Azalea (*Rhododendron* spp.), Button-bush (*Cephalanthus occidentalis*), Red Buckeye, Virginia Sweetspire (*Itea virginica*), New Jersey Tea (*Ceanothus americanus*), and Lantana as rich nectar sources. Be sure to plant the vines Woolly Pipevine (*Aristolochia tomentosa*) and Passionflower.

Even if the wooded area is too far from the yard to be included in the borders and beds there, there are many butterfly-attracting plants you can use to enhance the edges of the woods. This is an excellent place for many larval food plants which may not fit into your garden scheme, yet the adult butterflies will readily nectar at your garden flowers after being reared in the wooded area.

Choosing Plants

To select the proper plants to attract butterflies to your garden, you first have to know which butterflies you can expect. You need to know the species found specifically in your region, especially in choosing larval food plants. Before you begin thinking of plants to add, look at the butterflies listed here and their ranges. Also study the larval food plant list for the region or state in which you live, for this gives a more complete listing of larval food plants for each region or state as well as the butterflies which use them.

Referring next to the plants included here and both the larval and the nectar plant lists provided, make notes of favorite nectar and larval food plants of the butterflies for your area. Study the descriptions of the plants given here as well as those in gardening catalogs; then decide which ones you would like to try. Choose more species than you can use in order to give yourself more versatility when planning the garden, for you may not be immediately able to find the exact plants you want.

If you want to begin a long-term attracting program using both larval and nectar plants but your time and energy for garden work are limited, I suggest starting with only two or three of the nectar- and larval-attracting trees and shrubs during the first year. Perhaps add one or two choice species of perennials to already existing beds or borders and fill the additional open spaces with annuals. Even if there is no space in the borders for new plants, make no more new beds than you can easily mulch and water during the summer months. Instead, continue to improve your existing beds and, as time allows, properly prepare more new beds or enlarge already existing ones.

The season in which you begin your garden greatly influences your choice of plants. Ideally, you should start your garden in late summer or early fall, but a planting for butterflies can be made at any time. If you have started your garden in either spring or summer, by the time fall arrives you will probably have an even better idea of what you want growing in the garden.

Unless you already have beds with really good, loamy soils, do not plan to set out perennials the first spring or summer. These plants are long-lived, and much thought and care should go into their placement in properly prepared, permanent beds or borders. Instead, use annuals where they can be kept growing with commercial fertilizer; spend your time making plans for putting in new beds and improving the old ones. This will also give you an entire growing season to study plants growing in your area and evaluate them as to their suitability to your site.

Also, if you are not an accomplished gardener, you do not want to waste your time and money on selecting hard-to-grow seeds or plants. For spring and summer the first year, stick to the common, tried-and-true annuals such as single-flowered Marigolds (*Tagetes* spp.), Zinnias, Petunias, Madagascar Periwinkles (*Catharanthus roseus*), and Mexican Sunflower (*Tithonia rotundifolia*), which are easily grown from seeds or can be readily obtained at the local nursery. Use these annuals for wonderful groupings and drifts to make great splashes of color. There is enough variety in height and growth in annuals to make exceptional garden displays, as well as enough color and flower shape to please butterflies. Annuals can certainly be the backbone of the planting for the first season, and some of them are such butterfly favorites that you should allow for them somewhere in your garden every year.

As long as the flowers you plant are good nectar producers, the butterflies do not care whether they are annuals or perennials; just be sure there are lots of them. As I have stressed before, butterflies do not like a little bit of this and a little bit of that. They are attracted to large masses of the same color and fragrance. So whatever you plant, do it *en masse*. When butterflies find large groupings of good nectar-producing flowers, they will continue feeding from the plants until the flowering period has ended.

For your own sake, to cut down on yearly planting and maintenance, you will want to get your soils in topnotch condition and the borders established as quickly as possible with good nectar-producing perennials. Well-established borders start flowering earlier, and this is important since some butterflies are out in February and early nectar sources for them are vital.

If you have some established beds but are able to put out only one or two species of herbaceous perennials the first year, purchase a few good, failproof ones, such as Summer Phlox, Verbena, and Plumbago (*Plumbago* spp.). Save your big bucks for a few choice shrubs, such as Butterfly Bush, Bee-brush, Chaste Tree (*Vitex Agnus-castus*), and Lantana, for planting in the fall. Add one or two choice but easy larval food plants.

In choosing plants for butterfly usage, pay special attention to the bloom period length, especially for shrubs and perennials. Many times such plants flower only briefly; if the space in your garden is at a premium, plants having the longest flowering periods are certainly the most beneficial. On the other hand, many perennials may be trimmed back or perhaps naturally die back after flowering. In such a case, use them near plants which produce most of their vegetative growth and flowers either earlier or later.

Timing flowering periods is crucial for the butterfly gardener. A continuous production of flowers is absolutely mandatory, for a garden without nectar-producing flowers is going to mean a garden without food for the butterflies. Constant bloom is best guaranteed by always having at least one or two good ol' reliables, such as Lantana, Zinnias, and Mexican Sunflower. Then, if some of the new plants you are trying do not work well, you will still have something to draw in the butterflies.

You will probably purchase many of your plants from local nurseries. Generally, the plants are sold in containers; if buying a native species, look the plants over carefully. Most stock sold as container plants are still in the pots or cans in which they were raised. If lifted from the container, these plants should have a solid ball of earth filled with many fine rootlets showing on the outside of the soil ball. Occasionally, you run across so-called container plants, especially native species, which have recently been dug from a field or roadside and indiscriminately crammed into cans or pots for quick sale. Whenever you find plants treated this way, refuse to buy them. Furthermore, let the nurseryman know that the reason you are not buying the plant is because it was dug from the wild, depleting our natural wildflower resources, instead of being properly propagated to increase the natives. Rarely do such plants survive due to the stress of being improperly cared for. There are many nursery folks who are propagating their own native stock, and these places should be sought out and patronized. The importance of obtaining native plants from appropriate sources cannot be stressed enough.

Some firsthand information could possibly help you in making final choices of plants for your garden. To learn more of how a particular plant will grow in your area, visit and talk with knowledgeable and trustworthy nurserymen about a plant's good and bad features. Your local landscape architects and designers are gold mines of knowledge about certain plants. They are the ones who draw the plans for the home owner, purchase the plants, and guarantee their survival after planting. Talk to them about the species which do the best in your area or how they deal with the ones that are harder to grow. Naturally, have your list of chosen plants with you at all times so you can ask about specific ones. To avoid any

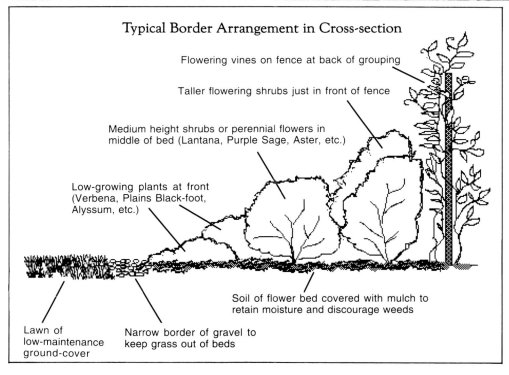

Typical Border Arrangement in Cross-section

Flowering vines on fence at back of grouping

Taller flowering shrubs just in front of fence

Medium height shrubs or perennial flowers in middle of bed (Lantana, Purple Sage, Aster, etc.)

Low-growing plants at front (Verbena, Plains Black-foot, Alyssum, etc.)

Soil of flower bed covered with mulch to retain moisture and discourage weeds

Lawn of low-maintenance ground-cover

Narrow border of gravel to keep grass out of beds

Above left. Tried-and-true annuals, such as the marigolds and globe amaranths here, are good choices for the beginning gardener.

Above. Plant such ranging plants as Columbine in front of trees to create your own wooded and protected area for woodland butterflies.

63

Purple coneflowers are dependable and cheery performers.

confusion when discussing plants and to prevent mistaken purchases, use both the scientific and the common names of the plant.

Visit arboretums, botanical gardens, city parks, university campuses, and trial gardens and talk with the gardening personnel there. At the same time, you can compare butterfly usage in areas where a wide range of plants are growing and flowering together. Drive around your town and make notes of plants you see and like. Anytime you are in the country, observe the wild plants that butterflies are using. If the butterflies are avidly nectaring on a plant a few miles from your house, chances are they will readily use it if it's growing in your yard.

Study the seed and plant catalogs thoroughly. Instead of treating them simply as lists of available plants, use them as textbooks. The descriptions given for each plant should give you a good idea of whether it will grow in your area and in your particular garden habitat. Pay special attention to the soil and moisture requirements for each plant and choose the ones with requirements most closely matching what you can provide.

No matter what time of year you get your garden started or the amount of work you first put into it, a richly productive garden is not going to be accomplished in one year. It requires patience and a lot of trial and error and will need to be developed over two or three seasons or even longer. Your garden is unique, like absolutely no other. Therefore, you will need to keep working with various plants until you find those that grow best in the area you have provided as well as those the butterflies show a particular fondness for. Eventually, when you have effectively combined your own favorites with what the butterflies need and want, you will have a garden that is truly beautiful and functional—for both you and the butterflies.

Preparing Beds

Butterflies do not like disturbances or radical changes in their feeding area, so the sooner shrubs and perennials can be planted and arranged satisfactorily, the better. And since the plants should remain relatively undisturbed once established, proper bed preparation is very important. If you take time and care in preparing the beds correctly, they will be a joy to work with. If you skimp at all, however, trying to keep the beds going will be a continual frustration, with weak and diseased plants and an unwanted expense in replacing dead ones. There are three major considerations: soil, watering, and mulching. These are all equally important for the health of the plants and for ease of future maintenance.

Soils

Soil is the growing medium and the basic source for nutrients readily available to plants. From the soil come the makings of foliage and flowers. You cannot properly prepare the soil in a bed until you understand the requirements of the plants you plan to use.

Some plants demand deep, dry, well-drained sand, while others want seepy muck. For the plants which require a very particular type of growing situation, plan to prepare a special bed for them. The majority of plants, including many natives, grow well in moderately rich, well-drained soils of a loose or porous texture.

For general garden beds, first mark off the outlines of the desired shapes, then spade the soil to a depth of several inches within the entire outlined areas. Most gardeners are finding that in a lot of situations, raised beds allow easier gardening and healthier plants. Raised beds greatly aid in drainage and can help alleviate problems with heavier soils.

Creating the perfect planting medium, in which most plants will grow their absolute best, takes time. But no matter what type of soil you are having to start with, whether deep sand, hard caliche, or the tightest of clays, organic matter is the best amendment available. Organic matter not only helps hold moisture in the soil but also slowly releases nutrients as the matter decomposes, thus providing the plants a steady source of the good things they need for healthy growth.

So, in the beginning stages of bed preparation, add plenty of organic matter

65

to the beds. Sphagnum moss, barnyard or horse manure, and compost are all effective. Work in well-rotted sawdust, chopped corn cobs, cotton burrs, peanut shells, or rice hulls. Half-deteriorated pine needles and bark chips are excellent. Visit the local fresh produce market where they shell pecans and peas and get the discarded hulls. In some cities there are organic matter composting programs that provide compost to the home gardener. If you have nothing but last year's leaves, run the lawn mower over them a couple of times, shredding them finely, then add them to the spaded soil. Add some sand and garden gypsum if the soil is heavy and full of clay particles.

If you suspect your soil is drastically lacking in something, make a soil test. Then add whatever is specifically needed, if anything. Finally, sprinkle in bone meal, blood meal, and cottonseed meal. After you have added every good thing you can think of to make the soil richer, loamier, and better-drained, turn the soil once more, mixing everything together thoroughly, level the bed, and set out your plants.

In designing your garden, if cost becomes a factor and you have to make a choice between some "extra" items, such as paving or edging materials, and a load of manure for the beds, go for the manure. The health and survival of every plant you put out depends to a large extent on what it is growing in, so you simply cannot afford to skimp on good soil. It will be no problem adding the extras the following season, but once beds are planted, it would be a major undertaking to completely redo the soil.

Watering

No matter how rich and loamy you have made your bedding soil, all those wonderful nutrients can be used by the plants only if there is adequate moisture. The most efficient and least troublesome way of providing the necessary moisture to the plants is with a watering system of some sort. Watering systems range from the simple to the elaborate. One simple system, of course, is the familiar old watering hose, which can be so frustrating, aggravating, and time-consuming that the watering may not be done adequately, if at all. On the other end of the spectrum is the elaborate (and expensive) network of underground lines complete with timers for automatically turning the water on and off.

One common method for watering gardens is through putting one or more sprinklers about the yard, generally placing them where some of the water hits the flower beds. Sprinklers waste a tremendous about of moisture due to evaporation, and they should never be used in the garden except in early mornings, allowing the foliage to become completely dried off before nightfall. Otherwise, you are risking invasion of all kinds of fungus diseases to the plants.

No sprinkler of any kind should ever be used to water a butterfly garden. Most sprinklers have to run from four to six hours to saturate the soil well enough to benefit the plants, and butterflies cannot feed from flowers while a sprinkler is spraying them with water. The water also dilutes the nectar, or possibly even washes it away entirely, so the butterflies will have to wait until the nectar flow is back to normal, which may take several hours. Even if the sprinklers have been used in the early morning hours, the nectar will have been affected. As often as gardens need to be watered during the hottest summer weather, the butterflies may be without food for a day or so at a time. This is too long. They will go somewhere else for their nectar.

There are a couple of systems which are not very expensive and actually work quite well in my own butterfly garden. One is a drip system. There are several brands of drip systems to choose from, but basically they are all the same. A solid, flexible plastic pipe is run underground from the faucet to the beds, while on top of the ground in the bed area are short lengths of much smaller flexible tubing running off the main pipe. At the end of each short length of tubing is an emitter or dripper, which allows the water to drip slowly, thoroughly saturating the soil.

The other system is a simple, flat soaker hose. Soaker hoses work on the same principle as the drip system except minute holes are prepunched at regular intervals on one side of a flat plastic tubing (this should be the lower side, the one touching the ground), with water coming out in a continuous stream, instead of a drop at a time as with the drip system. Only flat soaker hoses work—round ones simply act as misters or sprayers and are as detrimental to butterfly attraction as sprinklers. The soaker hose is less expensive than a drip system, is less trouble to install, and does not have a problem with clogged holes (a frequent occurrence with emitters). These hoses come in different grades and quality; if you opt for this system, I recommend getting quality hoses with good fittings. They will last for many years, and a hose with sturdy, nonleaking connections is worth every penny of the few extra dollars of initial cash outlay.

To install the soaker hoses, run permanent, round, flexible hoses underground from the faucet to each bed. Then attach one or two flat soaker hoses from a Y connector at the end of each underground hose, laying the soaker hoses on the surface of the flower bed and running them the length of the bed. The Ys at all connecting points should have off and on knobs.

After the soaker hoses are installed to your satisfaction (making sure the entire bed is being reached with the water), cover them with a deep layer of mulch. Covering with mulch hides the hoses from view, conserves moisture, and protects the hoses from deer, squirrels, and mice—animals with a special liking for plastic. Flexibility and light weight make the hoses easy to install, move, or rearrange later if needed, without damaging the plants.

When you have a soaker hose covered over with mulch, it is very easy to overwater your plants. Keep a hand digger stuck in a bed and constantly check on the amount of soil moisture. To check, stick the digger into the ground up to the handle and pull to one side. If the soil is satisfactorily moist to the top of the blade (to an approximate depth of six inches), then discontinue watering.

Once the plants in the beds have become deeply rooted and are growing well and the beds are properly mulched each year, there may no longer be a need for an intensive watering program. Most likely only an occasional watering during the hottest parts of the year will be necessary. But until that time, a good, reliable watering system is one of the best investments you can make to assure the survival of your butterfly plants.

Pine needles make an attractive and effective mulch.

Mulching

For easiest upkeep once you have planted your shrubs and perennials, a good mulch on the beds is the nicest thing you can do for yourself—and your plants. Not only does the proper mulch eliminate practically all weeding, watering, and fertilizing, but it keeps the soil from cracking due to moisture evaporation and helps keep the plant roots at a more even temperature to prompt healthy growth. Also, a proper mulch prevents the erosion of good topsoil during heavy rains and stops water from splashing back onto the foliage, which could spread soil-borne diseases. Soil-splattered plants not only are unsightly, but if the plants are low, the dirt may cover the flowers to such an extent that butterflies cannot use them for nectaring. Furthermore, organic mulch adds nutrients to the topsoil.

Do not add deep, permanent mulch to the beds until all plants are up and growing, especially if you use annuals with perennials. Until this time, some weeding may be necessary. If possible, bury the weeds you pull out. Often you can simply turn the extracted plants upside down and stuff them back into the holes you dug them from. If this is not possible, at least turn them upside down (exposing the roots so there will be no danger of rerooting) and leave them on the flower bed to act as a thin mulch until you can apply a deeper one. As the plants deteriorate, they add more good nutrients to the soil. A little soil sprinkled on top of the uprooted plants and a good watering a few days after they have sufficiently dried out will speed the rotting process. If the pulled plants cannot be left on the bed, by all means add them to the compost pile. However, plants which have already gone to seed should never be left on the beds, for all you will be doing then is planting more.

There are many materials which can be used as a permanent mulch. Organic mulches are popular, and those from wood or vegetable by-products are especially desirable. These attractive mulches decompose slowly, continually enriching the soil. If the organic matter is relatively fresh or new when applied, it is best to add a sufficient amount of a good nitrogen fertilizer because the mulch has a tendency to deplete the soil of nitrogen while decomposing.

Sawdust is often free for the hauling from a local sawmill. Whether you haul it yourself or buy it, select from the oldest, most rotted piles possible. The older sawdust is when applied, the faster it deteriorates into the soil. To avoid any nitrogen loss from using sawdust, add a little blood meal or cottonseed meal to the soil when applying.

Pine needles make a beautiful mulch, as does shredded pine bark. Mushroom compost is excellent where available and is usually relatively inexpensive since you haul it yourself. Consider cottonseed hulls or burrs as well as ground corn-cobs, peanut shells, rice hulls, and sunflower seed hulls.

Do not let any of the leaves in your yard get away. Rake them into low piles, run the lawn mower over them a time or two, then spread them about two or three inches thick over the beds and around the plants. Even if you cannot use all of the leaves that winter, keep the bags until spring. By then, what you placed on the beds in the fall will have partially decomposed and can be worked into the soil as humus. Then shred your saved leaves and apply a fresh mulch for the summer.

Be constantly on the lookout for tree-trimming trucks. These folks usually shred their trimmings and are always looking for a close, convenient dumping spot; your yard is probably much nearer than the city garbage heap. They are usually happy to deposit their chipped trimmings in your yard or driveway. These make an attractive top dressing for the beds and are slower to deteriorate than leaves.

If possible to obtain, a mixture of materials is less likely to compact on the beds, and it provides better aeration and water penetration. All of these materials have a natural, attractive appearance and last well when applied to a three-inch depth. Ideally, a three-inch organic mulch should be spread over a one-inch layer of organic fertilizer, such as well-rotted horse or chicken manure.

Using Native Plants

The use of native plants in the home landscape has been advocated for years, but only the true wildflower lover has taken the message to heart. In the eastern states, gardeners have created beautiful woodland gardens using native plants such as Mayapples (*Podophyllum peltatum*), Bleeding Hearts (*Dicentra eximia*),

69

and Jack-in-the-pulpit (*Arisaema triphyllum*). Only in the last twenty years or so have the words wildflower gardening come to be meaningful for the southern and southwestern states. We should take an interest in it, for nature has been more than generous in providing beautiful and varied species of trees, shrubs, and herbs. It is time we took a good look at our native plants, learned their ways and growth needs, and claimed them as our heritage.

Using these plants in our landscaping to attract butterflies has both practical and aesthetic advantages. Using native plants which have been observed to be useful to butterflies gives the gardener a better chance of bringing the insects into the garden and at the same time brings the natives closer so that their beauty can be more fully enjoyed and appreciated. To attract butterflies, you must plant the things they prefer, and certainly they are familiar with and have developed a liking for many of the natives. To combine the best-loved natives with the best-loved cultivated species is further guiding the garden toward becoming a butterfly paradise.

As an added bonus, most native herbaceous plants are perennials or self-sowing biennials or winter annuals. Once established, they provide you with an abundance of plants each year, both for your own space and usually with enough left over for sharing. The native species are already well adapted to the soil and climate in which they are growing. If planted in a similar situation in the garden, they are the least demanding plants in cost and amount of care. Native plants also have the advantage of giving a more natural appearance to the garden. By using the hardier native species, the flowering season often can be extended in the garden, both earlier and later.

One important advantage to a diverse planting of both native and cultivated species is that it provides natural checks and balances which help keep unwanted insects and diseases under control. Generally, native species suffer from fewer diseases than cultivated stock, so when both native and cultivated species are grown together, a single disease or insect is less likely to annihilate the garden.

Sources for Your Butterfly Garden

To obtain some of the special food plants recommended in this book (especially those needed for larvae), you may find it necessary to look beyond nurseries and mail order catalogs. Check with your local nurseries first. If they are not carrying native plants, ask if they can obtain the material for you.

Make sure the material they offer has been propagated from your region. Do not accept "native" material ordered from Utah or California; I tried that, and it doesn't work. You will be much better off using a locally grown second-choice plant rather than a first-choice plant which has been grown in, and is adapted to, other climates. Also, wild plants native to other regions may not be as good nectar producers when grown out of their natural range.

If you want plants that are not available from catalogs or nurseries, here are

Look for construction sites that might have suitable plants for a garden.

some suggestions. Keep a watch whenever you travel; anytime you see massive construction going on, stop and ask permission to dig the plants you need. Contact the local offices of the highway department and the county commissioners in your area to find out sites where road work is in progress or to be done in the future. The county agent may know of land being cleared. If you travel county and ranch or farm roads, you will frequently find fence rows in the process of being cleaned or cleared of the existing vegetation. Permission to remove plants from such sites is usually readily granted.

Local contractors or builders are another source for obtaining plants. Usually they know months in advance where large construction is to be done, and your digging a few plants beforehand is of little concern to them.

In some cities there are "plant rescue teams" that stay in contact with local contractors and dig choice plants before they are lost to construction. Usually these plants are placed in arboretums, city gardens, and zoos. Check with local garden clubs to find out about such rescue groups in your area. The garden clubs themselves are often good sources for native plants and seeds. Many of them have sales or exchanges throughout the year and would welcome your participation. Various other organizations have sales and exchanges, usually during the early spring or the late fall. A good source for information on such events are newsletters of native plant societies. You can also try the letter section of your state's gardening magazine to locate unpopular and little-known plants.

Don't forget friends, relatives, and even total strangers. Be always on the lookout for places to visit in the country as possible sources for needed species. Rare is the landowner who will deny you the privilege of taking a few plants generally considered weeds. If you find an extra-good spot of wildflowers, the landowner is almost always delighted to share some seed. Don't be shy about

Roadside flowers can make excellent additions to a butterfly garden.

knocking on doors. If you are driving down a road and you see a much-needed plant in someone's yard, stop and visit. Rarely will you walk away empty-handed.

In order to find the really good plants, such as a single-flowered form of a normally double-flowered species or an odd or unusual color form, you must look very carefully. When driving by a large stand of a specially needed species, stop the car and walk about among the flowers to look them over closely. Many times, there will only be a few of the odd ones in a mile or more of plants.

For just such times, you should always be prepared for seed collecting, digging, or gathering of some choice goodies. Make up a collecting basket or box and always have it handy. In the basket have scissors, clippers, a pocket knife, cheesecloth or nylon netting, twist ties, gloves, flagging, metal or plastic tabs or ties (for labeling), a waterproof pen, a small notebook, and transparent tape. Don't forget the state and county maps for marking the location of collecting sites. If space in the car trunk permits, always carry a sharpshooter shovel, several thin cardboard boxes, a bundle of newspapers, various sizes of both plastic and paper bags, and a couple of jugs of water (tightly sealed). Now you are ready for gathering seed or digging plants when you have the opportunity. Do not forget or neglect to ask permission before collecting. Some states have laws regulating plant taking. Be sure to check before digging in a new area.

It is very easy, especially when the opportunity to dig plants from a large area arises, to take things simply because they are pretty or *might* attract butterflies. In

Always get permission before collecting wildflowers.

such a situation be firm and be selective. Before digging one plant, you should consider such things as the plant's growth habit, how it will fit into your land-scaping scheme, how long its bloom period is, and, most important, how often and by how many species of butterflies it is used. This is not to say that you should not continually try new things, but you should certainly give serious thought to the planting space you have available, not filling it up with less-than-choice species.

One of the easiest methods of transplanting the smaller, more shallow-rooted plants from the wild is to spread a layer of soil in the bottom of a thin cardboard box and, as you dig, compactly place the plants in the box until full. Set the box in a rolled-down plastic bag and water the plants well. Then close the plastic bag until ready to plant. When ready to set the plants out in your garden, simply remove the box from the plastic bag and plant the entire box of plants. The box will eventually rot. You can use extra-heavy or doubled paper sacks in the same way, either cutting or rolling the tops down before placing the plants inside. Cut rolled-down tops off at ground level after planting.

Some native plants are more easily started from seed than by transplants. If you see an especially attractive plant along the roadside, perhaps one of excep-tional color or robustness, tie flagging tape around its base and also tie some of the tape to the base of some nearby object such as fence post or small bush. Give the plant time to set seed, then go back and gather them. Store the seeds in small

Wildflowers

paper bags (*never* plastic) in the refrigerator until proper planting time.

When purchasing wildflower seeds, buy only those packaged as individual species. You need to be very specific in your selections, choosing only the species which will do well in your garden situation and which have the flowers with the characteristics liked by butterflies, namely, nectar, fragrance, a good landing platform, and favored colors. The packaged mixes contain few species which are butterfly favorites, and you would be left with an array of plants that may be showy but are continually passed over by the butterflies.

Planting Your Butterfly Garden

Here are some general hints on planting select wildflower seed, whether in a scattered naturalized planting or as grouped individual species in the border. Following these suggestions is the best way to ensure a successful showing of healthy plants with plenty of bloom for the butterflies.

1. Before you collect or buy seed, very carefully study the area where you intend to plant. Make notes as to type of soil, amount of moisture, and how much sun or shade you have. Most wildflowers, especially the ones you plant for the butterflies, need at least six to eight hours of sun each day, so select your site carefully.

2. Study the wildflowers in your area, decide on a few that you want in the garden, and get seeds from a source as near your area as possible, even if it

74

means collecting the seeds yourself. Even though a plant may have an extensive range, seeds collected from plants in your area will have the highest germination rate and will grow and bloom better than plants from seeds collected elsewhere. Plants become adapted to soils, rainfall, and climatic conditions; when introduced into different habitats, they generally do not grow and flower as well.

3. To prepare the beds for planting, the first step is to till the soil. Soil should be broken up according to its type: three to four inches if the soil is tight clay, one to two inches if sandy loam. If the ground is exceptionally dry, soak it thoroughly, then wait two or three days before tilling.

4. Fall planting of seed is generally the best, as most species need to germinate in the fall in order to have developed strong root systems by spring. Some species need the winter's cold and moisture to break their dormancy.

5. Seeds can be planted using various methods, such as in rows, in groups of separate species, or in your own special mix broadcast by hand. If the seeds are very small, it is helpful to mix them with dry builder's sand to prevent their clumping. After sowing, the seeds should be covered with a thin layer of soil. The general rule here is to cover no deeper than three or four times the diameter of the seeds. One easy method for covering seeds is to flip over a rake and use the smooth edge to rake the soil over the seeds. This method covers a large percentage of the seeds.

6. Next comes a most important step. In order for the seeds to survive after germination, they must be in direct contact with the soil, so it is very important to firm the seed bed after covering. If a roller is not handy, the bed can be firmed by gently patting with the back of a flat shovel or a board.

7. After the soil has been completely firmed, gently but thoroughly soak the entire bed. All seeds need moisture to germinate, so keep the bed moist until the seedlings are up. Also, do not let the young seedlings dry out after sprouting. Don't overwater, but keep the area moist until all plants are well established and growing.

8. Do not overfertilize your wildflowers. Heavy fertilizing usually results in plant death or an extraordinary amount of foliage but no flowers. If you have planted the wildflowers in a mass or in an uncultivated area, probably no fertilizing will ever be necessary. If you have plants in the border where more lush growth is desired, use a very weak fertilizer solution occasionally through the growing season. As a general rule, however, wild plants bloom much better if nothing richer than a light top dressing of organic compost is used.

9. If the vegetation becomes unruly or too unsightly late in the season, instead of mowing or shredding, do as much as possible with a scythe or "yo-yo." This gets the vegetation down and the ripened seeds in contact with the soil but leaves the stems intact. Any chrysalids attached to the stems will most likely remain attached and survive. Many larvae seek shelter at the base of plants, and stems left standing fairly high afford some winter protection.

Above. A naturalized
butterfly garden

Left. A Zebra
Swallowtail sips nectar
from Globe
Amaranth.

Different species of wildflowers respond to different maintenance techniques. Some species respond better to mowing in the fall, others to mowing in the spring. Others can tolerate year-round mowing or even burning off, while others cannot. Disking and the time of year it is done also have effect. Each of these may be favorable to one kind of plant but fatal to another.

If you are naturalizing an area, try dividing it into sections and experiment with one of the preceding techniques to see what happens. You most likely will have a dominant species for each section, even if you planted the entire area with exactly the same mixture of species.

Perhaps you have already begun your wild or untamed area but now want to add some special butterfly plants to it. You certainly do not want to go in and retill the area, losing some of the species you already have established. The simplest way to plant now is to take a three-pronged hand digger, choose spots with the least vegetation, scratch the earth as much as possible, scatter the seeds into the disturbed area, and then move the soil back into place with the side of the tines or with your hand. Gently step on the area, firming the soil, then water thoroughly with a watering can.

One of the beauties of wildflowers is their ability to find their own niches—the places *they* like best. If you find something coming up in a different part of the garden from where you planted it, you might want to leave it there to see how it will do. If the conditions are conducive to the seed's sprouting, then the adult plant will most likely grow well also.

Get to know what the baby seedlings of the species you planted look like. Study the seed bed constantly; if you see several things which look similar, chances are they are what you planted. Become familiar with these babies so if you happen upon them in a different part of the garden, you will know what they are. You can then either nurture them or move them to a more desirable area.

Include one or two species of the taller native grasses in your garden plantings. Many of the Skippers are grass feeders in the larval stage, so, to complete their life cycles in your garden, they need the native grasses. It is unusual to find any of the common native grasses in a nursery, but a couple of small clumps should be easily obtained from a landowner or from a construction site. One or two good-sized clumps can be divided before placing in the borders, providing plenty of starters.

Landscape Plans

Here are sample garden designs for inspiration. Use your imagination and personal preferences in substituting plants and materials, adapting these ideas to fit your yard and area. When choosing plants, refer to the complete larval food plant list as well as the general nectar plant list—the plants listed are all known to be used by the butterflies in the area where they are given.

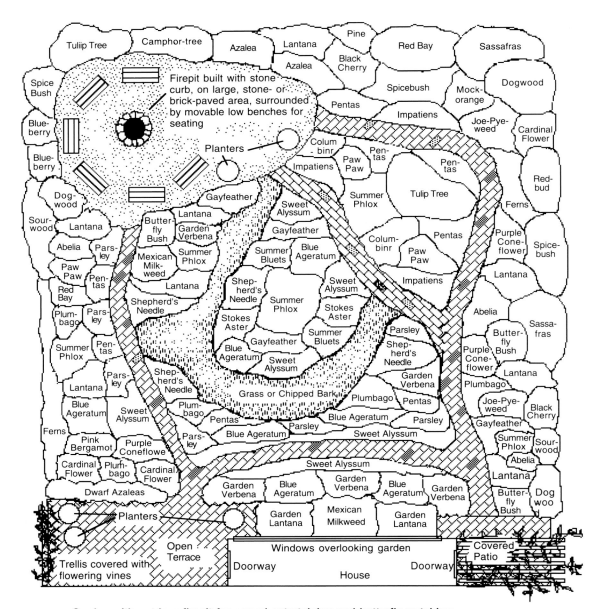

Garden with outdoor firepit for casual entertaining and butterfly-watching.

In addition to or in place of some of the plants shown here, you might want to choose from those shown elsewhere in this book, depending on your location. Also, if your site lends itself to more fences and/or trellises, keep in mind the colorful Bougainvilla, Climbing Hemp-weed, Passionflower and Woolly Pipe Vine.

Planters may be filled with Impatiens, Mexican Milkweed, Garden Lantana, Geranium, Garden Verbena, Garden Hibiscus, Zinnias, or Alyssum, depending on your light conditions and your preferences.

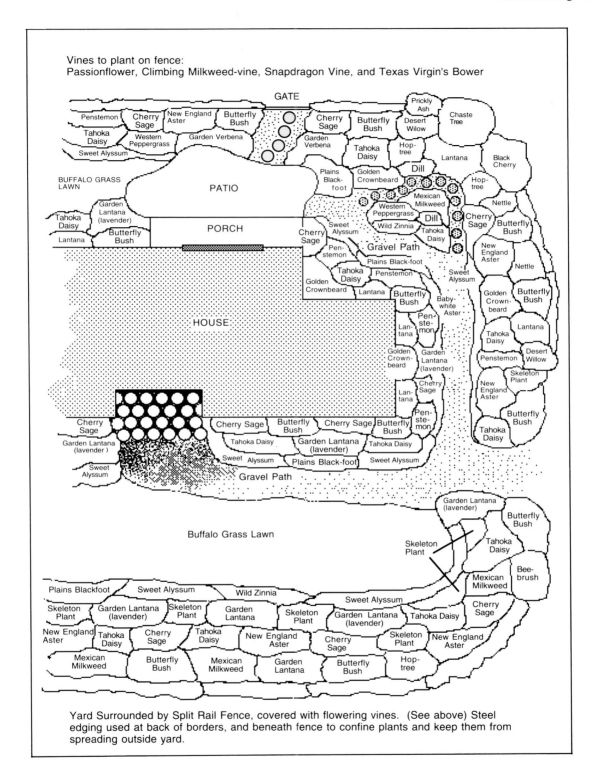

Vines to plant on fence:
Passionflower, Climbing Milkweed-vine, Snapdragon Vine, and Texas Virgin's Bower

Yard Surrounded by Split Rail Fence, covered with flowering vines. (See above) Steel edging used at back of borders, and beneath fence to confine plants and keep them from spreading outside yard.

High and Rolling Plains (Region 1)

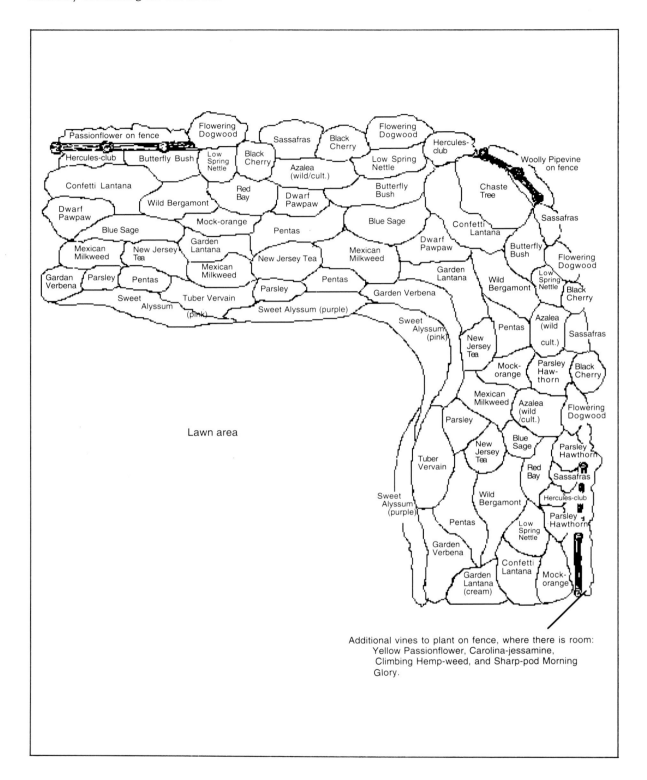

Lawn area

Additional vines to plant on fence, where there is room:
Yellow Passionflower, Carolina-jessamine,
Climbing Hemp-weed, and Sharp-pod Morning
Glory.

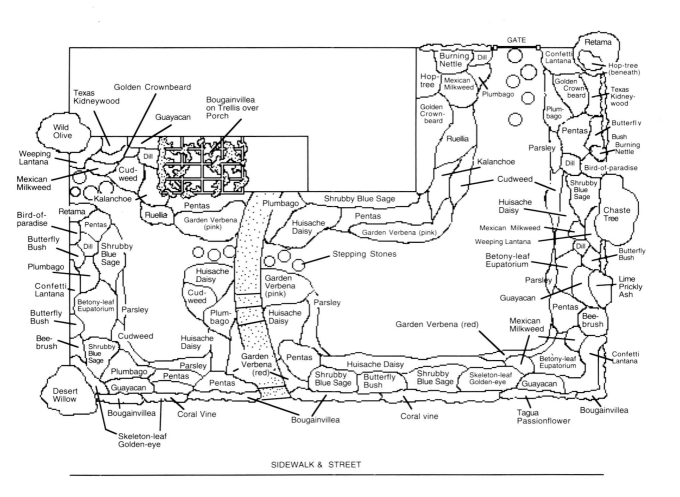

Chaparral and Rio Grande Valley (Region 3)

Vines on fence: Climbing Milkweed-vine, Slender-lobe Passionflower, Coral Vine, Snapdragon Vine, Texas Virgin's Bower

Chaste Tree

Desert Willow

Texas Lantana

Texas Kidneywood

Thoroughwort

Texas Lantana

Thoroughwort

Escarpment Black Cherry

Cherry Sage

Mexican Milkweed

Flame Acanthus

Bee-brush

Flame Acanthus

Garden Lantana (cream)

Garden Lantana (lavender)

Butterfly Bush

Parsley

Parsley

Garden Lantana (cream)

Cenizo

Narrow-leaf Gayfeather

Parsley

Dill

Flame Acanthus

Garden Verbena (pink)

HIGH END OF GARDEN

Garden Lantana (lavender)

Thoroughwort

Narrow-leaf Gayfeather

Lawn of Buffalo Grass

Other plants scattered in lawn area:
  False Garlic
  Drummond Wild Onion
  Blue-eyed Grass
  Celestials
  Wind-flower
  Two-flower Anemone
  Rain-lily
  Evening-star Rain-lily
  Mountain Pink
  Blue Gilia

Mexican Milkweed

Dill

Cherry Sage

Garden Verbena (pink)

Dill

Thorough-wort

Garden Verbena (lavender)

Cherry Sage

Mexican Milkweed

Mexican Milkweed

Parsley

Garden Lantana (cream)

Parsley

Garden Lantana (lavender)

Cherry Sage

Garden Verbena (lavender)

Garden Lantana (lavender)

Garden Lantana (lavender)

Garden Verbena (pink)

Garden Verbena (pink)

Escarpment Black Cherry

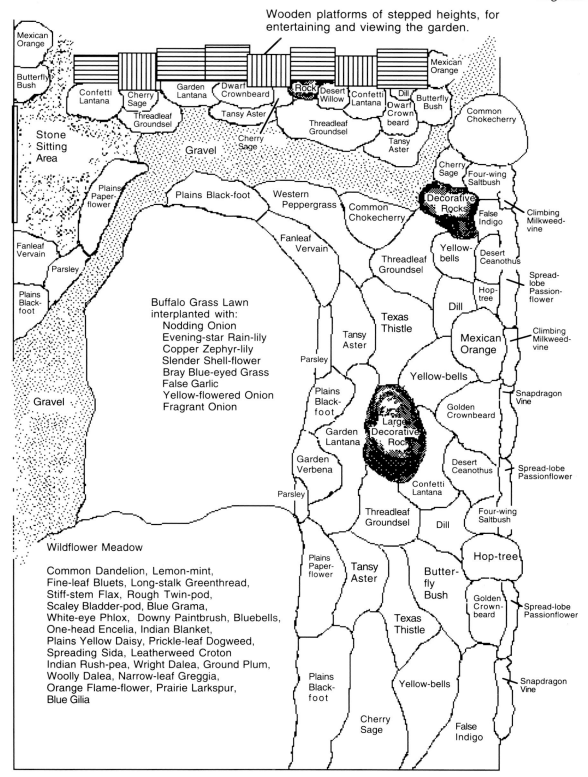

Wooden platforms of stepped heights, for entertaining and viewing the garden.

Mexican Orange

Butterfly Bush

Confetti Lantana

Cherry Sage

Threadleaf Groundsel

Garden Lantana

Dwarf Crownbeard

Tansy Aster

Rock

Desert Willow

Cherry Sage

Threadleaf Groundsel

Confetti Lantana

Dill

Dwarf Crown beard

Butterfly Bush

Mexican Orange

Common Chokecherry

Tansy Aster

Stone Sitting Area

Gravel

Plains Paper-flower

Plains Black-foot

Western Peppergrass

Common Chokecherry

Cherry Sage

Four-wing Saltbush

Decorative Rocks

False Indigo

Climbing Milkweed-vine

Fanleaf Vervain

Parsley

Fanleaf Vervain

Threadleaf Groundsel

Yellow-bells

Desert Ceanothus

Spread-lobe Passion-flower

Plains Black-foot

Hop-tree

Buffalo Grass Lawn
interplanted with:
Nodding Onion
Evening-star Rain-lily
Copper Zephyr-lily
Slender Shell-flower
Bray Blue-eyed Grass
False Garlic
Yellow-flowered Onion
Fragrant Onion

Texas Thistle

Dill

Mexican Orange

Climbing Milkweed-vine

Tansy Aster

Parsley

Yellow-bells

Plains Black-foot

Garden Lantana

Golden Crownbeard

Snapdragon Vine

Gravel

Large Decorative Rock

Garden Verbena

Desert Ceanothus

Spread-lobe Passionflower

Parsley

Confetti Lantana

Four-wing Saltbush

Threadleaf Groundsel

Dill

Wildflower Meadow

Plains Paper-flower

Tansy Aster

Butter-fly Bush

Hop-tree

Common Dandelion, Lemon-mint,
Fine-leaf Bluets, Long-stalk Greenthread,
Stiff-stem Flax, Rough Twin-pod,
Scaley Bladder-pod, Blue Grama,
White-eye Phlox, Downy Paintbrush, Bluebells,
One-head Encelia, Indian Blanket,
Plains Yellow Daisy, Prickle-leaf Dogweed,
Spreading Sida, Leatherweed Croton
Indian Rush-pea, Wright Dalea, Ground Plum,
Woolly Dalea, Narrow-leaf Greggia,
Orange Flame-flower, Prairie Larkspur,
Blue Gilia

Texas Thistle

Golden Crown-beard

Spread-lobe Passionflower

Plains Black-foot

Yellow-bells

Snapdragon Vine

Cherry Sage

False Indigo

CHAPTER FOUR

An Instant Butterfly Garden

I f you are really excited about the prospect of attracting butterflies, but it's too late in the season to dig beds or set out trees, there is a way you can still make a butterfly garden *almost* instantly, happily—with containers and the local nurseries.

Site Possibilities

Before heading for the nearest plant dealer, take a few minutes to give some thought to the possibilities of your yard. See exactly how you can make the best butterfly garden with the amount of time you want to spend on it.

To get some ideas, walk around your house and yard, noting areas where you can use pots or hanging baskets. There are many ways to make a small space become a haven for butterflies; with a little planning this is no great task, so give every nook and cranny a good, long look. The choice of a location for a container grouping is as important as for planting in beds or borders, so consider only open, protected locations in full sun. An area close to a water faucet or the end of a watering hose would be really handy, as potted plants need watering more often than bedded plants.

Following are a few site possibilities to keep in mind as you walk about, but don't be limited by these. No yard is exactly like another or used in the same way, so let your imagination soar. Choose what will work for your yard while providing the butterflies what they need. Keep in mind that the containers should be grouped, not spread out with one here and one there. As in the borders, mass plantings are most important with containers; three containers grouped together are much more effective than ten spaced twenty feet apart.

1. A sunny wall of the house, garage, or tool shed where baskets can be hung, with perhaps a strip of trellis fastened to the wall for climbing larval food plants and a grouping of pots or other containers on the ground beneath

2. One corner of the yard, or an area where a corner can be "made" with lengths of bamboo fencing, with a grouping of containers arranged in staggered heights

3. Outermost edges of uncovered porches, decks, or patios

4. Wooden or metal railings of stairways, balconies, or porches where pots or baskets can be hung

5. The immediate area around a mailbox post

6. Wooden fences, pillars, or posts where hanging baskets can be fastened in a staggered arrangement

7. Old wrought iron or metal tables, benches, or chairs or wooden picnic tables which are no longer used and where pots can be arranged

8. The edge of a driveway or walk or on steps or stairways where containers can be placed in a pleasing arrangement (and still allow passage)

A charming container garden of Petunias

Containers

Now that you have selected some garden sites where containers would work well, next consider the containers themselves. Gather all the hanging baskets, pots, or planting containers you possess and set them out where they are easy to see and work with.

Now it's imagination time again. Look around for such objects as concrete blocks, short tiles which can be stood on end, old wash pots, battered buckets, and bushel baskets. Make a note of flat stones or bricks lying about. Sturdy baskets from the house can be used. They will last only one season but are lovely when a plant in a plastic pot is placed inside.

Picturesque old stumps or pieces of driftwood can be incorporated into the grouping, not only as effective focal points but as convenient basking areas for the butterflies. If the arrangement of pots is to be on or near the ground, one of the salt or puddling areas previously described can be added. Make plans for this in your grouping.

In making your container selection, keep in mind that metal or plastic containers have a tendency to become exceptionally hot when placed in the sun; the plant roots may be burned from the overheated soil. Wooden or clay pots keep the roots much cooler, although clay is very porous, with rapid loss of soil moisture. Plants in clay pots will most likely need frequent watering. One way around this problem is to set one clay pot inside a larger clay pot, filling the area between the two pots with sphagnum moss or sand. If this filler is kept moist, it not only reduces evaporation but helps keep the plant roots several degrees cooler. Plants in plastic pots also benefit from the coolness of being placed in larger clay pots lined with moist sphagnum.

Wooden containers are probably the best for container plantings, but they have the drawback of being heavier than either plastic or clay. If the containers are very large, screw swivel rollers to the bottom. This not only makes them easier to move around but raises them off the ground and prevents rotting of the wood.

Measure the width and depth of your containers and the overall area where they are to be placed. Put as much of the arrangement together as possible and make a list of things which you need and don't have. Once you reach the nursery, the nurseryman can better advise you on the number of plants needed for each container.

Selecting Plants

Your choice of plants for this instant garden is limited to what the nursery folks have in stock at the time, but there should be enough available to attract butterflies within hours after you bring home and arrange the plants. Most nurseries have lovely, healthy baskets and containers of Lantana, Verbena, Petunias, and Sweet Alyssum. Get as many of these as you can use or afford. In

Verbenas work well in container gardens. Here, with American Painted Lady.

selecting the planted containers or baskets, it is as important here as in a regular garden planting to choose a few species and have many containers of the same thing, rather than have a dozen different pots of a dozen different species. Let the size, shape, and placement of the plants break up the monotony of the planting and be of interest to people. At the same time, the mass of a single nectar source will be of interest to butterflies.

If you want more containers or different species than are available in already planted containers at the nurseries, refer to your list of the containers you have,

87

Malachite and Lantana

note their size, and then purchase the needed number of bedding plants. If more hanging baskets are wanted, often wire baskets (the best kind) already lined with sphagnum moss are available. Be sure the moss is fairly thick, for if not the soil will be washed away during continual summer watering. You might want to purchase a small bag of sphagnum anyway because, in order to make the best use of the basket, you need to place plants between the wire mesh around the sides of the basket as well as in the top; extra sphagnum is needed to secure the side plants and close up any gaps after the plants are in place. Before adding any soil, place in the basket's bottom one of the plastic drip dishes ordinarily used beneath pots. This acts as a reservoir and cuts down on the amount of watering required.

If you are planting any really large containers such as wooden whiskey barrels, there is an easy way to save on the amount of soil you need. For container planting, the very best potting soils should be used, and planting can become very expensive when you have to fill several large containers. So, before adding any soil, place a large plastic pot upside down in the barrel. This takes up a lot of space yet leaves plenty of soil for the plants. It also lightens the planted container considerably, making it easier to move if necessary.

Every potted plant you have, whether purchased potted or planted yourself, should be mulched with medium- to small-sized bark chips. A bark mulch prevents rain from washing soil from around the roots and, more important, helps conserve moisture. Never use sphagnum for mulching, since it dries out very quickly when exposed to air; when dry, it even acts as a sponge, drawing water away from the roots of the plant.

Some plants which do well in containers, are commonly carried by nurseries, and are readily used by butterflies include shrubby-type perennials, such as Hibiscus (*Hibiscus* spp.), Cenizo (*Leucophyllum* spp.), and Barbados Cherry (*Malpighia glabra*). Less shrubby plants include Lantana and Verbena, which can be used in both pots or hanging baskets. More herbaceous perennials, such as single-flowered red and pink Geraniums (*Pelargonium* spp.), Lavender (*Lavendula latifolia*), Catmint (*Nepeta mussinii*), various Salvias, and Plains Blackfoot (*Melampodium leucanthum*), are excellent. Common annuals include Purslane (*Portulaca oleracea sativa*), Madagascar Periwinkle, Impatiens (*Impatience balsamina*), Wishbone Flower (*Torenia fournieri*), Pentas (*Pentas lanceolata*), single-flowered Marigolds and Zinnias, Multiflora Petunias, and purple-flowered Sweet Alyssum.

Food plants for some larvae can easily be grown in some of the containers. These you will probably have to pot yourself. Place four to six plants of Parsley (for the Eastern Black Swallowtail) in a low container to be placed in a prominent spot. Or plant a few of the taller growing Common Fennel (*Foeniculum vulgare*) or Dill in the middle of a pot (also for the Eastern Black Swallowtail), then plant Parsley around the rim for an edging. A pot or two of such a planting will add a ferny touch to an otherwise all-floral arrangement, making the overall area more attractive. Place a small trellis or a strong, decorative, many-branched stick in some of the pots and plant climbing vines of Dutchman's Pipe for the Pipevine Swallowtail, Passionflowers for the Gulf Fritillary, Zebra Longwing, and Julia, or Snapdragon Vine for the Buckeye.

A word of caution here. Do not move the plants about simply on a whim. Butterflies are very habitual; once a butterfly has found a food source, it comes back to it regularly for days. If the plant is moved very far away, the butterfly tends to become a little put out and may even quit coming to the plants entirely. This is another reason to keep plants in a grouping composed of several plants of the same species, and the plants of each type all of one color. This way, if the container of yellow Lantana in the most conspicuous spot stops flowering well, it can be exchanged for a better flowering one from the back of the grouping. The butterflies will not be as leery of the difference in appearance.

Maintenance

A plant in a container needs more attention than the same species planted in the garden. This does not mean you must do a lot of time-consuming work, but it does mean that you must look after the plants at least once a day. You must constantly monitor moisture, feeding, and placement to see that the plants remain healthy and full of flowers.

Since the objective here is mass in a very small area, the plants will be overcrowded aboveground, and the roots underground will have little room in which to expand. There is going to be much competition between the plants for what is available, and the soil will be quickly depleted of both nutrients and moisture.

For newly planted containers, you should use a root stimulator at the time of planting. After two weeks you should begin a regular feeding regime using a good, all-around fertilizer. A good combination is to apply a slow-release fertilizer at the time of planting, then once weekly apply a weak solution of liquid fertilizer. If you use a dry fertilizer, water before and after adding the granules. It is imperative that container plants receive adequate feeding, for without added food they quickly sicken and die.

Do not assume that if a little fertilizer is good, a lot is better. Like other living creatures, plants can suffer ill effects from overeating. Too much fertilizer causes a buildup of salts in the soil, which can inhibit growth or poison the plants, causing them to die.

Watering is the biggest chore for container gardening, but an absolutely necessary one. It usually has to be done daily, and during July and August twice a day may not be too often. It's not the easiest thing to do, either, especially for hanging baskets. The simplest arrangement is to have your containers as close to a faucet as possible and to install a hosereel on the house or a nearby fixture; then the hose can be conveniently unrolled for watering and rolled back up after finishing. A stout bamboo pole firmly wired to the last four or five feet of the hose allows you to reach the top of the baskets without a stepladder. If you do not have many containers, you can easily solve the watering problem by dropping a handful of ice cubes into the containers each day.

Making It Beautiful and Useful

You are now ready to begin planting and arranging in your chosen space. Both for the health of the plants and for attracting the attention of the butterflies, you should stagger the height of your plants. Place taller growing plants to the back or middle of the group. If you want low-growing plants at the back, use

Above. Zebra Swallowtail and Zinnia

Right. Tagua Passionflowers are stunning climbing vines.

raised pots. Some, such as the Lantana and Verbena, spread outward and so should be placed low and to the front or side of the grouping. Different heights can easily be obtained by using bricks, flat stones, or blocks of wood.

One of the wonderful things about container gardening is that you can rearrange the plants to suit the likes of the butterflies without disturbing the growth of the plants. If some of the plants begin to lag in producing flowers while others at the back of the grouping are more showy, move the back ones to the front.

If you are gardening in an arid region, you can place shallow terra cotta or plastic pans or drip trays beneath the pots to conserve liquid which may run out of the pots when you are applying water or fertilizer. Attached to the bottom of hanging baskets, pans or trays prevent dripping on the plants underneath and provide a longer period of available moisture. In rain-prone areas, excellent and immediate drainage may be required. Making large drainage holes and raising the pots off the ground by placing them on thin stones may be necessary. Clip all spent flower heads to ensure continued flowering. Some plants, such as Lantana and Verbena, benefit from clipping portions of the plants back to near the base, thus encouraging new growth.

At the end of the flowering season, do not let your perennial container plants go to waste. Empty your containers, separate the plants into small divisions, and plant these in the permanent border. You will most likely have enough plants to make a nice showing the next season and have an ample nectar source for the butterflies.

You may find that the concentrated container grouping was such a success, you want to repeat it the following year. Some of the butterflies which hibernated will remember the food source and will come to the same areas looking for food when they come out on warm days in the spring. Other species which emerge from the chrysalis stage in very early spring, such as the Sulphurs, Spring Azures, and Falcate Orangetip, will need an early nectar source. For these, some containers planted in late fall with Stocks (*Matthiola incana*), Pansies, Violets, Moss Phlox (*Phlox subulata*), or Calendulas (*Calendula officinalis*) are good to start the spring season. As warm weather approaches, replace these with plants which flower during the entire summer. For fall flowering, add some of the low-growing Asters (*Aster* spp.), Blue Mist-flower (*Eupatorium coelestinum*), and Thorough-wort (*Eupatorium havenense*).

Window boxes make charming and intimate gardens, and many styles of window boxes are available. When installed properly on the sunny sides of the house and filled with appropriate plants, window boxes can be very useful for attracting butterflies. They become even more so if baskets hung above and beds below the boxes are planted with butterfly-attracting plants.

Wonderful configurations can be made by stacking concrete blocks. If the gray color of the blocks is intrusive, paint them with a flat paint of soft, subtle earth colors; conceal them with rustic split logs, cork sheeting, rough cedar boards, or old bricks; or use the thinner, decorative concrete blocks as a false front for the less attractive planting blocks. Stack the planting blocks so that there are holes for filling with soil. If the holes are over two blocks deep, save soil by filling the bottom portion of the hole with a small plastic pot turned upside down, wadded-up plastic, gravel, or small styrofoam packing peanuts. You can use anything that is lightweight and will not rot. Otherwise, cut thin but stiff sheet metal to size and slip it beneath the top block. Drill some holes for drainage in the metal. Fill the holes in the top blocks with potting soil and then plant.

Constructing a Dry Bed

I use the term dry bed to describe a temporary flower bed where the soil does not come in contact with the ground. It is essentially a bottomless box lined with plastic sheeting and placed on top of concrete or some other impermeable surface. This alternative might be right for you if you have neither the time nor the inclination to care for bunches of flower beds or hanging baskets. Or it may be that your yard is too shaded for butterflies and the only really open, sunny spot is a driveway or a patio.

Constructing a dry bed is relatively simple. Select an area on a hard surface such as a concrete driveway, a wide walkway, or a brick or stone patio or porch. Begin to lay out your building materials, which can be railroad ties, rough cedar logs, sections of short half-logs, concrete blocks, old bricks, or stones. Place them in the bed configuration best suiting your needs and space. Designing the bed is the same as if you were digging one in the garden, except in this case you are placing it on top of a hard surface.

After you have the bed outlined to your satisfaction, be sure it is built at least eight to ten inches high; twelve to fourteen inches would be even better. Keep in mind that the bed will act exactly as a pot or container and must be filled with extra-rich potting soil; ordinary garden soil will not do. If the bed is deep, the bottom portion can be partially filled with small plastic pots turned upside down to conserve soil.

If you have placed the bed where drainage direction is important, heap up gravel or small round stones in the bottom of the bed on the side opposite the desired direction of drainage, slanting the bottom of the bed.

After the bed is built to the desired height and its drainage material is arranged, completely line the interior of the bed with an extra-heavy sheet of plastic, preferably clear type, placing it on top of the drainage material. Smooth the sheet into all the corners to conform it to the shape of the bed as much as possible. Do not split or cut the plastic to make it conform in shape, but fold it tightly and tape if necessary. After you have made this liner fit as well as possible, punch a few drainage holes in the bottom with an ice pick or a small nail.

Place a one- or two-inch layer of coarse gravel, pine bark, or wood chips in the bottom of the bed. Add a two-inch layer of sphagnum moss for moisture retention. Next begin to fill the bed with potting mix. The soil will be somewhat fluffy, so, to prevent settling, pour the soil out in layers, ever so gently patting down between layers. After the bed is filled with the soil, roll back the excess plastic around the edges and tuck it in neatly, leaving it about an inch below the top of the walls. You could do a little trimming here and there at this time.

Before the actual planting, place the potted plants in a position you think pleasing, then stand back and visualize what they will look like in a month or so. If some of the plants are the trailing type, place these toward the front or the outer edges; arrange taller plants either in the center or at the back. As you place the plants permanently, water them in with a root stimulator. After all planting is done, spray the entire area gently and briefly just to settle the soil and clean off the foliage.

If there are cracks in your building material which allow the plastic to be seen, stuff moist sphagnum moss gently in the cracks. Cover the entire top of the bed with pine bark or dark-colored wood chips. This greatly benefits in conserving moisture, which is quickly lost in this type of planting.

As this bed is truly an artificial one, having no bottom contact with garden soils, the combination of growing plants and evaporation depletes the soil moisture very quickly. Treat the bed as a large potted or container plant: do not neglect its daily watering and weekly fertilizing.

Collecting Caterpillars and Chrysalises

If you are impatient with the sometimes slow natural establishment of a wide assortment of butterflies in your garden, then you might consider collecting larvae or pupae. The number one rule to consider before beginning to collect is to be sure the species you want already exist in your area and would most likely eventually find their way into your garden. By bringing in these larvae or pupae, you are only speeding up the natural process.

The next thing to consider in introducing a species into your garden is the constant availability of an adequate food source. Before you seek out any larvae or pupae, it is important to know and have available the habitat and food preferences of both the larvae and the adults. Not only will it be necessary for the larval food plant to be in your own garden, but a plentiful, healthy source should be readily available no farther than one-quarter mile from your yard.

Now you are ready to start searching for caterpillars or pupae. Roadsides are one of the best areas for searching. Choose a little-used but paved road, if possible. Traffic on unpaved roads usually leaves a thick film of dust on the roadside vegetation, making the plants unpalatable to the larvae, so you will find few larvae near such roads. If you wish to collect away from a roadway or over a fence, be sure to ask permission from the landowner.

You should know food plant preferences and feeding habits of the larvae before the search begins. The looking is often long and tedious, but once you find a caterpillar, the excitement keeps you looking for others. Take caution here not to deplete a colony. Butterflies have a habit, in general, of depositing a number of eggs in a small area, so collecting all the existing larvae would not be hard to do.

When collecting caterpillars, clip a portion of the food plant with the larva clinging to it.

Take only one or two larvae from an area, then move on to other plants in a different area.

Once you find a caterpillar, clip a portion of the food plant with the larva clinging to it. It is most important to handle the caterpillar very gently if touching is required; the bodies of caterpillars are extremely soft, and handling can easily damage the internal organs.

Place the clipped foliage and caterpillar into a plastic bag. Sprinkle a few drops of cool water over the foliage and close the bag. If you are collecting different species, place them in separate bags. Try not to leave the larvae in the closed bags over four or five hours at the most, and never leave them in a hot, closed car. Immediately upon arrival at home, remove the foliage from the bag, place the caterpillar next to a leaf of its new food plant, and, using a cotton swab, or a camel's hair brush, touch the caterpillar at its rear, urging it to crawl onto the new plant.

If all goes well with your larvae, emergence of the adult butterflies in your garden will make it their home territory. If sufficient larval food plants are available, the adults will most likely breed, lay eggs, and establish a thriving colony.

Some butterfly gardening books list supply companies from whom you can purchase eggs or larvae of certain species. Do not order any of these eggs or larvae unless the company states plainly that the butterflies are from your own state. Many butterflies have evolved particular forms or varieties perfectly adapted to specific regions. For instance, the Zebra Longwing in Florida looks different from the Texas Zebra Longwing. They differ not only in appearance but also in their tolerance to humidity, rainfall, temperature, and other climatic factors. Release a bunch of the Florida Longwings in Austin, and chances are they would not survive a week. If you want to increase your garden's population or introduce some new species, collect the eggs, larvae, or pupae from within your own immediate area.

CHAPTER FIVE

Let Nature Do It: Butterfly-friendly Pest Controls

Establishing a garden to attract certain caterpillars and adult butterflies is also going to invite other insects which may not be so welcome. In the natural world there are no "good" bugs or "bad" bugs. In the following text, while I speak of the bad guys and show methods of removing them in order to better establish a garden for a particular insect, in this case the butterfly, in no way am I passing judgment on any living thing. Personally, I can, and do, appreciate the fortitude, mystery, and beauty of an aphid or Japanese beetle as quickly as the most gorgeous of butterflies.

Clearly, however, there are times in butterfly gardening when some species of insect becomes so numerous or damaging that it is detrimental to your purpose, and some sort of action needs to be taken. If you were to apply the usual methods of wide-scale eradication of the enemy, it is quite likely that you will also eliminate the butterfly larvae in the process. So, to keep the garden balanced in favor of the desired creatures, certain garden practices and a system of organic pest control are needed.

The best defense against any kind of pest insect or disease is to have the healthiest plants possible. It is the weak, malnourished plants that the bugs go for first. Provide your plants with a well-balanced diet through compost-rich soils, adequate moisture, and the sunshine needed for strong growth; the plants will be

Healthy plants are the best defense against pests. These Lantana plants benefit from good air circulation and an effective mulch.

less stressed and therefore less susceptible to harmful attack.

A pest outbreak is often triggered by the use of a potent, quick-release fertilizer or one of the miracle growth sprays which initiates tender, succulent plant growth. Plants are far less likely to be bothered if they are allowed to maintain a natural, steady growth pace by the use of compost in the soil and slowly deteriorating mulches.

Plants being grown out of their natural ranges or habitats may have a hard time adjusting and may be wide open to all kinds of insect attack. Plants which continually attract insect invasion should be promptly removed and replaced with tougher, more hardy species.

Give the plants in your flower beds plenty of room to breath. Good air circulation helps prevent many fungus diseases, such as mildew, crown rot, and black spot. Keep the garden clean by immediately removing severely infected plants, either by burning them or by burying them deeply in a new flower bed in the making.

97

There are many bacteria in good, rich compost, along with molds and fungi living in the soil, which provide various antibiotics to plants for fighting diseases, so use lots of compost in the beds. Treat only the plants showing actual damage, and apply treatment only to the areas affected.

There are many alternatives to indiscriminate usage of chemicals. For the health and safety of the butterflies and their larvae, apply a system using only natural controls, integrating physical controls, biological controls, and controls through the use of plants themselves.

Physical Controls

For some of the larger insects, hand removal may be the simplest and safest method. Fill a can or jar with a mixture of water topped with kerosene, and drop the insects into the liquid as you remove them from the plants. Grasshoppers are easily picked from plants at night. To capture sow bugs and pill bugs, moisten the ground and lay a board on the moist area. In early mornings and late evenings, lift the board and dispose of the clusters of bugs which have gathered.

Slugs and snails are reportedly attracted to saucers of stale beer. If this does not work, use a straw or pine needle mulch around the plants. These soft-bodied mollusks do not care much for the rough texture of the mulch, finding it difficult to move across. Bloodmeal and bonemeal sprinkled on top of the soil (or mulch) is also a deterrent to slug and snails as well as pill bugs, sow bugs, ants, aphids, deer, rabbits, and household cats. Wood ashes from the fireplace sprinkled thickly around plants act as a great deterrent to many pests. Other irritants to be strewn around plants include crushed dried hot peppers, camphor, powdered charcoal, builder's sand, and cedar shavings.

A potato sliced in half and buried about two inches beneath the soil's surface is a simple but effective trap for wire worms. After a couple of days, lift the potatoes and destroy the worms.

Ladybugs are beneficial insects that devour many common garden pests.

98

Traps made from plastic jugs containing sugar water flavored with Vanilla, Sassafras, Lemon, Anise (*Pimpinella anisum*), or Common Fennel will attract many flying and jumping insects. Place these near the infested plants. To trap grasshoppers, half-fill a wide-mouthed jar with this mixture and bury the jar to the rim in the ground. Other trap baits to try are a banana peel, a cup each of sugar and vinegar, and enough water to almost fill a gallon jug. A brew of mashed fruit, one or two cups of sugar, and some yeast for fermentation is especially attractive to Japanese beetles. Fill narrow-mouthed jugs no more than half full with these mixtures. Smaller insects crawl down into the jugs to get at the bait and drown, but butterflies normally do not enter.

Biological Controls

Along with some of the bad insects, there are others which are especially beneficial to a butterfly garden, and you should both protect and encourage their presence. Just as there are viruses, bacteria, and fungi that help keep plants healthy, there are also many insects which, during one or more stages of their life, attack and devour other insects which are damaging the plants. One of the most beneficial is a small beetle variously known as the ladybug, lady beetle, ladybird, or aphid wolf. Ladybug eggs, a bright yellow or orange, are attached in small clusters to plant leaves or stems, behind tree bark, or among debris scattered about on the ground. The larvae are flat, warty, and somewhat carrot-shaped, their grayish-black coloring spotted with blue and orange. Both the larvae and the adults eat aphids, leafhoppers, mealybugs, and scales. Each larva can devour up to four hundred aphids, and one adult ladybug may consume five thousand or more.

Lacewings are beautiful, delicate, fairy-like insects with clear, gauzy green wings and red eyes. The larvae, called ant lions or aphid lions, capture and suck the body fluids from aphids, mealybugs, thrips, mites, and cottony-cushion scales.

Ladybugs and lacewings can be purchased from some nurseries (see Appendix). When ordering, be sure to get the ladybugs which are already conditioned to eat aphids.

Larvae of the firefly or lightning bug are long, flat, and wormlike. These larvae, known as glowworms, can be seen on a summer's night moving among grasses, leaves, and plant stems, their bodies glowing from time to time, like the flying adults. The larvae are voracious nighttime predators, feeding especially on slugs, snails, and cutworms.

And keep a toad handy. Or two or three. In fact, keep several. A single toad can consume up to three thousand insects in a month, especially ants, sow bugs, and pill bugs. Having rather broad tastes, they also eat grasshoppers, cutworms, beetles, snails, and slugs.

There are several benefactors generally considered helpful in most gardens which are definitely not desired in a butterfly garden. Most of these are avid predators on eggs or larvae, including those of moths and butterflies. Some

The Praying Mantis is the butterfly's worst enemy.   A crab spider attacks an Antillean Blue.

predators which should not be encouraged to remain in a butterfly garden include most of the parasitic wasps (braconid, chalcid, ichneumon, and trichogramma), assassin bugs, stink bugs, robber flies, spiders, and praying mantises. Praying mantises are one of the most familiar insects sold as a biological pest control, and for a general garden I highly recommend their use over pesticides. But they have no place in a butterfly garden. Praying mantises are one of the worst enemies of butterflies, hiding among the foliage and seizing the insect as it approaches the flower to nectar.

Companion Plants

Some plants apparently thrive and are at their healthiest when placed in close proximity to certain other plants. The various benefits of such companion planting are not easy to explain. Perhaps it is due to certain nutrients being brought from a lower depth by one plant and thus made available to a more shallow-rooted plant. Perhaps it is shade provided to the roots of one plant by another during a critical growth period, or maybe one plant benefits from a

100

certain combination of room and light allowed by certain other plants. Or perhaps it is simply that plants like to be near their friends.

No exact, scientific explanation has been offered for the generally healthier effects obtained from such planting, but it does seem to work. Not only do plants appear to be larger and produce more flowers and fruit when placed in combination with certain other species, but they are noticeably less stressed when placed in small groups of their own kind, instead of being separated with one here and one there. It is not difficult to see the difference between the health of a solitary plant lost in the maze of a garden border and that of several plants of the same species placed in groups.

Repellent Plants

While the reason behind the obvious benefits of placing certain companion plants in close proximity to others may remain a mystery for the time being, there is another planting combination which is more easily understood. Repellent planting uses certain plants which, either by odor or the release of chemicals through their roots, ward off attack by certain insects. Scattering these plants among the butterfly-attracting plants helps keep undesired insects away.

Members of the Onion family are among the most useful repellent plants, with Garlic (*Tulbaghia violacea*) being an especially potent deterrent. Many of the *Alliums* or onions, both wild and cultivated, not only keep nearby plants free of insect pests, but the very attractive large, showy clusters of flowers are a great nectar source, drawing in numerous butterflies. As an added bonus for the garden, all of the *Alliums* can be eaten, except perhaps some of the ornamental ones.

The foliage of Four-O'clock (*Mirabilis jalapa*), Milkweed, Parsley, Dill, Rue (*Ruta* spp.), Fennel, and Anise is poisonous to many insects. When these plants are used among other plants, most insects tend to leave the nonpoisonous plants alone as well. Larvae of the Monarch, Queen, and Eastern Black Swallowtail have evolved methods for ingesting, storing and using certain plant poisons, but fortunately most of the harmful insects haven't. Other plants with foliage toxic to certain insects include Flax (*Linum* spp.), Wormwood (either *Artemesia absenthium* or *A. stelleriana*), Borage (*Borago officinalis*), Petunias, Larkspur, and Geraniums, especially white-flowered ones.

Many insects are repelled by the pungent odor of Nasturtiums. On the other hand, Nasturtiums *attract* almost all species of aphids. This can be good if the plants are placed where they can act as a trap crop for the aphids, keeping them away from other plants as well as making them easy to destroy.

Feverfew (*Chrysanthemum parthenium*) is a plant known and used since early times. Insects in general do not like its pungent foliage and avoid it. Nettles, important larval food plants for the Red Admiral butterfly, are also valuable both as companion plants and as repellent plants. Nettles greatly increase the potency of herbs planted among them, at the same time repelling aphids and plant lice. Tansy (*Tanacetum vulgare*) controls ants, which move aphids from one plant to another, and Marigolds can control nematodes in the soil. The tall, small-flowered Mexican Mint Marigold (*Tagetes lucida*) evidently exudes a repellent from the root system in greater potency than other Marigold species.

As far as I know, no in-depth research has been done on mixing repellent plants into a concentrated planting of butterfly plants. Most of the repelling qualities of these plants comes from the odors emitted through their foliage, especially when the foliage is crushed, and these odors may either make it hard or impossible for butterflies to find the nectar plants or make the general area so disagreeable the butterflies will not stay around. In using repellent plants it is best to constantly observe the actions of the butterflies about your garden. If you suspect that your repellent plants are doing more harm than good, remove them.

Natural Insecticides

As some plants have a natural repellent quality while growing, others (or sometimes the same ones) can be very effective when used as a spray, dust, or mulch. Some of these plants are not especially attractive, though, so they can be grown in out-of-the-way spots, not among your larval or nectar plants.

The best preventative for garden problems is to keep a close watch on the plants and catch the insects or diseases before they really get established. If you do this, often only a light spraying of a small portion of the plant will be required. If the infected plant is a nectar plant, hand-spray with a small bottle sprayer in such a manner as to keep the spray away from the flowers, thereby not disturbing the nectar source of the butterflies. If the foliage of a larval food plant is being damaged, use the spray and then, as soon as the infestation is over, wash the plant thoroughly with a garden hose.

For many of the following concoctions, using a blender is suggested, but do not use the household blender. If an old, no longer used machine is not available, simply mash the material until it is as mushy as possible. Chopped plant material can also be left to steep in warm water for several hours or placed in a jug and left in the sun for several days. The liquid you strain off is usually potent enough for use. Wear rubber gloves when chopping or blending the plants and also when spraying.

Use a small plastic sprayer bottle or a small commercial hand sprayer in order to confine the spray to exactly where it is needed. Two or three such sprayings with a weak solution are much more desirable in butterfly gardening than one extra-strong dose, which may be lethal to everything that touches it for weeks.

Keep in mind that even though these insecticides are concocted from plants, they are very potent and should never be used indiscriminately. Use much caution and apply them only to the pest-infected portions of the plants. Leave insecticides on plants only long enough to kill the pests, then thoroughly wash the plants with a soft dousing from the water hose.

The foliage of Petunias is toxic to some insects.

Natural Insecticide Sprays

⚒ You can make an excellent spray for spider mites by chopping the leaves, stems, and spent flowers of Flowering Tobacco (*Nicotiana* spp.) in a blender with enough water to make a liquid. Strain and add enough water for a spray.

You can make an even better spray by getting the strongest chewing tobacco on the market, combining one half cup of the tobacco with three cups of water, and simmering (not boiling) on very low heat for twenty or thirty minutes. Remove from heat and leave soaking in the same water for a couple of days. When ready to apply, strain through a nylon stocking before using in a sprayer. Try burying unused chewing tobacco around plants to help control underground pests such as wireworms, June bug larvae, nematodes, or cutworms.

⚒ A tea of chopped Burning Nettle (*Urtica urens*) makes a good spray for aphids. Use gloves and wear a long-sleeved shirt when gathering the Nettle. Some people are highly allergic to the sting of this plant, which can cause large blisters on the skin. After you have gathered the Nettle, chop in a blender. Remove to a glass jar or a jug, completely cover the chopped Nettle with water, cover the container tightly, and leave standing for several days or until the plant parts are well rotted. When ready to use, strain and mix one part of the tea to seven parts water.

103

Butterfly Weed (*Asclepias tuberosa*), notorious for attracting aphids

The leaves of Common Elderberry (*Sambucus canadensis*) contain oxalic acid and can make a tea which deters aphids.

A mixture of one-half cup of soft soap such as Ivory liquid (read the label carefully—non-soap detergents will not work), thoroughly mixed with two quarts of water is an excellent control for aphids. Soap is very strong; use a couple of mild applications instead of one strong one to lessen the risk of burning the plants. A potassium-based product now on the market under the brand name of Safer's Insecticidal Soap can be obtained at most plant nurseries. This special soap smothers its victims and is much less damaging to plants than household soaps.

Wash any soap mixture from the plants with a gentle sprinkling from the hose after the infestation is over, especially if used on *Asclepias* (notorious for attracting aphids). The Monarch and the Queen are going to be constantly needing the plants for egg laying. If there are eggs or larvae already on the plants, you can keep aphids under semicontrol by running your fingers along the stems and on the undersides of the leaves, crushing the soft-bodied insects. This does not completely eliminate the aphid colony, but does keep them controlled until the butterfly larvae have all pupated. Then you should thoroughly douse the plants with the soap-and-water mixture to completely eliminate the entire population.

Nasturtiums in the border are larval food for the Cabbage White and Great Southern White and a trap for aphids. When garden Nasturtium is ground in a blender in combination with Sage (*Salvia officinalis*), Wormwood, and Chamomile (*Anthemis nobilis*), along with enough water to make a spray, it is very effective in the control of white flies and aphids.

Brew the chopped stems and leaves of Wormwood (either *Artemisia absenthium* or *A. stelleriana*) into a tea and sprinkle the mixture on the ground and on young plants. The bitter taste repels slugs and snails.

Also, use Wormwood tea in combination with the water from soaked Quassia (*Picrasma excelsa*) chips for an especially potent control. Quassia chips may be purchased at the drug store or nurseries which carry natural control products. To make the spray, soak four ounces of chips in two gallons of water for several days. Then simmer slowly over very low heat for three or four hours; cool and strain before using. When combining this with the Wormwood spray, add one-half teaspoon of soft soap to a bottle full of the spray to make it stick to the plants better. Insects find the bitter taste of these brews totally unpalatable. Again, if used on any of the butterfly larval food plants, the spray should be thoroughly washed off as soon as the pest infestation is over.

Chop citrus peels in a blender with water, let stand for several hours, strain, and use on various insect pests. This is a good, all-around spray and may be tried on almost all chewing or juice-sucking insects. It is very strong and, if not diluted sufficiently, can severely burn foliage.

A mixture of three cloves of garlic, one medium onion, and a teaspoon of hot pepper combined in the blender with a quart of water is an excellent repellent for many insects, including aphids, thrips, and grasshoppers. Let the mixture stand for half an hour or so before straining. Use one part mixture to three or four parts water. These ingredients can also be mixed in a large jar of water and left to steep in the sun for several days before using.

Many gardeners have reported phenomenal success with an elixir called bug juice. To prepare this mixture, collect about a cup of the bugs causing the problem (or as many as possible in the case of small insects, such as aphids or mealybugs). Be sure to collect any that look weakened or sick. Place the insects in a blender, using the proportion of one-half cup of bugs to two cups of water, and blend until liquified. If a blender is not available, mash the insects thoroughly, then add the water, and let set for several hours. Strain through a sieve or cheesecloth, retaining all the liquid possible. Dilute the juice with four to eight parts water and then use as a spray.

Mix only what is needed at the time. Any juice left over can be frozen for a year or more. In order to get enough insects for this juice, you will have to have a pretty bad infestation. By having some of the proper juice on hand from the previous summer, you can use it at the first sign of the insects the next spring, before they become a real problem. This juice can also be prepared using either slugs, snails, or pill bugs; when the liquid is sprayed, poured, or sprinkled around the base of plants, it proves to be a powerful deterrent to these pests.

For an infestation of mealybugs, dip a cotton swab in alcohol and apply to each insect seen as well as to the axil of each leaf, where the eggs and very young are hidden.

If nematodes are a serious problem, consistent use of compost and natural fertilizer in the soils should eliminate them. Lime and fish fertilizer make a useful repellent. A teaspoon of sugar sprinkled into the planting hole before setting out plants such as annuals is also helpful.

✻ Stems and foliage of Common Fennel can be cut into two- or three-inch pieces and scattered in circles around plants as a thin mulch to keep snails away. Pill bugs and sow bugs may be controlled by sprinkling a weak lime solution (two pounds of lime dissolved in five gallons of water) around plants. Sprinkle corn-meal around plants where cutworm damage is apparent; cutworms love the meal, but they can't digest it and will die from overeating.

✻ One of the worst enemies to butterfly larvae and chrysalids is the fire ant. Fire ants become established after flying into an area during mating flights, which occur any time from spring through fall. They can also be brought to the garden in containers of nursery stock or even on plants dug from the wild. If you want to raise butterflies, you simply have to get rid of any and all fire ants anywhere near your food plants.

To eradicate fire ants, there are safe, nonchemical ways as well as chemicals specific to fire ants. Fire ants continually move their larvae and the queen about within the mound and in tunnels to regulate their temperatures. Midmorning to early evening is the best time to treat the mound in the spring, for the ants will have the larvae near the top of the mound to receive the warmth of the sun. During the summer months they are near the surface only during the cooler mornings and late evenings. At these times the colony can be destroyed by pouring boiling water on the mound. Use about three gallons per mound and be sure it's as hot as you can possibly get it. Do not disturb the mound in any way before pouring the water on; in fact, walk up to the mound slowly and quietly. Any earth tremors can send the ants deep within their tunnel, carrying both the queen and the larvae. To completely eradicate a colony, the queen has to be destroyed. Oils from citrus peels are very toxic to fire ants. Remove as much of the white inner lining of Orange (*Citrus sinensis*), Grapefruit (*C. maxima*), or Lemon (*C. limon*) as possible. Run the outer rind through a blender with enough water to blend nicely. Add more water and pour this on the fire ant mound. Safer's Insecticidal Soap can also be blended with water and poured on the mound.

The toxins Pro-Drone and Logic Fire Ant Bait affect only fire ants. Scattered about the mound, the bait is picked up by the ants, carried underground, and fed to the young. The bait is a growth inhibitor; with the young not developing properly, the colony is eventually eliminated.

The Heavies

If a really terrible insect infestation becomes established in the garden and you have already tried various methods (and there are many more than discussed here), consult your local nurseries for other control methods. In any selection of chemical insecticides, always choose short-term ones. Try using a slightly weaker solution than recommended the first time. Use it late in the evening, and hope for an overnight miracle. If the pests appears to be dead the next morning, wash the plant down immediately, reducing the chance of any larvae or adult butterflies being harmed during the day while feeding.

Ants are a serious threat to larvae and chrysalids. Janais
Patch larva.

Perhaps one of the most effective yet less toxic of the insecticides is
Pyrethrin. This is an extract of the toxins from the dried flowers of a daisylike
perennial formerly in the genus *Pyrethrum* but now known as *Chrysanthemum
cineraiifolium.* Some seed and plant sources now offer seeds of this Chrysanthemum, so gardeners can grow their own insecticidal plants, sprinkling the dried,
crushed flowers around infested plants. Pyrethrin is especially effective against
aphids, thrips, leafhoppers, and many beetles.

Sometimes Pyrethrin is used mixed with such chemicals as ryonia and
rotenone. While they are nonpersistent in the environment, all of these other
extracts are extremely high in their toxicity and are nonselective, killing most
things they come in contact with. Any such poison should be used with the
greatest caution.

The new rage in pesticides today are the systemics. Systemic poisons are
usually placed in the ground around a plant either as liquid, powder, or tablets.
As the substance dissolves, it is taken up by the roots of the plant and carried into
all plant parts. The poisons infiltrate the leaves and stems of the plants as well as
the pollen and nectar of the flowers, meaning sure death not only to larvae but
adult butterflies as well. Furthermore, if these chemicals are placed in the soil,
they will, by the water movement and soil disturbance, be carried to other parts
of the garden, eventually contaminating many more plants than the ones originally used on. It is my suggestion to leave the systemics at the store.

Another product which should never be used in a butterfly garden is *Bacillus thuringiensis,* commonly referred to as BT. This bacterial pathogen works
internally, causing paralysis and death within twenty-four hours to all butterfly
larvae (and other critters) which eat even a small amount of any part of the plant
the bacterium has been used on. This product is sold in liquid, dust, and granular
forms, and is marketed under the brand names of Dipel, Thuricide, Biotrol,
Attact, Bactisphere, and Soilserv Bacillus Bait. Do not use any of these products
in your butterfly garden.

107

CHAPTER SIX

A Special South Texas Garden

Gardeners in the semitropical area of the Rio Grande Valley have an excellent opportunity for attracting to their gardens some of the rarest and most beautiful species of butterflies to be found in the region. Not only are there several species which are permanent Texas residents only in the Valley area, but there are some even less common species which come into South Texas from Mexico and South America, and will, under favorable conditions, remain and breed, often for several years in a row. This northward movement, added to the already abundant species breeding there, also gives this area the highest number of total species for the state.

There are probably several environmental factors which determine the residence and breeding status of these uncommon Central and South American butterflies, but two of the most important factors are the occasional periods of freezing temperatures and the scarcity of larval food plants. A severe freeze may completely eliminate a population of these exotic species of butterflies, but even so, they again come northward and repopulate the Valley area usually within a year or so.

Other than providing protection through the planting of windbreaks, there is little that can be done to prevent the extermination of the butterflies during hard freezes, but by planting appropiate food plants, their numbers can surely be increased during the years between the devastating freeze periods.

Bright red Shrimp Plants will attract the rare Cuban Crescentspot to your garden.

As most of the native vegetation has been replaced with crop plants in the Valley area, these tropical butterflies encounter difficulties in locating a plentiful supply of the appropriate food plants on which to lay their eggs. This shortage limits the range, distribution patterns, and number of individuals. Only in areas where an adequate source of the larval food plants is available will there ever be a chance of a colony becoming well established. By incorporating the necessary food plants in home gardens, a gardener greatly increases the chances of getting colonies of these "special" butterflies to remain and breed.

Many of the larval food plants for these more uncommon species of butterflies have either been almost entirely eliminated from the Valley area through clearing practices or, in a few instances, may never have been abundant members of the flora there. Very few of the needed plants are going to be readily available at nurseries, and, due to their scarcity within the remaining areas of native vegetation, the plants cannot be obtained easily from the wild. The best method of obtaining many of the plants listed here will be through gathering seeds or taking cuttings from native plants. You can place special orders for some plants from Mexico through a local nursery which offers such plants. Take a list of the plants which you would like to purchase to your local nursery expert and ask their help in obtaining them. Or, visit the local chambers of commerce and get names and phone numbers of local nature, birding, and garden clubs. Contact these folks for sources and methods of obtaining the plants you need.

The following list is not in any way the "final word" on the butterflies to be found in the lower Rio Grande Valley. Each year, as more collecting is done and more researchers become interested and involved in the butterflies in that region, new species are continually being added. And, as with all such work, the more that is learned about the distribution, habitats, and life cycles of a wildlife species, the status as to their abundance is continually changed and updated. Some of the recent collections are proving that, indeed, many butterfly species can be found there and are substantiating old, disputed records of much earlier collections. Are these rarely reported butterflies really that uncommon for the area and only to be found once every fifty years or so—or have they actually been there but, not knowing their life histories, observers have not searched at the proper time or in the proper habitat? Obviously, more in-depth work must be done before the answers to such questions can be given. Take this list, then, as a guideline—to be substracted from and added to while more research is completed on these uncommon species.

I've compiled the following list from current literature and my own observations in the field. It includes those species which, at the present time, are known to breed (in Texas) only in the lower Rio Grande Valley. Refer to the landscape drawing for ideas on incorporating these special larval food plants in the home garden. I've only listed a butterfly when its food plant is known. Many other species of butterflies stray or wander into the lower Valley (probably) to breed, but their food plants are not presently known. Others wander in—some quite regularly—but do not breed there. These species are not listed. Most of these plants are native species, but a few from other areas (noted) you can possibly purchase from nurseries.

Butterflies for South Texas

Butterfly	Food Plant
Astraptes, Dull (*Astraptes anaphus*)	Kudzu (*Pueraria montana*)
Astraptes, Flashing (*Astraptes fulgerator*)	Chaste Tree (*Vitex agnus-castus*)
	Coyotillo (*Karwinski humboldtiana*)
Black, Crimson-banded (*Biblis hyperia*)	Noseburn (*Tragia volubilis*) (Brazil)
	Noseburn, Brush (*Tragia glanduligera*)
	Noseburn, Catnip (*Tragia ramosa*)
Blue Wing (*Myscelia ethusa*)	Adelia (*Adelia vaseyi*) (Mexico)
	Croton (*Croton niveus*) (El Salvador)
	Croton, Bent-leaf (*Croton reflexifolius*) (El Salvador)
Buckeye, Dark (*Junonia nigrosuffusa*)	Stemodia (*Stemodia tomentosa*)
	Gerardia, Purple (*Agalinis purpurea*)
	Gerardia, Seaside (*Agalinis maritima*)

Butterfly	Food Plant
Calico, Gray-skirted (*Hamadryas februa*)	Noseburn (*Tragia* spp.) (prob. in Texas)
Cracker, Central American (*Hamadryas guatemalena*)	Noseburn (*Tragia* spp.) (prob. in Texas) Dalechampia (*Dalechampia scandens*) (El Salvador)
Crescentspot, Cuban (*Anthanassa frisia*)	Dicliptera, Perennial (*Dicliptera brachiata*) Dicliptera, Rio Grande (*Dicliptera sexangularis*) Ruella, Violet (*Ruella nudiflora*) Shrimp Plant (*Beloperone guttata*)
Daggerwing, Banded (*Marpesia chiron*)	Artocarpus (*Artocarpus* spp.) (Mexico) Chlorophora (*Chlorophora* spp.) (Mexico) Fig, Common (*Ficus carica*)
Daggerwing, Ruddy (*Marpesia petreus*)	Fig, Short-leaf (*Ficus brevifolia*) (Florida) Fig (*Ficus padifolia*) (Mexico) Fig, Common (*Ficus carica*)
Emperor, Rio Grande Valley (*Asterocampa clyton louisa*)	Hackberry, Sugar (*Celtis laevigata*)
Fatima (*Anartia fatima*)	Ruellia, Violet (*Ruellia nudiflora*)
Flasher, Mad (*Astraptes gilberti*)	Bauhinia (*Bauhinia divaricata*) (Mexico)
Greenwing, Blue-eyed (*Dynamine dyonis*)	Noseburn, Catnip (*Tragia ramosa*)
Hairstreak, Azia (*Tmolus azia*)	Acacia, Wright (*Acacia wrightii*) Leadtree, Great (*Leucaena pulverulenta*) Mimosa, Vine (*Mimosa malacophylla*)
Hairstreak, Columella (*Strymon columella*)	Croton, One-seeded (*Croton monanthogynus*) Portulaca, Shaggy (*Portulaca pilosa*) Sida, Alkali (*Malvella leprosa*) Indian-mallow (*Abutilon permolle*) (Florida) Hibiscus (*Hibiscus denudatus*)
Hairstreak, Goodson's (*Cyanophrys goodsoni*)	Rouge-plant (*Rivina humilis*)
Hairsteak, Mexican Gray (*Strymon bebrycia*)	Balloon-vine, Common (*Cardiospermum halicacabum*)
Hairstreak, Miserabilis (*Cyanophrys miserabilis*)	Retama (*Parkinsonia aculeata*)
Hairstreak, Reddish (*Strymon rufofusca*)	False-mallow (*Malvastrum coromandelianum*)
Hairstreak, White (*Strymon albata*)	Indian-mallow (*Abutilon fruticosum*)
Hairstreak, Xamia (*Xamia xamia*)	Stonecrop, Texas (*Lenophyllum texanum*)
Lantana Butterfly, Smaller (*Strymon bazochi*)	Lantana, West Indian (*Lantana camara*) Lippia, Scented (*Lippa graveolens*) Lippia, White (*Lippia alba*)
Laure (*Doxocopa laure*)	Hackberry, Spiny (*Celtis pallida*)
Leafwing, Tropical (*Anaea aidea*)	Croton, Low (*Croton humilis*) Croton, Narrow-leaf (*Crotonopsis linearis*) Croton, Soliman (*Croton soliman*)
Longtail, Brown (*Urbanus procne*)	Grass, Common Bermuda (*Cynodon dactylon*)

Butterfly	**Food Plant**
Longtail, Teleus (*Urbanus teleus*)	Grass, Guinea (*Panicum maximum*)
	Grass, Johnson (*Sorghum halepense*)
	Paspalum, Thin (*Paspalum setaceum*)
Malachite (*Siproeta stelenes*)	Ruellia, Violet (*Ruellia nudiflora*)
	Water-willow (*Justicia americana*)
	Water-willow, Runyon (*Justicia runyonii*)
	Yerba Papagayo (*Blechum brownei*) (Florida)
Metalmark, Falcate (*Emesis emesia*)	Caesalpinia, Mexican (*Caesalpinia mexicana*)
Orange, Banded (*Dryadula phaetusa*)	Passionflower, Blue (*Passiflora caerulea*)
Patch, Rosita (*Chlosyne rosita*)	Dicliptera, Rio Grande (*Dicliptera sexangularis*)
	Dicliptera, Perennial (*Dicliptera brachiata*)
Pavon (*Doxocopa pavon*)	Hackberry, Spiny (*Celtis pallida*)
Pixie (*Melanis pixe*)	Guamuchil (*Pithcellobium dulce*)
Purplewing, Dingy (*Eunica monima*)	Ash, Prickly (*Zanthoxylum* spp.) (Mexico)
Queen, Tropic (*Danaus eresimus*)	Cynanchum (*Cynanchum unifarium*)
	Milkweed, Mexican (*Asclepias curassavica*)
Silverspot, Mexican (*Dione moneta*)	Passionflower, Slender-lobe (*Passiflora tenuiloba*)
	Passionflower, Tagua (*Passiflora foetida*)
	Passionflower, Yellow (*Passiflora lutea*)
Sister, Mexican (*Adelpha fessonia*)	Hackberry, Lindheimer (*Celtis lindheimeri*)
	Hackberry, Net-leaf (*Celtis reticulata*)
	Randia (*Randia rhagocarpa*)
Skipper, Brown-banded (*Timochares ruptifasciatus*)	Barbados Cherry (*Malpighia glabra*)
Skipper, Brown-margined White (*Heliopetes macaira*)	Drummond Wax-mallow (*Malvaviscus arborea*)
Skipper, Falcate (*Spathilepia clonius*)	Inga (*Inga edulis*) (Brazil)
	Bean (*Phaseolus* spp.) (Brazil)
Skipper, Fawn-spotted (*Cymaenes odilia*)	Grass, Guinea (*Panicum maximum*)
Skipper, Guava (*Phocides palemon*)	Guava (*Psidium guajava*)
	Guava, Strawberry (*Psidium cattleianum*)
Skipper, Hoary (*Carrhenes canescens*)	Hibiscus (*Hibiscus* spp.) (El Salvador)
Skipper, Malicious (*Synapte malitiosa*)	Grass, Guinea (*Panicum maximum*)
Skipper, Olive-clouded (*Lerodea dysaules*)	Grass, Common Bermuda (*Cynodon dactylon*)
Skipper, Purple-washed (*Panoquina sylvicola*)	Cane, Sugar (*Saccharum officinarum*)
	Grass, Carpet (*Axonopus compressus*)
	Grass, Johnson (*Sorghum halepense*)
	Rice (*Oryza sativa*)
Skipper, Russet (*Panoquina hecebolus*)	Cane, Sugar (*Saccharum officinarum*)

Butterfly	Food Plant
Skipper, Violet-banded (*Nyctelius nyctelius*)	Cane, Sugar (*Saccharum officinarum*) Corn (*Zea mays*) Rice (*Oryza sativa*)
Skipper, Violet-patch (*Monca tyrtaeus*)	Paspalum (*Paspalum* spp.)
Skipper, Window-winged (*Xenophanes tryxus*)	Drummond Wax-mallow (*Malvaviscus arborea*) Malachra (*Malachra fasciata*) (Brazil)
Snout, Southern (*Libytheana carinenta*)	Hackberry, Spiny (*Celtis pallida*)
Swallowtail, Astyalus (*Heraclides astyalus*)	Lemon (*Citrus limon*) Orange, Sweet (*Citrus sinensis*)
Swallowtail, Ornythion (*Heraclides ornythion*)	Lemon (*Citrus limon*) Orange, Sweet (*Citrus sinensis*)
Swallowtail, Red-spotted (*Priamedes anchisiades*)	Amyris, Texas (*Amyris texana*) (probably) Lemon (*Citrus limon*) Casimiro (*Casimiroa edulis*)
Swallowtail, Thoas (*Heraclides thoas*)	Rue, Common (*Ruta graveolens*)
Tiger, Isabella (*Eueides isabella*)	Passionflower, Slender-lobe (*Passiflora tenuiloba*) Passionflower, Tagua (*Passiflora foetida*) Passionflower, Yellow (*Passiflora lutea*)
White, Giant (*Ganyra josephina*)	Cappari (*Capparis frondosa*) (Mexico) Forchammeria (*Forchammeria hintonii*) (Mexico)
Yellow, Boisduval's (*Eurema boisduvalidana*)	Senna, Coffee (*Cassia bicapsularis*)
Yellow, Mimosa (*Pyrisitia nise*)	Lysiloma (*Lysiloma latisiliqua*) Mimosa (*Mimosa pudica*)

CHAPTER SEVEN

Butterflies for the South

The following is a sampling of the many species of butterflies to be found in the South. Some, such as the Gray Hairstreak (*Strymon melinus*) and the Eastern Black Swallowtail (*Papilio polyxene*), can be found in gardens throughout during the entire growing season. Others, such as the Olympia Marblewing (*Euchloe olympia*) and King's Hairstreak (*Satyrium kingi*), can be found in only small specialized areas and for only short periods of time each year.

The butterflies here were chosen for some unusual interest, to show the variability of our area's insects or simply because they are beautiful. There are many butterflies more common than some shown here, but space does not allow their inclusion.

No scientific order was followed in the arrangement of species within this section. Instead they are placed generally by size for ease in identification—beginning with one of the largest butterflies occuring in the area, the Giant Swallowtail (*Heraclides cresphontes*), and ending with one of the smallest, the Western Pygmy Blue (*Brephidium exilis*). In a few instances, I have placed look-alikes near one another for easy comparison.

114

There are sets of information at the beginning and the end of each description to help you become more familiar with each butterfly's life cycle.

⚘ **Common and Scientific Names:** In most instances, the common names are the ones used by Robert Michael Pyle in *The Audubon Society Field Guide to North American Butterflies*. A major exception is with the Hackberry butterflies (*Asterocampa* spp.); their scientific names follow Dr. Timothy Friedlander's recently completed, exhaustive work on this genus, in some instances reducing species to a subspecies level. For clarity, I have included the subspecies names in this work. The other butterflies' scientific names used in this text follow *A Catalogue/Checklist of the Butterflies of America North of Mexico* by Lee D. Miller and F. Martin Brown, the work most generally accepted by professional lepidopterists.

⚘ **Range:** The first range given includes all the states (within the area covered in this book) where the butterfly is known to occur and breed.

The first number(s) for the Texas range indicates the region(s) where that particular butterfly is known to breed within the state (refer to map). The number(s) following in parentheses indicates the region(s) where the butterfly does not normally breed but wanders and may be seen in gardens during some portion of the growing season. Some species, due to climatic conditions or their whims, wander into other regions where, if conditions are favorable, the female deposits some eggs. This results in what is termed a partial brood, meaning that only a part of the female's normal egg mass is deposited in that area. In some instances, the resulting butterflies may survive to establish a colony for a short time, but they are usually eventually eliminated by some climatic factor, such as a freeze.

⚘ **Flight Time:** "All year" refers to butterflies that spend part or all of their life cycle in the warmer portions of Florida and in the Rio Grande Valley area of Texas, where they continue to fly and perhaps breed the year-round or it may indicate species which partially hibernate during the coldest days of winter but can be seen during warmer, non-freezing days. The months indicate when that particular species flies and breeds after spending the winter in some other form.

⚘ **Broods:** The exact number of broods remains unknown for many species. Even with some of the better understood species, climatic factors play a major role in the number of broods produced each year. The numbers here are according to the best information available.

⚘ **Overwinters:** Given here is the stage or diapause period in which the butterfly spends the winter or period of coldest weather. The overwintering stages vary with the species (and region) and may be either egg, larva, chrysalis, or adult. Many species in Florida and the Rio Grande Valley area have no diapause, continuing to fly and breed year round. If the butterfly also breeds in regions or states where a resting period is required, this stage is indicated in parentheses.

⚘ **Egg:** A general, rather than an in-depth description is given here, due to the fact that most eggs are so small that a microscope is required to examine the features in detail.

⚘ **Larva:** A larva goes through several molts during this cycle, with each instar appearing quite unlike the previous one. Here I describe the last instar, unless otherwise noted.

⚘ **Food Plants:** Plants eaten by the caterpillars.

⚘ **Note:** An additional bit of information.

GIANT SWALLOWTAIL
(*Heraclides cresphontes*)

Family: *Papilionidae*
Size: 3 3/8-5 1/2 inches
Range: All
   Texas: 2, 3, 4 (1, 5)
Flight Time: All year (May-November)
Broods: Many
Overwinters: Adult (pupa)

The Giant Swallowtail is easily recognized, being the only large, common swallowtail with brownish-black on the upper wing surface and yellow on the lower surface. The brownish-black upper surface is marked by two broad yellow bands meeting near the tip of the forewing; the lower surface is yellow splashed with black bands, veins, and borders. A row of blue iridescent crescents decorates the black band on the hindwing. Tails on the hindwings are long, spoon-shaped, and yellow-centered.

Normally a strong, high flier, the Giant Swallowtail is easily enticed down to flowers, drinking from them long and thirstily. It is especially fond of Butterfly Bush (*Buddleia davidii*) and Lantana (*Lantana* spp.), flying about leisurely from one bush to the other. It also partakes of the fluids of mud, fruit juices, and manure.

The larva commonly feeds on leaves of citrus trees and is referred to as an orange puppy or orange dog. It is not hard to see the resemblance to a puppy as the caterpillar lies stretched out on a leaf in the sun. The caterpillar's osmeteria, or scent organs, are yellow and emit a most unpleasant odor when the caterpillar is handled.

The female is a prolific egg producer; one can lay four or five hundred eggs during her lifetime.

Egg: Usually pale green, but sometimes yellowish; laid singly on new growth, generally near the leaf tip; sometimes deposited on branch near young foliage.

Larva: Brownish- or greenish-maroon with white or cream markings; shiny, resembling bird droppings. The larva rests exposed on upper or lower sides of leaves or along young branches. It does not make any sort of nest or shelter.

Food Plants: Hercules'-club (*Zanthoxylum clava-herculis*), Lime Prickly Ash (*Z. fagara*), Prickly Ash (*Z. hirsutum*), Grapefruit (*Citrus maxima*), Lemon (*C. limon*), Lime (*C. aurantifolia*), Sour Orange (*C. aurantium*), Sweet Orange (*C. sinensis*), Hop-tree (*Ptelea trifoliata*), Common Rue (*Ruta graveolens*), Rue (*R. chalapensis*)

Parts Eaten: Young to midmature foliage

TIGER SWALLOWTAIL
(*Pterourus glaucus*)

Family: *Papilionidae*
Size: 3 1/8-5 1/2 inches
Range: All
  Texas: 2, 3, 4
Flight Time: April-November
Broods: Many
Overwinters: Pupa

The yellow-and-black tigerlike striping of this butterfly makes it easy to recognize. When in flight or nectaring with its wings raised, it can be confused with the Giant Swallowtail, which is similar in size and underwing coloring. However, the four tiger stripes trailing downward from the leading edge of the forewing are distinctive enough for identification. The lower wing surface of the Tiger also differs in having its row of several blue and red dots set within a smudgy black marginal band of the hindwing; the dark-colored band of the Giant is placed in the middle of the hindwing and contains numerous blue dots but only two red dots. You won't confuse their upper surfaces, though, for the upper wing surface of the Tiger is yellow with the same four black, trailing stripes parallel to the body, while the Giant's is black with yellow stripes placed in a very different pattern.

An interesting dimorphism occurs in Tiger Swallowtails. Some of the females are black, appearing to be the unpalatable Pipevine Swallowtail (*Battus philenor*). The black coloration normally occurs only from female eggs laid by a black mother. Male eggs from the same black mother produce yellow males.

The Tiger Swallowtail is a strong flier, at times flying very rapidly, at other times slowly, soaring with the wings at an angle. It often flies high in the trees in the wild, frequently along watercourses or along forest borders. It visits flowers readily, sometimes barely clutching the flower with the feet and with the wings fluttering rapidly, similar to the other Swallowtails. At other times it may cling below the nectar source with wings spread flat, thoroughly working the flowers. When nectaring at especially rich sources such as Azalea (*Azalea* spp.), Butterfly Bush, Butterfly Weed (*Asclepias tuberosa*), or Glossy Abelia (*Abelia grandiflora*), it closes the wings and crawls among the flowers, slowly extracting every minute drop of nectar. It may also occasionally be found on carrion. Male Tiger Swallowtails are fond of wet areas and often gather in groups to obtain salts from the moisture. This puddling behavior is practiced by many species of butterflies.

Both the male and the female participate in the courtship ritual, with much fluttering and flying about before landing and actually mating. During the courtship flight, the male releases a perfumelike pheromone, which acts as an aphrodisiac to excite the female for mating. If the pair are disturbed during copulation, the female flies carrying the male.

Top. Tiger Swallowtail
Above. Female Tiger Swallowtail, dark form

117

Egg: Yellow-green, round, large for butterfly eggs; laid singly on leaf of food plant.

Larva: The young larva is shiny, mottled in browns, with white saddle across back, much resembling a fresh bird dropping. The mature larva is green, the head portion enlarged, banded crosswise with a solitary narrow yellow band bordered by a black stripe, and with two yellow and black eyespots. Larva eats at night. During the day they rest on a silken mat on top of a leaf, with the leaf edges pulled together to form a tent.

Food Plants: Arizona Ash (*Fraxinus velutina*), Carolina Ash (*F. caroliniana*), Green Ash (*F. pennsylvanica*), White Ash (*F. americana*), Black Cherry (*Prunus serotina*), Common Chokecherry (*P. virginiana*), Common Peach (*P. persica*), Mexican Plum (*P. mexicana*), Apple (*Malus pumila*), Camphor-tree (*Cinnamomum camphora*), Common Catalpa (*Catalpa bignonioides*), American Hornbeam (*Carpinus caroliniana*), Eastern Cottonwood (*Populus deltoides*), Mock Orange (*Styrax americana*), Sassafras (*Sassafras albidum*), Sweet Bay (*Magnolia virginiana*), Tulip-tree (*Liriodendron tulipifera*), Common Lilac (*Syringa vulgaris*), Hop-tree (*Ptelea trifoliata*), Spicebush (*Lindera benzoin*)

Parts eaten: Leaves

Note: The Tiger Swallowtail is very similar in coloring to the Two-tailed Tiger Swallowtail (*P. multicaudata*). Identification is best determined by the addition of the short but conspicuous second tail near the body of the Two-tailed Tiger Swallowtail.

PALAMEDES SWALLOWTAIL
(*Pterourus palamedes*)

Family: *Papilionidae*
Size: 3 1/8-5 1/2 inches
Range: All except Arkansas, Oklahoma, Tennessee
   Texas: 2, 3
Flight Time: April-October
Broods: Several
Overwinters: Pupa

A large, slow-flying denizen of the more moist wooded or semishaded gardens, this splendid Swallowtail sails among the shrubbery, casually taking nectar from many different species of flowers. Where there are good stands of flowers such as the Azaleas, Pickerelweed (*Pontederia cordata*), Yellow Iris (*Iris pseudacorus*), Purple Loosestrife (*Lythrum salicaria*), or Thistle, Palamedes Swallowtails congregate in numbers and are very showy. They also visit Phlox (*Phlox* spp.), Madagascar Periwinkle (*Catharanthus roseus*), Verbena (*Verbena* spp.), or just about any nectar producing flowers, preferring areas where masses of one species are growing instead of going from one species of plant to another.

There are several Swallowtails with similar coloring and markings, but the Palamedes is distinguished by its large size and long, creamy yellow to orangy-red stripe on the lower surface of the wings along the base and parallel to the body. This stripe is large and easily seen as the insect is feeding, for usually in taking nectar it does not rest on the flower but hovers above the blossom with fluttering wings, lightly grasping the petals with its feet. Other identifying markings are the large abdomen striped in black and yellow, and the upper surface of the hindwings, bearing an unbroken yellow band.

Palamedes Swallowtails roost communally at night in swampy areas of Georgia, with several taking shelter together high in trees or branches of tall Red Bay (*Persea borbonia*) trees.

Egg: Pale yellowish or greenish; laid singly on the undersurface of a young leaf.

Larva: Young larva is blotched brown and white, shiny. Mature larva is green on upper portion of body, velvety brown or buff on lower side. Portion of body behind head enlarged and with two black eyespots circled in orange. Larva lives in a tent made by making a bed of silk along the midrib on upper surface of a leaf and drawing the sides together.

Food Plants: Red Bay (*Persea borbonia*), Sassafras (*Sassafras albidum*), Sweet Bay (*Magnolia virginiana*), and the cultivated Avocado (*Persea americana*)

Parts Eaten: Leaves

SPICEBUSH SWALLOWTAIL
(*Pterourus troilus*)

Family: *Papilionidae*
Size: 3 1/2-4 1/2 inches
Range: All
  Texas: 2, 4 (1)
Flight Time: March-November
Broods: Several
Overwinters: Pupa

Often seen about edges of woodlands, along banks of streams, and in open fields and flower gardens, the Spicebush Swallowtail seeks out low-growing flowers in a slow, easy flight. All the Swallowtails seem to prefer flowers which form heads or clusters, such as Butterfly Bush, Lantana, Beebalm, Bergamot, Butterfly Weed, Phlox, and Verbena. When a Swallowtail finds choice plants, it remains for a long period, going from one flower cluster to another. While feeding, it continues to flutter its wings, lightly grasping the flower with the feet. It has been suggested that the Swallowtail does this in order not to tip the flower with its heavier body and perhaps spill the nectar.

This is a beautiful butterfly with a majestic flight, covering ground quite rapidly when the need arises. Ordinarily, though, it flies about with an up-and-down motion, frequently sailing with motionless, outspread wings and veering around as if guided by the tails. It is usually quite wary, whether in flight or feeding, and not easily approached.

Some of the Spicebush Swallowtail's most used nectar sources include Azaleas (both cultivated and native), Butterfly Bush, Sweet Pepper-bush (*Clethra alnifolia*), Lantana, Carolina-jessamine (*Gelsemium sempervirens*),

various Asters (*Aster* spp.), Butterfly Weed, Cardinal Flower (*Lobelia cardinalis*), Globe Amaranth (*Gomphrena globosa*), Golden Crownbeard (*Verbesina encelioides*), Joe-Pye-weed (*Eupatorium fistulosum*), Pineapple Sage (*Salvia elegans*), Spreading Dogbane (*Apocynum androsaemifolium*), Summer Phlox (*Phlox panaculata*), and Verbena.

Spicebush Swallowtails are also great moisture lovers and frequently congregate around mud puddles, patches of wet dirt, or along the edge of a stream.

In coloration this butterfly mimics the unpalatable Pipevine Swallowtail, but the Spicebush Swallowtail differs in having a row of large white or pale bluish spots along the edges of

119

both fore- and hindwings on the upper surface (dots on the Pipevine Swallowtail are very small or nonexistent). Also, the iridescent sheen of the hindwings is reduced to a wide band on the Spicebush. In the female this sheen is a lovely blue; in the male it has a distinct green cast. A prominent round spot of orangy-red occurs on the trailing or inner edge of each hindwing, but these can rarely be seen in flight. There are two rows of orange or red dots on the lower surface of the hindwing, instead of the one row of the Pipevine Swallowtail.

Egg: Greenish-white; laid singly on underside of food plant leaf.

Larva: Green above, with pale tan or gray-ish-beige beneath. Rows of small blue dots cover the body. There are large orange eyespots on the enlarged, "humped" portion of the body behind the head, one pair the largest and with large black dots beneath, forming the pupil of the "eye." The mature larva is large, up to 1 5/8 inches long. During the day it rests on a silken mat on the upper surface of a leaf with the sides of the leaf pulled together. It feeds at night.

Food Plants: Camphor-tree (*Cinnamonum camphora*), Red Bay, Sassafras (*Sassofras albidum*), Sweet Bay (*Magnolia virginiana*), Tulip-tree (*Liriodendron tulipfera*), and Spicebush (*Lindera benzoin*)

Parts Eaten: Leaves

EASTERN BLACK SWALLOWTAIL
(*Papilio polyxenes*)

Family: *Papilionidae*
Size: 2 5/8-3 1/2 inches
Range: All
  Texas: Throughout
Flight Time: February-November
Broods: Several
Overwinters: Pupa

The Eastern Black Swallowtail is adapted to many situations within open country. This is a common butterfly of fields and meadows, cultivated farmland, parks, golf courses, and flower gardens. It seems to show no preference between dry uplands and moist marshes, as long as the area is open and not wooded.

A great lover of flowers, it likes to drift among the plants lazily, taking nectar and pausing frequently to bask with wings fully outspread. It is especially attracted to gardens which have both plentiful flowers and good stands of Common Fennel (*Foeniculum vulgare*), Dill (*Anethum graveolens*), or Parsley (*Petroselinum crispum*), its larval food plants. Favored nectar plants include blossoms of fruit trees such as Apple and Common Peach along with Lantana, Thoroughwort (*Eupatorium havense*), Butterfly Weed, Indian Blanket (*Gaillardia pulchella*), New England Aster (*Aster novae-angliae*), Phlox, Purple Loosestrife, various Thistles, and Zinnias (*Zinnia* spp.).

The female of the Eastern Black Swallowtail closely mimics the Pipevine Swallowtail, gaining an advantage from the Pipevine's toxicity. The upper wing surfaces of the female are mostly black, with two rows of creamy or pale yellowish dots bordering both wings and with a wide iridescent bluish band between the rows of dots. The upper band of yellow dots is often absent or very faint. The upper wing surface of the male is generally black with two rows of large, very prominent bright yellow spots. The rows of spots are separated on the lower wings by a narrow wash of metallic blue. The lower wing surfaces of both sexes are similar to those of the Spicebush Swallowtail, being black with two rows of orangy-red spots separated by a band of widely spaced blue dots. Rows of small yellow dots line the black abdomen. A solitary large, black-centered red or orangish spot in the lower angle of each hindwing occurs on both upper and lower surfaces.

The insect is often seen in moist areas or around mud puddles, methodically sucking up the moisture with its accumulated salts. To seek mates, a male patrols a chosen area or occasionally claims a perching place from which to fly out to inspect whatever passes by. He changes his perching site frequently, usually not using the same space more than two or three days. The female flies to a hilltop (or to the highest terrain around) to mate, with a male usually in

Eastern Black Swallowtail

pursuit. Once at the mating ground, the male and female flutter near one another briefly, then land, where they copulate. If the female lives longer than a week, she often mates a second time.

Egg: Cream to yellowish, becoming reddish near top; somewhat oval, smooth; laid singly on a flower bud or leaf of food plant.

Larva: The young larva may be various shades of brown, or perhaps black and white with a wide white saddle. The mature larva is up to 2 inches long, basically green with wide, crosswise bands of black, the bands interspersed with yellow dots or slashes. The larva does not eat its cast skin after molting, as is common with many species.

Food Plants: Nuttall Mock Bishop's-weed (*Ptilimnium nuttallii*), Ribbed Mock Bishop's-weed (*P. costatum*), Thread-leaf Mock Bishop's-weed (*Ptilimnium capillaceum*), Prairie Parsley (*Polytaenia nuttallii*), Texas Dutchman's Breeches (*Thamnosma texana*) and cultivated Common Fennel, Dill, and Parsley seem to be the favored food plants. Others less commonly used include Anise-root (*Osmorhiza longistylis*), Common Rue, Rue, Forked Scale-seed (*Spermolepis divaricata*), Garden Parsnip (*Pastinaca sativa*), Queen Anne's Lace (*Daucus carota*), Rattlesnake-weed (*Daucus pusillus*), Stalky Berula (*Berula erecta*), Spotted Cowbane (*Cicuta maculata*), Water-parsnip (*Sium suava*), Wild Celery (*Apium graveolens*), Wild Chervil (*Cryptotaenia canadensis*) and Yellow Pimpernel (*Taenidia integerrima*).

Parts Eaten: Almost all aboveground parts of plant except tough stem

Note: Queen Anne's Lace is often listed as a major food source (and is included here), but I have yet to find a caterpillar on this rough plant.

PIPEVINE SWALLOWTAIL
(*Battus philenor*)

Family: *Papilionidae*
Size: 2 3/4-3 3/8 inches
Range: All
  Texas: 2, 3, 4 (1, 5)
Flight Time: March-November
Broods: Many
Overwinters: Pupa

The Pipevine is one of our most common and most easily recognized Swallowtails, with the upper surface of the forewings being a solid dark gray or black and the hindwings overlaid with metallic blue or turquoise scales. The metallic sheen on the wings of the male is usually brighter and covers a larger area than on

121

Pipevine
Swallowtail

tough, enabling it to survive after being bitten or tasted. As an added protection, the red dots along the abdomen emit an acrid, unpleasant odor when the insect is molested.

The Pipevine Swallowtail has a swift flight but stops often to visit flowers. This butterfly seems to prefer pink to purple hues, although yellows and oranges are almost as readily used. Some of its favorite nectar sources are fruit tree blossoms, Azaleas, Butterfly Bush, Golden Corydalis (*Corydalis aura*), and Southern Corydalis (*C. micrantha*) in early spring; Lantana, Butterfly Weed, the summer-flowering Chicory (*Chicorium intybus*), Globe Amaranth, Mexican Sunflower (*Tithonia rotundifolia*), Sand-verbena (*Abronia* spp.), Summer Phlox, Texas Thistle (*Cirsium texanum*), Wild Bergamot (*Monarda fistulosa*), Verbena; and the fall-flowering Cardinal Flower, Frostweed (*Verbesina virginica*), Golden Crownbeard, New England Aster and Pineapple Sage.

Pipevine Swallowtails often roost in loose groups at night in a tree or a large-leaved shrub, hanging from the branches and undersides of the leaves. Males seek mud puddles and spend much time there.

Egg: Reddish-brown, large, spherical; laid singly or in small groups on underside of host leaf, along leafstalk, or occasionally along stem of plant. Although each grouping usually consists of only a few eggs, almost every leaf and stem of the plant may be utilized.

Larva: The young larva is brownish. The larvae remain in small groups during the first two or three instars, dispersing as they become older. Mature larva is up to 2 1/4 inches long, soft-bodied, and ranging in color from almost orange to dark maroon. Long, floppy tubercles extend along the body, with four longer ones on segments of the body just behind the head. The larva feeds at night as well as during the day.

Food Plants: All native species of *Aristolochia* are used as well as most cultivated species. The female occasionally lays eggs on the cultivar Calico Flower (*Aristolochia elegans*), but young larvae will die on it. In the last instars (or almost-mature stages), the larvae can survive on Calico Flower, although they do not like it much.

Parts Eaten: Leaves or, in some instances, the entire aboveground portions of the plant

the female. Two rows of very narrow, somewhat inconspicuous, creamy to yellow dashes rim the margins of both wings but are usually more prominent on the hindwings. The lower surface of the hindwing has a wide row of large orangy-red dots bordered with bands of metallic blue scaling.

The Pipevine Swallowtail retains some of the poisonous properties of its larval food plant and is most unpalatable to its bird and lizard enemies. Three other Swallowtails—the Spicebush, females of the Eastern Black, and black females of the Tiger—along with the Red-spotted Purple have evolved their coloring to closely resemble the Pipevine, obtaining protection through this mimicry. The dark-phased female of the Tiger Swallowtail is the closest in coloring and markings, but the Tiger can instantly be recognized by the bright orange spots on the upper surface of the hindwings near the tip of the abdomen, which are lacking in the Pipevine. The scent scales of the male Pipevine Swallowtail are in a slender, pocketlike depression along the inner edge of the hindwings and are quite noticeable on close inspection. As with the Monarch, the body of the Pipevine Swallowtail is very

ZEBRA SWALLOWTAIL
(*Eurytides marcellus*)

Family: *Papilionidae*
Size: 2 3/8-3 1/2 inches
Range: All
  Texas: 2
Flight Time: March-October
Broods: 3, possibly more
Overwinters: Pupa

There is no confusing this Swallowtail with any other. The wings are sharply striped in black and greenish-white, beautifully accented with red and blue dots on both surfaces of the wings near the excessively long tails.

Zebra Swallowtails rarely emigrate, usually remaining in the area of the earlier stages of their life cycle. While they are palatable to all forms of predators, their worst enemy seems to be spiders, both the ones which lie in wait on flowers and the web builders.

The Zebra Swallowtail remains low to the ground in flight. Although it flaps its wings slowly, because of its size it moves very quickly and with an erratic, bobbing motion. It does not remain long in one place but flits from flower to flower, sipping briefly. Males are especially fond of congregating at mud puddles. Both the male and the female often use the underside of Pawpaw leaves (their larval food plant) for roosting at night and resting during inclement weather.

The Zebra Swallowtail shows a variation of color during the season. The brood relationships are extremely complex and have been given different names. Early spring forms have short wings and short tails and are light in coloration; this brood is the most numerous. Summer forms are larger, with darker coloring and longer wings and tails. The butterflies which emerge latest in the season are the largest and darkest of all. Some larvae from each brood hibernate until the next year, causing still more confusion in the coloring of those seen on the wing.

This butterfly does not seem to adapt very well to urban development, needing wilderness conditions for breeding. However, if some larval food plants are provided in yards near natural stands of Pawpaw, the female readily uses the ones in gardens along with the wild plants for depositing her eggs.

Egg: Pale green; deposited singly on the underside of a leaf.

Larva: Pale green with crosswise rows of tiny black dots and narrow bands of pale yellow and blue. Wider and darker bands of yellow, black, and blue occur directly behind the head. Some larvae may be mostly black, with narrow orange and white lines across the body and with the head solid black. The larva rests on the underside of a leaf or at the base of a plant.

Food Plants: Big-flower Pawpaw (*Asimina obovata*), Common Pawpaw (*Asimina triloba*), Dwarf Pawpaw (*A. parviflora*), Netleaf Pawpaw (*A. reticulata*), Slim-leaf Pawpaw (*A. angustifolia*), Small-flower Pawpaw (*A. parviflora*), Woolly Pawpaw (*A. invicona*)

Parts Eaten: Leaves

123

RED-SPOTTED PURPLE
(*Basilarchia astyanax*)

Family: *Nymphalidae*
Size: 3-3 3/8 inches
Range: All
    Texas: 2, 4, 5
Flight Time: March–November
Broods: One to many
Overwinters: Third instar larva

Commonly seen flying along forest edges, woods' paths, and water courses, this butterfly is a great lover of flowers and visits parks and gardens where good nectar sources are available. But having a rather catholic taste in food choices, it can just as readily be seen feeding on sap, fruit, decaying wood, fungi, honey-dew, dung, or dead animals.

When mating, the male does not patrol but instead chooses a perch in the open on trees or tall bushes and waits for the female to fly by.

Similar to the Pipevine Swallowtail in its plainness and lack of conspicuous markings, the Red-spotted Purple is nonetheless very striking, with a beautiful iridescent sheen of blue across the outer portion of the black wings on the upper surface, with the blue most noticeable on the basal portion of the hindwings. Faint, iridescent reddish patches near the tips of the forewings are visible under certain lighting. The undersurface is distinguished by a cluster of red markings near the body in addition to a row along the outer red- and black-banded margins. When trying to separate the two in the field, note the absence of tails on the Red-spotted Purple.

Even though it is in an entirely different family, the Red-spotted Purple has evolved to mimic the poisonous Pipevine Swallowtail and thus obtains protection from birds and other predators.

Egg: Grayish to pale green; laid singly on the uppersides of young leaves of food plants.

Larva: Cream to greenish with reddish or brownish saddle-patch on the back; area behind the head enlarged or "humped" and bearing two small, brushlike horns or bristles.

Food Plants: Black Poplar (*Populus nigra*), White Poplar (*P. alba*), Large-toothed Aspen (*P. grandidentata*), Quaking Aspen (*P. tremuloides*), Eastern Cottonwood (*P. deltoides*), Swamp Cottonwood (*P. heterophylla*), American Hornbeam (*Carpinus caroliniana*), Eastern Hop-hornbeam (*Ostrya virginiana*), Black Cherry (*Prunus serotina*), Common Chokecherry (*P. virginiana*), Apple (*Malus pumila*), Common Pear (*Pyrus communis*), American Basswood (*Tilia americana*), and Common Deerberry (*Vaccinium stamineum*)

Parts Eaten: Foliage, preferably young or immature

MOURNING CLOAK
(*Nymphalis antiopa*)

Family: *Nymphalidae*
Size: 2 7/8-3 3/8 inches
Range: All
    Texas: Throughout
Flight Time: All year
Broods: One to several
Overwinters: Adult

This butterfly is so distinctively colored and patterned there can be no confusion as to its identity. Basically the wings are a rich brownish maroon which takes on a purplish sheen when viewed in a certain light. The wing margins are conspicuously angled and rimmed in a pale velvety yellow border with an inner row of large, brilliant blue spots. The undersurface of the wings is a dull, grayish-black with an irregular, dirty cream or pale yellowish border.

This is the largest and one of the most striking of the Anglewings. The range of the Mourning Cloak is extraordinary, wandering as far north as Alaska, as far south as South America, and even to England, where it is known as the Camberwell Beauty. Its flight is strong and erratic, but the insect will often remain on the ground until almost stepped on, then leap into the air in a circling flight, only to settle down again close to its original position. This flight is often accompanied by a rattling noise and a conspicuous click as it closes its wings on alighting. The Mourning Cloak has a habit of resting head downward with wings closed over the back on tree trunks or posts, but often basks on the ground or on low shrubbery in the sun with wings expanded. When resting on the ground with wings closed, it is almost impossible to see.

Mourning Cloaks are one of the hibernators, but you can often see them flying around on sunny days during the winter even though there may be snow on the ground. If the temperature reaches 45 degrees or more on a sunny winter day, they often come forth for a bit of tree sap, then back to a crack or crevice until the next "warm" day. They are one of the first butterflies to visit sap flows in the early spring. Trees which have been "tapped" by the Yellow-bellied Sapsucker are favorite feeding places. Mourning Cloaks generally are not great visitors to flowers, preferring open woodlands, but they will occasionally nectar among flowers, usuallly later in the year. They are especially fond of nectar from the flowers of Milkweed and Goldenrod.

Egg: Whitish, becoming darker before hatching; laid in one layer of 200 or more, forming a wide ring around a twig of the food plant tree.

Larva: Velvety black with raised white dots and several rows of branching black spines or bristles on the body and with a row of red spots along the back.

Food Plants: Black Willow (*Salix nigra*), Peach-leaved Willow (*S. amygdaloides*), Sandbar Willow (*S. exigua*), Silky Willow (*S. sericea*), Weeping Willow (*S. babylonica*), Large-toothed Aspen (*Populus grandidentata*), Quaking Aspen (*P. tremuloides*), Eastern Cottonwood (*P. deltoides*), Black Poplar (*P. nigra*), White Poplar (*P. alba*), Eastern Hop-hornbeam (*Ostrya virginiana*), American Basswood (*Tilia americana*), Common Pear (*Pyrus communis*), American Elm (*Ulmus americana*), Siberian Elm (*U. pumila*), Slippery Elm (*U. rubra*), Common Hackberry (*Celtis occidentalis*), Net-leaf Hackberry (*Celtis reticulata*), Red Mulberry (*Morus rubra*), White Ash (*Fraxinus americana*), Yellow Birch (*Betula lutea*), Meadowsweet (*Spiraea alba*), Hops (*Humulus lupulus*), and Sheep Sorrel (*Rumex acetosella*)

Parts Eaten: Young foliage

MONARCH
(*Danaus plexippus*)

Family: *Danaidae*
Size: 3 1/2-4 inches
Range: All
    Texas: Throughout
Flight Time: March-December
Broods: Many
Overwinters: Adult in Mexico

The Monarch is probably the best known and most easily recognized butterfly in North America. The upper surface of its wings is a rich burnt orange with black veins and borders, the borders liberally sprinkled with a double row of small white dots. The male also has a conspicuous black hindwing dot, which is a cluster of special scent scales. From these scales the male can emit a strong fragrance, which attracts nearby females for mating. The female lacks these black scent scales and is generally a little darker in color. The lower wing surface of both sexes is lighter, duskier orange, with a black, white-dotted marginal border.

Moving in a slow, rather deliberate, soaring flight, Monarchs begin to return from their wintering grounds in early March, just as Milkweeds, the larval food plants, are showing fresh young growth. The females have mated before leaving their wintering grounds. By the time they reach their destination they are ready to begin depositing their eggs.

The Monarch larva feeds on many species of *Asclepias* as well as some other genera of the Milkweed family. Most members of the Milkweed family are poisonous; the plants contain cardiac glycosides, or heart poisons. These chemicals are carried over from the larval stage to the adult butterfly, especially in the female,

125

Monarch

making the insect unpalatable to predators. However, some species of *Asclepias*, and other genera as well, have very low toxin concentrations, leaving the adult butterfly relatively unprotected. Given a choice, a female Monarch finds the most poisonous plants on which to lay her eggs.

During the breeding season, the Monarch's favorite habitats are open fields, meadows, and flower gardens. It is a great lover of flower nectar and freely visits many different species. In the fall it seems especially fond of Lantana, Roosevelt Weed (*Baccharis neglecta*), Thoroughwort, Blue Mist flower (*Eupatorium coelestinum*), Frostweed, Golden-eye (*Viguiera dentata*), Goldenrod (*Solidago* spp.), Mexican Sunflower, New England Aster, and Verbena. In many instances, Milkweed serves not only as the larval food source but as a favorite nectar source as well. Butterflies are one of the pollinators of Milkweed, as can be observed from the not infrequent presence of pollen dangling from their legs.

The Monarch has a strong, powerful flight and moves about among the flowering plants with much deliberation. Its sight is exceptional and it is not easily approached, especially in the spring. On the southward migration during autumn, Monarchs are often tired and anxious to feed, so they can be observed more closely then.

The fall Monarch migration is a familiar sight to everyone, especially to those traveling during this period. They commonly move southward with cold fronts, similar to the movements of geese. In some areas at certain times, there are continuous, seemingly unending lines often a mile or more wide.

During their autumn movements, Monarchs spend the nights roosting in trees in large groups. Each evening near sunset, they begin to drop from the sky to settle on lower leaves and branches. Incredibly, the same trees are used year after year. This phenomenon is as unexplainable as the Monarchs' eventual return to the exact same spot and trees where their ancestors had spent the previous winter.

Egg: Creamy to pale green, with many lengthwise ridges and crosslines; cone shaped; usually laid singly on undersurface of leaf. If plant is large, more than one leaf is used.

Larva: Conspicuously striped crosswise with narrow black, yellow, and white bands, and with two long, black, threadlike segments near the head and two shorter segments near the rear.

Food Plants: Various members of the Milkweed family, especially Antelope-horns (*Asclepias asperula*), Green Milkweed (*A. viridis*) and Mexican Milkweed (*A. curassavica*). Almost all other species are used, as well as Climbing Milkweed Vine (*Sarcostemma cynanchoides*) and Net-leaf Milkvine (*Matelea reticulata*). Butterfly Weed is often listed as a food plant, but because of its roughness and a very low concentration of toxins, it is rarely used.

Note: The Queen, which is closely related to the Monarch, also feeds on Milkweeds in the larval stage and is poisonous as an adult. The Queen does not migrate but spends the winter in the pupal stage. The nonpoisonous Viceroy, which belongs to another family and feeds on Black Cherry, Eastern Cottonwood, and Willow in the larval stage, has evolved coloration similar to the Monarch and thereby gains protection.

VICEROY
(*Limenitis archippus*)

Family: *Nymphalidae*
Size: 2 5/8-3 inches
Range: All
  Texas: All except 1
Flight Time: April-October
Broods: Three or more
Overwinters: Third instar larva

Of the same genus as the Red-spotted Purple, the Viceroy is totally different in coloration and mimics the poisonous Monarch in the northern portion of its range. In the southern portions of its range it often mimics the various color phases of the Queen, which may be more common than the Monarch and is also distasteful. General coloration of the Viceroy, above and below, is a rich, russet-orange with conspicuously wide black venation. A distinctive black line curves across the lower wings above the black-bordered margins. Both wings are bordered in wide, white-dotted black bands with a group of white dots near the tips of the forewings.

The Viceroy is very fond of a wide variety of flowers but is especially attracted to white ones such as Button-bush (*Cephalanthus occidentalis*) and the fall-flowering vine Climbing Hemp-weed (*Mikania scandens*), Heath Aster (*Aster ericoides*), Late-flowering Boneset (*Eupatorium serotinum*), and Plains Black-foot (*Melampodium leucanthum*). While nectaring, the Viceroy usually keeps its wings partially expanded, differing from the Monarch, which usually feeds with its wings closed. The Viceroy basks frequently with half- or fully opened wings. Flight of the Viceroy consist of a series of rather rapid wing beats alternating with a period of gliding, enabling the insect to cover ground in a slow, erratic pattern. This butterfly prefers open fields, meadows, and sunny gardens, but likes a bit of moisture. It is one of the most commonly seen species along open, sunny stream banks or along edges of marshes if there are flowering plants around. Not only does the Viceroy take nectar readily, but it also sips moisture from sap, mud, rotting wood, fungi, dung, and aphid honeydew.

Egg: Pale green or yellow, flattened, oval-shaped; laid singly, usually on upper side of tips of young leaves of the food plant.

Larva: Mature larva mottled brown and olive, with creamy white saddle patch on the back, shiny, resembling fresh bird dropping. Region behind head enlarged or "humped" with two short feathery black horns.

Food Plants: Black Willow (*Salix nigra*), Coastal-plain Willow (*S. caroliniana*), Sandbar Willow (*S. exigua*), Silky Willow (*S. sericea*), Weeping Willow (*S. babylonica*), Large-toothed Aspen (*Populus grandidentata*), Quaking Aspen

127

(P. tremuloides), Black Poplar (P. nigra), White Poplar (P. alba), Eastern Cottonwood (P. deltoides), Swamp Cottonwood (P. heterophylla), Apple (Malus pumila), Black Cherry (Prunus serotina), Common Pear (Pyrus communis), and Gopher-apple (Chrysobalanus oblongifolius)

Parts Eaten: First spring larvae often feed at night on the catkins (inflorescences) of some species; later larvae eat tips of leaves, preferably young ones.

ZEBRA LONGWING
(Heliconius charitonius)

Family: Nymphalidae
Size: 3-3 ⅜ inches
Range: Florida, Texas
  Texas: 3, 4 (1, 2, 5)
Flight Time: All year (April-November)
Broods: Many
Overwinters: No diapause (pupa)

It would be hard to confuse this distinctively marked and colored butterfly with any other. Bold black-and-yellow zebra stripes cross the upper surface of the long, narrow wings. Two rows of yellow dots border the lower edges of the hindwings. The lower surface of both wings is much lighter, with a cluster of bright crimson spots near the bases of both wings. Banding is similar on the lower surface, but the yellow becomes more creamy colored. A beautiful rosy-pink patch decorates the tip of the hindwing.

The Zebra Longwing does not usually stray far from its place of emergence but may occasionally wander widely from spring to fall. Its flight is rather slow, with more sailing and drifting than flapping of the wings, but when disturbed or alarmed it can move quickly and usually darts into low shrubbery. It prefers white or bluish flowers; Desert Lantana (Lantana macropoda), Weeping Lantana (Lantana montevidensis), Thoroughwort, Blue Plumbago (Plumbago lapensis), Fragrant Mist-flower (Eupatorium odoratum), Sand-verbena, and Verbena are favorites, along with the yellow-flowered Golden-eye.

The Zebra Longwing and the Crimson-patched Longwing (Heliconius erato) are two of the few butterflies with the ability to use pollen as a food source. Gathering minute amounts of

128

pollen on the knobby tip of the proboscis, the butterfly releases a drop of fluid to dissolve the pollen; the insect is then able to drink the liquid in the usual manner. Pollen is extremely rich in protein, and this special food enables the female to lay an unusually large number of eggs—up to one thousand eggs over a long lifetime of three months or more.

Adults choose low shrubbery for roosting, with both males and females gathering in a small group. They return to the same site night after night. The Longwings are thought to be the most intelligent among the butterflies. Freshly emerged adult Longwings readily learn the locations of good flower sources and communal roosting sites by association with the older insects.

The male chooses only a small territory for patrolling for females. He is also attracted to female pupae by scent; just before the female is ready to emerge, the male opens her shell with his abdomen and mates with the still unreleased female. He then deposits a repellent pheromone on the tip of the female's abdomen, which repels other males and thereby prevents her from mating again.

Egg: Pale yellow, becoming darker; ribbed; laid singly or in occasional clusters on very young terminal leaves.

Larva: Pure white dotted with brownish black, with six rows of branching, shiny black spines. The larva feeds at night.

Food Plants: Passionflower (*Passiflora incarnata*), Bracted Passionflower (*P. affinis*), Slender-lobe Passionflower (*P. tenuiloba*), Tagua Passionflower (*P. foetida*), and Yellow Passionflower (*P. lutea*)

Parts Eaten: Especially young leaves, but occasionally buds, flowers, tendrils, and young fruits

MALACHITE
(*Siproeta stelenes*)

Family: *Nymphalidae*
Size: 2 1/2-3 3/4 inches
Range: Florida, Texas
    Texas: 3 (1, 4, 5)
Flight Time: All year
Broods: Several
Overwinters: No diapause

A freshly emerged Malachite is one of the most beautiful butterflies. Unfortunately, the green fades in the sunlight and is not nearly so brilliant within a day or so after emergence. There is no mistaking the Malachite for any other, though, for the green and brownish markings are very distinctive. The dark brownish-black of the upper wing surface is richly spotted and banded with dark jade or emerald green. The lower wing surface is beautifully patterned in tawny orange or rusty brown, with spots and bands of a lighter, pearly green highlighted with black. A short but prominent tail is present on the hindwings. The female is usually lighter in coloring than the male.

The Malachite frequents flower gardens and can be seen even in cool weather visiting favorite nectar sources. For this beauty, have an abundance of Barbados Cherry (*Malpighia glabra*), Mexican Poinciana (*Caesalpinia mexicana*), Lantana, Coral Vine (*Antigon leptopus*), Blue Plumbago, Tropical Sage (*Salvia coccinea*) and Verbena in your garden. In Mexico one of

129

the best flowers for nectaring is Male Mujer (*Cnidoscolus palmeri*), a member of the Spurge family. It is closely related to the more familiar Bull Nettle (*Cnidoscolus texanus*) and like the Bull Nettle, is clothed with stinging hairs. This butterfly also makes use of various other substances as food sources, such as mud, dung, rotting fruit, and rotting leaf litter. At night, several adults roost communally on the undersides of leaves and branches on low shrubbery.

In seeking females with which to mate, the male perches on vegetation and waits for passing females. He occasionally patrols an area, slowly flying back and forth.

Egg: Dark green; laid singly or in small groups of two or three on lower surface of very young food plant leaves or plant seedlings.

Larva: Velvety black with many branching spines. The head has two long, red or black horns curving backward.

Food Plants: Violet Ruellia (*Ruellia nudiflora*) (and probably other Ruellias), Waterwillow (*Justicia americana*), and Runyon Water-willow (*J. runyonii*)

Parts Eaten: Leaves

LARGE WOOD NYMPH
(*Cercyonis pegala*)

Family: *Satyridae*
Size: 2-2⅞ inches
Range: All
    Texas: 1, 2, 4
Flight Time: May-September
Broods: One (or more)
Overwinters: Newly hatched larva

Although called a Wood Nymph, this butterfly is not much of a true forest dweller. It much prefers brushy roadsides, woodland edges, trails, or even grassy meadows. It is a great lover of flowers and visits them often, seeming especially fond of Button-bush, Bonesets (*Eupatorium* spp.), Golden-eye, Joe-Pye-weed, Milkweed, and Thistles. The life span of this butterfly is usually only five to ten days.

The flight of this butterfly is usually short and with an appearance of being slow and weak, yet it is very erratic and extremely difficult to follow. The Large Wood Nymph commonly sits fully exposed with folded wings on a leaf or branch. If disturbed it will take off, often dropping into the grass or flying into thick shrubbery, where it alights on the underside of a leaf or a branch and is almost impossible to find again.

To see this butterfly with wings spread is an uncommon sight, for it seems a bit reluctant to show the rich, dark chocolate-brown coloring and brighter yellow banding of the upper surface. The lower surface is just as pretty, though, with the wings mottled with fine, barklike striations. The forewing bears a wide yellow band decorated with two large eyespots of white or blue circled with black. The female is usually larger than the male, with a softer, lighter brown coloring and paler but bigger eyespots. Both sexes have a series of smaller dots edging the hindwings.

To bask, the Large Wood Nymph tilts the folded wings to one side, almost laying them flat. When warm enough on one side, it flips the wings over, warming the other side.

Egg: White, cream, or yellow, becoming pale brownish, with brown or pink mottling; elongated and larger in middle, deeply ribbed. The female deposits between 200 and 300 eggs singly on or near grasses.

Larva: Pale yellowish or greenish, striped lengthwise with green and yellow lines and covered with short, fuzzy hairs. The rear of the caterpillar has two reddish tails.

Food Plants: Various grasses, including Redtop (*Tridens flavus*), Wild Oat (*Avena fatua*), and several of the Bluestems in the genus *Andropogon*

Parts Eaten: Leaves

GOATWEED BUTTERFLY
(*Anaea andria*)

Family: *Nymphalidae*
Size: 2 3/8-3 inches
Range: All except North Carolina, South Carolina
   Texas: Throughout
Flight Time: All year (February-December)
Broods: Continuous (many)
Overwinters: No diapause (adult)

The large, robust Goatweed Butterfly is one of the Leafwing butterflies and with an underwing coloring of softly mottled grays or purplish-browns, it does much resemble a dried and withered leaf. The tips of its forewings are pointed; the hindwings are somewhat scalloped and with short tails. This irregularity, along with the Goatweed Butterfly's habit of resting on the ground with the folded wings at a decided slant, adds even more to its illusion of being a fallen leaf. In such a position it is very difficult to see, and it often flies from directly beneath your feet. If captured and handled, it usually plays possum, falling over on its side and pretending to be dead. This butterfly habitually rests on the ground or on tree trunks; when taking flight, the bright red-orange color of its upper wing surface is quite unexpected, giving it an edge in escaping predators.

Food fare of the Goatweed Butterfly is usually made up of tree sap, juices of fruits, or moisture from dung or decaying wood. Its proboscis is rather short, so it can gain nectar from only a few flower species. It is a frequent inhabitant of the garden, however. When not feeding, it frequently chooses a warm spot on a tree trunk, where it rests head downward.

The adult Goatweed Butterfly does not die during the cold winter months but becomes partially inactive, taking refuge inside unheated buildings, behind loose boards or tree bark, or in protected crevices of trees or posts.

Egg: Greenish cream; laid singly on the underside of a food plant leaf.

Larva: Grayish green, covered in minute points or bumps, and tapering toward the rear. In the later instars, the larva pulls the lengthwise edges of a leaf together, making a loose

131

tent open at both ends. When using some of the smaller-leaved species of *Croton*, it pulls several leaves together, making a tent but still leaving the top and bottom portions open.

Food Plants: Leatherweed Croton (*Croton pottsii*), One-seed Croton (*C. monanthogynus*), Silver Croton (*C. argyranthemus*), and Woolly Croton (*C. capitatus*)

Parts Eaten: Leaves

QUESTION MARK
(*Polygonia interrogationis*)

Family: *Nymphalidae*
Size: 2 3/8-2 5/8 inches
Range: All
   Texas: Throughout
Flight Time: All year (February-November)
Broods: Continuous (many)
Overwinters: No diapause (adult)

The Question Mark is not a frequent visitor to flowers, but it is easily attracted to mud, tree sap, carrion, and rotting fruit. It is especially fond of spoiled fruit and actually becomes intoxicated if the fruit has fermented. The Question Mark spends most of its time along the edges of semishaded trails, in woodland openings, or along shrubby borders, preferring the shaded coolness to sunlit areas. During winter the adult takes shelter in boxes and cans, or behind loose boards and tree bark, coming out to fly around during the warmer days.

The Question Mark is one of the Anglewings, so called because of its ragged outline and the mottled brown, violet-sheened coloring of the wings' surface. They are also referred to as Deadleaf or Leafwing butterflies.

Normally, it rests with its wings folded above the back. If basking, it tips over until almost lying flat on the ground. When doing so, the Question Mark is camouflaged so well it is hard to distinguish it from rocky ground or fallen leaves—the type of area it prefers for resting.

The upper surface of the wings is brightly colored, being basically orange, with black dots, spots, and mottling in the outer portion. The hindwings are tailed, with a violet-gray sheen and with violet extending around the wings to form a narrow border. The lower surface of the hindwing bears a small silver streak somewhat in the form of a printed question mark.

Egg: Pale green, longer than wide, ribbed; laid singly or in strings of up to eight, attached either to the upper or lower surface or along the margins of young leaves of the food plant.

Larva: The mature larva is basically reddish-brown to black, with numerous orange-brown, branched spines covering the head and body. The young larva is somewhat gregarious.

Food Plants: American Elm (*Ulmus americana*), Cedar Elm (*U. crassifolia*), Siberian Elm (*U. pumila*), Slippery Elm (*U. rubra*), Winged Elm (*U. alata*), Net-leaf Hackberry (*Celtis reticulata*), Sugar Hackberry (*C. laevigata*), and the herbs False-nettle (*Boehmeria cylindrica*) and Tall Wild Nettle (*Urtica gracilis*)

Parts Eaten: Young leaves

GULF FRITILLARY
(*Agraulis vanillae*)

Family: *Nymphalidae*
Size: 2 1/2-2 7/8 inches
Range: Alabama, Florida, Georgia, Louisiana, Mississippi, South Carolina, Texas
  Texas: 2, 3, 4 (1, 5)
Flight Time: All year (April-December)
Broods: Continuous (many)
Overwinters: Adult (pupa)

The tropical or semitropical Gulf Fritillary is one of the most common yet spectacular butterflies found in the South. The upper surface of both wings is a bright tawny orange with prominent black veins and markings, with a group of three silver dots near the body on the forewing. The lower surfaces of both wings are a soft, rich brown heavily splashed with silver spots and bars. A large patch of coral pink in the basal portion of the forewing is usually visible, or at least partially so at all times. To watch a group of these insects as they fly about, flashing their silver in the sun, is a breathtaking sight long remembered.

Even though they are genetically placed with the Longwings, which include the Zebra Longwing and the Julia, the Gulf Fritillary does not have the exceptionally long, narrow wings so characteristic of these other species.

The Gulf Fritillary is a fast flier but usually stays within a few feet of the ground while searching for nectar plants. It is quite addicted to flower visiting and works good nectar sources continually, hardly leaving the plants during the day. It is extremely fond of Butterfly Bush, Lantana, Thoroughwort, Golden-eye, Mexican Sunflower, New England Aster, Texas Thistle, Zinnia, and Verbena. This butterfly is one of the few readily attracted to white flowers, and it also visits red ones. Both of these colors are the least used by most butterflies.

If there are several vines of Passionflower in the garden or nearby (the ones native to the area are best) and available as a larval food source, you will have a continuous parade of Gulf Fritillaries during the entire season. Where both larval food and nectar sources are available, there is continual egg laying by the females, with great overlaps of emerging adults.

The insects contain toxic body juices from the poisonous larval food and generally go unmolested by predators. For protection during the night, they often roost in small groups near the ground on blades of grass or on the leaves and lower stems of herbaceous plants.

The adults do not stray far from the larval food plants for most of the year, although they occasionally migrate long distances northward. They do not breed there since *Passiflora* does not grow in cold climates.

Egg: Pale yellow, becoming golden brown; oblong, ribbed; laid singly on pratically any part of the food plant but especially on the underside of a leaf.

Larva: Striped lengthwise in muddy maroon and bluish-black and covered with branching black spines; the two spines on the head much longer and curved backward.

Food Plants: Almost all *Passiflora*, but the native species preferred, especially Passionflower (*Passiflora incarnata*), Tagua Passionflower (*P. foetida*), and Yellow Passionflower (*P. lutea*). The evergreen cultivated Blue Passionflower (*P. caerulea*) is much utilized where available.

Parts Eaten: Mostly leaves but sometimes buds, flowers, and young fruit

Note: Where it overwinters as an adult, the Gulf Fritillary becomes greatly reduced in numbers during periods of severe cold. Due to the abundance of native food plants and favorable climatic factors most of the time, though, they are able to reestablish rather quickly.

VARIEGATED FRITILLARY
(*Euptoieta claudia*)

Family: *Nymphalidae*
Size: 1 3/4-2 1/4 inches
Range: All except Oklahoma, Tennessee
Texas: Throughout
Flight Time: All year (March-December)
Broods: Continuous (many)
Overwinters: No diapause (pupa)

The Variegated Fritillary is a tawny orange and black butterfly, with black markings covering the upper surfaces of both wings in bars, dots, lines, and dashes to form a rather complex pattern. Somewhat of a narrow, zigzag black band marks the middle of both wings. The lower surfaces of both wings are a mottling of white and brown, with a large orange area near the body on the forewing and a smaller patch on the hindwing. This insect does not have the silver markings on the lower surface of the wings as do the true Fritillaries.

Its relationship to the true Fritillaries is shown through its use of Violets and Pansies as larval food plants. It also shows a close relationship to the Longwings because the larva uses the Passionflower as a food plant. The Variegated Fritillary is known to use a wide assortment of plants other than these, and in Texas it is most frequently found on Flax.

These butterflies are usually not present in great numbers at any one time in a garden, and even when present they may be easily confused with the more common Gulf Fritillary unless the underside of the wings is seen. The Variegated Fritillary is a fast flier and rather far ranging, but it readily comes to gardens where a good supply of nectar plants is available, usually remaining if proper plants are available for egg deposition. Whether feeding, mating, or searching for plants on which to lay eggs, it usually flies close to the ground in a hovering or darting manner. These butterflies annually migrate as far north as Wyoming but are not residents there.

Egg: Cream to pale green; ribbed; laid singly on a leaf or stem of the food plant.

Larva: Striped in orange-red and white and with six rows of dark-colored branching spines, the front pair of spines larger and pointing forward over the head.

Food Plants: In Texas the genus *Linum* is apparently the most preferred, with almost all of the *Linums* being used, especially Blue Flax (*Linum lewisii*), Grooved Flax (*L. sulcatum*), Meadow Flax (*L. pratense*), Rock Flax (*L. rupestre*), Stiff-stem Flax (*L. berlanderi*), Texas Flax (*L. medium*), and Tufted Flax (*L. imbricatum*). Other food plants include Common Fennel (*Foeniculum vulgare*), Passionflower (*Passiflora incarnata*), Blue Passionflower (*P. caerula*), Tagua Passionflower, Erect Spiderling (*Boerhaavia erecta*), Scarlet Spiderling (*B. coccinea*), Spreading Spiderling (*B. intermedia*), Whorled Nod-violet (*Hybanthus verticillatus*), and probably any or all of the genus *Viola*.

BUCKEYE
(*Junonia coenia*)

Family: *Nymphalidae*
Size: 2-2 ½ inches
Range: All except Tennessee, Arkansas, Oklahoma
  Texas: 2, 3, 4, 5 (1)
Flight Time: All year (February-October)
Broods: Continuous (two or more)
Overwinters: No diapause (pupa)

The Buckeye is easily recognized by the large blue and black eyespots set near an orange border on the upper surfaces of both wings. Otherwise, the wings are generally tawny to dark brown, overlaid with various iridescent colors, and with one white band and two smaller lengthwise orange bars on the forewings. Beneath, the forewing somewhat resembles the upper surface, while the hindwing is beautifully mottled in soft rose-browns and tans. The large eyespots on this butterfly give it another common name, the Peacock Butterfly.

A very common butterfly, the Buckeye ranges practically throughout North America south of the Canadian border. The Buckeye is a rapid flier and tends to be nervous and wary when approached. It usually flies low to the ground, alternately gliding and flapping its wings. It migrates northward but is not able to overwinter there, and in the fall there are massive southward movements.

The male Buckeye is not as active as the female, sitting for long periods on the ground or on low shrubbery, basking and waiting for passing females. A male chooses a special perch from which he patrols a territory; and within the chosen boundaries he takes quick flights to intercept passing females or pugnaciously attack other males or any other intruder, no matter its size or description. While most individuals live only an average of ten days, the flight period is continuous in the southern portion of the Buckeyes' range. The ones which have overwintered in the adult stage are among the first butterflies to emerge from hibernation in the spring in the rest of the range.

The Buckeye likes to bask with wings spread wide in early mornings or after inclement weather. It is also fond of mud puddles, spending much time there. It is equally fond of flowers and is found in almost all gardens as well as other open areas where flowers are plentiful.

Egg: Dark green; ribbed; laid singly, usually on upper side of a leaf of the food plant.

Larva: Generally black with lengthwise rows of cream or white and with numerous black, branching spines; the rows of spines nearest the underside of the body are conspicuously orange at the base.

Food Plants: Almost all species of the genera *Agalinis*, *Castilleja*, *Linaria*, *Plantago*, or *Phyla* with *Agalinis*, *Castilleja*, and *Linaria* being the most commonly used in Texas. Others used include Snapdragon Vine (*Maurandya antirrhiniflora*), American Bluehearts (*Buchnera americana*), American Brooklime (*Veronica americana*), Runyon Ruellia (*Ruella runyonii*), Seymeria (*Seymeria cassioides*), and Snake-herb (*Dyschoriste linearis*).

Parts Eaten: Flower buds, young fruit, leaves

WHITE PEACOCK
(*Anartia jatrophae*)

Family: *Nymphalidae*
Size: 2-2 3/8 inches
Range: South Florida, South Texas
    Texas: 3 (1, 2, 4, 5)
Flight Time: All year (May-August)
Broods: Many
Overwinters: No diapause

While the White Peacock breeds only in the lower Rio Grande Valley and southern Florida, it migrates northward and may possibly be seen anywhere during the summer months. However, it is not a regular migrant to some areas and is never noted for massed groups or noticeable numbers at any one time. It is common within its breeding range, though, and can be seen around any patch of wildflowers or in a garden, especially if there is water or areas of extra moisture nearby. It is especially common around irrigation canals and dripping faucets or leaking water lines.

Closely related to the Buckeye, with which it often flies, the White Peacock differs in having the upper surface of the wings washed with a pearly sheen, making the butterfly appear almost white in flight. The white shades into buff, marked with orange crescents which form a border along the wing margins. The hindwings are shortly and bluntly tailed. The undersurface is somewhat less white, with numerous scrawled lines, bands of orange, and various shades of light browns. Both surfaces bear one large black eyespot on the forewing and two smaller, widely separated ones on the hindwing. Summer broods are darker than spring and fall broods.

The White Peacock is not a strong flier and remains low, seeking flowers near the ground. Easily approached if your movements are slow, the White Peacock is a fascinating subject to watch while it is feeding. Once it finds a good nectar source, it slowly crawls from flower to flower, seeming completely absorbed in nectar gathering. If disturbed, it flutters and glides to the next flower to continue on with its feeding. Once really frightened, it flies into nearby grasses or shrubbery, closes its wings, and immediately disappears.

In seeking females, the male patrols back and forth in a rather erratic flight interspersed with periods of gliding. The male also perches on low, exposed branches of shrubbery or a blade of grass near the larval food plant to await a passing female. To reject a male, the female lands and leans her wings from side to side until the male leaves.

Egg: Pale yellow; laid singly on underside of food plant leaf or on nearby vegetation.

Larva: Dark brown to black, with white or silver spots forming crosswise bands, with four rows of black or orangish spines. Head with two long, curved, clubbed horns.

Food Plants: Common Frog-fruit (*Phyla nodiflora*), Diamond-leaf Frog-fruit (*P. strigillosa*), Northern Frog-fruit (*P. lanceolata*), Texas Frog-fruit (*P. incisa*), Coastal Water-hyssop (*Bacopa monnieri*), Ruellia (*Ruella occidentalis*), and Violet Ruellia (*R. nudiflora*). Probably several other Ruellias are used as well.

Parts Eaten: Foliage

GREAT SOUTHERN WHITE
(*Ascia monuste*)

Family: *Pieridae*
Size: 1 3/4-2 1/4 inches
Range: Alabama, Georgia, Louisiana, Mississippi, Texas
    Texas: 3 (1, 2, 4, 5)
Flight Time: All year (May-November)
Broods: Continuous
Overwinters: No diapause

This large, white butterfly is easily identified due to its lack of any prominent markings on the lower surface of the wings, except the veins and some scaling, which are dusted in soft charcoal. The upper surface of the wings is strikingly edged with dark gray or black half-diamonds. The tips of the antennae of this butterfly are a lovely light blue. The females are of two color forms, depending upon day length; the spring and summer broods, living in longer days, are dark gray, and the late summer and fall broods, in shorter days living, are white like the males.

Often when areas become overpopulated or food becomes scarce for other reasons, Great Southern Whites migrate northward. During migration flights the insects apparently continue on their course in a steady flight and in an unchanging direction, rarely stopping to nectar at flowers at all. Otherwise, both males and

females sip flower nectar, with the females beginning to feed earlier in the day.

Great Southern Whites are common at all times in southern Florida and the Rio Grande Valley area, where they breed almost throughout the year. They can readily be seen along edges of the coastal marshes, beaches, and in

Top. White Peacock
Above. Great Southern White

137

tidewater areas searching for nectar plants or Batis, their larval food plant. Further inland, they are readily observed about gardens or along roadsides during the warmer months where they breed but do not winter in any form.

Egg: Pale yellow; elongated but wider in middle, ribbed; laid singly or in clusters of up to fifty on certain food plants. Eggs can withstand inundation by salt water for short periods of time.

Larva: Gray to brownish green or yellow, with several stripes of maroon, purplish green, or dark gray.

Food Plants: Batis (*Batis maritima*) along coastline; inland a wide range of both cultivated and wild members of the Mustard family (*Cruciferae*), such as Broccoli (*Brassica oleraceae italica*), Brussels Sprouts (*B. o. gemnifera*), Cabbage (*B. o. capitata*), Cauliflower (*B. o. botrytis*), Bird's Rape (*B. rapa*), Garden Radish (*Raphanus sativus*), Nasturtium (*Tropaeolum majus*), Shepherd's Purse (*Capsella bursa-pastoris*), and Virginia Peppergrass (*Lepedium virginicum*)

Parts Eaten: Leaves

Note: The Giant White (*Ganyra josephina*), a resident only in the Rio Grande Valley area, is white but is larger (largest of North American Whites) and has a distinctive black spot on both surfaces of upper wings.

AMYMONE
(*Mestra amymone*)

Family: *Nymphalidae*
Size: 1 3/8-1 5/8 inches
Range: Texas
  Texas: 2, 3, 4, 5 (1)
Flight Time: March-December
Broods: Several
Overwinters: No diapause (larva)

Common in the Rio Grande Valley and breeding as far north as Austin and possibly Waco in Texas, the Amymone sometimes wanders to Minnesota in great numbers. This is an easily identified butterfly, with the upper surface of both wings being gray at the base near the body, dusted with a pearly white sheen in the middle section, and with a wide charcoal band on the tips of the forewings. A bright orangy-yellow band edges the hindwings. The lower surface of the wings is brownish-orange, with large, irregular creamy white spots forming bands. Broods occurring during periods of unusual moisture are reportedly darker in general coloration. The soft, subtle coloring of a freshly emerged adult is truly beautiful, but the colors quickly fade, scales are lost, and the fragile wings easily become tattered and torn.

The flight of the Amymone is slow and sailing, with few wing beats. The butterfly never flies far when disturbed. It prefers to stay close to the ground, taking nectar from low-growing flowers and slowly making its way from plant to plant. If really frightened, the Amymone quickly darts into nearby vegetation and disappears. This butterfly is at home wherever the flowers are, whether dense woodlands or the edges of hot, sunny areas.

Egg: Pale yellow. It has not been described further.

Larva: Body brown with green diamond shapes on back and with eight rows of spines; head with two longer spines, each of which ends with a knob or crest of smaller spines.

Food Plant: Catnip Noseburn (*Tragia ramosa*)

Parts Eaten: Foliage

CHECKERED WHITE
(*Pontia protodice*)

Family: *Pieridae*
Size: 1 1/4-1 3/4 inches
Range: All
  Texas: Throughout
Flight Time: All year (February-November)
Broods: Continuous (many)
Overwinters: No diapause (pupa)

The overall coloration of the Checkered White varies considerably, differing from habitat to habitat and with the seasons; also, the male is less marked than the female. The upper wing surface of spring broods is white with charcoal-gray or brown markings and washes. The veins of the lower surface are lined and speckled in brown or olive green. The summer male is solid snowy white, with the exception of a small black dot on the upper surface of the forewing and light beige or pale brown tracery on the lower surface. Summer females usually have much lighter markings than the spring brood. All color gradations of gray, brown, tan, and olive can and do occur in the Checkered White, yet the patterning and flight characteristics are such that identification is not difficult.

Checkered Whites frequent open, sunny spaces and can commonly be found in gardens, fields, vacant lots, and along roadsides. They are great puddlers and hundreds can be seen at times around small areas of water or temporarily moist areas in a roadway. The Checkered White flies in a fast, skipping manner. If disturbed, it flits away into an open area instead of taking refuge among trees or brush. In seeking females for mating, the male flies back and forth near the food plants. Both sexes use ultraviolet reflection instead of scent to identify the opposite sex. The male and the female have different pigments in their wing scales, resulting in ultraviolet light's being reflected by the female and absorbed by the male. These butterflies are known to readily disperse after emerging, traveling many miles to form new colonies where their weedy food plants are plentiful. Normally, their life span is about seven days, but they can live longer in cool weather.

Egg: Yellow, becoming orange; spindle shaped; laid singly on bud, flower, or young leaf of a food plant.

Larva: Blue-green speckled with black, with four lengthwise yellow stripes; downy, with soft, fine hairs.

Food Plants: Numerous genera of the Mustard family, including Broccoli (*Brassica oleraceae italica*), Brussels Sprouts (*B. o. gemnifera*), Cabbage (*B. o. capitata*), Cauliflower (*B. o. fotryris*), Bird's Rape (*Brassica rapa*), Charlock (*Sinzpis arvensis*), Shepherd's Purse (*Capsulla bursapastoris*), Tansy-mustard (*Descurainia sophia*), Pinnate Tansy-mustard (*D. pinnata*), Hairy-pod Peppergrass (*Lepedium lasiocarpum*), Prairie Peppergrass (*L. densi florum*), Virginia Peppergrass (*L. virginicum*), and Western Peppergrass (*L. montanum*). Other species reportedly used include Sweet Alyssum (*Lobularia maritima*), Field Pennycress (*Thlaspi arvense*), Garden Radish (*Raphanus sativus*), Rocky Mountain Bee Plant (*Cleome serrulata*), Spectacle-pod (*Wislizenia refracta*), and Tumble Mustard (*Sisymbrium altissimum*).

Parts Eaten: Flower buds, flowers, fruits, leaves, tender stems

Note: Both the invasion of the Cabbage White (*Artogeia rapae*) and the agricultural pattern of people are changing the distribution of the Checkered White, continually forcing it to find new areas. With expanding farming practices in the western states, along with the accompanying introduced or "weedy" members of the Mustard family, the Checkered White has had no problem becoming established there. Often populations build to serious numbers in some areas, where the Checkered White may be considered a pest.

139

FALCATE ORANGETIP
(*Falcapica midea*)

Family: *Pieridae*
Size: 1 3/8-1 1/2 inches
Range: All except Florida
    Texas: 1, 2, 3, 4
Flight Time: March-May
Broods: One
Overwinters: Pupa

One of the earliest butterflies to appear each spring, the Falcate Orangetip can be seen flying low to the ground about garden shrubbery and along the edges of open woodlands. It is very local in distribution, but once one is spotted, there are often several in the same area.

Undaunted by unpredictable spring weather, the Orangetip is on the wing even on very cool or partially cloudy days. The male seems to never perch, continually flying back and forth and often along the same route day after day. Its stops for nectar are numerous but usually very brief. The female is usually seen less often than the male but seems to visit flowers more often. She spends a lot of time hovering about, low to the ground, going in and out of brambles, and inspecting numerous plants for the proper ones for egg deposition. The normal flight of the Orangetip is composed of a short period of slow sailing or gliding, then a series of quick, jerky wing beats, then more sailing.

For the most part, the upper wing surface of the Falcate Orangetip is a soft, snowy white. The forewings of the male bear a solitary, elongated black dash midway in from the margins, and the wings are tipped with a bright orange patch. The forewings of the female bear the same black dash. The lower wing surface of both sexes is similar, with the forewings white, black-dotted, and with a patch of greenish-brown mottling near the tip. The hindwings are beautifully marbled in greenish-brown or yellowish-brown. The forewings of both sexes are conspicuously hooked (falcate) at the tips. This curving and the orange patch on the wings of the male give this butterfly its common name.

Being only a spring visitor to the garden, flower preferences are those in full bloom by March and April. Some which are regularly visited are Dewberry (*Rubus* spp.), Bluets (*Hedyotis* spp.), Dakota Vervain (*Verbena bipinnatifida*), Rose Vervain (*V. canadensis*), False Garlic (*Nothoscordum bivalve*), Phacelia (*Phacelia congesta*), Spring Beauty (*Claytonia virginica*), Violets (*Viola* spp.), Wild Onions (*Alliums* spp.), Yellow Star-grass (*Hypoxis hirsuta*), Yellow Wood-sorrel (*Oxalis dillenii*), and various members of the Mustard family.

Egg: Yellow-green, becoming orange; elongated; laid singly, usually at the base of a flower, with rarely more than one egg per plant.

Larva: Basically yellow-green, with a conspicuous orange stripe down the center of its back and with blue, white, and yellow stripes along its sides. The larvae are cannabilistic in early stages.

Food Plants: Best known Texas food plants are Brazos Rockcress (*Arabis petiolaris*), Prairie Peppergrass (*Lepedium densiflorum*), and Virginia Peppergrass (*L. virginicum*). Other plants reportedly used in Texas are Bitter-cress (*Cardamine parviflora*), Hairy Bitter-cress (*C. hirsuta*), Mouse-ear Cress (*Arabidopsis thaliana*), Mustard, Rocket Mustard (*Sisymbrium irio*), Spring-cress (*Cardamine rhomboidea*), and Sickle-pod (*Arabis canadensis*).

Parts Eaten: Buds, flowers, seed pods

140

CLOUDLESS GIANT SULPHUR
(*Phoebis sennae*)

Family: *Pieridae*
Size: 2 1/8-2 3/4 inches
Range: All except Arkansas, North Carolina, Oklahoma, Tennessee
   Texas: 2, 3, 4 (1, 5)
Flight Time: All year (March-December)
Broods: Continuous (many)
Overwinters: No diapause (larva)

The brightest and lightest in color of our yellow butterflies—and one of the easiest to identify—is the Cloudless Giant Sulphur. Both the upper and the lower surfaces of the wings are a beautiful clear yellow with only a few markings or spots. Females are usually dark yellow in the winter but almost white in the summer. Fall broods have varying amounts of black markings along the wing margins. The folded wings are normally held at such an angle that their outer edges form an almost straight line from tip of forewing to base of hindwing; the Cloudless Giant Sulphur is the only one of our common yellow butterflies to form such a distinctive shape.

A very strong flier, the Cloudless Giant Sulphur moves about the garden very rapidly. If approached too closely, it will fly for quite a distance before coming to rest again. These butterflies are frequent visitors to the gardens and can be seen working the flowers throughout the day. They are much more common, and come to the garden in greater numbers, during the late summer and fall months.

Although not able to tolerate cold northern winters, Cloudless Giant Sulphurs migrate northward each summer, rearing two or more broods where breeding conditions are favorable. By the end of summer, local southern populations may also have built to intolerable numbers, at which times they too migrate northward in large groups. They may travel as far north as Maine and Montana. With the arrival of cooler temperatures, however, they begin a return flight southward, where at least some of them overwinter. In many areas each fall, you can see their impressive flights, but they are never quite as spectacular in numbers or frequency, as the migratory flights of the Monarchs.

Since the Cloudless Giant Sulphur is found in almost every open habitat, the plants it uses for nectaring are very diverse. Some of the most common ones include Butterfly Bush, Buttonbush, Lantana, Thoroughwort, Morning Glory (*Ipomoea* spp.), Butterfly Weed, Golden-eye, New England Aster, Pentas (*Pentas lanceolata*), and Zinnias. This is another of the butterflies which use red flowers extensively, often being seen around Drummond Waxmallow (*Malvaviscis arboreus*), Cherry Sage (*Salvia greggii*), Cedar Sage (*S. roemeriana*), Pineapple Sage, and Tropical Sage.

As with other yellows, Cloudless Giant Sulphurs like to congregate around mud puddles, and they spend a lot of time taking moisture from such areas.

The male patrols his territory all during the day seeking females. Once he finds a receptive

141

female, the male approaches and touches her with his wings, using his scent brushes to release pheromones. Once mated, the joined pair usually flies off, the male flying and the female passive beneath.

Egg: White or cream, later turning orange or red; laid singly on flower bud or young leaf of food plant.

Larva: Yellowish to greenish, striped along sides, and with rows of small black dots across the back. Sometimes the larva may be orangy-yellow, with narrow crosswise bands of greenish-gray interspersed with rows of tiny black dots. The larva hides during the day in a nest formed of silk and leaves of the food plant.

Food Plants: Senna (*Senna pendula*), Argentine Senna (*S. corymbosa*), Coffee Senna (*S. occidentalis*), Maryland Senna (*S. marilandica*), Sickle-pod Senna (*S. obtusifolia*), Two-leaved Senna (*S. roemeriana*), Partridge Pea (*Chamaecrista fasciculata*), and Sensitive Pea (*C. nictitans*)

Parts Used: Leaves

Note: The greener form of the caterpillar seems to be the most common from Central Texas eastward, with the yellow form more frequent westward. There are several intermediate, varying colorations and markings of this caterpillar. Any caterpillar found on one of the *Sennas* is most likely one of the Sulphurs, Yellows, or Whites.

DOGFACE BUTTERFLY
(*Zerene cesonia*)

Family: *Pieridae*
Size: 1 7/8-2 1/2 inches
Range: All except Arkansas, North Carolina, Oklahoma, South Carolina, Tennessee
   Texas: Throughout
Flight Time: All year (April-December)
Broods: Continuous (many)
Overwinters: No diapause (adult)

From a distance the Dogface Butterfly can be mistaken for the Common Sulphur (*Colias philodice*), but a close inspection of the upper surface of the wings quickly distinguishes one from the other. The Dogface Butterfly is aptly named because, instead of the almost even black border of the upper wing surface of the Sulphur, the black in the border of the Dogface Butterfly is such that the remaining yellow of the wings forms a "poodle" or "dog face." A black dot within each yellow forewing patch forms the "eye" of the dog. The lower wing surface of the Dogface Butterfly is generally greenish yellow, with a black-rimmed white dot on the forewings and a red-rimmed white dot on the hindwings. Rosy or magenta scaling along the veins and along the wing margins of a fresh specimen is usually conspicuous. This rose coloring becomes even more noticeable in the winter form. Forewing tips of the Dogface Butterfly are prominently pointed, in contrast to the rounded

tips of the Common Sulphur.

The flight of the Dogface Butterfly is swift. Its stay around each flower is usually rather brief, although it spends much time in the garden sipping nectar. It is frequently seen around red flowers, such as Drummond Waxmallow, Cardinal Flower, and various *Salvias*.

Both sexes of this butterfly stay around mud puddles for hours. If disturbed, they usually circle around briefly, then return to the moisture. When not nectaring or puddling, the male patrols his territory in search of females. Once he finds a receptive female, the male attracts her both by ultraviolet light reflected from the outer portion of the dog's face on the forewings and by scent pheromones.

Egg: Yellowish green, later turning dark red; laid singly on underside of leaf of food plant.

Larva: Mostly green but may be cross-banded or striped lengthwise with yellow or black or both; sometimes striped lengthwise with a white band containing orange dashes.

Food Plants: Bearded Dalea (*Dalea pogonathera*), Black Dalea (*D. frutescens*), False Indigo (*Amorpha fruticosa*), Texas Kidneywood (*Eysenhartia texana*), Alfalfa (*Medicago sativa*), Leavenworth Vetch (*Vicia leavenworthii*), Purple Prairie Clover (*Dalea purpureum*), Soybean (*Glycine max*), White Clover (*Trifolium repens*)

Parts Eaten: Leaves

LITTLE YELLOW
(*Eurema lisa*)

Family: *Pieridae*
Size: 1-1½ inches
Range: All
　Texas: Throughout
Flight Time: All year (February-December)
Broods: Continuous (many)
Overwinters: No diapause (pupa)

Although small in size, the Little Yellow makes up for it in numbers and is probably the South's most plentiful butterfly. It is on the wing year-round in the southern portions of its range. By midsummer it is encountered in every field, meadow, garden, and open woodland, and along almost every roadside. It is not a fast flier and stays low to the ground, where it visits flowers readily and also seeks areas of moisture. Inclement weather does not seem to bother the Little Yellow, for it can be seen flying on windy and cloudy days. It is not uncommon to find it in great numbers, alone or with Hairstreaks, Blues, Common Sulphurs, or Dogface Butterflies, taking moisture from mud puddles or seepage areas.

The basic color of the male is usually a clear yellow, with a solid black border on the upper surface of the wings. The female is usually a little larger in size and with spotted borders. Occasionally a female is chalky white or creamy white with black markings. The undersurface of both sexes is yellowish-green, with minute dark speckling and brownish blotches and smudges. The female has a large, dark-colored, but indistinct spot near the tip of the hindwing.

Although Little Yellows migrate to the more

northern states during the summer and even produce two or more broods there, they cannot survive the harsh winters. Each fall the adults either fly southward or perish, with new adults again flying northward the next year.

A courting male patrols constantly during the day seeking females. The upper surface of the wings of the male reflect ultraviolet light, and he also uses pheromones to attract a mate.

Egg: Minute, pale green when deposited; laid singly on upper surface of food plant leaf.

Larva: Pale green, marked lengthwise with white and green lines; downy, with fine, short hairs.

143

Food Plants: Partridge Pea (*Chamaecrista fasciculata*), Sensitive Pea (*C. nictitans*), Coffee Senna (*Senna occidentalis*), Maryland Senna (*S. marilandica*), Big Bend Bluebonnet (*Lupinus havardii*), Sandyland Bluebonnet (*L. subcarnosus*), Texas Bluebonnet (*L. texensis*), and Deer Pea Vetch (*Vicia ludoviciana*)

Parts Eaten: Leaves

HACKBERRY BUTTERFLY
(*Asterocampa celtis celtis*)

Family: *Nymphalidae*
Size: 2-2½ inches
Range: All
   Texas: 2
Flight Time: All year (March-October)
Broods: Several
Overwinters: Adult (third instar larva)

The Hackberry Butterfly is one of our most common butterflies but is not one to visit flowers very often. On occasion it has been seen gathering fluids from blossoms in the wild, but mostly it feeds on tree sap, rotting fruit, honeydew, carrion, and mud.

Even if the Hackberry Butterfly is not a great flower visitor, it likes to patrol open areas and also bask. If there are any Hackberry trees in or near your garden, you will see the Hackberry Butterfly making frequent forays into the open areas. And if you provide damp sand and rotting fruit, it will be a common visitor to your garden. It is especially fond of fermented dewberries, mulberries, overripe bananas, peaches, pears, and persimmons. It also loves canned fruit cocktail, especially if a shot of rum has been added. While feeding on this stuff, the insect becomes so engrossed in sipping the juices that you can approach closely enough to actually move it about with your fingers without its taking flight.

The Hackberry Butterfly is a medium-sized butterfly, with the upper wing surface colored a most distinctive orange and olive-brown; the black outer wing tips are dotted in white. Patterning and coloring of the lower surface of the wings is complex and variable, with markings of brown, black, and purplish-gray and with eyespots on both wings.

This butterfly is always found in close association with its food plant, Hackberry (*Celtis* spp.), with the female leaving the trees only while searching for food or basking. Frequently the female will sun with wings spread wide, especially if she is carrying a heavy egg load. The female commonly basks in this position on low vegetation in an open area, where the male "dive-bombs" her in courtship before mating. The male also perches on Hackberry trees, awaiting passing females, or occasionally wanders a short distance, patrolling for feeding females. Some sites are more attractive to the male for perching than other sites, and an occupant's perching rights are often contested by another male. The male Hackberry Butterfly is usually the last butterfly you'll see in the day, continuing to fly until almost dark.

From his perching area, the male frequently flies out to inspect moving objects—especially if the object is shiny. His main objective is to find a female, of course, but he has a tendency to be curious about any moving object, no matter what its size or color.

This butterfly normally perches on the trunk of the host tree until disturbed, then flies to another perching site, such as a fence post or the handle of the hoe you are using. Often it alights on your arms or hands, seeking the salts from perspiration.

Egg: Cream to pale green; laid singly or in small groups on underside of leaf or occasionally on stem near the leaves.

Larva: Leaf-green, with faint yellow length-wise stripes bordering a zigzag yellow line. The body is tapered at both ends, forked at the rear and with two small, branched spines on the head. Each of the upper straight yellow lines ends at a branched spine on the head and a "tail" at the rear. The middle instar larva of the last brood hibernates in crevices along a tree trunk or in leaf litter until the following spring.

Food Plants: Known to use all kinds of Hackberry (*Celtis* spp.) within its range.

Parts Eaten: Leaves of young trees or new growth on older trees

Note: In the western half of Texas the Hackberry Butterfly is replaced with the Western Hackberry Butterfly (*A. celtis antonio*). Here, the Western Hackberry Butterfly can be confused with the Pale Emperor (*A. clyton texana*), but the Pale Emperor has no eyespots on either surface of the upper wings.

PALE EMPEROR
(*Asterocampa clyton texana*)

Family: *Nymphalidae*
Size: 2-2 5/8 inches
Range: Texas
  Texas: 1, 2, 3, 4
Flight Time: All year (March-October)
Broods: Several
Overwinters: Adults (third instar larva)

The Pale Emperor is the West Texas form of the Tawny Emperor (*A. clyton*), which ranges throughout the eastern states. Both the Pale and Tawny Emperors are very similar to the Hackberry Butterfly in all aspects, but with the orange and black coloring of the wings reversed. The best field marks to look for are the blue eyespots on both the upper and lower surfaces of both the fore- and hindwings of the Hackberry Butterfly—the Pale and Tawny Emperors have dots only on the hindwings. Also, the bodies of the Pale and Tawny Emperor are usually orange or reddish brown, whereas the body of the Hackberry Butterfly is much darker and generally gray.

The Pale Emperor has a very swift and powerful flight, but it can and frequently does glide slowly from tree to tree. Generally, it does not

145

fly very far between stops, except the male may fly some distance back and forth from his perching area and the closest larval food plants, where the females usually stay. Mating flights are most often performed from the middle of the day to late evening. The Pale Emperor likes large, mature trees—especially if they bear fruit abundantly.

As with the other Hackberries, the Pale Emperor basks often, opening its wings wide to fully partake of the sun's warmth. It is commonly seen resting head downward, especially liking to perch on leaves in full sun and on tree trunks, fence posts, rocks, paved roads, and people.

This insect's food preferences are similar to those of the other Hackberry Butterflies, and they all are frequently found imbibing liquid from the same source. Sometimes there are so many individuals gathered together, they jostle each other about, each one trying to get the best position. The Pale Emperor also spends a lot of time around mud puddles, either with others of its own kind or with various Sulphurs, Hairstreaks, or Swallowtails.

Egg: Cream to greenish with thick sculpturing of usually twenty ridges; laid in large, moderately tightly packed cluster or layer on underside of leaf or occasionally on bark of host tree.

Larva: Pale green with two wide, yellowish lines down back separated by a very narrow blue line; downy, with short hairs, forked at rear, and with two spiny horns on head. The larvae are gregarious in early instars and can commonly be found in groups of fifty or more. The third instar larvae of the last fall brood hibernate.

Food Plants: Known to use all species of Hackberry (*Celtis* spp.) in the state within the insect's range, except Spiny Hackberry (*C. pallida*).

Parts Eaten: Leaves

SNOUT BUTTERFLY
(*Libytheana bachmanii*)

Family: *Libytheidae*
Size: 1 5/8-1 7/8 inches
Range: All
  Texas: Throughout
Flight Time: All year (April–frost)
Broods: Many
Overwinters: Adult (pupa)

Snout Butterflies are curious creatures, still closely resembling their primitive ancestors. The two palpi which protect the proboscis are exceptionally long, projecting forward from the head and resembling a "snout" or the beak of a bird. The Snout Butterflies are the only butterflies in North America with such long palpi, and is our only genus representing the family of butterflies known as the Long-beaks.

To make its appearance even more unusual, both forewings and hindwings are square-tipped as if deliberately clipped, giving the insect a curiously angular look. There are several subspecies of this butterfly, with research showing that gradations exist from one subspecies to the next. Coloring varies with the subspecies, but generally the upper surface is blackish brown with orangy brown patches and white spots toward the tips of the forewings. Lower surface of the forewings is orangish brown in the basal portion, but this area is usually hidden when the insect is at rest. Hindwings are a mottled grayish brown overlaid with iridescent scales reflecting greens, pinks and lavenders. In general, females are lighter in hue than the males. The two forelegs of the male are undeveloped, making him appear to have only four legs, but all six legs of the female are well developed.

Snout Butterflies have not developed any type of mimicry but have evolved an almost perfect leaf like camouflage. When at rest, they fold the wings together and direct the body parallel to a twig, where the wing coloring and shape much resembles a leaf. The forward projecting palpi and antennae appear as the petiole or "stalk" of a leaf.

Their flight is very swift and rather jerky or fluttery and usually low to the ground, although they will go several feet high to nectar on flowering shrubs and trees. They are regular visitors to flowers and often gather by the dozens at a flowering plant extra-rich in nectar, such as Gum Elastic (*Bumelia lanuginosa*), Plum (*Prunus americana*), and Peach. They are equally attracted to muddy streams and lake margins and are often seen at such sites in the company of various Sulphurs and Swallowtails. They are rather wary and do not usually allow a close approach.

The Snout Butterflies are strong voyagers and massive numbers of them travel northward each year in late summer. These butterflies do not have a return flight southward and perish with the onset of winter.

Egg: Pale green; laid singly on petiole or underside of the leaf on young, terminal growth of food plant.

Larva: Generally dark green with yellow stripes, the enlarged segment behind head with a pair of black tubercles basically ringed with yellow. Coloring and markings vary greatly according to subspecies.

Food Plants: All native Hackberries (*Celtis* spp.)

Parts Eaten: Foliage

PAINTED LADY
(*Vanessa cardui*)

Family: *Nymphalidae*
Size: 2-2 1/4 inches
Range: All
  Texas: Throughout
Flight Time: All year (March-November)
Broods: Continuous (many)
Overwinters: No diapause (adult)

The Painted Lady is the most widespread of all the butterflies in the world. It bears other descriptive common names, such as the Cosmopolitan and the Thistle Butterfly, the first from its almost worldwide distribution, the second from its favorite food plant. This butterfly is a most familiar sight, being one of the first seen in early spring and one of the last in the fall, or all year round in the southern part of its range. In most of its range, it spends the winter months tucked away in some crevice, inactive except on the very warmest days. It is a common visitor to the garden all during the flowering season but is usually seen in greater numbers in the autumn.

The upper wing surface of the Painted Lady is a complex mottling of black and pinkish-orange, with a sprinkling of white dots near the tips of the forewings. The pattering on the lower surface is even more complicated, being a mixture of golds, tans, black, and white. A row of small eyespots and a narrow blue band occur near the margins of the hindwings. In coloration and markings the Painted Lady is very similar to its near relative, the American Painted Lady (*Vanessa virginensis*), but differs by having four or five small black dots on the

lower surface of each hindwing, whereas the American Painted Lady has only two very large black dots with blue centers.

The Painted Lady occurs in almost all environments, as long as they are open, sunny, and

147

covered with flowers. It cannot overwinter in any stage where the temperatures are severe; not moving southward as do some other species, they perish. But by February or March the overpopulated southern broods begin moving north and east from their warmer Southwestern wintering grounds; by late spring the Painted Lady has once again become a common sight throughout North America.

Despite their wide distribution, Painted Ladies do not congregate when feeding. Almost always there is only one or two in the garden at a time, unless they are around the larval food source. They are easily attracted to the garden by flowers of the Sunflower family, such as New England Aster, Mexican Sunflower, Purple Coneflower (*Echinacea purpurea*), and the single Zinnias.

Courtship flights of these butterflies are usually quite elaborate and preferably take place on open hilltops or at least the highest terrain possible. After mating, the female returns to lower ground and seeks out stands of Thistle to lay her eggs.

Egg: Pale green; elongated, and wider in middle; laid singly on the upper surface of a leaf.

Larva: Grayish brown or black, with numerous narrow crosswise lines and rows of branched spines. Larva lives in silk nest formed by folding leaves of the food plant together and binding with silk.

Food Plants: Some of the most commonly used are Texas Thistle (*Cirsium texanum*), Swamp Thistle (*Cirsium muticum*), Wavy-leaf Thistle (*C. undulatum*), Nodding Thistle (*Carduus nutans*), Barnaby Star Thistle (*Centaurea solstitialis*), and Milk Thistle (*Silybum marianum*). Other species used include Western Mugwort (*Artemisia ludoviciana*), Calendula (*Calendula officinalis*), Milfoil (*Achillea millefolium*), Annual Sunflower (*Helianthus annuus*), Garden Lettuce (*Lactuca sativa*), Borage (*Borage officinalis*), Cryptantha (*Cryptantha angustifolia*), Hollyhock (*Althaea rosea*), Little Mallow (*Malva parviflora*), High Mallow (*M. sylvestris*), Common Mallow (*M. neglecta*), Alkali Sida (*Malvella leprosa*), Cotton (*Gossypium hirsutum*), Beet (*Beta vulgaris*), Lamb's-quarters (*Chenopodium album*), Soybean (*Glycine max*), Alfalfa (*Medicago sativa*), Garden Bean (*Phaseolus vulgaris*), Burning Nettle (*Urtica urens*), Tall Wild Nettle (*U. dioica*), Tree Tobacco (*Nicotiana glauca*), English Plantain (*Plantago lanceolata*), Garden Radish (*Raphanus sativus*), Muskmelon (*Cucumis melo*), and American Elm (*Ulmus american*).

Parts Eaten: Leaves

AMERICAN PAINTED LADY
(*Vanessa virginiensis*)

Family: *Nymphalidae*
Size: 1 3/4-2 1/8 inches
Range: All
  Texas: Throughout
Flight Time: All year (April-November)
Broods: Continuous (many)
Overwinters: No diapause (adult)

Inhabiting almost all open areas, including gardens, the American Painted Lady is found wherever flowers are abundant. It does not seem particularly attracted to special colors or species and freely visits whatever flowers are available. It occasionally flies along woodland trails or borders, but this is because of particular flowers found there, such as Wild Azaleas or Asters, not because of a preference for shade. When nectaring it habitually holds its wings open or at least partially so, moving warily about, constantly changing position. You can occasionally see it basking on bare earth with wings widely spread. The best time to see the undersurface of the folded wings is to find one in the late evening, its having gone to roost, in early mornings before it takes flight, or in cool or inclement weather, when it takes shelter beneath a leaf or a blade of grass. At such times the intricate markings, the large blue-centered eyespots, and the brilliant pink forewing patch can be closely observed and appreciated. The upper wing surfaces of the American Painted Lady are a dark pinkish-orange, with dark markings across the tips of the forewings which are sprinkled with a few white dots. A row of small blue eyespots circled in black follows the margins of the hindwings, these dots connected or running together to form a band.

If startled, this butterfly takes off in sudden, erratic flight, but often returns in a few moments to the former site if there is no further movement. It frequently dashes out at other butterflies which approach the flower it is feeding on, fluttering its wings until the intruder seeks other flowers or leaves the area entirely. With the arrival of the first really cold nights, it begins seeking snug, protected places where it will remain inactive during the winter months.

Egg: Pale green or yellowish; barrel shaped; laid singly on upper surface of food plant leaf.

Larva: Greenish with black marbling or velvety black with groupings of several narrow crossbands of yellow. Black, branching spines with red dots at the bases and two large white dots occur in each black portion. The larva lives inside a nest made of the food plant. The young larva spins plant hairs and small bits of the inflorescence into shelters, while the older larva uses larger bits of the inflorescence and leaves to make the nest larger and more compact. The larva often pupates inside the nest.

Food Plants: Fragrant Cudweed (*Gnaphalium obtusifolium*), Purple Cudweed (*Gamochaeta purpureum*), Bighead Evax (*Evax*

American Painted Lady

prolifera), Many-stem Evax (*Evax verna*), Silver Evax (*E. candida*), and Pussy's Toes (*Antennaria parlinii*) are the preferred food plants. Many more genera and species are generally listed as being used.

Parts Eaten: Buds, flowers, young leaves

RED ADMIRAL
(*Vanessa atalanta*)

Family: *Nymphalidae*
Size: 1 3/4-2 1/4 inches
Range: All
　Texas: Throughout
Flight Time: All year (March-October)
Broods: Continuous (many)
Overwinters: No diapause (adult)

First described in Europe by Linnaeus in 1758, the Red Admiral is one of the best known and most widespread butterflies. It is one of the most common species occurring in city parks, gardens, and shrubby fields and along woodland edges and brushy roadsides.

The Red Admiral is similar to the Painted Lady in being widespread along with its larval food plant. Few plants have a wider distribution than Nettles, and where Nettles grow, the Red Admiral is almost always found. During the summer months the Red Admiral strays as far

north as Alaska, and it is one of the fifteen species of butterflies in Hawaii, where it is now a common resident, arriving there about 1882.

The bright, simple coloring of the Red Admiral makes for easy identification. The upper surface of the wings is a soft velvety black, with the forewings crossed with a diagonal band of orangy-red or vermillion and the tips sprinkled with white dots. A narrower band of the same orange-red color borders the curved hindwings. When resting with the wings open, the banding of fore- and hindwings seems connected, forming two bowed or curved lines which almost complete a circle. The banding also appears on the undersurface of the forewing but is much lighter in color, appearing more pink than red.

The Red Admiral can be seen on warm days in winter sipping the sap of trees or the juice of wild fruits which have been burst open by

149

Red Admiral

salts from human perspiration, often alighting on exposed legs, arms, or hands. It feeds on a variety of substances, including sap, fruit, and dung, as well as regularly visiting flowers.

This insect is a fast flier and has a tendency to wander far from where it was reared. This is probably because the Nettle food plants grow in semishaded areas, but as an adult it must seek masses of nectar-producing flowering plants in more sunny areas. The male is very territorial and extremely aggressive, defending his chosen resting site against all intruders.

If you can allocate an out-of-the-way, semishaded spot for a patch of Nettle, the larval food plant, you will see these butterflies much more frequently in your garden. In the fall they gather around crushed fruit if provided; if the fruit has begun to ferment, the more they seem to enjoy it. Often they appear drunk and have difficulty flying.

Egg: Pale green; barrel shaped, faintly ribbed; laid singly on upper side of young food plant leaf, but many leaves on the same plant may be used.

Larva: Extremely variable but usually blackish. Body has many bumps and branching spines. The larva makes a silken nest or tent of leaves.

Food Plants: Burning Nettle (*Urtica urens*), Low Spring Nettle (*U. chamaedryoides*), Tall Wild Nettle (*U. dioica*), False-nettle (*Boehmeria cylindrica*), Hammerwort (*Parietaria pensylvanica*), and Pellitory (*Parietaria floridana*)

Parts Eaten: Leaves, within the silken nest

freezing. It habitually rests head downward on vertical surfaces and, when its wings are closed, is extremely difficult to see. It is one of the first to emerge from hibernation in the spring, spending much time on the ground at moist areas or basking on flat surfaces with opened wings. The Red Admiral is particularly fond of

GOLDEN-BANDED SKIPPER
(*Autochton cellus*)

Family: *Hesperiidae*
Size: 1 5/8-2 inches
Range: All except Oklahoma
   Texas: 2, 3, 5
Flight Time: February–September
Broods: Two to several
Overwinters: Pupa

Not only is the Golden-banded Skipper one of the less common Skippers, but it is also one of the most wary of insects. Even when one flits into view it is usually difficult keeping it in sight for it's extremely alert and generally will not tolerate a close approach. When disturbed, it takes

off with strong wing beats and in very rapid flight, usually flying quite a distance or even out of sight before alighting again. Even though this skipper ranges throughout the eastern states, populations are usually small, very local, and often widely separated.

The overall blackish brown coloring of this Skipper is highlighted by wide, unbroken golden yellow bars or bands across both the upper and lower surfaces of the forewings. A small white dot occurs near the tip of each forewing. Fringe of the hindwings is brown-and-white checkered in upper portion, becoming brownish near the body. The lower surface of the hindwings is gray-frosted with two bands of darker spots near the margins.

The Golden-banded Skipper readily takes nectar, preferring plants in open, moist woodlands near streams, woodland lakes, or humid ravines. It should be looked for on heavy nectar producers such as Azaleas, Button-bush, False Indigo (*Amorpha fruticosa*), Hawthorns (*Crataegus* spp.), some Viburnums (*Viburnum* spp.), wild berries (*Rubus* spp.), wild Hydrangeas (*Hydrangea* spp.), Ironweed (*Vernonia* spp.), Milkweed, and Self-heal (*Prunella vulgaris*). In the garden it often uses flowering shrubs and trees such as Common Lilac (*Syringa* spp.), Glossy Abelia, Ninebark (*Physocarpus opulifolius*), and Sourwood (*Oxydendrum arboreum*).

Egg: Pale yellow becoming tan or brownish; usually laid in cluster of two or three but occasionally in string of as many as seven or eight, usually at base of food plant leaf.

Larva: Yellowish green, yellow dotted or speckled, and with a broad, clear yellow line along each side. Head reddish brown with two eyelike yellow dots. Larva feed at night, hiding during the day in rolled or tied leaf tents. As the larva become larger and go to larger leaves, they cut the silken threads which bound the old nest together, removing signs of their presence.

Food Plants: Most commonly Hog Peanut (*Amphicarpa bracteata*), although Pigeon-wings (*Clitoria mariana*) and Purple Stylisma (*Stylisma aquatica*) are given in the literature as probable food sources. Wright Bean (*Phaseolus wrightii*) is given for the western portion of Texas.

Parts Eaten: Foliage

SILVER-SPOTTED SKIPPER
(*Epargyreus clarus*)

Family: *Hesperiidae*
Size: 1 3/4-2 3/8 inches
Range: All
  Texas: 2, 4, 5
Flight Time: Almost all year
Broods: Few to many
Overwinters: Pupa

The Silver-spotted Skipper is one of our widest ranging butterflies, almost equaling the Painted Lady in its distribution. It is equally at home in wilderness areas, parks, suburban gardens or along country roadsides. Its flight is very strong, swift, jerky, and erratic. It is generally very pugnacious in character and will attack just about anything in its range, especially other butterflies, no matter which species they happen to be.

This is one of our largest Skippers and easily recognized in the field. The Silver-spotted Skipper is brownish in coloring, but the upper surface of the long forewings has a broad, indistinct band of clearish orangy yellow dots. This band is often hidden by the large hindwings, as the butterfly usually rests with the wings folded above the body. The large hindwings are mostly filled with a large, irregularly shaped patch of silvery white.

Males often engage in impressive aerial combat flights. From early morning until around noon, the males remain on favorite perch sites in open areas to await passing females, and when a female is sighted, the male launches out and trys to persuade her to alight for copulation. Often the female is sighted by more than one male and the aerial battle is on. Generally the female continues her flight. In the afternoons, you can see males hanging upside down from beneath leaves when not nectaring.

The Silver-spotted Skipper frequently appears around mud puddles as it sips the moisture there, as well as in open, sunny areas, where it seeks nectar. It visits many species of flowers, briefly visiting one then quickly flying to another.

Egg: Green, reddish on top; round, laid singly on upper side of food plant leaf.

Larva: Yellow or greenish with darker patches or speckles, and with black lines across body; head dark brownish red with two large, orange-red oval spots. Larva builds a shelter by binding leaves of the food plant together with silken threads.

151

Food Plants: Black Locust (*Robinia pseudo-acacia*), Clammy Locust (*R. viscosa*), Honey Locust (*Gleditisia triacanthos*), Bristly Locust (*R. hispida*), New Mexico Locust (*R. neomexicana*), False Indigo (*Amorpha fruticosa*), Ground Nut (*Apios americana*), Hog Peanut (*Amphicarpaea bracteata*), Kudzu (*Pueraria lobata*), Wisteria (*Wisteria macrostachya*), Chinese Wisteria (*W. sinensis*), Garden Bean (*Phaseolus vulgaris*), Thicket Bean (*P. polystachios*), Round-head Bush Clover (*Lespedeza capitata*), Wild Licorice (*Glycyrrhiza lepidota*), and Wild Pea (*Lathyrus palustris*). Almost all of the Tick-clovers (*Desmodium* spp.) are used.

Parts Eaten: Foliage

HOARY EDGE
(*Achalarus lyciades*)

Family: *Hesperiidae*
Size: 1½-1¾ inches
Range: All
  Texas: 2, 4
Flight Time: April-December
Broods: Many
Overwinters: Larva

The Hoary Edge is another common and widely distributed Skipper, similar in appearance to both the Golden-banded and Silver-spotted Skippers. The dark, blackish brown triangular-shaped forewings are marked by four or five yellow-orange, squarish spots forming a glassy band. The area between the bands (the area seen protruding above the hindwing when the butterfly is at rest) is of a lighter shade of brown. The lower surface of the hindwings is mottled black and dark brown, with the outer half conspicuously frosted in a large, white patch. The irregular shape and amount of "frosting" of this patch gives it a "smeared" effect.

While not as fast or strong a flier as its two look-alikes, the Hoary Edge is a mover, and when not basking or perched and waiting for females, the male seems never to be still for long. Its stay at any one flower is brief, but it will continue to nectar in an area at length if not disturbed.

Frequently seen around flowers, these butterflies are continually alert—dipping into the middle of a blossom and then quickly backing out, looking around, and going back in for more feeding. They use many different plants, but obviously prefer those in open, sunny spots. The best places to look for these beauties are along the outer edges of wide roadsides where unmowed plants are in flower.

For a courting territory, males usually choose small openings within woodlands or along woodland edges, brushy fence rows, or the sunny edges of shrubby areas in parks or gardens where they perch on outer twigs or leaves and wait for passing females. Females fly by in search of nectar-filled flowers and the males fly out, circling around them, fluttering their wings and releasing certain scent pheromones. Often the female is sighted by more than one male and the males then begin contesting the rights of territory. Courting is forgotten until one of the males is persuaded to leave.

Egg: Whitish or creamy; laid singly beneath leaves of the food plant.

Larva: Pale to dark green, with the body covered in minute bumps, a broad, blue-green stripe down the back, and a narrow stripe along each side composed of yellowish orange dots.

Food Plants: False Indigo (*Amorpha fruticosa*), Hairy Bush Clover (*Lespedeza hirta*), Little-leaf Tick-clover (*Desmodium ciliare*), Large-bracted Tick-clover (*D. cuspidatum*), Nuttall Tick-clover (*D. nuttallii*), Canadian Tick-clover (*D. canadense*), Paniceled Tick-clover (*D. paniculatum*), Bare-stem Tick-clover (*D. nudiflorum*), Prostrate Tick-clover (*D. rotundifolium*), Trailing Tick-clover (*D. glabellum*)

Parts Eaten: Foliage

152

LILAC-BANDED LONGTAIL
(*Urbanus dorantes*)

Family: *Hesperiidae*
Size: 1½-2 inches
Range: South Florida, South Texas
    Texas: 3 (2, 4)
Flight Time: All year (April-October)
Broods: Three or more
Overwinters: No diapause

The Lilac-banded Longtail is readily identified by the long, pointed forewings and the hindwings which conspicuously narrow into long, slender tails. The upper surface of the wings is generally dark to grayish-brown, with an overall iridescent glimmer of lilac or rosy-lavender covering the hindwings. A grouping of irregularly placed translucent spots occurs on the forewings. The lower surface of the forewings is dark gray, the hindwings frosty-gray with dark brown spots and banding. The lower surface of both wings is beautifully tinged purple with iridescent scaling, but darker and more conspicuous on the hindwings.

This butterfly is found in the coolness of shade more often than in the sun, but this does not mean it cannot be found in gardens. It is a great lover of flowers: It simply feeds for long periods, then darts into the foliage or to a shaded tree trunk to keep cool between feedings. The Lilac-banded Longtail stays close to the more shrubby parts of the garden, making frequent forays out into the open. It is a strong flier and rapidly zips back and forth across pathways or small openings before finally settling down on a flower to feed.

It takes nectar from Lantana, Verbena, Huisache Daisy (*Amblyolepis setigera*), Indian Blanket, Missouri Ironweed (*Vernonia missurica*), Mist-flower, Morning Glory, Narrow-leaf Gayfeather (*Liatris mucronata*), Phacelia, Skeleton Plant (*Lygodesmia texana*), Lemon Mint (*Monarda citriodora*), Summer Phlox, and Texas Thistle as well as many others.

While the Lilac-banded Longtail is a common resident only in the southern portion of Florida and the Rio Grande Valley area of south Texas, it emigrates as far north as Kansas and may breed there in some areas where the food plant is available. It cannot overwinter in any form in the colder climes, and large numbers perish each year.

Egg: Shiny, iridescent green; flattened on both top and bottom, ridged.

Larva: Yellowish green to reddish orange, with lighter colored spots; downy, with short hairs; head black.

Food Plants: Pigeon-wings (*Clitoria mariana*), Garden Bean (*Phaseolus vulgaris*), Lima Bean (*Phaseolus limensis*), Purple Bean (*P. atropurpureus*), and probably Butterfly Pea (*Centrosema virginianum*)

Parts Eaten: Leaves

153

BRAZILIAN SKIPPER
(*Calpodes ethlius*)

Family: *Hesperiidae*
Size: 1 3/4-2 1/4 inches
Range: Alabama, Florida, Georgia, Louisiana, Mississippi, Texas
   Texas: 2, 3, 4
Flight Time: All year (April-December)
Broods: Several
Overwinters: No diapause

An inspection of any patch of Cannas (*Canna* spp.), especially in city gardens, will probably yield this large Skipper in all its stages. Look for rolled leaf edges, large portions of the leaves eaten, or adults zipping about nectaring on the flowers.

The Brazilian Skipper certainly has a personality all its own, and the more you watch this butterfly, the more intriguing it becomes.

Quick in flight and almost secretive, it alights, then appears to be watching to see if you have noticed. Then it quickly flies to another perch in plain sight to do the same thing. The game seems endless.

The Brazilian Skipper is an especially fast flier, with strong, powerful wing beats. It often basks with wings spread in the "airplane" pose, at which times the beautiful markings of translucent spots on both wings are very conspicuous against the dark brown scaling. When the wings are folded, the hindwings are marked with three translucent dashes, and the forewings appear to be marked with two smaller ones. The forewings of this butterfly are very long and pointed.

Favorite flowers for nectaring include Lantana, Cannas, Globe Amaranth, Periwinkles, Petunias, and Summer Phlox.

At times there may be so many larvae on the food plants that practically all of the leaves will be eaten. Often these Skippers disperse to great distances, lay their eggs, then immediately leave for yet another area. Especially susceptible to viruses, entire colonies are periodically wiped out.

Egg: White to greenish white becoming reddish; laid singly or in small clusters on upper surface of highest leaves of food plant.

Larva: Later instar larva is large, translucent grayish green with a dark and light line along each side, its head orange and black. Larva rests during the day in a leaf stitched together with silk to form a rolled tent, from which it emerges at night to feed.

Food Plants: All Cannas (*Canna* spp.) as well as Powdery-thalia (*Thalia dealbata*)

Parts Eaten: Leaves, usually the midmature ones first

Note: Green-leaved Cannas with red flowers are reportedly preferred over the red-leaved plants for egg deposition by the females, but I have found them to show no preference. When a number of caterpillars are feeding, their nighttime chomping can be heard for some distance.

154

SICKLE-WINGED SKIPPER
(*Achylodes tharso*)

Family: *Hesperiidae*
Size: 1 5/8-1 7/8 inches
Range: Texas only
  Texas: 3 (2, 4)
Flight Time: All year (May-October)
Broods: Continuous (many)
Overwinters: No diapause

This is one of the largest and most unusual-looking skippers to be found. There is hardly any mistaking the Sickle-wing, for its size, coloring, and shape are most distinctive. The wings are wide and rounded, with the forewing indented just below the hooked tip, forming a "sickle." The surface of the upper wings is blackish brown to mahogany-brown, with pale areas of purplish gray forming bands and irregular groupings of spots. A beautiful iridescent sheen of coppers and lavenders covers both wings. The undersurface of the wings is similar but lighter. The female is lighter in overall coloration and appears somewhat more mottled, instead of banded as in the male, but the hooked forewing tips and overall violet sheen easily separate this skipper from all other skippers

The Sickle-winged Skipper visits flowers often, especially those close to shrubby borders or around clusters of trees. It moves about with an unusual jerky flight, until it alights on a flower to nectar or on a leaf, where it rests with wings spread tightly against the surface. During midday or periods of extremely high temperatures, it is not uncommon to see it fly to the cooler underside of a leaf after nectaring.

These skippers are year-round residents in the Rio Grande Valley area, but in some years they make flights through the eastern half of the state and as far north as Kansas and Arkansas during the summer and fall months. They are especially attracted to Bee-brush (*Aloysia gratissima*), Lantana, Texas Kidneywood (*Eysenhardtia texana*), Field Mint (*Mentha arvensis*), Globe Amaranth, Missouri Ironwood, and Mist-flower.

Egg: Not described in any of the literature; laid singly on upper side of food plant leaf.

Larva: Yellowish green or grayish blue, with darker stripe down back and broad band of yellow dashes along each side. The larva lives in a silk-lined nest made in a leaf.

Food Plants: Lime Prickly Ash (*Zanthloxylum fagara*) and possibly some *Citrus*

Parts Eaten: Leaves

JUVENAL'S DUSKYWING
(*Erynnis juvenalis*)

Family: *Hesperiidae*
Size: 1 1/4-1 3/4 inches
Range: All
  Texas: All except 3

Flight Time: February-May
Broods: Usually one
Overwinters: Last instar larva

155

Juvenal's Duskywing is a widespread and common butterfly throughout the eastern half of the United States. Their favorite habitat seems to be the edges of small openings in deciduous or mixed hardwoods. They can also frequently be found in shrubby areas of gardens where they remain resting on the foliage except when feeding or courting. Courting males can usually be found perching about head-high where they await passing females.

Overall coloring, both above and below, of this Duskywing is a blackish brown. The upper surface of the forewings is blotched, with several glassy white spots and indistinct, irregular bands of darker brown or blackish spots, and with the hindwing becoming a lighter brown toward the basal margins. Undersurface of both wings is similar but somewhat lighter in color. Background coloring of the female is lighter than the male, causing the markings to appear darker and more distinct. Its large size and coloring help to separate this butterfly from all other Duskywings except Horace's Duskywing (*E. horatius*), which is quite similar.

Juvenal's Duskywing visits flowers freely, drifting from plant to plant with a rather slow, soft flight, but you can spot it just as readily taking moisture from mud puddles or dung. When basking, it usually seeks a bare patch of sunny ground and rests with the wings spread wide.

Egg: Cream, greenish white to pale green, later becoming pink to salmon-red; laid singly on young leaves and seedlings of larval food plant.

Larva: Pale green to dark green with a yellow stripe along the sides, thickly covered with yellowish hairs arising from minute bumps; head yellow, orange, or red.

Food Plants: White Oak (*Quercus alba*), Swamp Chestnut Oak (*Q. michauxii*), Black Oak (*Q. velutina*), Shin Oak (*Q. mohriana*), Bur Oak (*Q. macrocarpa*), Post Oak (*Q. stellata*), Black-jack Oak (*Q. marilandica*), Water Oak (*Q. nigra*), Northern Red Oak (*Q. rubra*), and Chinquapin Oak (*Q. muhlenbergii*). Probably many more species of Oak are used than listed here.

Parts Eaten: Foliage

JANAIS PATCH
(*Chlosyne janais*)

Family: *Nymphalidae*
Size: 1¾-2 inches
Range: Texas
    Texas: 3 (1, 4)
Flight Time: All year (June-November)
Broods: Several
Overwinters: No diapause

The Janais Patch is an extraordinarily beautiful butterfly, and its uncommoness makes it even more so. It basically has a soft, velvety black color, with very large, prominent patches of red to reddish-orange on the upper surface of the hindwings and a sprinkling of white dots on the forewings. The lower surface of the forewings is black, heavily dotted in white, while the hindwings are banded in creamy yellow, reddish-orange, and black. A row of white dots lies within the black band.

The Janais Patch is almost always present in the Rio Grande Valley area, but severe winters can wipe it out. When this happens, it only takes a year or two to become recolonized from Mexico, once again a welcome sight in gardens and woodlands and along watercourses. In most years it is a breeding resident as far north as San Antonio, wherever the larval food plant is available. During the summer or early fall months, it occasionally strays as far north as the Rolling Plains area.

The Janais Patch is very specific in its larval food plant, feeding only on Flame Acanthus (*Aniscanthus quadrifidus*). It also uses this plant as a nectar source, along with Button-bush, Bee-brush, Annual Sunflower (*Helianthus annuus*), and other good nectar-producing plants near its food plant. While breeding, it does not venture far from the Flame Acanthus, preferring to use its flowers for nectaring instead of flying long distances to other sources. Where there is a colony of plants established, there is a great overlap of the breeding cycles, with courtship, egg laying, pupation, and adult emergence all going on at once.

Egg: Cream to pale yellow; laid in clusters on undersides of leaves of food plant.

Larva: White to pale metallic grayish green with many rows of branched, black spines; up-per portion of head orange-red.

Food Plant: Flame Acanthus (*Aniscanthus quadrifidus*)

Parts Eaten: Buds, flowers, young leaves

Above. Janais Patch

Left. Janais Patch laying eggs

157

BORDERED PATCH
(*Chlosyne lacinia*)

Family: *Nymphalidae*
Size: 1 5/8-1 7/8 inches
Range: Texas
   Texas: 2, 3, 4, 5 (1)
Flight Time: All year (March-December)
Broods: Continuous (many)
Overwinters: Adult (third instar larva)

The Bordered Patch is one of our most variable butterflies, making it a little difficult to identify, especially on the wing. However, within its range it is usually abundant and is a frequent visitor to flowers, thus offering many opportunities for closer inspection.

The Bordered Patch is very showy, both with wings open and closed. The upper surface of both wings is basically black, with a wide band of bright orange. Rows of tiny white dots edge both the band and the wing margins. The lower surface of the wings is black, banded, and dotted in cream or pale yellow and orange.

An avid flower visitor, the Bordered Patch visits almost anything in bloom. It is especially attracted to white and yellow flowers, such as Bee-brush, Dewberry, Thoroughwort, Annual Sunflower, Fleabane (*Erigeron* spp.), Golden-aster (*Heterotheca subaxillaris*), Golden-eye, Golden Crownbeard, Hairy Wedelia (*Wedelia hispida*), and Indian Blanket. When in bloom and available, Golden-aster and Golden Crownbeard seem to be the top choices for nectaring. It is not uncommon to see several of these butterflies working a large stand of these plants, with a lot of chasing of "intruders" of other species as well as frequent mating pursuits. The males feed on mud, carrion, and dung, as well as flower nectar.

The reproductive cycle of this butterfly is impressive. The female may lay up to five hundred eggs during her lifetime, and the entire life cycle, from egg to adult, is completed in thirty days.

Egg: Pale greenish or yellowish becoming reddish; laid in clusters of more than a hundred on the underside of food plant leaves.

Larva: Quite variable, ranging from an all orange to orange-red form, to an all black form with white stripes on the back, to a black form with an orange-red interrupted stripe down the center of the back. Younger larvae are gregarious and usually remain in groups until the fourth or fifth instar, when they begin to disperse.

Food Plants: Annual Sunflower (*Helianthus annuus*), is the major food plant from spring until late summer, with Golden Crownbeard (*Verbesina enceloides*), becoming the major choice from late summer until the end of the breeding season in November or December. Giant Ragweed (*Ambrosia trifida*) is used if one of the first- or second-choice plants is nearby. Plants occasionally used include Brown-eyed Susan (*Rudbeckia hirta*), Bush Sunflower (*Simsia calva*), Frostweed (*Verbesina virginica*), Golden-eye (*Viguiera dentata*), Hairy Wedelia (*Wedellia hispida*), and Weak-stem Sunflower (*H. debilis*).

Parts Eaten: Buds, flowers, leaves, tender stems

TEXAN CRESCENTSPOT
(*Anthanassa texana*)

Family: *Nymphalidae*
Size: 1-1½ inches
Range: All except North Carolina, Oklahoma, Tennessee
    Texas: 2, 3, 4, 5 (1)
Flight Time: All year (March-November)
Broods: Many
Overwinters: No diapause (larva)

With a low, strong, fluttering flight, the Texan Crescentspot moves from one clump of flowers to another. Once on a good nectar source, such as the fall-flowering Thoroughwort or Frog-fruit (*Phyla* spp.), however, it remains for a long period, basking in the warm sun while lazily feeding from the plentiful flowers. Many confrontations with bees, wasps, and other butterflies take place, all of them vying for the freshest flowers and most nectar, but the Texan Crescentspot usually sends them scurrying with strong flicks of its wings.

Basically a dark brownish-black in color, the upper surface of the wings of the Texan Crescentspot is heavily dotted in white, the dots large, somewhat squarish, and forming two rows on the hindwings. Orangish bars and splotches combine to form bright patches at the bases of the wings near the body. The lower surface of the forewings has white markings near the tip, and the hindwings are generally more buff-colored and marked with black lines and dots. A white band crosses the wings about midway. The female is usually larger than the male. The body and wing area near the body is overlaid with iridescent greenish, copper, and purple scaling.

The Texan Crescentspot is a denizen of low, open, shrubby-type areas, such as along the edges of thin, rocky woodlands or along open, chaparral or thorn-shrub trails. It also readily inhabits flower gardens for nectar and will remain in the area if some shrubs or low trees are about, providing it an escape site. It can be found at various altitudes, being at home on tops of low mountains, along the shrubby edge of a foothill stream, or in flat, arid chaparral. Favorite flowers

for nectaring include Texas Kidneywood, Thoroughwort, Engelmann Daisy (*Engelmannia pinnatifida*), Golden-eye, Indian Blanket, New England Aster, and the Wild Onions.

In seeking mates, the male Texan Crescentspot usually perches on an exposed twig, rock, or grass blade in a low habitat such as a gully, an open area between hills, or along a mountain stream. From his chosen perch within his territory, he flies out to inspect everything that passes by and fiercely chases off other butterflies, especially other male Crescentspots. Females are an exception, of course; when one flies into a male's territory, he begins an elaborate courtship dance, flying loops behind and above her, attracting her attention and hopefully persuading her to mate.

Some individuals of the first spring broods of Texan Crescentspots have a tendency to wander, and specimens are occasionally seen as far north as Minnesota, east into Illinois, and west into California.

159

Egg: Appearance undescribed; laid in clusters on underside of leaves of food plant.

Larva: Young larva is greenish-brown, with four rows of pale-colored, flattened bumps or tubercules, each bump bearing a hair. Mature larva is yellow-brown, with the sides striped in black and white; one white band is broad and mottled with greenish and brown. Spines on lower portion of body greenish white, all the others brown.

Food Plants: Flame Acanthus (*Aniscanthus quadrifidus*), Flamingo Plant (*Jacobinia carnea*), Shrimp Plant (*Beloperone guttata*), Southwest Bernardia (*Bernardia myricaefolia*), Hairy Tube-tongue (*Siphonoglossum pilosella*), Long-flowered Tube-tongue (*S. longiflora*), Perennial Dicliptera (*Dicliptera brachiata*), Rio Grande Dicliptera (*D. sexangularis*), Snakeherb (*Dyschoriste linearis*), Ruellia (*Ruellia occidentalis*), Carolina Ruellia (*R. caroliniensis*), Drummond Ruellia (*R. davisiorum*), Mexican Ruellia (*R. brittoniana*), Water-willow (*Justicia americana*), Runyon Water-willow (*J. runyonii*), Warnock Water-willow (*J. warnockii*)

Parts Eaten: Leaves

PEARLY CRESCENTSPOT
(Phyciodes tharos)

Family: *Nymphalidae*
Size: 1-1½ inches
Range: All
   Texas: Throughout
Flight Time: All year (March-November)
Broods: Continuous (many)
Overwinters: No diapause (third instar larva)

The Pearly Crescentspot is one of our most abundant and familiar small butterflies. In almost any open field, meadow, flower garden, or roadside, this little gem can be seen flying low, taking nectar or sipping moisture from wet ground. The male patrols for females with which to mate or perches with closed wings on a bare branch, rock, or grass blade, darting out to inspect everything that passes by. It is especially fond of darting at other butterflies being photographed and sending them off in terrified flight.

The upper surface of the wings is primarily

orange, with numerous black blotches, lines, and spots. The bases of both wings are intricately marked with networks of fine curving or scrawly lines. A row of small black dots borders the hindwings near the margins. The female has more black than the male, and both sexes are darker in the early spring form. The lower surface of the forewing is pale orange, with black and cream patches vaguely forming a border, while the hindwing is softly mottled in cream and yellows, with fine brown curvy lines. Along the darker border of the hindwing is a conspicuous purplish brown patch surrounding a pearly crescent or boomerang-shaped mark.

The Pearly Crescentspot often uses the same plants for nectaring as it uses for egg deposition and is almost always found around whatever Aster is in flower at the time. It also visits other members of the Sunflower family, preferring them to the deeper throated flowers since its proboscis is short, making nectar gathering difficult. While feeding, it moves about with wings opened flat or almost so and characteristically raises them up and down while continually turning its body around and around in slow circles. Its flight is usually very low, hardly rising above the grasses or flowers. For protection it usually darts down among plant stems and debris close to the ground.

Egg: Pale green; laid in a mass, sometimes in a layer, on the underside of basal leaves of the food plant.

Larva: Dark reddish or chocolate brown, lined with yellow, and covered with numerous branching spines. Gregarious when young.

Food Plants: Many species of Asters, especially Heath Aster (*Aster ericoides*), Tall Aster (*A. prealtus*), Texas Aster (*A. texanus*), and New England Aster are used wherever planted.

Parts Eaten: Leaves, at first only the lower surface but later the entire leaf

THEONA CHECKERSPOT
(*Thessalia theona*)

Family: *Nymphalidae*
Size: 1-1 5/8 inches
Range: Texas
    Texas: 3, 4, 5
Flight Time: April-October
Broods: Many
Overwinters: Half-grown larva

The Theona Checkerspot is never found very far from *Leucophyllum* spp., its larval food plants. This, its weak flight, and its distinctive coloration make for easy identification. The upper wing surfaces of this butterfly are dark grayish or blackish, with orange spots forming bands. A row of pale yellow or cream-colored rectangles forms a wide band across both wings, with another row of orange rectangles just below it, making both wings double-banded. Both wings are bordered in black with a double row of small white dots. The lower wing surfaces are a series of bands of white or cream and reddish-orange. The bands are highlighted by conspicuous black veins. The abdomen is black with very narrow yellow crosswise bands or lines.

This is a butterfly of open country. In its natural habitat it flies slowly among scattered shrub-

bery of the brushlands or chaparral, stopping to take nectar from blossoms of low-growing herbs. Often after a shower it spends much time around mud puddles or concave rocks where

161

the moisture remains standing. Natural seepage areas are an excellent place to look for the adult in the wild. For the home garden within its range, good nectar sources, a group planting of *Leucophyllum*, and a constantly moist area readily bring it in.

The Theona Checkerspot enters the United States from Mexico along two different routes, forming two distinct populations. One population enters the United States from western Mexico along the Pacific, with the Texas population entering along the Gulf Coast from eastern Mexico. I have found this butterfly to be very common anywhere good stands of *Leucophyllum* are growing.

Egg: Cream colored; laid in cluster beneath leaf of food plant. Often several leaves of the same plant are used.

Larva: Velvety brownish-black, dotted and banded with cream, and with many branching spines. The young larvae have a tendency to stay together in close groups, almost completely defoliating certain portions of the food plant.

Food Plants: Big Bend Silver-leaf (*Leucophyllum minus*), Cenizo (*L. frutescens*), and Violet Silver-leaf (*L. violaceum*). Possibly Paintbrush (*Castilleja* spp.)

Parts Eaten: Leaves

COMMON CHECKERED SKIPPER
(*Pyrgus communis*)

Family: *Hesperiidae*
Size: 3/4-1 1/2 inches
Range: All
  Texas: Throughout
Flight Time: All year (March-November)
Broods: Continuous (several)
Overwinters: No diapause (larva)

This is probably the most common skipper in North America. It is also one of the earliest to fly in the spring, visiting whatever is in bloom at the time.

Coloration of this butterfly is very variable, occasionally causing some confusion in identification. Basically, the upper surface of both wings is a dark gray, banded and checkered with white. The lower surface of both wings is much lighter, variously mottled in grays and white. Wing margins are fringed, and the fringe is checkered with gray and white. Long, hairlike scales produce a bluish or turquoise sheen on the body. The male is somewhat lighter in color than the female.

Frequently visiting flowers in short, fast, direct flights, this skipper often stops to bask with wings spread wide. While feeding, it continually turns round and round and with frequent up-and-down movements of the wings. It normally remains low to the ground.

Favorite flowers used for nectaring include Cat's-claw Mimosa (*Mimosa biuncifera*), New

Jersey Tea (*Ceanothus americanus*), Thoroughwort, Dewberry, Antelope-horns (*Asclepias asperula*), Bluets, Bur-clover (*Medicago polymorpha*), False Garlic, Frog-fruit, Golden Crownbeard, Hedge-parsley (*Torilis arvensis*), Indian Blanket, New England Aster, Purple Prairie Clover (*Dalea purpurea*), Spring Beauty, Verbena, Violets, White Sweet Clover (*Melilotus albus*), and Zinnias.

The male is seemingly very territorial and has

been described as being "pugnacious." It is interesting to watch as he "defends" his area, darting out at everything that passes by. He either perches on some exposed twig or branch to await passing females or patrols a regular path, flying slowly back and forth from one boundary to the other. Once he encounters a female, he follows in pursuit until either having mated or having been rejected.

Egg: Greenish, changing to cream just before hatching; laid singly on a bud or an upper surface of a young leaf of a food plant.

Larva: Mostly tan to brown, with darker stripe down back and light brown and white stripes along sides; downy, with short whitish hairs. Lives in rolled-up leaves.

Food Plants: Caliche Globe-mallow (*Sphaeralcea coccinea*), Copper Globe-mallow (*S. angustifolia*), Woolly Globe-mallow (*S. lindheimeri*), Velvet-leaf Butterprint (*Abutilon theophrasti*), Common Mallow (*Malva neglecta*), High Mallow (*M. sylvestris*), Hollyhock (*Althaea rosea*), Three-lobe False-mallow (*Malvastrum coromandelianum*), Flower-of-an-hour (*Hibiscus trionum*), Crested Anoda (*Anoda cristata*), Alkali Sida (*Malvella leprosa*), Arrow-leaf Sida (*Sida rhombifolia*), Prickly Sida (*S. spinosa*), Spreading Sida (*S. abutifolia*), Showy Sida (*S. lindheimeri*), Violet Sida (*Meximalva filipes*), Carolina Modiola (*Modiola caroliniana*), and Tall Poppy-mallow (*Callirhoe leiocarpa*)

Parts Eaten: Leaves

GREAT PURPLE HAIRSTREAK
(*Atlides halesus*)

Family: *Lycaenidae*
Size: 1 1/4-1 1/2 inches
Range: All
  Texas: 2, 3, 4, 5
Flight Time: All year (February-November)
Broods: Continuous (many)
Overwinters: Adult (pupa)

Among the North American Hairstreaks, the Great Purple is very unusual in its coloring, being basically black overlaid with blue. Wing scaling on the upper surface is one of the most brilliant iridescent blues found in any of the butterflies in the South, making this one of our most beautiful. The lower wing surface is not quite so lavish in coloring, being more of a purplish gray, with spots of bright red on the base of the wing near the body and a patch of metallic blue and green spots near the tail. There is a large patch of brilliant blue at the base of the forewing, but it is usually hidden by the hindwing. The upper portion of the abdomen is black with white dots; the rear portion is a spectacular bright reddish orange. The male is more brilliantly colored than the female.

Commonly visiting flowers, the Great Purple Hairstreak can readily be found in gardens if certain conditions are favorable. During most of the year, it does not wander far from trees infested with the semiparasitic Mistletoe (*Phorandendron* spp.), its larval food plant. So,

if there are trees near your garden—usually Elm (*Ulmus* spp.), Hackberry (*Celtis* spp.), Honey Mesquite (*Prosopis glandulosa*), Live Oak (*Quercus virginiana*), or Juniper (*Juniperus* spp.)—with a healthy and thriving growth of Mistletoe, the Great Purple Hairstreak will be a

163

regular visitor to nearby flowers. In some areas greater numbers of these butterflies can be seen in the spring or early summer, but there are almost always at least a few around, and any time this striking beauty is sighted is a special treat.

Some flowers regularly visited for nectar include fruit tree blossoms (both wild and cultivated) such as Peach and Plum. Others include Honey Mesquite, Redbud (*Cercis* spp.), Agarita (*Mahonia trifoliata*), Roosevelt Weed, Texas Kidneywood, Texas Snakewood (*Columbrina texensis*), Thoroughwort, various Asters, Englemann Daisy, Frostweed, Globe Amaranth, Golden-eye, Goldenrod, Hedge-parsley, Kalanchoe (*Kalanchoe* spp.), Texas Thistle, White Clover, Wild Onions and Woolly Ironweed (*Vernonia lindheimeri*).

The male is quite long-lived for a Hairstreak, often surviving three weeks or more. His chosen area for pursuing mates is usually very local, such as one particular tree and a very small surrounding territory. He usually perches in the open near the top of the tree from midday to dusk.

Egg: White and shiny; somewhat rounded, but flattened on top and bottom, with deep depression on top. The outer surface is covered with tiny bumps arranged in more or less regular horizonal rows.

Larva: Pale green, with a darker stripe down the back and a yellowish stripe along each side; velvety, with very short yellowish orange hair; slug shaped.

Food Plants: Christmas Mistletoe (*Phorandendron tomentosum*) on Ash (*Fraxinus* spp.), Eastern Cottonwood (*Populus deltoides*), Elm (*Ulmus* spp.), Hackberry (*Celtis* spp.), Honey Mesquite (*Prosopis glandulosa*), Oak (*Quercus* spp.), Sycamore (*Platanus occidentalis*), and Willow (*Salix* spp.); Juniper Mistletoe (*Phorandendron juniperinum*), and Juniper (*Juniperus* spp.).

Parts Eaten: Leaves

WHITE M HAIRSTREAK
(*Parrhasius m-album*)

Family: *Lycaenidae*
Size: 1 1/8-1 1/2 inches
Range: All
   Texas: 2, 4
Flight Time: February-December
Broods: Three to many
Overwinters: Pupa

Like most of the other Hairstreaks, the White M Hairstreak is an avid feeder on flower nectar and crawls from flower to flower when it finds a good nectar source such as Willow Baccharis (*Baccharis salicina*). While feeding, it is relatively docile, but if startled takes off in rapid, often erratic flight. Although widely distributed and seen in many different habitats, its range is apparently more southern, and nowhere or at any time is it abundant. Peak emergence occurs usually in the early spring months of March and April. In the fall the butterflies are again frequently seen but are usually very local in distribution and in groups. In the fall this butterfly will often be in the company of other Hairstreaks around a good nectar source, so close observation is necessary to separate the different species present.

You can identify the White M Hairstreak most easily by the large and conspicuous M or W (depending on which way you are viewing the wing) on the hindwings that is formed by narrow white and black bands. At the base of the two long, narrow tails are large red and blue areas. The upper sides of the wings are a brilliant, iridescent blue with wide black borders along the wing margins. Occasionally this butterfly will partially open the wings while nectaring or basking, but more often even basking is done with the wings closed and turned sideways to the sun. The beauty of the upper sides is generally viewed only briefly as the butterfly alights and takes off in flight.

Egg: White

Larva: Olive or light yellowish green, with darker green stripe along the back and with seven dull, dark green, slanting stripes along each side; body downy; head black, smooth.

Pupa: Brown with brown blotches and with a black ridge along the abdomon segments which squeaks when the pupa moves. Pupa overwinters, probably in the leaf litter beneath host Oak trees.

Food Plants: Probably any species of Oak (*Quercus* spp.), but especially trees with narrow or very lobed leaves, such as Live Oak (*Q. virginiana*) and Shumard Oak (*Q. shumardii*)

Parts Eaten: Foliage, especially immature or the tenderest portions of mature leaves

GRAY HAIRSTREAK
(*Strymon melinus*)

Family: *Lycaenidae*
Size: 1-1 1/4 inches
Range: All
    Texas: Throughout
Flight Time: All year (April-November)
Broods: Continuous (many)
Overwinters: No diapause (pupa)

This is probably our most common Hairstreak, being found in a wide range of habitats and throughout the season from earliest spring to freezing weather or all year, depending on the range. Anywhere there are flowers, the Gray Hairstreak can be seen flying swiftly about. At times the larvae are so numerous they cause serious damage to cultivated beans, corn, or cotton. The larvae sometimes bore into young flower buds of cotton, seeking the high-protein pollen, and are known as the Cotton Square Borer.

The Gray Hairstreak is colored with soft blackish or bluish-gray scaling on the upper surface of both wings and with an orange spot on each hindwing. Below, the wings are a soft dove-gray, with black and white lines forming narrow bands; two large, orange-red and blue patches containing two black spots form "eyes" near the tails on the hindwings. The gray coloring is darker in the spring specimens, and the male is darker than the female. The male also has orange along the abdomen.

As with other Hairstreaks, this one moves the tailed and eyed portion of the wings about while feeding, simulating a head complete with eyes and antennae in case of attack by a predator. In basking, it generally only partially opens the wings and rarely spreads them completely for any length of time. In the afternoons, the male perches on a low tree limb or shrub to await passing females for mating.

Many species of flowers are used by this Hairstreak for nectaring, especially Chaste Tree (*Vitex agnus-castus*), Milfoil (*Achillea millefolium*), various Milkweeds, Phlox, Plains

Black-foot, Tansy Aster (*Machaeranthera tanacetifolia*), Verbena, and White Sweet Clover. It is an avid partaker of the nectar of Parsley Hawthorn (*Crataegus marshallii*), and the Wild Plums (*Prunus* spp.).

Egg: Pale green; laid singly on a bud or young flower of a food plant.

Larva: May range from white to various shades of pink, purplish, or reddish brown, but usually green; white or rose stripes line the sides.

Food Plants: Larval food plants of this butterfly are extensive, with over ninety species being recorded as utilized. However, members of the Legume family (*Fabaceae*) and Mallow family (*Malvaceae*) are preferred. Some of the more commonly used are Alfalfa (*Medicago sativa*), Peanuts (*Arachis hypogaea*), and Cotton (*Gossypium hirsutum*). Others include Althea (*Hibiscus syriacus*), False Indigo (*Amorpha fruticosa*), Garden Bean, Lima Bean, Garden Pea (*Pisum*

165

sativium), Hairy Bush Clover (*Lespedeza hirta*), Texas Bluebonnet (*Lupinus texensis*), Scarlet Pea (*Indigofera minuata*), White Clover (*Trifollium repens*), White Sweet Clover, Common Mallow (*Malva neglecta*), Little Mallow (*M. parviflora*), Running Mallow (*M. rotundiflora*), One-seed Croton (*Croton monanthogynus*), and Silver Croton (*C. argyranthemus*). Parsley Hawthorn (*Crataegus marshallii*), Texas Persimmon (*Diospyros texana*), Desert Lantana (*Lantana macropoda*), and Yellow-bells (*Tecoma stans*) are sometimes used.

Parts Eaten: Flower buds, immature fruits, occasionally young leaves

HENRY'S ELFIN
(*Incisalia henrici*)

Family: *Lycaenidae*
Size: 7/8-1 1/8 inches
Range: All
Texas: 2, 3, 4, 5
Flight Time: February-May
Broods: One
Overwinters: Pupa

Although it has a wide distribution, Henry's Elfin is very local within its range—even when found, there never seem to be very many of them. I was fortunate to have a colony at my butterfly garden in Brazos County, but I still never saw but one or two each year. I almost always saw them around the Farkleberry (*Vaccinium arboreum*) bushes along the driveway and almost always taking moisture from the ground. When disturbed they quickly flew into the woodland shrubbery and disappeared.

This butterfly will rarely be found anywhere except near its larval food plant. Such shrubby or brushy areas along woodland edges and openings in deciduous or pine hardwood forest are much to its liking, but it can also be found in swampy, shady deciduous woodlands—habitat of the lower growing Blueberries (*Vaccimium* spp.).

The best way to find these little beauties is to walk slowly and quietly to one of their larval food plants and then gently shake it. If a colony of butterflies has become established in the area, more than likely some will fly out, for when not taking nectar, courting or laying eggs, they are usually hidden among the foliage.

Upper surface of both wings of the Henry's Elfin is a dark grayish brown with reddish scaling. The basal two thirds of the surface of the forewing is a rich, dark brown with a lighter brown covering the marginal third. The two areas are separated by thin, interrupted lines of black and white. The lower surface of the hindwing is dark blackish brown with brownish scaling, followed by bands of lighter brown then bluish gray near the wing margin. The two brown areas are separated by thin black and white lines as in the forewings; the lighter brown and grayish area by a row of dark brown or blackish crescents. Short, stubby, tail-like projections are conspicuous on the hindwings and help in the identification of this species.

This butterfly visits the blossoms of many spring flowers freely, but especially those of its larval food plants, the Blueberries, Farkelberries, Huckleberries, Redbud (*Cercis canadensis*), and Texas Persimmon (*Diospyros texana*).

Egg: Pale green becoming white, ridged; laid singly on flowers or near leaf buds.

Larva: Green to reddish or maroon with lengthwise lines and comma-shaped dashes along the sides.

Food Plants: Black Huckleberry (*Gaylussacia baccata*), Blueberry (*Vaccinium vacillans*), Highbush Blueberry (*V. corymbosum*), Farkleberry (*V. arboreum*), Redbud (*Cercis anadensis*), American Plum (*Prunus americana*), Black Cherry (*P. serotina*), Fire Cherry (*P. pennsylvanica*), Sand Cherry (*P. pumila*), American Holly (*Ilex opaca*), Dahoon (*I. cassine*), Yaupon (*I. vomitoria*), Maple-leaf Viburnum (*Viburnum acerifolium*), Texas Mountain Laurel (*Sophora secundiflora*), and Texas Persimmon (*Diospyros texona*). Texas Bluebonnet (*Lupinus texensis*) is sometimes used. Favorite genera seem to be *Gaylussacia*, *Vaccinium*, and *Cercis* where available. Probably many more species of the former two are used than listed here.

Parts Eaten: Flowers and young fruits

166

Pygmy Blue is very common, flying slow and low to the ground, visiting the smaller flowers. The upper wing surface is a rich reddish-brown, with iridescent blue scaling near the body. The brown of the undersurface is interrupted with small white striations in the outer portion of the forewings, then becoming mixed with blue-gray near the body. A row of black spots lines the margins of the hindwings, the lower spots centered with iridescent blue-green. The wings are delicately fringed in white. The female is generally a little larger than the male and somewhat browner.

Despite the fragile appearance of this tiny mite, it emigrates northward each year while rearing broods, but it cannot survive the harsh winters and must start over each year. Its appearance in certain breeding areas is also somewhat sporadic, as in some locales it is abundant in a particular year, then absent the next. Perhaps it depends on food plants of a certain age, but this is not known.

Low-growing or sprawling plants with flowers close to the ground are the ones which attract this butterfly. Also, because its proboscis is very short, the Western Pygmy Blue uses only flowers with shallow nectaries. Some favorite flowers are Agarita, Thoroughwort, Wild Onions, Bluets, Dakota Vervain, Frogfruit, Phlox, Phacelia, Zinnia, and various Asters, especially New England Aster.

The male slowly and continuously flies back and forth over the larval food plants during the day, seeking females with which to mate.

Egg: Pale bluish green becoming white; laid singly on almost any part of the food plant, particularly on the upper leaf surface.

Western Pygmy Blue

Larva: Variable; most commonly creamy white to pale green, covered with tiny, white-tipped brown bumps and yellow and pinkish stripes on back and sides. When touched by ants, the larva produces a honeydew which is eaten by the ants.

Food Plants: Australian Saltbush (*Atriplex canascens*), Four-wing Saltbush (*A. semibaccata*), Horse-purslane (*Trianthema portulacastrum*), Lamb's-quarters (*Chenopodium album*), Narrow-leaf Goosefoot (*Chenopodium leptophyllum*), Seepweed (*Suaeda monquinii*), Tumbleweed (*Salsola iberica*), Virginia Glasswort (*Salicornia virginica*), and Winged Sesuvium (*Sesuvium verrucosum*)

Parts Eaten: Flowers, fruits, leaves, stems

169

CHAPTER EIGHT

Larval Food Plants

ere and in the next chapter are some of the best larval and nectar food plants to use in your own butterfly garden—space prohibits describing all of the useful plants of the South and Southeast. If you use a plant shown here and have poor results in attracting butterflies, the best thing to do is to consult the more complete lists of food plants that follow, as well as the list given in any of the good field guides. If one of the plants listed there is more prolific in your area than the plants shown or listed here, start watching the plants for larvae and larval usage. If you want to know locations of the plants, call members of local garden clubs, members of the Sierra Club, or the biology departments of high schools, colleges, or universities. If you live close to a university, visit the entomology department. Usually someone there is knowledgeable about butterflies and can tell you the preferred larval food choices for particular species in your area.

Become familiar with the "weeds" of your area which are known food plants. Each time you pass through a place where they are growing abundantly, take a close look at them; you will often find larvae. If you are unable to recognize some of the plants of the truly weedy type, visit the herbaria of high schools or universities and study the dried plant specimens.

Both the larval and nectar food plants have been separated into categories, beginning with trees and continuing with shrubs, vines, and herbs, and placed in alphabetical order by common name.

Each nectar and larval food plant description includes the following:

🦋 **Common and Scientific Names:** When choosing common names, my *Wildflowers of Texas* was consulted; then *Checklist of the Vascular Plants of Texas* by Stephen L. Hatch, Kancheepuram N. Gandhi, and Larry Brown; *A Synonymized Checklist of the Vascular Flora of the United States, Canada and Greenland* by John T. Kartesz and Rosemarie Kartesz; and *Manual of the Vascular Flora of the Carolinas* by Albert E. Radford, Harry E. Alyles, and C. Ritchie Bell. For the scientific names of Texas plants I have followed Hatch, Gandhi, and Brown; for the eastern species not in Texas, I have followed Kartesz and Kartesz.

🦋 **Bloom Period:** Dates given for both the larval and nectar plants are for the flowering period. For the larval food plants, in most instances it is the foliage which most larvae use, and this is available to them over a longer period, usually throughout the entire breeding season.

🦋 **Range:** For a larval food plant, only the states where the plant can be found and can be used (as far as known) *and* where the butterflies which use the plant as a larval food source are known to breed are given here. In the Texas range, the first numbers indicate the natural range of the plant in the state by the region where the butterfly breeds and would use the plant as a larval food source. The number(s) in parentheses indicate additional regions of the plant's natural range in Texas but where the butterfly does not breed. Before experimenting with the range of a larval food plant, make sure the butterfly which would use it already occurs in your area.

When the word "Throughout" is given in the range, the plant either occurs naturally throughout the state or, in the case of a cultivar such as Dill or Butterfly Bush, may be grown in the garden throughout the state.

General ranges given for the nectar plants are those states where the plant grows naturally. Many of the natives are now being offered by nurseries and are slowly becoming available over a wider range. For a cultivar, escape, or naturalized species, the ranges given are where the plant can be either found growing semi-wild or can be cultivated. The first number in the Texas range indicates where the plant can most likely be grown and do well; the number in parentheses gives a range where the plant can also be found, although perhaps not as extensively.

🦋 **Height:** These measurements are, in most instances, the extremes from lowest to highest as found in nature. Often in a garden situation, growth is faster and a greater height is achieved due to the greater nutrient and moisture availability.

🦋 **Class:** This rating has been given the plants in order to better understand the plant and to help in its location. If "native," then the plant may have to be obtained from the wild. If "escape" or "naturalized," then it may be purchased or occasionally found in the wild along with the native species. If "cultivar," then the plant needs to be obtained from a mail-order catalog or a local nursery.

171

Trees

BLACK CHERRY (*Prunus serotina*)
Rose Family (*Rosaceae*)

Bloom Period: March-April
Range: All
   Texas: Throughout
Height: To 100 feet
Class: Native

A beautifully shaped tree with scaly bark on the lower portion of the trunk; the bark in the upper portion is streaked horizonally in shiny, silvery grays and soft blacks. The bark is very aromatic. Leaves are glossy, bright green. Small, creamy white flowers appear in long, drooping racemes in early spring, followed by black fruit.

The fruit is edible when fully ripe and dark black, but avoid red half-ripe fruit as it contains hydrocyanic acid, a respiratory poison.

Cultivation: Plant this tree in a moist, well-drained situation. It grows in a variety of soils. Plants may be started from seed or cuttings or dug from the wild. They are commonly offered by nurseries dealing in native plants, and this is by far the easiest way to get healthy, fast-growing plants.

If you want to try plants from seed, gather the ripe fruit, remove the pulp from the seed, and allow the seed to air-dry for a day or so. Layer the dried seed in moist perlite and place in the refrigerator until ready to plant. Sow the seeds in prepared beds in early fall, then cover the beds lightly with mulch.

Foliage of Black Cherry is sometimes attacked by moth caterpillars. One of them, commonly called the tent caterpillar, forms large webs or tents of silk in the angles of the branches. Close, continual inspection of the trees in early spring and immediate control is the best remedy. When the webs are first sighted, squash the mass by running your hands up and down the branches. If these caterpillars are not removed, especially from a small tree, the tree becomes stressed and is sometimes unable to recover from its loss of foliage.

Used By: Coral Hairstreak, Henry's Elfin, Red-spotted Purple, Spring Azure, Striped Hairstreak, Tiger Swallowtail, Viceroy

Parts Eaten: Immature leaves; larvae prefer the foliage on younger trees.

Note: The flowers of Black Cherry are used as a nectar source by many species of butterflies. However, the bloom period is short, lasting only two or three weeks.

HERCULES'-CLUB (*Zanthoxylum clava-herculis*)
Citrus Family (*Rutaceae*)

Bloom Period: April-May
Range: All
   Texas: 2
Height: To 15 feet
Class: Native

A large shrub or small tree with broad, rounded crown and dark green, glossy foliage. Leaves large, divided into several leaflets. Large, terminal clusters of numerous small, greenish white flowers are followed by clusters of hard fruits resembling unground peppercorns. There are corky prickles on the trunk and lower branches, and the upper branches and leaves often bear reddish black prickles. All parts of the tree are strongly aromatic when crushed.

Cultivation: This is an easily grown tree, not particular as to soils. Give adequate moisture, especially during summer, for the healthiest and fastest growth. Habitually a stout or chunky appearing tree, Hercules'-club rarely needs pruning. It grows relatively fast up to about seven or eight feet.

New plants are readily obtained by removing the outer husk from the fruit and planting the inner black, shiny seeds in the fall. If you want to provide larval plant food immediately, though, the best thing is to obtain plants two or three feet in height from the wild. These are small enough to transplant easily, yet they produce enough foliage for food. This is not a plant usually found in nurseries, so try to find a construction site or a kind landowner. Look for the plants especially along fence rows where they have been planted naturally by birds.

Hercules'-club may sometimes be attacked by white flies when in a garden setting, but frequent and forceful spraying of the underside of the leaves with a garden hose usually discourages the pests.

Used By: Giant Swallowtail
Parts Eaten: Young to midmature foliage
Note: The young larvae of the Giant Swallowtail, which appear very similar to bird droppings, rest on the leaves in plain sight, methodically consuming them one by one. During the heat of the day, they often crawl to the undersides of leaflets or rest along small branches out of the sun. They do not make any sort of nest or shelter.

RED BAY (*Persea borbonia*)
Laurel Family (*Lauraceae*)

Bloom Period: May-June
Range: All except Tennessee, Arkansas, Oklahoma
   Texas: 2, 3
Height: To 25 feet
Class: Native

A large shrub or very small tree, usually with many trunks from the base, forming a large clump. The foliage is thick, leathery, and evergreen, bright green on the upper surface and somewhat whitish or silvery underneath. The leaves are very aromatic when crushed. The

173

Red Bay

good drainage. Unless you have a sloping lot, loamy soil alone does not provide enough drainage. The best planting program here is to use wide, raised beds. The beds should be at least one foot above the surrounding area and wide enough to give the plant enough area for root growth. A bed six by six feet is large enough for a number of years. Dig the original soil to a depth of two to three feet and refill with a mixture of sandy loam and rich compost, shredded leaves, or well-rotted sawdust. A mixture of sand and coarse pine bark worked into the soil is excellent, keeping the soil loose, aerated, and well drained. Give Red Bay a little extra water now and then, due to the extra drainage. In the second year after planting, if the shrub is well established and growing nicely, trim a few of the branches back occasionally to promote new growth. The plant will resprout into a clump of new stems with a lot of new growth.

The Red Bay is susceptible to a leaf gall which disfigures the leaves and makes them nonusable for butterfly larvae. At the very first sign of infestation, spot-spray with a mild Sevin solution. After a week or so, hose the plant down to remove the spray, or the plants will not be used for egg deposition.

flowers are small, creamy, and borne in small clusters from leaf axils. The small fruits are dark blue to black, each containing a solitary seed.

Cultivation: While Red Bay normally grows in naturally moist or wet areas, it can easily be grown in the garden in just about any soil with just a bit of extra care. Use no commercial fertilizer with this one. Instead, work lots of well-rotted leaves or compost into the soil and add a mulch of shredded leaves or pine straw.

Another requirement for Red Bay is extra-

Used By: Palamedes Swallowtail, Spicebush Swallowtail

Parts Eaten: Young vegetative growth

SASSAFRAS (*Sassafras albidum*)
Laurel Family (*Lauraceae*)

Bloom Period: March-April
Range: All
  Texas: 2
Height: To 90 feet
Class: Native

Thinly branched, well-shaped, small deciduous tree rarely attaining its maximum height. Twigs bright green, limber, and breaking easily. Leaves extremely variable in shape and may be one-lobed, mitten shaped, or distinctly three-lobed. Showy clusters of greenish yellow flowers appear before the leaves or just as the leaves begin to unfold. Male and female flowers occur on the same or separate trees. Showy blue

174

fruits are borne on thickened, cuplike red pedicels, ripening in late fall. Almost all parts of this plant are aromatic.

Cultivation: To obtain plants of Sassafras, collect the attractive blue fruits when ripe, anytime between August and October, and sow in the garden by late November. Getting a fair-sized sapling from seed may be a bit slower than desired; on the other hand, well-established plants root-sprout readily and soon need thinning or transplanting. Young saplings or root sprouts can easily be transplanted from the wild if moved in early fall. Better yet, well-established container-grown plants are frequently offered by nurseries and are the surest way of having adequate food plants.

While Sassafras can eventually become large, for many years it remains a shrub or small tree. Sassafras grows best and produces the most foliage if given moist, rich, well-drained, sandy loams on the acid side and plenty of sun.

Under normal conditions the lower branches of the Sassafras continually die and fall off as the tree grows taller. To ensure that the plant retains optimal heights for egg laying and to increase foliage, you may do light trimming from time to time.

Very light applications of fertilizer in the spring and early summer produce more foliage, but be careful not to overfertilize the Sassafras—in this case, a little goes a very long way!

Used By: Palamedes Swallowtail, Spicebush Swallowtail, Tiger Swallowtail

Parts Eaten: Foliage, preferably young to midmature

Note: In the fall the leaves of the Sassafras turn wonderful shades of yellow, orange, rose, pink-purple, and red, so try to plant in groups of three or more in the garden, placing them where they can be easily seen and admired.

Shrubs

BLACK DALEA (*Dalea frutescens*)
Legume Family (*Fabaceae*)

Bloom Period: June-October
Range: Texas
   Texas: 1, 3, 4, 5
Height: 3-4 feet
Class: Native

Open, spreading or somewhat rounded, thornless, hardy shrub. Leaves composed of many tiny, silvery-green leaflets conspicuously dotted on the lower surface with minute glands. The foliage is very aromatic when crushed. Flowers magenta and white, with several compressed into shortened terminal spikes or clusters. Flowering is usually very prolific, and the plants are often almost solid masses of beautiful color.

Cultivation: The Black Dalea is a native to dry, rocky, limestone soils and is generally found growing mixed with other brushy-type shrubs. It is an excellent nectar source for many species of butterflies.

This is not one to be found in nurseries, so to

get plants you have to dig, take cuttings, or plant seed. Unless the plants are very small, I would not suggest digging. Instead, take semi-woody tip cuttings in summer or early fall from the more succulent growth of the current season. Dip cuttings in hormone rooting powder and place in sand under a plastic frame. Place rooting container in open, light shade and keep moist but not soggy.

By far the easiest method of obtaining plants of Black Dalea is by planting seeds. Collect seed pods after they have become plump and brown. Plant the seeds immediately after gathering, either in a seeding bed from which the seedlings can be transplanted or directly into the spot where the plants are to remain. If seeds are to be carried over the winter, wait to gather them until they are as ripe as possible and then air-

dry them several days after removing from the pods. Fumigate the seed, then refrigerate for the winter. Sow the seeds in spring after the danger of frost is past.

Black Dalea does quite well even in the poorest of soils and under almost droughty conditions, so do not kill it with kindness in the garden. See that the plants get a good start by placing them in a sunny location with well-drained soils, adding lime if necessary but not fertilizer. Provide the plants with moisture until well established, then water occasionally during the summer if needed, but basically leave them alone. Black Dalea produces more flowers if trimmed severely each spring.

Used By: Dogface Butterfly
Parts Eaten: Leaves

CENIZO (*Leucophyllum frutescens*)
Figwort Family (*Scrophulariaceae*)

Bloom Period: Summer
Range: Texas only
  Texas: 3, 4, 5
Height: To 8 feet
Class: Native

Cenizo (meaning "the color of ashes" in Spanish) is a densely branched shrub with distinctive grayish foliage. The entire plant is covered with fine whitish hairs, which make it very soft to the touch and give it its unusual coloration. The flowers are somewhat bell shaped and range in color from various shades of pinks to lavenders and purples.

Cultivation: The Cenizo does not transplant well from the wild but can easily be raised from cuttings of the current season's growth. Container plants are being offered by almost every nursery and are available in a wide variety of leaf and flower colors and in dwarf forms. Not all forms are winter hardy for all areas, so purchase plants recommended by a knowledgeable nurseryman.

Use these plants in a dry, well-drained site, preferably with rocky or gravelly soils. If drainage is a problem, raise the beds. Once they are well rooted, a deep, thorough watering during extended droughts is beneficial, but over-

watering produces a straggly, sprawling, tender plant that will winterkill. Contrary to popular belief, it is not rain or watering which controls the flowering of Cenizo, but humidity.

All of the *Leucophyllums* need alkaline soils. Add dolomitic limestone to acid soils, and if more calcium is needed, adding gypsum would be appropriate. Do not use peat moss in the area where the Cenizo is growing, as it would make the soil acid. Cenizo is generally hardy and disease resistant and usually needs nothing but the proper soil for producing spectacular plants. The only serious problem is with cotton root rot, a fungus to which all Cenizos are highly susceptible.

Place several Cenizos together in small groupings, use as hedges, or arrange as the background of a border. These are slow growers, so if you are using them in the last two situations, buy large plants, as small plants may be shaded out by the plants in the front. Do not crowd the Cenizo wherever you plant it, for it likes the drying breezes. If the plants need shaping to keep in bounds, trim during spring or summer. The plants bloom on old wood as well as new growth, so do not trim to try and force flowering, and take out only what is needed for shaping.

Used By: Theona Checkerspot

Parts Eaten: Foliage preferred; buds and flowers if the larvae run out of leaves

CHRISTMAS MISTLETOE (*Phorandendron tomentosum*)
Mistletoe Family (*Viscaceae*)

Bloom Period: November-March
Range: All
   Texas: 2, 3, 4, 5 (1)
Height: To 3 feet
Class: Native

A parasitic, clumped shrub growing on deciduous trees. The small, thick, leathery leaves may be either yellowish or dull, dark green. Minute, inconspicuous male and female flowers occur in short, stiff racemes later followed by pearly white to creamy translucent berries on the female plants.

Cultivation: New plants of Christmas Mistletoe are normally started from bird droppings. The fruits or berries consist of a mass of gluey mucilaginous material surrounding the solitary seeds, seeds which, even after being eaten, remain whole within some of the glutinous substance and readily become attached to whatever they come in contact with.

Christmas Mistletoe depends on its host tree for certain nutrients. As the seeds sprout, they send minute hairlike tendrils beneath the bark layer, where they are able to absorb the liquid sap of the tree. If a weak or diseased tree becomes heavily infested with the shrub, the tree can actually be killed. However, one or two clumps on a healthy tree usually will neither weaken nor kill the tree.

These plants use several species of trees as hosts, with some of the common ones being Ash, Cottonwood, Elm, Hackberry, Honey Mesquite, Willow, and almost all of the Oaks.

Christmas Mistletoe is a plant of open lands and will be found most often on trees in pastures, along roadsides, at woodland edges, or in thin woodlands.

When trying to propagate Mistletoe, your first requirement is to have a healthy host plant that is preferably a few years old. Then, in mid- to late winter, gather Mistletoe berries and mash them all over the branches and trunk of the tree. Several species of birds savor the berries, in particular Bluebirds, Cedar Waxwings, and Robins. If you spot a flock of these birds, gather some of the seed-filled droppings and smear these on the tree where you want Mistletoe to grow. Often the percentage rate of germination is greatly increased for seeds which have passed through an animal's digestive tract.

If more than six clumps of plants begin to grow, remove all but three or four after the first year or two. It will do no good to weaken or kill the tree. Each clump of Mistletoe will be either male or female, so if you want berries for decorative purposes, wait to remove the unwanted clumps until they begin to bear fruit, leaving plants of each sex on the tree.

Used By: Great Purple Hairstreak

Parts Eaten: Flowers and leaves

Note: Berries of all of the Mistletoes are toxic to humans and should never be eaten.

SMALL-FLOWERED PAWPAW (*Asimina parviflora*)
Custard-apple Family (*Annonaceae*)

Bloom Period: April

Range: All except Oklahoma and Tennessee
  Texas: 2

Height: 2-8 feet

Class: Native

Stout, irregularly branched, tropical-appearing deciduous shrub bearing large, thick, leathery, dark green leaves. Stems, branches, and young growth usually covered with soft, reddish brown hairs. The solitary flowers are small, purplish or brownish, appearing in early spring before or with first leaves. The two- to three-inch banana-shaped fruits turn black or dark brown when ripe.

Cultivation: The Pawpaw is an interesting plant for the garden but not one to use for showiness. It is an ideal background plant for the semishaded part of the garden and blends in well with such other natives as Hoary Azalea (*Rhododendron canescens*), Parsley Hawthorn (*Crataegus marshallii*), Red Bay, Sassafras, and Spicebush.

Small-flowered Pawpaw prefers somewhat acid, moist but well-drained, sandy-loam soils. It grows quite well in the garden under these conditions but cannot tolerate dry, hard soils. It can survive in full sun but does best in open, airy semi-shade.

Propagation is usually by seed or cuttings. Pawpaws are sometimes offered as nursery potted plants. They are extremely deep rooted and are very difficult to dig from the wild. If plants are being destroyed and you want to attempt transplanting, though, choose the very youngest plants and dig deeply and carefully to get as much root as possible. Cut top growth back two thirds or more and plant in carefully prepared sites. Dig the planting holes much larger than the root balls and add lots of half-rotted pine needles and sharp sand. Soil taken from where the plants were growing is ideal. After planting, add a deep mulch of pine needles. Keep the plants moist but not soggy until new growth begins.

Used By: Zebra Swallowtail

Parts Eaten: Foliage. The larvae feed at night or during the day if it's cloudy, at other times resting near the base of the plant.

FLAME ACANTHUS (*Anisacanthus quadrifidus*)
Acanthus Family (*Acanthaceae*)

Bloom Period: June-Frost
Range: Texas only
  Texas: 4 (1, 2, 3)
Height: 2-4 feet
Class: Native

Many-branched, deciduous shrub usually wider than high. Branches slender and brittle, with small, widely spaced, pale green, opposite leaves. Numerous slender, tubular flowers of bright firecracker red or deep orange form open, terminal racemes.

Cultivation: A very drought-tolerant plant and one of the easiest of our natives to grow in the home garden if given an exposed, sunny site with dry soils. It is exceptionally disease resistant. Flame Acanthus is one of the last to put forth leaves each spring but one of the last to loose its leaves in the fall. The flowering period is intermittent but continuous, with the heaviest flowering during the hottest, driest periods of late summer and on into fall.

You may easily obtain new plants from seeds, seedling transplants, or cuttings. Two to four seeds are formed in each capsule; the plants bear seed throughout the summer and fall after each flowering period. Once they begin ripening, you need to collect the capsules almost daily until you have the amount of seeds needed. The seeds should be thoroughly dried after gathering and stored until the following spring. Seeds germinate readily without any pretreatment. After all danger of frost is past, plant in a prepared site in the garden and keep moist but not soggy. Flame Acanthus readily reseeds, and you can easily move new plants from around the mother plant.

Use this as a specimen planting, placing at least three plants in a prominent area of the lawn or entrance way, or use for a solid hedge. Otherwise, mix with other shrubs in a border. They are very striking when grown in barrels for the porch or patio. When trimmed or shaped, the branches become thicker and more dense, but in many instances the more natural look, even if less branched, is more appealing in a garden planting. To obtain both more branching and still retain a natural shape, cut the entire plant back to approximately six inches above ground level after a hard freeze or in very early spring.

Used By: Janais Patch, Texan Crescentspot
Parts Eaten: Buds, flowers, young foliage

HOP-TREE (*Ptelia trifoliata*)
Citrus Family (*Rutaceae*)

Bloom Period: March-July
Range: All
  Texas: Throughout
Height: 2–25 feet
Class: Native

A large, rounded shrub with several stems or sometimes a small tree, with aromatic bark and foliage. Leaves alternate, divided into three separate leaflets of various shapes. Small greenish white flowers in clusters in spring are followed

179

by conspicuously winged, wafer-thin, circular fruits coming to full maturity in late summer or early fall.

Cultivation: If not in flower or fruit, the Hop-tree can be mistaken for a small Ash. It is easy to grow either from fall- or spring-planted seeds or from cuttings. Gather seeds in late summer or early fall and plant them in your garden immediately. Mark the planting area well—seedlings do not show until the follow-

ing spring. You can also obtain good results by placing the seeds in layers of moist Perlite, peat moss, or sand and refrigerating during the winter until ready to plant in the spring. Small plants are also easy to transplant from the wild if you take care to obtain the deep taproot. Occasionally, this plant is carried by nurseries, especially those dealing in native species.

The Hop-tree is not especially particular as to soil and makes do under near-drought conditions after becoming sufficiently rooted. It tolerates some shade but forms much lusher growth in full sun and with adequate moisture. Trimming or pruning also produces a bushier plant and keeps it to shrub size. If preferred, trim out all the stems except one or two for a small tree form.

Some gardeners object to the odor of this plant, likening it to the scent of a skunk. If you find the odor offensive, place the plant in a part of the garden where you will not brush or bruise it when you pass by.

Used By: Giant Swallowtail, Tiger Swallowtail, Two-tailed Tiger Swallowtail

Parts Eaten: Foliage

Note: While the flowering period is not long lasting, the blossoms are used for nectaring by many species of butterflies, especially Hairstreaks and Skippers.

NEW JERSEY TEA (*Ceanothus americanus*)
Buckthorn Family (*Rhamnaceae*)

Bloom Period: April-June
Range: All
   Texas: 2
Height: 1-4 feet
Class: Native

Small, delicate shrub, woody at the base, with slender, spreading herbaceous branches. Flowers small, white, in frothy terminal racemes. Plants are often multitrunked from the base.

Cultivation: New Jersey Tea is not easily transplanted from the wild because of excessively large, burl-like rootstocks, but it can be readily propagated from seeds or cuttings. Plants are occasionally offered by nurseries; when you can find them there, this is the best way of obtaining plants. If you want to gather

180

seeds, watch the capsules carefully. Immediately upon ripening, the capsules split and throw the seeds quite a distance from the plant; the seeds are then practically impossible to find on the ground. Tie small squares of nylon netting around almost-mature capsules, thus preventing loss of the seeds. Getting these seeds to germinate is often difficult. Soaking the seeds in hot water before planting sometimes helps. Layering them in moist Perlite or peat moss for two to three months before planting might also help. For best results, try both methods or any other way you can think of.

New Jersey Tea roots from shoots of the current season's growth. Be careful of the very brittle roots when moving the newly rooted cuttings to permanent beds. For better formed plants, pinch the tops of the cuttings when transplanting.

Normally growing in sandy soils, New Jersey Tea is tolerant of a variety of soils in a garden situation if given enough moisture and excellent drainage. It is best used in a lightly shaded portion of a perennial border, along a shady path, or in filtered sun at the edge of a woodland. Plant in groupings of three to five, as butterflies are more attracted to large patches of color and are better able to detect the chemical fragrance of the foliage when it is in masses. The bloom period lasts only two to three weeks, but the seed capsules which form later are a beautiful brown and remain on the plant until the next year. After plants begin showing good growth in the early spring, pinch or trim them back for bushier growth and to keep the plants lower.

Used By: Spring Azure, Mottled Duskywing
Parts Eaten: Foliage
Note: New Jersey Tea is a nectar source for several species of butterflies.

PARSLEY HAWTHORN (*Crataegus marshallii*)
Rose Family (*Rosaceae*)

Bloom Period: March-April
Range: All
Texas: 2
Height: To 25 feet
Class: Native

Usually low-growing, tough, deciduous shrub with silvery-gray bark peeling off in patches and revealing the reddish brown inner layer. Leaves distinctively lobed, similar to leaves of the garden Parsley. Clusters of white flowers cover the branches before or with first leaves. Anthers red, conspicuous, making the flowers appear almost pink from a distance. Flowers followed by small, applelike fruits, which turn a brilliant scarlet in late fall.

Cultivation: The Parsley Hawthorn, as are almost all of the *Crataegus*, is easily grown from stratified seed; cuttings are not very successful. Seeds should be soaked in water for several days until swollen. Then layer the seeds in moist Perlite in an airtight plastic bag and place in the refrigerator for four to six weeks. Container plants are offered by some local nurseries as well as through some catalogs.

Tag very young wildings in the summer or

fall when easily identified, then move them after they become dormant in the winter. The Parsley Hawthorn has an extra-long taproot; take care not to break or cut this taproot when transplanting. In the garden, plant in loose, loamy garden soils, fertilize occasionally, and give adequate moisture. Well-established plants can survive brief periods of drought, but prolonged summer dryness can cause the fruit to fall prematurely.

Use this shrub along a naturalized woodland edge or as a specimen planting. It can be left as a single stem by trimming root sprouts that occur. If you want a bushier plant, cut back to three or four inches from the ground when two or three years old. New growth results in several stems for a low-branched specimen. To achieve an immediate clumped effect, place three or four small plants together.

For easiest planting, remove approximately one-fourth of the soil from one side of the plants in one-gallon containers. Place all three (or four) of the plants in the same hole, placing the sections where the soil was removed close together and leaning the trunks of the plants slightly away from the center. When finished planting, the trunks should look like a slightly spread, upside-down tripod.

Rarely does the Parsley Hawthorn attain the maximum height given here, perhaps doing so only after many years. It usually remains a slow-growing, low- to medium-height shrub or low tree. With good garden care, there should be no problem growing this shrub well outside its normal range.

Used By: Gray Hairstreak
Parts Eaten: Foliage
Note: When in flower, the Parsley Hawthorn attracts numerous butterflies for nectaring, especially various Hairstreaks, Skippers, and the Zebra, Tiger, and Palamedes Swallowtails.

TEXAS KIDNEYWOOD (*Eysenhardtia texana*)
Legume Family (*Fabaceae*)

Bloom Period: April-October
Range: Texas only
   Texas: 3, 4, 5
Height: To 10 feet
Class: Native

Loosely upright, many branched, ferny-appearing shrub with few to several stems from base. Leaves are a rich, dark green, divided into numerous tiny leaflets, which produce a delightful aromatic fragrance when touched. Numerous small, white or creamy-colored, fragrant flowers are clustered in slender racemes from the leaf axils or near the branch tips.

Cultivation: Texas Kidneywood is easy to propagate from either seeds or softwood cuttings. If you want to use seeds, gather the pods after they have turned brown and are at least partially dry. Place the pods in an open container, on a wire screen surface, or in an open paper bag until completely dry. After drying, remove the seeds from the pod or leave the pods intact. Place the seeds or pods in a paper bag, add a moth ball, a few naptha flakes, or a portion of an insect strip, seal tightly, and store at room temperature until spring.

After danger of frost, plant the seeds in the garden where plants are to remain. To break dormancy, pour boiling water over the seeds and let stand until the water cools, then plant. Seedling growth is slow at first, but water occasionally with a weak soluble fertilizer. Once the roots become established, top growth becomes quite rapid.

You can take softwood or semihardwood cuttings in summer and early fall. Remove bottom leaves from a four- to six-inch cutting, dip in rooting powder, and place either in flats or individual pots. Cuttings should be rooted in three to four weeks, at which time you should individually pot them for the winter. Plant out in the garden the following spring.

Small plants may be dug from the wild and transplanted either in fall or spring, but take care to get a good ball of earth around the roots. Moist soils naturally hold more firmly, so transplanting would be best after a rain. Before planting, trim the stems and branches back at least two thirds in order for the plant to be able to establish a good root system.

Texas Kidneywood is now available at many nurseries offering native plants. Buying there would be the best and fastest way of obtaining plants already established and large enough to furnish food for larvae.

Use Texas Kidneywood as a specimen plant, as a delicate hedge to line a walk or driveway, or in groupings at the back of a border. It is especially lovely in groups of two or three in a mixed planting with other native shrubs. This is a plant used both as a larval food source and for nectaring, so give it a prominent position in your plantings. Place it in full sun.

In the wild it is found in calcareous soils but does quite well in sandy or loamy soils. In its native haunts and under normal growing conditions, heaviest flowering is usually in May and again in August and September, but it almost always blooms after a rain. In the garden an occasional heavy soaking during the drier months usually promotes a burst of flowering. An occasional addition of organic fertilizer can help during the growing season but is not mandatory.

Used By: Dogface Butterfly
Parts Eaten: Foliage

YELLOW-BELLS (*Tecoma stans*)
Catalpa Family (*Bignoniaceae*)

Bloom Period: April–November
Range: Florida, Texas
   Texas: 3, 4, 5
Height: To 8 feet
Class: Native

Upright, many-branched, deciduous shrub, often with few to several stems and forming a clump. The opposite leaves are divided into five to thirteen leaflets. Large yellow, trumpet-shaped flowers form showy, elongating terminal clusters.

Cultivation: Yellow-bells—or Esperanza, as it is also commonly called—is one of our most beautiful native shrubs. In the last few years, it has been offered by many nurseries which sell native plants and has found its way into gardens throughout the warmer states. This wide distribution demonstrates its ability to readily adapt to a wide range of habitats and various growing conditions.

You can obtain plants either at nurseries or by starting from seeds or cuttings. The seeds are contained in long, slender pods; gather them when the pods become beige or brownish in color. Seeds which are planted fairly soon after gathering have better germination. You can obtain good results with cuttings by taking four-inch-long branch sections approximately one fourth of an inch across, dipping them in a rooting hormone powder, and potting them. Keep potted plants under plastic until well rooted. Cuttings taken in midsummer will be rooted and ready for transplanting to the garden by fall.

Not especially particular as to soil, Yellow-bells likes to stay a little on the dry side. Plant in average, well-drained soils and water only in times of drought, and this plant will ask nothing more. This is an airy, graceful shrub in its growth habit, blending beautifully with native and cultivated plants alike. Use it at the back of the border or in a hedge planting along with Bee-brush, Bird-of-paradise (*Caesalpinia gillesii*), Butterfly Bush, Desert Willow (*Chilopsis linearis*), Texas Kidneywood, and any of the Lantanas.

Used By: Gray Hairstreak

Parts Eaten: Flowers and fruits, rarely young foliage

Vines

SNAPDRAGON VINE (*Maurandya antirrhiniflora*)
Figwort Family (*Scrophulariaceae*)

Bloom Period: April-December
Range: Texas only
   Texas: 3, 4, 5
Height: 3-15 feet
Class: Native

A delicate, climbing or trailing, much-twining herbaceous perennial vine with very small, smooth, triangular or three-lobed leaves. Beautiful violet or purple snapdragonlike flowers occur solitarily from leaf axils.

Cultivation: The Snapdragon Vine is an easily grown plant which is not particular to soils, doing well in whatever is provided. It is drought tolerant and a good choice for the drier, more neglected sites in your garden. It is a prolific grower, producing numerous slender stems which quickly cover its support. Snapdragon Vine is not generally offered by nurseries, but you can raise it from seed. Gather the thick, brown, corky-winged seeds in late summer or early autumn, and plant them either in November or December or in early spring. Germination is somewhat unpredictable, so sow plenty of seeds and at various times. If spring-planted, the vines often bear flowers by midsummer the first year. Not cold tolerant, the foliage is killed by the first hard frost but reappears in early spring.

Easily adaptable, this vine does equally well twining through a hedge, trailing over a rock, shrub, or fence, or cascading from a hanging basket. You could give it a special trellis of its own. If you desire continued bloom, bring potted plants inside in the fall before frost and place them in a sunny window for winter bloom. Gradually move the plants outside again in spring as the weather warms. This vine needs only a light support and does not weigh down plants it happens to use in its reach for the sun. It is an excellent choice in any kind of container planting.

Used By: Buckeye

Parts Eaten: Foliage. Damage is usually minimal, as the Buckeye lays eggs singly or few to a plant.

TAGUA PASSIONFLOWER (*Passiflora foetida*)
Passionflower Family (*Passifloraceae*)

Bloom Period: April–November
Range: Texas only
   Texas: 3
Height: To 20 feet
Class: Native

A strong, vigorous vine covered throughout with soft grayish or brownish hairs. Leaves light green, three-lobed, with the middle lobe the longest. Intricately shaped flowers of whitish lavender and purple. Flowers subtended by large, beautifully dissected, feathery-appearing bracts. Bracts remain after flowering, partially enclosing the red fruit pods.

Cultivation: This hardy vine grows best in sandier soils and delights in adequate moisture and a sunny position. Light applications of high-phosphorous fertilizer in spring and again in fall increase the number of flowers. Do not overfertilize, though, as the chemical structure of the foliage would change and not be acceptable as larval food.

The Tagua Passionflower grows equally well if left to trail on the ground or if given a support to climb. It makes a beautiful "summer cover" for woodpiles or the brushpiles often provided by birdwatchers as escape areas for birds. The vines are especially attractive when trained to climb on a low wooden fence at the back of a perennial border.

You may plant seeds in the fall or spring. After the pods begin loosing their red color and become brown, gather and leave them in an open paper bag in a warm area until completely dry and crisp. Crush the pods and remove the seeds. Store the seeds in a dark, dry area in a sealed container until spring. Plant them in prepared sites after the ground has become warm. Seeds may also be planted in the fall, with plants appearing in late spring. New plants are easy to take from around a mother plant because mature plants send out numerous sprouts from widely spreading underground roots.

Used By: Crimson-patched Longwing, Julia, Gulf Fritillary, Mexican Fritillary, Variegated Fritillary, Mexican Silverspot, Zebra Longwing

Parts Eaten: Buds, foliage, young fruits

Related Species: As far as is known, every native species of *Passiflora* is used as a larval food source by the Longwing butterflies within their breeding range. Choose the ones for your garden that grow naturally in your area or try some which grow just outside your range. Most of the larvae which normally feed on native Passionflowers also use many of the cultivated sorts, some of which have gorgeously colored flowers. Before purchasing a cultivated or ex-

185

otic plant, inspect the stems carefully and run your fingers along the stems and leaves. If they have rough hairs, do not purchase for butterfly usage. As a protective measure, some tropical species of *Passiflora* have evolved sharply pointed, recurved hairs which puncture the skin of caterpillars and eventually kill them.

TEXAS VIRGIN'S BOWER (*Clematis drummondii*)
Crowfoot Family (*Ranunculaceae*)

Bloom Period: April-October
Range: Texas only
   Texas: 3, 4, 5 (1)
Height: 10-20 feet
Class: Native

A climbing or sprawling semiwoody, slender-branched vine. Leaves pale green, usually divided into five to seven leaflets. Small, greenish white flowers, either solitary or borne in terminal clusters, which later form conspicuous and showy feathery seedballs.

Cultivation: This is an easily propagated vine, either by seeds or by cuttings. The fluffy seed masses remain on the plant for some time after ripening, so obtaining the brown, mature seed is usually no problem. Place the seeds in a paper bag and let them dry for a few days. To stimulate germination, *Clematis* seeds require a prechilling (stratification) process. Place the seeds between layers of moist sand in a container, seal the container in a plastic bag, and leave the bag in the refrigerator from two to three months. The seeds may then be planted directly in the ground after all danger of frost has passed. Healthy, viable seeds germinate in one to two weeks. If planted in a pot, transplant the vine to the garden when its roots have filled the container.

You can take cuttings from a mature plant anytime during the growing season. Clip a four- to five-inch section of a branch, strip off the lower leaves, dip the lowest node in rooting hormone, and insert into sand or vermiculite. Cuttings should be rooted within forty-five days, at which time you may pot them for planting in the garden the following spring.

Texas Virgin's Bower is easy to transplant if you dig in early spring or late fall. Dig deeply, and retain a good ball of soil if possible. Clip all aboveground vegetation to about six inches from the crown before digging. Failure to do so often results in the stems being broken off too close to the ground, causing crown damage.

First-year plants are slow to become established and will probably not flower until the second year. Once they are established, however, growth can become lush and rampant and may even require trimming to keep in bounds. These plants thrive in rich garden soils and do not necessarily need fertilizing. Each spring, work organic matter into the soil around the plants, and give an occasional thorough soaking during the growing season, if needed.

If left to climb upward on their own, these plants may become a bit top-heavy by midsummer. To keep them low, trim young growth back until quite bushy, then occasionally trim out some of the longer branches. Healthy plants immediately put out new growth just below where they were clipped. This vine is easy to train and is attractive on arbors, trellises, or fences. If you clip it for use on a wire fence, the dense branches make an excellent seasonal screen. But Texas Virgin's Bower is perhaps at its loveliest when left to freely clamber over a low split-rail fence or to sprawl across a jumbled pile of rocks.

Used By: Fatal Metalmark
Parts Eaten: Foliage

WOOLLY PIPEVINE (*Aristolochia tomentosa*)
Birthwort Family (*Aristolochiaceae*)

Bloom Period: March-May
Range: All
   Texas: 2
Height: To 50 feet
Class: Native

A high-climbing, deciduous vine with large, handsome, heart-shaped leaves. The leaves are usually woolly with whitish hairs. The elongated, oddly curved flowers blend an unusual shade of dark purple and greenish yellow and are shaped somewhat like a Dutch pipe.

Cultivation: The Woolly Pipevine is not too demanding as to soils because it grows naturally in deep sands along upland streams and also in river bottom flood plains. What it does require is good drainage and adequate moisture but with a period of dryness between soakings. Best growth and foliage are produced if planted with the roots in dense shade and where the vines can climb a support to be in bright, filtered sun. It does very well planted at the edge of thick, tall shrubbery or small trees which it can use as a support. Vines die back to the ground each year, but spring growth is rapid and vigorous on healthy, well-established plants. The largest leaves are always the youngest ones, near the tips of the branches.

Propagation is best by seeds or by taking cuttings or runners. The seed pods are large but cannot be found very often. Pipevine Swallowtail larvae relish the young pods of the Swanflower (*Aristolochia erecta*) and probably eat the pods of this species as well.

If you find a plant in the wild with flowers which look old enough to have been pollinated, then you might try sleeving. Take small pieces of nylon netting, cover each flower, and close the open end around the stem a couple of inches below each flower with a band. When the pods are mature, clip and spread on paper towels until completely dry and beginning to release the seeds. When ready to plant, soak the seeds in distilled water for at least twenty-four hours, changing the water every twelve hours. Have the water hand-hot when first adding the seeds. As each seed swells, remove and sow it immediately, before it has time to dry out. Plant the seeds in a professional germinating mix, barely covering the seeds and keeping the soil moist with distilled water. Place a piece of clear plastic over the pot and place it in an area with lots of light. Light is very important to the germination of all species of *Aristolochia*.

Mature plants of Woolly Pipevine put out long underground roots or runners with many Ys or Ts, and often a new plant forms at these joints. If well rooted, these runners can be clipped on each side of the newly rooted joint. If you are collecting from the wild, have a container filled with a commercial potting soil with you and plant immediately. Moisten with rainwater with a bit of root stimulator added. Place

187

some sticks around the edge of the pot (taller than the plant) and cover with a clear plastic bag. Fasten below the rim of the pot with twine or a rubber band. Do not let the plastic touch the plant. Keep the soil moist. After the plant is firmly established and showing new growth, gradually remove the plastic. Do not let these plants remain too long in containers as they will grow only roots and make no top growth. You can place runners in shallow trenches in the garden, but take extra care to see that they never dry out until well rooted.

Woolly Pipevine is slow to come into flower; it may be two years or more before it blooms. Since these plants are being grown for their foliage, however, the flowers are not important to the caterpillars. Applications of compost or manure from time to time increase foliage.

Used By: Pipevine Swallowtail

Parts Eaten: All aboveground parts of the plant

Herbs

ANTELOPE-HORNS (*Asclepias asperula*)
Milkweed Family (*Asclepiadaceae*)

Bloom Period: March-November
Range: Oklahoma, Texas
   Texas: 1, 2, 4, 5
Height: 8-24 inches
Class: Native

Low, upright to widely sprawling herbaceous perennial, usually with several unbranched stems from the base and forming mound-like clumps. Leaves opposite or almost so, long, slender, the edges often folded together. The greenish flowers numerous and crowded into rounded, solitary terminal clusters.

Cultivation: Rarely are any of the *Asclepias* other than Butterfly Weed and Mexican Milkweed (*A. currassavica*) offered by nurseries. Antelope-horns does not transplant well because of its deep, brittle roots, but it is easy and fast to grow from seed. You can plant the seed immediately after collecting them or hold them over in cold storage until spring. The taproot grows very fast, so you should transplant the seedlings as soon as true leaves appear.

Take three- to four-inch tip cuttings before the plants begin flowering. Remove the lower leaves and insert the cuttings into moist, pure sand or a sand and peat mix. Make a tent from clear plastic to cover the cuttings and keep them moist. Cuttings should be rooted within six weeks.

Antelope-horns is very hardy once established and usually does quite well under normal garden conditions. It grows better and is less prone to stem rot if the soil is of the sandier, somewhat gravelly type. Good, fast drainage is important. Place it in full sun, give little or no fertilizer, and water only during periods of drought. Trim back well-established plants to three or four inches above ground level in June, and they will put forth new shoots and bloom again in the fall. If you have several plants, rotate cutting continually during the entire season, thus providing a constant source of new growth for larvae.

Used By: Monarch, Queen

Parts Eaten: Young foliage, occasionally flower buds

CALICHE GLOBE-MALLOW (*Sphaeralcea coccinea*)
Mallow Family (*Malvaceae*)

Bloom Period: May-October
Range: Oklahoma, Texas
Texas: 1, 4, 5
Height: To 3 feet
Class: Native

An upright or occasionally sprawling, low-growing herb having a perennial root and one to several woody-based annual stems. The leaves are thick, alternate, and usually deeply three-lobed. Flowers are orange-pink, five-petaled, and loosely arranged in open, branching clusters along the stem.

Cultivation: You may propagate this herb either by seed or by division. To collect seeds, clip mature seed pods and place them in a paper bag. Allow them to dry in a warm area for several days until all moisture is gone and the capsules are completely opened. Shake the seeds loose or break the capsules open, releasing the seeds. If insects are present in the seed pods, add an insect strip to the bag and close tightly for two weeks. Remove the cleaned, treated seeds and store in a refrigerator until spring. Sow the seeds thinly in a prepared bed after all danger of frost is passed. Growth will be rapid, and you may transplant seedlings to permanent places in the garden when they have three to four leaves.

It is very easy to divide established clumps. Dig either in late fall or early spring. With a sharp knife or spade, separate the clump, leaving one stalk and a ball of roots in each section. Replant, placing the sections two to three feet apart. If you divide in the spring, apply a mild soluble fertilizer once weekly until the new clumps are established and growing nicely.

This is a plant well suited to the drier areas of the garden: it actually grows best and is very long-lived in loose, extremely sandy soils. In tight soils it will die out in three or four years. If planted in richer, more moist soils than its normal habitat, it will rot at ground level and die.

Use Caliche Globe-mallow in scattered groups in beds or borders, along walkways, or in any type of naturalized situation. The unusual coloring of their blossoms is especially lovely when used with Fragrant Gaillardia (*Gaillardia suavia*), Leatherweed Croton (*Croton pottsii*), Mist-flower, Plains Black-foot, Western Pepper-grass (*Lepedium montanum*), Woolly Paper-flower (*Psilostrophe tagetina*), or the cultivated Plumbago or cream-colored Garden Lantana.

Used By: Common Checkered Skipper, Small Checkered Skipper

Parts Eaten: Foliage

Note: A very similar plant, Copper Globe-mallow (*S. angustifolia*), with narrow, unlobed leaves, is used by the larvae of several species of butterflies. If you desire this plant in your garden, propagate by seed only, as it is almost impossible to dig this plant without breaking its unusually deep taproot.

189

CANNA (*Canna* × *generalis* cultivar "The President")
Canna Family (*Cannaceae*)

Bloom Period: May-December
Range: All except Oklahoma
   Texas: 2, 3, 4 (1, 5)
Height: To 6 feet
Class: Cultivar

Upright, colony-forming perennial from large bulb. Leaves thick and lush, the foliage quite similar to a banana plant. Flowers large, red, with several forming a terminal spike which extends above the foliage. Petals of various widths, with some upright and some recurved, giving the blossom a completely disorganized appearance.

Cultivation: Plant Canna bulbs in March or April, spaced twelve to twenty-four inches apart. Divide established clumps at this time. You can also raise plants from seeds if you scar the seeds with a file and soak them in warm water overnight. Plant the seeds vertically, about two inches deep. They should sprout in about two weeks.

Cannas grow in almost any soil and habitat, but blooms are more plentiful and colorful if the plants have rich soil and full sun. They demand good drainage; otherwise, the new growth will rot at soil level. When foliage is about eight inches high, apply a complete fertilizer, such as 12-24-12, around the plants at the rate of one to two pounds per one hundred square feet of bed; this amounts to a very light sprinkling. Once established, healthy clumps need to be dug and divided about every three years. With just a little care as to proper watering and feeding, Cannas come back year after year, the clumps becoming larger and the blossoms lovelier with each season.

Used By: Brazilian Skipper
Parts Eaten: Leaves
Note: Be prepared for your plants to look a little ragged at times, for once Brazilian Skipper larvae start on the plants, they consume a surprising amount in a short time. They also cut large portions of the edges of leaves and roll up in them, like using them for blankets.

CUDWEED (*Gamochaeta pensilvanica*)
Sunflower Family (*Asteraceae*)

Bloom Period: February-May
Range: Alabama, Florida, Georgia, Louisiana, Mississippi, North Carolina, South Carolina, Texas
   Texas: 2, 3, 4
Height: 4-16 inches
Class: Naturalized

Low annual or biennial with usually several stems from base and forming rounded mounds. The alternate leaves are densely silvery-woolly on lower surface, a brighter green and less woolly on upper surface. Fresh foliage fragrant when crushed. Disk flowers minute, whitish or yellowish, few, in small heads, with several heads grouped in short, spikelike arrangements in axils of upper leaves.

Cultivation: Not a showy plant with brilliant displays of flowers, but its green- and silver-colored foliage makes Cudweed a beautifully subtle companion to brighter colored flowers, such as Zinnias, Petunias, or Indian Blanket. Cudweed is a strong, hardy plant and one easy to raise from seed. When the seeds begin to ripen, the entire tip of the plant will look cottony or fluffy. The seeds should be ripe and ready for harvesting a few weeks after flowering. When ready to gather, grasp the entire fluffy mass on each stem and strip it gently but firmly from the plant. Otherwise, clip the entire seed-bearing portion of the plant. Place the seed and its fluff in a paper bag and store it in a cool, dry place until ready to plant.

Sow the seeds in early fall either where they are to grow or in a bed for transplanting later. Plants will be ready for transplanting by late fall or can be moved as late as the last of January. Moving after this would not give the plants time to become fully established and would usually result in small, nonmounding plants. The healthiest and best formed specimens are those you plant in early fall where they are to stay; as the seeds come up, thin the plants to approximately a foot apart. Try saving some seeds and planting them around the first of May. Since it is the young, tender plant growth which larvae use, the availability of young plants later in the season could possibly extend the length of breeding and rearing of the butterflies in your garden.

Cudweed is a drought-hardy plant which grows its finest in full sun in well-drained soils. If growing it in ordinary garden soil, no fertilizer should be necessary. In fact, overfertilizing and overwatering will cause excessive growth, resulting in weak, sprawling, rather unattractive plants. When growing under such conditions, the plants will not be as readily used by female butterflies for egg deposition, if at all. Cudweed grows in open, semishaded conditions, but the plant generally will not produce as many stems, and the clump will not be as full or mound-forming.

Use Cudweed in open areas or toward the front of beds or borders where it can be readily found by searching females. Do not crowd the plants, but group five to seven plants together, with several groupings scattered about the garden.

Above.
Cudweed

Used By: American Painted Lady

Parts Eaten: Buds, flowers, young foliage

Note: Female American Painted Ladies lay their eggs on the younger foliage, and the young larvae make silk nests in the upper leaf clusters. If you see your plants all matted together at the top, don't panic. Instead, share the good news with a friend: You have just succeeded in attracting the American Painted Lady to your garden.

191

DOWNY PAINTBRUSH (*Castilleja sessiliflora*)
Figwort Family (*Scrophulariaceae*)

Bloom Period: March-May
Range: Oklahoma, Texas
  Texas: 1, 4, 5
Height: 4-12 inches
Class: Native

Low, upright perennial covered with soft, velvety hairs. Often there are several stems from the base which form a large, showy clump. Almost all of the leaves pink or purple tinged, gradually becoming smaller as they extend upward and finally becoming the colorful bracts subtending the flowers in upper portion of the stalk. The long, tubular flowers may be pinkish, purplish, yellowish, or greenish, extending somewhat beyond the subtending bracts.

Cultivation: All of the Paintbrushes are almost impossible to transplant, but there should be no problem starting the plants in your garden from seeds if you take some care. Gather seeds as soon as the capsule becomes dry and before it splits, releasing the numerous tiny seeds. Let the seeds air-dry for a few days, then store them in the refrigerator for fall sowing. When ready to plant, mix the seeds with fine sand for better distribution. Indian Paintbrush is thought to be partially parasitic on the roots of grasses during the early stages of its growth, so plant the seeds of this species in raked areas next to a clump of native grass for best results.

The percentage of germination will probably be small, but if only one or two plants come up and flower, they usually reseed quite well. A good colony should be established within two or three years. Since little is actually known about the propagation or life cycle of this plant,

for best results try planting some seeds as soon as they are ripe, some in early summer, and some in the fall. Also, try them among native grasses as well as in perennial beds.

Downy Paintbrush normally grows in dry, rocky, or sandy soils, so in your garden try to give it a habitat as near natural as possible. Neither fertilize nor overwater.

Used By: Buckeye, Fulvia Checkerspot
Parts Eaten: Upper portion of plant
Related Species: There are many species of *Castilleja*, and at least one of them, the annual Texas Paintbrush (C. *indivisa*), is used from Central Texas eastward by the larvae of the Buckeye. Many others are probably used.

FERN ACACIA (*Acacia angustissima*)
Legume Family (*Fabaceae*)

Bloom Period: June-October
Range: Arkansas, Louisiana, Oklahoma, Texas
  Texas: Throughout
Height: 2½-3 feet
Class: Native

An upright to sprawling, deep-rooted perennial with one to several stems from a woody, persistent base. Stems rarely branching, but the plants put out numerous underground woody, creeping roots and form small colonies. Alternate, bright green leaves are usually divided into nine to twelve pairs of segments with each segment bearing eighteen to thirty pairs of tiny leaflets. The leaflets are not prominently nerved on lower surface, are sensitive and will fold together when touched, in rain, and at night. Ball-like clusters of numerous white to creamy yellow flowers are held on stalks arising from leaf axils in upper portion of stem. Flower stalks are shorter than subtending leaves with flower heads remaining intermingled with the fernlike foliage.

Cultivation: Fern Acacia is well adapted to a wide variety of soils and climatic conditions as is shown by its wide distribution. In the wild this plant can be found along roadsides, in open woodlands, in prairie grasslands, or along bluffs, ledges, or outcrops of limestone or shale, often above streams and frequently in shade. In its natural habitat it seems to prefer either tight, heavy calcareous clay or alkaline soils but can frequently be found in sand. It is a hardy plant which once established will take care of itself and continue to multiply quite readily. It does not multiply at a very rapid rate, however, so the plants do not become obnoxious or hard to control.

In the northern portion of its range, Fern Acacia will usually be killed to the ground each winter, but in the southernmost areas will continue as an evergreen, at most losing only some of its leaves.

Plant Fern Acacia in full sun, giving it good soil and an adequate amount of moisture to get it growing well. Once established it should not need any special attention. A light application of natural fertilizer or rich compost will enhance both growth and flowering, but do not overdo it. Overfertilizing and too much moisture will cause excessive foliage growth, fewer flowers, and, eventually, crown-rot—resulting in death of the plants.

The easiest method to obtain a start of Fern Acacia is by seed. The brownish seed pods are borne singly in the upper portion of the plant, are from two to three inches long, less than

Fern Acacia

one-half inch wide, and very flat. They open promptly after becoming fully ripe, so observation of the wild plants in order to gather seed at the proper time will be necessary. Seed which are at least three-fourths brown in color can be gathered and stored in a cool, dry area for a few days or until completely brown and the pods begin to split.

Seed of Fern Acacia have very hard outer coats and germination can be very slow. To hasten the process, after gathering the seeds, let them dry for two to four months in a cool, dry area. Refrigeration is not necessary. When ready to plant, pour boiling water over the seed and let them soak for at least twenty-four hours. Fern Acacia seed are very durable and show a good viability after many years of storage or even lying uncovered on the ground.

Used By: Acacia Skipper, Antillean Blue, Mexican Yellow, Reakirt's Blue, and Texas Acacia Skipper

Parts Eaten: Buds, flowers, and young foliage

GOLDEN CROWNBEARD (*Verbesina enceloides*)
Sunflower Family (*Asteraceae*)

Bloom Period: February-Frost
Range: Texas only
   Texas: 2, 3, 4, 5 (1)
Height: To 5 feet
Class: Native

An upright to sprawling, rather coarse, usually much-branching plant with grayish-green, odoriferous foliage. Large yellow flower heads are terminal on long, slender stalks.

193

tions in the garden. Also, even though the butterflies nectar on this plant ravenously, they will temporarily leave the area when the plants have been disturbed.

Trimming from time to time may be necessary to keep the plant in bounds, but this only makes for a sturdier, more bushy plant with even more flowers. Keep as many of the spent flowers clipped as possible, as fruit production will slow down the forming of new flowers. If left undisturbed, Golden Crownbeard will eventually form large colonies for an absolutely spectacular autumn show. Since the plants are so robust, in a garden situation treat them almost as a shrub. They blend beautifully with Bee-brush, Bird-of-paradise, Butterfly Bush, Thoroughwort, Confetti Lantana (*Lantana camara forma confetti*), Weeping Lantana, Summer Phlox, or any of the tall, blue-flowered *Salvias*. Front them with Blue Plumbago, Mistflower, Narrow-leaf Gayfeather, Tansy Aster, Texas Thistle, Woolly Ironweed, or Zinnias.

Used By: Bordered Patch
Parts Eaten: Foliage

Note: According to recent studies, Golden Crownbeard is the preferred larval food choice of the Bordered Patch for rearing of the late summer and fall broods, with Annual Sunflower (*Helianthus annuus*) being first choice for the spring and early summer broods. For best results in attracting this butterfly as a resident, provide a patch of both plants in the garden.

While Golden Crownbeard grows throughout the Southeast and is an excellent nectar source, with many different species of butterflies visiting it while in bloom, it is used as a larval food source by the Bordered Patch only in Texas.

Cultivation: The main problem usually encountered with this plant is that it may be too easily grown. From Austin southward it often does not winterkill, or will freeze only to ground level. With the first warm days, new growth shoots forth and the plants may be flowering again by March or early April. It also reseeds atrociously, so there is never a shortage of new plants. Seedlings may be transplanted anytime. Golden Crownbeard will survive under the most trying conditions, but for lush, full-flowering plants, give a light fertilizer (any kind will do) occasionally and a bit of extra watering during summer drought periods. Use these plants toward the back of your border—preferably in an out of the way place. The foliage has a rather foul odor when disturbed, which makes for unpleasant working condi-

HEATH ASTER (*Aster ericoides*)
Sunflower Family (*Asteraceae*)

Bloom Period: October-December
Range: All except Florida
  Texas: Throughout
Height: To 3 feet
Class: Native

194

Basically upright, many-branched perennial with numerous arching or reclining branches.

Plants spread from underground stems, forming colonies. Leaves along the branchlets are very numerous and crowded, short, stiff, very narrow, and heathlike. Flower heads consist of yellow disk flowers and white ray flowers; the heads are numerous and almost cover the plant during time of flowering.

Cultivation: The Heath Aster is adapted to many soil types and amounts of drought or moisture. It is also a strong, hardy plant, multiplying well. When planted in full sun, it makes an exceptional autumn-flowering plant. It performs beautifully under any garden conditions, but grows taller and more lush when given fairly good soil and a bit of moisture.

Heath Aster is easy to propagate from root sprouts. When you find a colony of plants, there almost always are numerous young plants around the mother clump. You may loosen these by inserting a spade and gently lifting. Clip the young plant from the main plant, leaving a plentiful cluster of rootlets on the lifted plant.

To start plants from seeds, gather the dried seed heads after the first frost. Plant seeds immediately in prepared beds where the plants are to remain, or transplant them in late spring. Sow the seeds thickly, as the viability of Aster seeds is never very good. If plants come up too close together, transplant them to other areas. Seedlings benefit from a weekly application of a weak liquid fertilizer solution until they become well established and growing; then they normally require no further fertilizing. You can also propagate this Aster by taking tip cuttings of young growth in early spring, dipping them in a rooting hormone, and inserting in a mixture of equal parts peat and sand. Cover the cuttings and container with plastic to retain a high humidity until rooted.

Old clumps of Heath Aster may decline in vigor when they become excessively crowded.

Heath Aster

For healthier, more robust plants, dig and divide the clumps every three or four years.

Give the Heath Aster plenty of room in the border, where the graceful "weeping" branches can droop and spread. When in flower, the plants appear as large masses of snowy white, forming a wonderful backdrop for various purple and yellow fall-flowering species. Try Heath Aster backed with the purple-flowered New England Aster and fronted with the native yellow-flowered Broom Groundsel (*Senecio riddellii*), Woolly Paper-flower, or the single-flowered Marigold (*Tagetes* spp.).

Used By: Pearly Crescentspot
Parts Eaten: Leaves

LINDHEIMER SENNA (*Senna lindheimeriana*)
Legume Family (*Fabaceae*)

Bloom Period: June-November
Range: Texas only
   Texas: 4, 5
Height: To 6 feet
Class: Native

Upright, strong, many-stemmed perennial from a woody base. The leaves are divided into four to eight pairs of small leaflets. Golden yellow flowers, several, and borne in terminal clusters held well above the foliage. Almost the entire plant is covered in shiny, velvety hairs.

When disturbed, the foliage is strongly—and to some, unpleasantly—scented.

Cultivation: The Lindheimer Senna produces an abundance of long pods which are filled with small "beans." Gather these seeds when mature and either plant them in late fall or store them in the refrigerator and plant the following spring. As this is a perennial, sow where it is to remain in the garden, especially if planting the seeds in the fall. Sow spring-planted seeds either directly in the garden or in pots to be transferred to the garden later. Germination is best if you plant the seeds immediately after harvesting and before the pods are totally dry.

When the plants are up and showing true leaves, use a weak soluble fertilizer about every two weeks until well established. Discontinue all fertilizing after plants are showing a lot of healthy growth. Lindheimer Senna does not need an overabundance of moisture, but an occasional deep soaking during July and August ensures good growth and nice flowering.

Because of its height and its growth habit of producing several stems from the base, this plant is ideal at the back of the border or for an annual hedge. Frost kills the plants back somewhat, but new growth begins again in early spring. Trimming the plants back even further, to approximately six or eight inches above the ground, in late fall after a frost promotes even more growth the following year.

This plant may do well just outside its natural range and is certainly worth a try. If you are transplanting it to an entirely different habitat, then gather some limestone rocks along with the seeds or plants. In the garden, place the plants among a grouping of the rocks and even work some large limestone gravel into the planting hole. This provides aeration to the roots and makes the plant feel more at home.

Used By: Sleepy Orange

Parts Eaten: Buds, young foliage

LOW SPRING NETTLE (*Urtica chamaedryoides*)
Nettle Family (*Urticaceae*)

Bloom Period: February-July

Range: All except North Carolina

   Texas: 2, 3, 4

Height: 2-2½ feet

Class: Native

An upright or somewhat lax, slender annual, usually branching near the base and from the main stem. Leaves thin, opposite, long-stalked along lower portion of stem, sometimes purplish on lower surface. Tiny, greenish white flowers in clusters from axils of upper leaves. Almost entire plant covered with short, stiff, stinging bristles.

Cultivation: This is not a plant offered by the nursery trade and not one to be planted for any kind of showiness. But a Nettle you must have if you would attract the Red Admiral as a resident. The best method of propagation is probably by digging young plants. Since this is one of the more "weedy" species and one most folks are trying to get rid of, anyone who has a colony growing on their property will probably be quite happy for you to dig a few—or a lot. When handling the plant, wear thick gloves and a long-sleeved shirt, for any contact between this plant and bare skin results in a most painful sting which lasts for hours.

Ideally, Low Spring Nettle should be given a place of its own. A semishaded area beneath high-branched shrubbery or small trees, or in the afternoon shade provided by a fence or building, would work quite well. If you have to plant it in a bed or border, place it where it can be left alone and not have to be worked around. It likes fairly rich, well-drained loamy soils, but it can tolerate sand or clay as long as shade and moisture are provided. To promote new growth and provide a longer period of usable larval food, cut some of the plants back to about six inches above the ground. Do this at regular intervals of every two weeks or so.

If growing conditions are suitable, Low Spring Nettle will reseed itself each year. If it begins to spread beyond its designated area, remove young plants as they come up. Thin to eight to twelve inches apart, if needed, for healthier plants with more useful foliage. The plants are easy to contain by planting in a twenty-gallon plastic pot with the bottom removed; sink the pot to ground level before filling with soil and planting.

Used By: Red Admiral
Parts Eaten: Young foliage

PARTRIDGE PEA (*Chamaecrista fasciculata*)
Legume Family (*Fabaceae*)

Bloom Period: May-December
Range: All except Arkansas, North Carolina, Oklahoma, Tennessee
    Texas: 1, 2, 3, 4
Height: 1-5 feet
Class: Native

An upright, smooth to hairy, usually many-branched annual herb, with leaves composed of many small leaflets and appearing almost fern-like. Foliage of this plant partially closes when touched. The yellow flowers, with five petals of unequal size, open in short clusters along the branches. Only one flower within each cluster opens at a time.

Cultivation: The Partridge Pea is easily established in sandy or loamy soils anywhere in its range by simply scattering a few seeds. It is rather late to come up in the spring, but it grows rapidly once sprouted. This plant does not transplant well, so sow seeds where you desire the plants. This may cause a bit of a problem if the plants are to be in a border since the seeds need to be planted in the fall but the plants do not come up until late spring. The best way is to choose the desired site for the plants and scatter the seeds generously in the bed in September. Mark the area with metal tags, wooden stakes, or whatever method you choose. In the spring after the seeds have sprouted and the plants are about four inches high, pull out or thin the plants into

the configuration you desire. For a solid mass of mature plants (or a continuous border effect), leave the plants standing approximately three feet apart.

Under normal garden conditions of richer soil and more water than normal, these plants become almost twice as large as in the wild. They also grow larger and are much healthier if there is not severe competition with other plants, so give them plenty of space. If you find the plants

197

crowded later in the season, simply pull out a few. The remaining ones will spread out and remain lower and stockier instead of growing tall and becoming spindly.

This is an excellent plant to use in "natural" or untended areas, as well as in the border. Simply scatter a handful of seeds along fence rows, along roadsides, next to the garage, or at the back of the lawn. Rake in well, then gently tamp the surface.

Gathering ripe seeds of the Partridge Pea may be a little tricky. Upon ripening, the long, flat pods split, with each side making a couple of twists and flinging the seeds for several feet. Since it does not take but a few seeds to get a start of this plant for your garden, gathering good seeds is worth a little extra effort. The best way is to enclose the almost mature pod in a little bag made of a square of cheesecloth or nylon net wrapped around the seed pod and closed at the base with a cord or band. Another method is to gather the seed pods after they have turned dark brown but before they have

split. The ratio of plants obtained per seed gathered will not be nearly as great with this method since some seeds may still be immature, so be sure to plant plenty.

At the end of the growing season, if you let the Partridge Pea mature its seeds, there should be an abundance of new plants the following year. However, due to the method of dispersal, the next season's plants may not be exactly where you would like them. To be sure you have plants in areas of your choice, gather some seeds and plant them there.

Partridge Pea is quite attractive when used in small groups or as a somewhat continuous row in a long border. Some studies have shown that butterflies have a tendency to choose the more isolated plants for egg deposition, so you might try the plants in various situations to determine the best usage in your area.

Used By: Cloudless Giant Sulphur, Orange Sulphur, Little Yellow, Sleepy Orange

Parts Eaten: Buds, flowers, leaves

PERENNIAL DICLIPTERA (*Dicliptera brachiata*)
Acanthus Family (*Acanthaceae*)

An erect or somewhat sprawling, rather coarse perennial usually with many slender branches. Leaves opposite, long-stalked, tapering onto the stem at base. The conspicuously two-parted flowers range from pink to pale lavender to purple and are borne in small clusters from the leaf axils, mostly toward tip portions of branches or stems.

Cultivation: Perennial Dicliptera is a welcome addition for those semishaded areas of the garden. While it can tolerate some sun, it does best in an open, lightly shaded setting or where it receives sun only in the mornings. Naturally, when growing in the sun, plants require more watering than when growing in the shade. It is a hardy plant; once started, it continues to self-seed and needs pratically no attention. Although a naturally moist portion of the garden is the ideal location, Perennial Dicliptera can adjust to a wide range of soil and moisture conditions. When grown in moist but well-drained organic soil, Perennial Dicliptera outdoes its performance in nature.

Bloom Period: July-December
Range: Alabama, Florida, Georgia, Louisiana, Mississippi, Texas
   Texas: 2, 3, 4
Height: 14-28 inches
Class: Native

198

If Perennial Dicliptera does not receive sufficient amounts of moisture during times of drought or prolonged periods of dryness, the lower leaves will wither and die, leaving the plants looking rather scraggly. Fertilizing these plants is not demanded, but a light application of manure now and then keeps the plants exceptionally healthy and lush.

Not offered by nurseries and not easy to grow from cuttings, Perennial Dicliptera is best started by digging or from seed. These plants almost always grow in large colonies, often in creek or river bottoms, so taking two or three small plants does not endanger its continued existence. For best survival, take small plants and replant them immediately. And take only a few plants, for they quickly multiply and you will soon have plenty.

Seeds are usually ripe by mid-October, but some early-blooming plants may yield seeds before then. Gather the capsules as soon as they are mature. Little is known about the seed propagation of Perennial Dicliptera, so plant seeds at various times to ensure seedlings. Plant some seeds as soon as thoroughly dry after gathering; store some in the refrigerator until the ground is warm in the spring and plant some then. You should get enough seedlings to begin a colony. Once started, they should continue to reseed themselves.

As this is a larval food plant, allow it to form as large a patch as possible. Combine it with other shade-tolerant species, such as Bee-brush, Flame Acanthus, Thoroughwort, Yellow Passionflower (*Passiflora lutea*), Cardinal Flower, Heath Aster, Texas Aster, Goldenrod, and Mistflower.

Used By: Cuban Crescentspot, Texan Crescentspot, Rosita Patch

Parts Eaten: Leaves

PRAIRIE PARSLEY (*Polytaenia nuttallii*)
Parsley Family (*Apiaceae*)

Bloom Period: April-June
Range: Arkansas, Louisiana, Mississippi, Oklahoma, Tennessee, Texas
   Texas: 2
Height: To 3 feet
Class: Native

An upright, stout, usually several-branched biennial. Leaves are mostly near the base, with each leaf divided into several broad segments. The tiny yellow flowers are numerous, grouped into half-round, terminal clusters.

Cultivation: Obtain plants of Prairie Parsley by either sowing seeds or transplanting young plants. Since this is a biennial, which means the plants come up one year and bloom the next, you must take care not to destroy the tiny seedlings while working the beds.

Seeds should be mature about a month after flowering, so keep a close watch on the plants to get good, healthy, mature seeds. Collect the entire head when the seeds are light tan or yellowish. Thrash the head over an open paper bag or large tray, then blow or pick as much debris out as possible. Store the seeds in a dry, sealed, labeled container and place in the refrigerator.

The following June, sow the seeds in prepared beds where the plants will remain or in individual pots for transplanting later. Seedlings should be up within a few days. Water occasionally with a weak soluble fertilizer. Transplant a potted

199

plant to its permanent location when roots have filled the pot.

Once started, growth is usually rapid, forming large rosettes of leaves aboveground and sending the long taproot deep into the soil. The plants overwinter as rosettes and flower the following spring. If you broadcast seeds in a natural area instead of regular beds, make sure to cover the seeds with soil.

Prairie Parsley grows in a good garden loam in many areas but does not do well in extreme limestone, caliche, or acid soils. A light application of fertilizer now and then makes for studier plants, as does a little extra water. Since plants may become more lush under garden conditions, they may need staking. These are sun-loving plants, so place them in full sun and give them plenty of room to breathe and spread out. Almost all of the foliage is near the ground, and even this may be disappearing at bloom time, so use this plant toward the middle or back of the border and plant something in front of it.

Prairie Parsley reseeds itself readily, so, once it is established in an area, there will be an abundance of new plants appearing in late summer. These seedlings may be moved while still very young; due to the long taproot, however, moving is not advisable if seedlings are more than two months old.

Used By: Eastern Black Swallowtail
Parts Eaten: Foliage
Note: In order for the butterfly to lay her eggs on the leaves, this plant needs to be in a fairly open area, so do not crowd the plants. And place them in small groups in order for her to have a selection of leaves. She likes to deposit one egg to a leaf, but she will leave two or three eggs per plant and use several plants in a group.

PURPLE GERARDIA (*Agalinis purpurea*)
Figwort Family (*Scrophulariaceae*)

Bloom Period: August-November
Range: All except Oklahoma
　　Texas: 2
Height: 2-4 feet
Class: Native

An erect to somewhat sprawling, many-branched annual, bearing few, small, almost needlelike leaves. Branches very slender, wiry, and widely spreading. The pale pink to dark lavender, somewhat tubular flowers open one or a few at a time from upper leaf axils.

Cultivation: Purple Gerardia is another of our beautiful natives which is not offered by nurseries. The plants are supposedly partially parasitic on the roots of grasses and perhaps other herbs, but they may need host plants only for the first weeks of growth. Little is actually known about the cultivation of this native in the home garden.

Gather the seed capsules as soon as they start to become brownish in color and before they split, releasing the numerous tiny seeds inside. Finish air-drying in an open paper bag or on paper towels. Since so little is known about its growth requirements, stagger the planting of the seeds to be on the safe side. Plant some immediately after they are completely dry, plant some in late fall, and save some seeds in cold storage for planting in the early spring. Try stratifying some of the seeds by placing them in layers in moist sand or between moist paper towels. Put them in a resealable plastic bag in the refrigerator for two or three weeks before planting. When sowing, try some in the flower beds and some in a more naturalized area where native grass roots are available. Once the seedlings are up, do not try transplanting them until their roots are well developed.

Withhold fertilizer until the plants are well up and growing, then use sparingly. Keep the soil moist, especially during droughty summer months. Purple Gerardia grows in a wide diversity of soils and habitats, so it should do well in just about any good garden situation. Plant in full sun for best flowering.

Purple Gerardia will not be showy in the border until late summer or early fall, so plant with summer-flowering species, such as Brown-eyed Susan (*Rudbeckia hirta*), Indian Blanket, Kansas Gayfeather (*Liatris pycnostachya*), Milkweed (any species), Pentas (*Pentas lanceolata*), Texas Thistle, Tuber Vervain (*Verbena rigida*), single Zinnias, or any of the low-growing Lantanas or Verbenas. Some good companions for fall would be Asters (any species), Climbing Hemp-weed, Blue Lobelia (*Lobelia siphilitica*), Goldenrod, Golden Crownbeard, Mist-flower, and any of the blue-colored *Salvias*.

Used By: Buckeye

Parts Eaten: Buds, foliage, young fruit

Note: The larvae feed during the day. They are extremely well camouflaged and make no effort to hide.

SILVER CROTON (*Croton argyranthemus*)
Spurge Family (*Euphorbiaceae*)

Bloom Period: April-September
Range: Alabama, Florida, Georgia, Louisiana, Mississippi, Texas
   Texas: 2, 3
Height: To 2 feet
Class: Native

Low, bushy, somewhat reddish stemmed perennial with slender leaves conspicuously silver on lower surface. Small white flowers form feathery terminal clusters. The male flowers appear near the tip of the cluster, with the female flowers below.

Cultivation: Silver Croton does not transplant well even when dug under the most ideal circumstances, and rarely survives when taken from the wild. The best way to obtain plants is by seed. Capsules of Silver Croton split open when ripe, flinging the seeds for several feet. Thus, to get a good supply of seeds, collect large, firm, but unopened capsules and let them finish maturing in a paper bag. When gathered before fully ripe, there is the possibility of some not maturing properly and not becoming viable, so gather more seed than the number of plants you need. Plant immediately, either directly in the garden or in small pots for transferring later. Keep the planting medium moist but not saturated, as excessive moisture will cause the seeds to rot.

Silver Croton has a very deep root system that needs plenty of aeration. Its permanent growing soil should be as sandy as possible. If your garden soil is not naturally sandy, then mix a large quantity of sand in the area where the plants are

Purple Gerardia

Silver Croton

to grow. They do best when there is plenty of room to breathe, yet they like the company of their own kind, so always plant in groups of at least three to five and space the plants so they will be barely touching when mature. After they have become root-established, there is no need to fertilize; water only sparingly.

In most of its range, Silver Croton dies down to ground level each fall but puts out new growth in the spring. It readily reseeds if the

201

soil and other growing factors are favorable, so there will be plenty of new plants each year. Unwanted plants will need to be removed to prevent overcrowding.

STIFF-STEM FLAX (*Linum berlandieri*)
Flax Family (*Linaceae*)

Bloom Period: February-September
Range: Alabama, Arkansas, Texas
   Texas: Throughout
Height: 8-20 inches
Class: Native

An upright or somewhat sprawling smooth annual with very small, stiffly upright leaves. Stems usually several, many-branched, and forming rounded clumps. Flowers are few to numerous and form open, terminal clusters, with one flower opening at a time in each cluster. Petals golden yellow or copper colored, splashed with reddish near the base.

Cultivation: Nice, healthy clumps of this plant appear to be "all flowers," for the blossoms are quite large in comparison to the tiny leaves and delicate stems. The flowers of many *Linums* have a tendency to fall early in the day or shatter when touched or blown by the wind. The flowers of Stiff-stem Flax remain open and

Used By: Goatweed Butterfly, Gray Hairstreak
Parts Eaten: Flower buds, foliage

windproof until at least midafternoon, making it a good subject for the border as well as caterpillar food.

Stiff-stem Flax is not offered by any nursery that I know of, nor are the seeds available. Transplanting these plants is just about impossible, so to start them in your garden, you must gather your own seeds. Gather the seed pods as soon as they begin to turn a light brown or beige color. Place in an open paper bag until the capsules are completely dry and are easy to open. Plant the seeds as soon as dry; scatter them about in the area where you want plants, then rake the seeds in thoroughly. Lightly tamp the soil and sprinkle gently until the ground is thoroughly moistened. Otherwise, wait until a week of fall rains is forecast and plant the seeds before the rains begin. Seedlings should appear shortly, live through the winter, and flower the following season.

Although tolerant of a fairly wide range of growing conditions, Stiff-stem Flax thrives in sandy, well-drained soils kept on the dry side. An occasional soaking during the summer, if conditions are dry, keeps them producing more flowers. Grow the plants in an open, sunny exposure, and they develop a tight, rounded habit. A lightly shaded setting will do, but the clumps will be looser, more spreading, and with fewer flowers. Also, they will be less likely to attract butterflies for egg laying.

Stiff-stem Flax is most attractive when used toward the front of a bed or border along with Common Horehound (*Marrubium vulgare*), Dwarf Crownbeard (*Verbesina nana*), Indian Blanket, Tuber Vervain, Western Peppergrass, Woolly Paper-flower, Dwarf Crownbeard (*Verbesina hana*), Indian Blanket, and Common Horehound (*Marrubium vulgare*).

Used By: Variegated Fritillary
Parts Eaten: Almost all aboveground parts of the plant

TEXAS FROG-FRUIT (*Phyla incisa*)
Vervain Family (*Verbenaceae*)

Bloom Period: March-November
Range: Texas only
   Texas: 2, 3, 4, 5 (1)
Height: To 10 inches
Class: Native

Low, creeping or trailing, mat-forming perennial rooting at the nodes. The leaves are long, slender, and conspicuously toothed. Numerous tiny white flowers form a small terminal cluster, with the flowers opening in a circle. New circles continue to open during the season, with the flowering portion eventually becoming elongated.

Cultivation: Wherever you encounter this plant, there is a large patch with the creeping branches rooting at each node. The best method of obtaining plants is simply to clip one of the branches near the main root and gently loosen the roots along the branch. When replanting, in order to obtain the most coverage for the largest area, cut the long branch between each node and plant each rooted section separately.

Texas Frog-fruit is not particular as to soils but does exceptionally well in rich garden loam with good drainage. A little extra moisture and occasional fertilizing make for faster and more luxurious growth.

Once the plants have spread and have sufficiently covered the ground, take branches to start plants in new areas. While this plant spreads and multiplies rapidly and quite readily, it never becomes obnoxious or uncontrollable. Cutting back to the desired area with either clippers or a hoe is all that is needed to keep it in bounds.

Virtually disease resistant, Texas Frog-fruit is an ideal plant for edgings, as a groundcover, or to replace problem spots in lawns. You can also use it in beds which have been mulched. The branches will not root as readily since they will not be in contact with the soil, instead spreading out into most attractive designs and patterns.

Texas Frog-fruit grows in semishade but produces thicker, more compact foliage if planted in full sun. Also, plants in an open, sunny area are more readily used by butterflies for egg deposition.

Used By: White Peacock, Buckeye, Phaon Crescentspot
Parts Eaten: Foliage

TEXAS THISTLE (*Cirsium texanum*)
Sunflower Family (*Asteraceae*)

Bloom Period: May-July
Range: Oklahoma, Texas
   Texas: Throughout
Height: To 5 feet
Class: Native

An upright, bristly-spiny biennial or perennial, with usually only one stem but many-branched. Leaves are long, slender, and covered with fine, woolly hairs on lower surface and appearing silver—a beautiful contrast to the bright green, smooth upper surface. Flowers small, numerous, pink to rose-purple, clustered in showy, terminal, somewhat rounded heads.

Cultivation: This is an easy plant from seed.

203

Gather the seeds when fully ripe and "fluffed up" on the plant. Sow immediately or at least by early September. Plants will come up in the fall and form rosettes which live over the winter. Texas Thistle readily reseeds, so a good colony of plants forms the following year. Remove unwanted plants as soon as they come up in the fall. In flower beds, thin the plants, leaving from two to three feet between each plant for sufficient growing space. A small colony is a better attractant than solitary plants scattered through a border or bed.

Plant in full sun and keep somewhat on the dry side. They become scraggly and have a tendency to fall down, with the lower foliage developing mildew or turning brown if placed in shade or receiving too much moisture. Plant toward the middle or back of the border or away from foot traffic, as the plants are rather prickly. Often these plants are not impressive in the wild, but under garden conditions of rich soil and adequate moisture, they become magnificent specimens. They are prolific bloomers, and you can lengthen the season by keeping the faded blossoms trimmed off. Cut the long flower stalk just above the leaf node below the flower, and new flowering stalks will form. This trimming back to the node keeps the plant lower and bushier; removing spent flowers prevents an invasion of plants the following season.

Used By: Painted Lady

Parts Eaten: Foliage. The larva makes a nest of several leaves, gathering them together with strands of silk.

Note: Texas Thistle (as are other Thistles) is an excellent nectar source for many species of butterflies, especially Swallowtails.

VIOLET RUELLIA (*Ruellia nudiflora*)
Acanthus Family (*Acanthaceae*)

Bloom Period: March-December
Range: Texas only
   Texas: 2, 3, 4
Height: To 2½ feet
Class: Native

An upright to semisprawling perennial from woody base. Stem usually solitary or may be several and clump-forming as plant ages. Several lavender to purple trumpet-shaped flowers form a showy terminal cluster, with few to several clusters per plant. Flowers open about sunrise, then fall from plant in afternoon heat.

Cultivation: Depending upon which part of this plant's range you live in, you may have a normal-acting perennial or an evergreen. In the northern part of its range, it dies back to the ground each year, while in the Rio Grande Valley area, it may remain green and flowering all

204

year if the winter is mild. Violet Ruellia grows in most types of soil except dry, sandy ones, but soil supplemented with organic matter promotes larger, more floriferous specimens.

To start plants, collect the dried seed capsules as soon as they become a light to medium brown and before they begin to split. Sow in prepared areas of your garden immediately. Germination is slow, and seedlings will probably not show until the following spring. Once up, the seedlings are fast growing. Weekly applications of an all-purpose fertilizer enhance their growth.

You can expect some flowering the first year, but more abundant flowering comes from the fully mature plants of the second season. Give mature plants adequate moisture and light dressings of fertilizer twice a year for really spectacular flowering. Clip off spent blossoms until you want a seed-set, usually in late summer or early fall.

A semishaded setting is recommended for Violet Ruellia, such as woodland edges or in borders beneath taller growing plants. Violet Ruellia is especially lovely when combined with Cherry Sage, Flame Acanthus, Thoroughwort, Western Peppergrass, Woolly Paper-flower, and any of the Verbenas.

Used By: Buckeye, Cuban Crescentspot, Fatima, Malachite, White Peacock

Parts Eaten: Foliage

VELVETLEAF (*Wissadula amplissima*)
Mallow Family (*Malvaceae*)

Bloom Period: April-December
Range: Texas only
  Texas: 3, 5
Height: To 4 feet
Class: Native

A stout, upright, usually many-branched perennial which becomes semiwoody at base. Leaves to eight inches long and almost as broad, covered in short hairs, making them thick, soft, and velvety to the touch. Numerous five-petaled, yellow-orange flowers appear solitarily or in leafy clusters, with one or two opening at a time in each cluster.

Cultivation: Obtain plants of Velvetleaf for your garden either from seeds or cuttings. Gather seeds in the fall immediately upon their ripening. Air-dry the seeds thoroughly, then place them in a paper bag with an insect strip or a moth ball for a couple of weeks. Remove and place in a sealed container and store in the refrigerator until spring. After all danger of frost has passed, plant seeds either directly in the garden where the plants are to stay or in small pots for later transplanting. Cover the seeds with one-fourth to one-half inch of soil. Mark the location well, for sometimes it may take two years for the seeds to germinate.

You may take six-inch-long cuttings from strong growing tips of a healthy plant, dip them in a rooting medium, then plant them in well-

drained soil. Before dipping into the rooting medium, cut to just below a node and remove all but the top leaves. Cuttings are best taken in early summer in order for the plants to become established before fall. The success rate is not very high with cuttings, either, so try rooting more than will be needed. Extras will always be welcomed by other gardeners attracting butterflies.

Cut back well-established and strong-growing plants to ground level during the winter months each year to encourage a robust, bushy habit and more flowering. Do not fertilize older plants, for this would encourage lank, spindly growth, with the foliage prone to powdery mildew. Also, keep them on the dry side, for mature plants cannot tolerate an overabundance of moisture. Butterflies will not use weak, sickly foliage for egg deposition.

You may move these plants with some success. If you see plants being destroyed by construction of some sort, ask permission to dig a few. Before replanting, cut the tops back to about six inches above ground level; keep well watered until new growth appears and the root system is well established. For the first few weeks after transplanting, use a very weak soluble fertilizer about once every two weeks. Provide a bit of shade in the form of leafy branches or tented newspapers the first few days to help reestablish the plants.

Used By: Common Steaky Skipper, Laviana Skipper, Scarce Streaky Skipper, Texas Powdered Skipper

Parts Eaten: Foliage

WESTERN PEPPERGRASS (*Lepidium montanum*)
Mustard Family (*Brassicaceae*)

Bloom Period: February-August
Range: Texas
Texas: 1, 4, 5
Height: To 28 inches
Class: Native

Low, upright or somewhat sprawling perennial, woody at the base, usually with several stems, and forming a large, rounded clump. Flowers numerous, white, in elongating terminal racemes, making the plants appear as mounds of snow.

Cultivation: Plants of Western Peppergrass do not transplant well except in a very young stage, and then you should take a large amount of soil with the roots. For a large number of plants, it is best to sow seeds in late fall where you want plants, then thin to desired stands. This plant is not particularly soil selective, but the soil must be very well drained and the plants kept on the dry side after they are up and growing well. Plant in full sun, as flowering will be drastically reduced in shade and the plants will become leggy and sprawl excessively. Also, do not overwater these plants.

Because of the beautiful mounding effect when you grow these plants in full sun, you can use Western Peppergrass in groupings of five or seven throughout the beds or as a continual irregular border for a most dramatic effect. Or use it as a higher than average edging in front of taller flowering perennials and shrubs, such as Purple Coneflower and Confetti Lantana. Shear off spent flowers for continual bloom. Also, as flowers begin to fade, cut some plants back about one half to one third to induce new growth, providing plenty of tender larval food. Plants remain green throughout the winter if you cut them back after the first frost.

Used By: Checkered White

Parts Eaten: Buds, flowers, young seed pods, leaves

206

WHITE CLOVER (*Trifolium repens*)
Legume Family (*Fabaceae*)

Bloom Period: March-November
Range: All
    Texas: 2, 3, 4
Height: To 6 inches
Class: Naturalized

A low, creeping, shallow-rooted perennial forming large mats or patches. The long-stalked leaves are numerous and parted into three separate leaflets. Many small, pale pink or white flowers are tightly congested into long-stalked terminal clusters.

Cultivation: White Clover is not a difficult plant to get started, and one some folks would like to get rid of. In some areas it is an unwanted "weed" in the lawn or garden, but when growing along roadsides and in abandoned areas, it is quite lovely. Plants of White Clover start easily from seed. Gather the seed heads after they have turned brown and place them in an open paper bag for a few days until completely dry. Shake the seeds loose and store them in the refrigerator until spring.

Plants are also easy to obtain from a rooted branch from a mature plant. Gently dig the roots loose at each node along the branch, then clip it loose from the mother plant. When replanting in the garden, clip the branch between each node and plant each rooted section. Even if no roots are showing at the node, make a shallow depression, lay the branch in the depression, and cover it with soil. It usually quickly roots and forms a new plant.

White Clover is best adapted to loamy soils a little on the heavy side with clays and silt. However, do not let your soil type stop you from trying this one, for it grows on caliche, limestone, sand, or salt. What it does like is a little extra moisture and good drainage. Occasional fertilizing through the growing season promotes lusher vegetation.

Once established, White Clover readily reseeds and needs very little care. To keep it within desired bounds, simply hoe back each spring. In the flower garden it should not become obnoxious or uncontrollable. White Clover can be most effective in problem areas where grass or other groundcovers do not grow well. Use it in low areas where moisture has a tendency to stand, on badly eroding slopes, or in just about any area where nothing else grows. This plant dies out during the summer but returns with the cooler fall weather and in some areas remains green all winter.

Used By: Common Sulphur, Orange Sulphur, Dogface Butterfly, Eastern Tailed Blue, Fairy Yellow, Gray Hairstreak, Northern Cloudywing, Reakirt's Blue, and probably others

Parts Eaten: Leaves, flowers, young fruits

Additional Larval Food Plants

The following lists include more larval food plants than shown and described in the text in order to broaden the scope of exciting possibilities for attracting butterflies to your garden. Plants have been placed on each list with the areas where the butterflies which use them normally occur for breeding, not necessarily where the plants naturally occur within the region. Even though a plant may grow all over the region, there is no need to plant it in the garden as a larval food source if the butterfly which uses it does not breed there.

As this is a food plant list and not a complete listing of the butterflies which occur in the South, many species of butterflies which may be found in the region are not given here. This is because their food plants are unknown or because the literature searched gave only the plant genus and no species. This is especially true for many of the butterflies which come into the Rio Grande Valley from Mexico. These butterflies and their food plants have been dealt with under the section on a Special South Texas Garden and in the special Florida listing.

Sometimes a plant listed, such as the Junipers, Oaks, Agaves, and some of the grasses, may be a dominant component in a particular habitat. Such plants are listed not to consider first for planting but as ones not to destroy if they already exist in or around your garden. In most instances, the butterflies which use such plants require a number of plants for breeding, and one or two plants in your garden would not be adequate. If the plants are available in sufficient numbers nearby to support a colony, you will most likely get the butterflies around the nectar plants in your garden.

As with the nectar and larval food plants shown and described elsewhere, the plant species are placed here in separate categories of trees, shrubs, vines, and herbs and listed in alpabetical order by common name. The listing is followed by where it appears in the South and the regions of Texas where it appears. The butterfly larvae which eat the plant in those areas then follows.

Tree	Range	TX Regions	Butterfly
Amyris, Sez (*Amyris elemifera*)	FL		Giant Swallowtail
Apple (*Malus pumila*)	All	2,4	Gray Hairstreak
			Spring Azure
			Red-spotted Purple
			Viceroy
	TX	2,4	Tiger Swallowtail
		2	Striped Hairstreak
Ash, Arizona (*Fraxinus velutina*)	TX	4	Tiger Swallowtail
		4,5	Two-tailed Tiger Swallowtail
Ash, Green (*Fraxinus pennsylvanica*)	All	3	Tiger Swallowtail
	TX	1,2,3	Two-tailed Tiger Swallowtail
Ash, White (*Fraxinus americana*)	All	2,4	Mourning Cloak
		2	Tiger Swallowtail
	AR,GA,NC, SC,TN		Hickory Hairstreak
	All ext FL, LA,OK,TX		Baltimore
Aspen, Quaking (*Populus tremuloides*)	TN,TX	5	Mourning Cloak
			Red-spotted Purple
			Viceroy
Avocado (*Persea americana*)	FL,TX	2,3	Palamedes Swallowtail
Bay, Red (*Persea borbonia*)	All ext AR,OK,TN	2,3	Spicebush Swallowtail
			Palamedes Swallowtail
Bay, Sweet (*Magnolia virginiana*)	All ext OK	2	Tiger Swallowtail
			Spicebush Swallowtail
	TX	2	Palamedes Swallowtail
Beech (*Fagus grandifolia*)	GA,NC,SC, TN		Early Hairstreak
Birch, Yellow (*Betula alleghaniensis*)	GA,NC,SC, TN		Faunus Anglewing
			Mourning Cloak
Boxelder (*Acer negundo*)	All	2,4	Banded Hairstreak
Camphor-tree (*Cinnamonum camphora*)	AL,FL,GA, LA,MS,TX	2	Spicebush Swallowtail
	TX	2,3	Tiger Swallowtail
Catalpa, Common (*Catalpa bignonioides*)	All	2,4	Tiger Swallowtail
Cherry, Black (*Prunus serotina*)	All	2,4,5	Spring Azure
		2	Striped Hairstreak
		2,4,5	Red-spotted Purple
		2,3,4,5	Viceroy
		1,2	Coral Hairstreak
	TX	2,4,5	Henry's Elfin
		2,3,4	Tiger Swallowtail
		4	Two-tailed Tiger Swallowtail

209

Tree	Range	TX Regions	Butterfly
Cherry, Common	AR,NC,OK,	2	Tiger Swallowtail
(*Prunus virginiana*)	TN,TX	1	Coral Hairstreak
		2	Striped Hairstreak
		5	Red-spotted Purple
		2,5	Spring Azure
Cherry, Fine	GA,NC,TN		Striped Hairstreak
(*Prunus pensylvanica*)			
Chestnut, American	AL,FL,GA,		Banded Hairstreak
(*Castanea dentata*)	LA,MS,NC,		Hickory Hairstreak
	SC,TN		
Cottonwood, Eastern	All	All	Mourning Cloak
(*Populus deltoides*)		2,4	Red-spotted Purple
		2,3,4	Viceroy
	TX	2,3,4	Tiger Swallowtail
Dogwood, Flowering	All	2,4	Spring Azure
(*Cornus florida*)			
Ebony, Texas	TX	3	Cassius Blue
(*Pithecellobium			Coyote Skipper
flexicaule*)			Orange Giant Sulphur
Elm, American	All	All	Question Mark
(*Ulmus americana*)		2,4	Comma
		All	Mourning Cloak
		All	Painted Lady
Elm, Cedar	AR,FL,LA,	3	Mourning Cloak
(*Ulmus nassifolia*)	MS,TN,TX	2,3,4	Question Mark
Elm, Siberian	All	1,2,4	Mourning Cloak
(*Ulmus pumila*)			Question Mark
Elm, Slippery	All	1,2,3,4	Mourning Cloak
(*Ulmus rubra*)			Question Mark
Elm, Winged	All	2,4	Question Mark
(*Ulmus alata*)			
Grapefruit	FL,TX	3	Giant Swallowtail
(*Citrus maxima*)			
Hackberry, Common	All ext FL	1	Snout Butterfly
(*Celtis occidentalis*)			Question Mark
			Mourning Cloak
	TX	1	Pale Emperor
Hackberry, Net-leaf	TX	1,3,4,5	Mourning Cloak
(*Celtis reticulata*)		1,3,4	Pale Emperor
		1,3,4,5	Question Mark
		1,3,4,5	Snout Butterfly
		1,4	Tawny Emperor
		1,3,4,5	Western Hackberry Butterfly
Hackberry, Sugar	All	All	Question Mark
(*Celtis laevigata*)			Snout Butterfly
		2	Hackberry Butterfly
		1,2,4	Tawny Emperor
		1,2,3,4	Mourning Cloak
	TX	1,2,3,4	Pale Emperor
		1,3,4,5	Western Hackberry Butterfly

Tree	Range	TX Regions	Butterfly
Hawthorn, Copenhagen (*Crataegus intricata*)	All ext AR,FL,LA, TX		Striped Hairstreak
Hawthorn, Waxy-fruit (*Crataegus pruinosa*)	AR,GA,TN		Striped Hairstreak
Hercules-club (*Zanthoxylum clava-herculis*)	All ext TN	2	Giant Swallowtail
Hickory, Bitternut (*Canya cordiformis*)	AR,GA,NC, SC,TN		Hickory Hairstreak
Hickory, Black (*Carya texana*)	AR,LA,OK, TX	2,3,4	Banded Hairstreak
Hickory, Shagbark (*Carya ovata*)	All	2	Banded Hairstreak
	AR,GA,NC, SC,TN		Hickory Hairstreak
Hickory, Swamp (*Canya glabra*)	All ext OK	2,4	Banded Hairstreak
Hickory, Swamp *cont.*	AR,GA,NC, SC,TN		Hickory Hairstreak
Hop Hornbeam, Eastern (*Ostrya virginiana*)	All	2	Mourning Cloak Red-spotted Purple
Hornbeam, American (*Carpinus caroliana*)	All	2	Striped Hairstreak Red-spotted Purple Tiger Swallowtail
Huisache (*Acacia smithii*)	TX	3	Marine Blue
Juniper, Ash (*Juniperus ashei*)	OK,TX	1,4,5	Olive Hairstreak
	TX	5	Juniper Hairstreak
Juniper, Common (*Juniperus communis*)	GA,LA,NC, SC		Olive Hairstreak
Juniper, Eastern Red (*Juniperus virginiana*)	All	2,3,4	Olive Hairstreak
Juniper, Rock (*Juniperus ashei*)	TX	4	Juniper Hairstreak Olive Hairstreak
Lemon (*Citrus limon*)	FL,TX	3	Giant Swallowtail Gray Hairstreak
Lime (*Citrus aurantifolia*)	FL,TX	3	Giant Swallowtail
Locust, Black (*Robinia pseudo-acacia*)	All ext OK,TX		Zarucco Duskywing
	All ext FL	2	Common Sulphur
	All	2	Silver-spotted Skipper
	AR,GA,NC, OK,SC,TN		Dreamy Duskywing
Locust, Clammy (*Robinia viscosa*)	AL,GA,NC, SC,TN		Silver-spotted Skipper
Locust, Honey (*Gleditsia triacanthus*)	All	2	Silver-spotted Skipper

Tree	Range	TX Regions	Butterfly
Mesquite, Honey (*Prosopis glandulosa*)	AR,LA,TX	1,3,4,5	Reakirt's Blue
	LA,TX	3,4	Antillean Blue
	TX	3,5	Leda Hairstreak
	LA,TX	3,5	Long-tailed Skipper
	AR,LA,TX	3,5	Marine Blue
Mimosa (*Albiza julibrissin*)	AR,LA,MS, TN,TX	3,4	Reakirt's Blue
Mock-orange (*Styrax americana*)	All	2	Tiger Swallowtail
Mountain Laurel, Texas (*Sopora secundiflora*)	TX	2,3,4,5	Henry's Elfin
Mulberry, Red (*Morus rubra*)	All	1,2,3,4	Mourning Cloak
Oak, Arizona (*Quercus arizonica*)	TX	5	Araxes Skipper
			Juvenal's Duskywing
			Short-tailed Arizona Skipper
			Southern Duskywing
Oak, Black (*Quercus velutina*)	All	2	Juvenal's Duskywing
			Horace's Duskywing
	All ext FL	2	Edward's Hairstreak
Oak, Blackjack (*Quercus marilandica*)	All	2,4	Juvenal's Duskywing
		2,4	White M Hairstreak
		1,2,3,4	Horace's Duskywing
Oak, Bur (*Quercus macrocarpa*)	AL,AR,LA, MS,OK,TN, TX	2,3	Banded Hairstreak
		1,2,4	Sleepy Duskywing
			Juvenal's Duskywing
		2	Edward's Hairstreak
Oak, Chinquapin (*Quercus muhlenbergii*)	AL,FL,LA, MS,NC,OK, SC,TN,TX	1,2,4	Horace's Duskywing
Oak, Emory (*Quercus emoryi*)	TX	5	Early Hairstreak
			Juvenal's Duskywing
			Short-tailed Arizona Skipper
Oak, Laurel (*Quercus laurifolia*)	All ext OK	2	Horace's Duskywing
			Northern Hairstreak
Oak, Live (*Quercus virginiana*)	All ext OK,TN TX	3,4	Gray Hairstreak
		2,3,4	Northern Hairstreak
		2,4	White M Hairstreak
		2,3,4	Horace's Duskywing
	FL,GA		Southern Hairstreak
Oak, Northern Red (*Quercus rubra*)	All ext FL, TX		Banded Hairstreak
			Juvenal's Duskywing
			Horace's Duskywing
Oak, Post (*Quercus stellata*)	All	1,2	Juvenal's Duskywing
		1,2,3	Horace's Duskywing
		1,2,3,4	Northern Hairstreak
Oak, Southern Red (*Quercus falcata*)	All	2	Horace's Duskywing
			Banded Hairstreak
			White M Hairstreak

Tree	Range	TX Regions	Butterfly
Oak, Water (*Quercus nigra*)	All	2	Juvenal's Duskywing
			Horace's Duskywing
			White M Hairstreak
			Northern Hairstreak
Oak, White (*Quercus alba*)	All	2	Juvenal's Duskywing
			Banded Hairstreak
			White M Hairstreak
	TX	2	Edward's Hairstreak
Oak, Willow (*Quercus phellas*)	All	2	Horace's Duskywing
			White M Hairstreak
Orange, Sour (*Citrus aurantium*)	FL,TX	3	Giant Swallowtail
Orange, Sweet (*Citrus sinensis*)	FL,TX	3	Giant Swallowtail
Peach, Common (*Prunus persica*)	All	2,3,4	Tiger Swallowtail
Pear, Common (*Pyrus communis*)	All	2,4	Mourning Cloak
		2,3,4	Viceroy
		2,4	Red-spotted Purple
Pecan (*Carya illinoensis*)	All	All	Gray Hairstreak
Persimmon, Texas (*Diospyros texana*)	TX	3,4,5	Gray Hairstreak
			Henry's Elfin
Plum, American (*Prunus americana*)	All	1,2	Coral Hairstreak
		2	Striped Hairstreak
		2,4,5	Spring Azure
Plum, Mexican (*Prunus mexicana*)	AL,AR,LA, MS,OK,TN, TX	2,4	Tiger Swallowtail
Pine, Loblolly (*Pinus taeda*)	All	2	Eastern Pine Elfin
Pine, Sand (*Pinus clausa*)	AL,FL,MS		Eastern Pine Elfin
Pine, Scotch (*Pinus sylvestris*)	All	2	Eastern Pine Elfin
Pine, Shortleaf (*Pinus echinata*)	All	2	Eastern Pine Elfin
Pine, Virginia (*Pinus virginiana*)	AL,GA,NC, SC,TN		Eastern Pine Elfin
Poplar, Black (*Populus nigra*)	All	2,3,4	Red-spotted Purple
			Viceroy
		2,4,5	Mourning Cloak
	AR,GA,NC, OK,SC,TN		Dreamy Duskywing
Poplar, White (*Populus alba*)	All	2,5	Red-spotted Purple
			Viceroy
			Mourning Cloak
Redbud (*Cercis canadensis*)	All	2,4,5	Henry's Elfin

Tree	Range	TX Regions	Butterfly
Sassafras (*Sassafras albidum* var. *molle*)	All	2	Spicebush Swallowtail Tiger Swallowtail
	All ext AR,OK,TN	2	Palamedes Swallowtail
Soapberry (*Sapindus saponaria* var. *drummondii*)	AR,OK,TX	All	Soapberry Hairstreak
Sweetleaf (*Symplocos tinctoria*)	All ext OK	2	King's Hairstreak
Tulip-tree (*Liriodendron tulipfera*)	All ext AR,OK,TX	2	Tiger Swallowtail Spicebush Swallowtail
Walnut, Black (*Juglans nigra*)	All	2,4	Banded Hairstreak
Walnut, River (*Juglans microcarpa*)	OK,TX	4	Banded Hairstreak
Walnut, White (*Juglans cinerea*)	AL,AR,GA, MS,NC,SC, TN		Banded Hairstreak
	AR,GA,NC, SC,TN		Hickory Hairstreak
Willow, Black (*Salix nigra*)	All	2,4	Banded Hairstreak
		All	Mourning Cloak Viceroy
Willow, Peach-leaved (*Salix Amygdaloides*)	AR,TX	1,4,5	Mourning Cloak
Willow, Pussy (*Salix humilis*)	GA,SC,NC, TN		Faunus Anglewing
Willow, Sandbar (*Salix exigua*)	AR,LA,MS, OK,TN,TX TX	All 2,3,4,5 2,4,5	Mourning Cloak Viceroy Red-spotted Purple
Willow, Silky (*Salix sericea*)	AL,AR,GA, NC,SC,TN		Mourning Cloak Viceroy
Willow, Tall Pussy (*Salix discolor*)	NC,TN		Mourning Cloak Viceroy
Willow, Weeping (*Salix babylonica*)	All	2,4	Mourning Cloak Viceroy

Shrubs	Range	TX Regions	Butterfly
Abutilon (*Abutilon lignosum*)	TX	3	Laviana Skipper Texas Powdered Skipper
Acacia, Wright (*Acacia wrightii*)	TX	3,4,5	Marine Blue
Acanthus, Flame (*Aniscanthus quadrifidus*)	TX	3,4	Janais Patch Texan Crescentspot
Althea (*Hibiscus syriacus*)	All	All	Gray Hairstreak
Azalea, Flame (*Rhododendron calendulaceum*)	GA,MS,NC, SC,TN		Striped Hairstreak
Azalea, Hoary (*Rhododendron canescens*)	AR,NC,TN		Gray Comma
Bear-grass (*Nolina erumpens*)	TX	4,5	Sandia Hairstreak
Bernardia, Southwest (*Bernardia myricifolia*)	TX	3,4	Alea Hairstreak Texas Crescentspot
Blackbead, Cat-claw (*Pithecellobium unquis-cati*)	FL		Antillean Blue
Blueberry, Early Lowbush (*Vaccinium pallidum*)	AL,GA,NC, SC,TN AL,AR,GA, MS,NC,SC, TN		Brown Elfin Henry's Elfin
Blueberry, Highbush (*Vaccinium corymbosum*)	All AL,GA,NC, SC,TN	2	Striped Hairstreak Spring Azure Henry's Elfin Brown Elfin
Brasil (*Condalia hookeri*)	TX	3	Snout Butterfly
Bugbane, Black (*Cimicifuga racemosa*)	AL,AR,GA, MS,NC,SC, TN		Spring Azure
Buckeye, Mexican (*Ungnadia speciosa*)	TX	4,5	Henry's Elfin
Cenizo (*Leucophyllum frutescens*)	TX	3,4,5	Theona Checkerspot
Cherry, Barbados (*Malpighia glabra*)	TX	3	Cassius Blue White Patch
Chokeberry, Black (*Aronia melanocarpa*)	AL,GA,MS, NC,SC,TN		Striped Hairstreak
Crameria (*Krameria pauciflora*)	TX	5	Mormon Metalmark
Dahoon (*Ilex cassine*)	AL,FL,GA, LA,MS,NC, SC,TX	2	Henry's Elfin

215

Shrubs	Range	TX Regions	Butterfly
Dalea, Bearded	TX	All	Dogface Butterfly
(*Dalea pogonathera*)		3,4,5	Reakirt's Blue
Dalea, Black	TX	1,3,4,5	Dogface Butterfly
(*Dalea frutescens*)			
Deerberry, Common	All	2	Red-spotted Purple
(*Vaccinium stamineum*)			
Dogwood, Alternate-leaf	AL,AR,FL,		Spring Azure
(*cornus alternifolia*)	GA,MS,NC,		
	SC,TN		
Eupatorium, Fragrant	TX	3	Lost Metalmark
(*Eupatorium odoratum*)			
Farkleberry	All	2	Henry's Elfin
(*Vaccinium arboreum*)			Striped Hairstreak
Flamingo Plant	AL,FL,GA,	3	Texan Crescentspot
(*Jacobinia carnea*)	LA,MS,TX		
Gooseberry, Appalachian	NC,TN		Gray Comma
(*Ribes rotundifolia*)			
Gooseberry, Missouri	AR,TN		Gray Comma
(*Ribes missouriense*)			
Guayacan	TX	3,4,5	Gray Hairstreak
(*Guaiacum angustifolia*)		3,5	Lyside
Hackberry, Spiny	TX	3,4,5	Snout Butterfly
(*Celtis pallida*)			Western Hackberry Butterfly
		3	Red-bordered Metalmark
Hawthorn, Parsley	All	2	Gray Hairstreak
(*Crataegus marshallii*)			
Hazel-nut, Beaked	GA,NC,SC,		Early Hairstreak
(*Corylun cornuta*)	TN		
Holly, American	All	2	Henry's Elfin
(*Ilex opaca*)			
Holly, Yaupon	All ext TN	2,4	Henry's Elfin
(*Ilex vomitoria*)			
Hop-tree	All	2,3,4	Tiger Swallowtail
(*Ptelea trifoliata*)			Giant Swallowtail
	TX	1,3,4,5	Two-tailed Tiger Swallowtail
Huckleberry, Black	AL,GA,NC,		Brown Elfin
(*Gaylussacia baccata*)	SC,TN		
	AL,AR,GA,		Henry's Elfin
	LA,MS,NC,		
	SC,TN		
Indigo, False	All	All	Dogface Butterfly
(*Amorpha fruticosa*)			Gray Hairstreak
			Silver-spotted Skipper
		2,4	Hoary Edge
Kidneywood, Texas	TX	3,4,5	Dogface Butterfly
(*Eysenhardtia texana*)			
Lantana, Hammock	FL,TX	3	Painted Lady
(*Lantana microcephala*)			

Shrubs	Range	TX Regions	Butterfly
Lantana, Texas (*Lantana horrida*)	LA,MS,TX	2,3,4,5	Painted Lady
Lantana, Weeping (*Lantana montevidensis*)	AL,FL,GA, LA,MS,TX	3,4	Painted Lady
Lantana, West Indian (*Lantana camara*)	All	1,2,3,4	Painted Lady
Lechuguilla (*Agave lechuguilla*)	TX	4,5 5	Pecos Giant Skipper West Texas Giant Skipper
Lilac, Common (*Syringa vulgaris*)	All	2,4	Tiger Swallowtail
Locust, Bristly (*Robinia hispida*)	All	2	Silver-spotted Skipper
Mistletoe, Christmas (*Phoradendron tomentosum*)	All	2,3,4,5	Great Purple Hairstreak
New Jersey Tea (*Ceanothus americanus*)	All	2	Spring Azure Mottled Duskywing
Pawpaw, Common (*Asimina triloba*)	All	2	Zebra Swallowtail
Pawpaw, Dwarf (*Asimina pygmaea*)	AL,FL,GA		Zebra Swallowtail
Plum, Chickasaw (*Prunus angustifolius*)	All	1,2	Coral Hairstreak
Possumhaw (*Viburnum nudum*)	All ext OK	2	Spring Azure
Prickly Ash (*Zanthloxum hirsutum*)	AR,TX	3,4	Giant Swallowtail
Prickly Ash, American (*Zanthoxylum americanum*)	All ext NC,OK,TX		Giant Swallowtail
Prickly Ash, Lime (*Zanthloxum fagara*)	FL,TX	3	Giant Swallowtail Sickle-winged Skipper
Privit (*Lingustrum vulgare*)	TX	1,3,4,5	Two-tailed Tiger Swallowtail
Redroot (*Ceanothus herbaceus*)	All ext FL	2,4	Spring Azure Mottled Duskywing
Rock-spiraea (*Petrophytum caespitosum*)	TX	4,5	Spring Azure
Screwbean, Dwarf (*Prosopis reptans*)	TX	3	Clytie Hairstreak Tailed Orange
Senna (*Senna pendula*)	FL,TX	3	Cloudless Giant Sulphur
Senna, Argentine (*Senna corymbosa*)	GA,LA,MS, SC,TX	2,3,4	Cloudless Giant Sulphur
Service-berry, Canadian (*Amelanchier canadensis*)	AL,GA,NC, SC,TN		Striped Hairstreak
Shrimp Plant (*Beloperone guttata*)	AL,FL,GA, LA,MS,TX	2,3	Texan Crescentspot

Shrubs	Range	TX Regions	Butterfly
Silver-leaf, Big Bend (*Leucophyllum minus*)	TX	5	Chinati Checkerspot Theona Checkerspot
Spicebush (*Lindera benzoin*)	All	2,4	Spicebush Swallowtail Tiger Swallowtail
Sumac, Fragrant (*Rhus aromatica*)	All ext FL,TN	2	Red-banded Hairstreak
Sumac, Wing-rib (*Rhus copallina*)	All	2	Red-banded Hairstreak
Thoroughwort (*Eupatorium havanense*)	TX	4	Rawson's Metalmark
Tobacco, Tree (*Nicotiana glauca*)	AL,FL,TX	3,4,5	Painted Lady
Wax Myrtle, Southern (*Myrica cerifera*)	All ext TN	2	Red-banded Hairstreak
Wild Buckwheat, Wright (*Eriogonum wrightii*)	TX	1,5 5	Acmon Blue Mormon Metalmark Rita Blue
Yellow-Bells (*Tecoma stans*)	FL,TX	3,4,5	Gray Hairstreak
Yucca, Aloe (*Yucca aloifolia*)	AL,FL,GA, LA,MS,NC, SC FL,GA,SC		Yucca Giant Skipper Cofaqui Giant Skipper
Yucca, Arkansas (*Yucca arkansana*)	AR,LA,OK, TX	2,3,4	Yucca Giant Skipper
Yucca, Giant (*Yucca faxoniana*)	TX	5	Colorado Giant Skipper
Yucca, Lousiana (*Yucca louisianensis*)	AR,LA,OK, TX	2	Yucca Giant Skiper
Yucca, Mound-lily (*Yucca gloriosa*)	AL,FL,GA, MS,NC,SC		Yucca Giant Skipper
Yucca, Narrow-leaf (*Yucca glauca*)	AR,TX TX	1,4 1,4	Yucca Giant Skipper Strecker's Giant Skipper
Yucca, Trecul (*Yucca treculeana*)	TX	3,4,5 5	Yucca Giant Skipper Ursine Giant Skipper
Yucca, Weak-leaf (*Yucca filamentosa*)	All ext OK FL,GA,SC	2	Yucca Giant Skipper Cofaqui Giant Skipper

Vines	Range	TX Regions	Butterfly
Balloon-vine, Common (*Cardiospermum halicacabum*)	TX	3	Silver-banded Hairstreak
Bean, Amberique (*Strophostyles helvula*)	All	2,4	Southern Cloudywing
Bean, Slick-seed (*Strophostyles leiosperma*)	AL,AR,FL, LA,OK,TN, TX	2	Southern Cloudywing
Butterfly Pea (*Centrosema virginianum*)	All	2	Southern Cloudywing
	All ext OK,TX	2	Zarucco Duskywing
	OK,TX	2	Funereal Duskywing
	FL,TX	3	Lilac-banded Longtail
Calico Flower (*Aristolochia elegans*)	FL,TX	3	Polydamas Swallowtail
		2,4	Pipevine Swallowtail
Groundnut (*Apios americana*)	All	2,4	Silver-spotted Skipper
		2	Southern Cloudywing Spring Azure
Heartseed, Tropical (*Cardiospermum corindum*)	TX	3	Silver-banded Hairstreak
Honeysuckle, Japanese (*Lonicera japanica*)	All ext FL,LA,OK, TX		Baltimore
Honeysuckle, Trumpet (*Lonicera sempervirens*)	All	2	Spring Azure
Hops (*Humulus lupulus*)	AL,AR,FL, GA,NC,SC		Comma Question Mark Spring Azure Mourning Cloak Red Admiral
Kudzu (*Pueraria montana*)	All ext OK	2	Silver-spotted Skipper
	TX	2	Spring Azure
Milkpea, Downy (*Galactia regularis*)	FL,TX	3,4	Cassius Blue
Milkweed-vine, Climbing (*Sarcostemma cynanchoides*)	OK,TX	All	Monarch Queen
Muskmelon (*Cucumis melo*)	All	2,3	Painted Lady
Passionflower (*Passiflora incarnata*)	AL,FL,GA, LA,MS,SC, TX	2,3,4	Gulf Fritillary
	All	3,4	Zebra Longwing
		2,3,4	Variegated Fritillary
	FL,TX	2,3,4	Julia
	TX	3	Mexican Fritillary

Vines	Range	TX Regions	Butterfly
Passionflower, Blue (*Passiflora caerula*)	AL,FL,GA, LA,MS,SC, TX	2,3,4	Gulf Fritillary
	All	2,3,4	Variegated Fritillary
	FL,TX	2,3,4	Julia
Passionflower, Corky-stem (*Passiflora suberosa*)	FL,TX	3	Gulf Fritillary Zebra Longwing
Passionflower, Purple (*Passiflora edulis*)	FL		Gulf Fritillary
Passionflower, Yellow (*Passiflora lutea*)	AL,FL,GA, LA,MS,SC, TX	2,3,4 3,4	Gulf Fritillary Zebra Longwing
	FL,TX	2,3,4	Julia
	TX	3	Mexican Fritillary Crimson-patched Longwing
Peanut, Hog (*Amphicarpaea bracteata*)	All	2	Golden-banded Skipper Silver-spotted Skipper Gray Hairstreak
	AL,FL,GA, LA,MS,SC		Long-tailed Skipper
Pipevine (*Aristolochia duoir*)	All	2,3	Pipevine Swallowtail
	FL,TX	3	Polydamas Swallowtail
Pipevine, Marsh (*Aristolochia pentandra*)	FL,TX	3	Polydamas Swallowtail
Pipevine, Woolly (*Aristolochia tomentosa*)	All	2,3	Pipevine Swallowtail
Snapdragon Vine (*Maurandya antirrhiniflora*)	TX	3,4,5	Buckeye
Snoutbean, Hairy (*Rhynchosia tomentosa*)	All ext OK	2	Southern Cloudywing
Snoutbean, Least (*Rhynchosia minima*)	AL,FL,GA, LA,TX	3,4	Antillean Blue
	TX	2,3	White-striped Longtail
Sweet Pea (*Lathyrus odoratus*)	AR,OK,TX	3,5	Marine Blue
Virgin's Bower, Texas (*Clematis drummondii*)	TX	3,4,5	Fatal Metalmark
Wisteria (*Wisteria frutescens*)	All	2	Silver-spotted Skipper
	All ext OK,TX		Zarucco Duskywing
	AL,FL,GA, LA,MS,SC,TX	3	Long-tailed Skipper
Wisteria, Chinese (*Wisteria sinensis*)	All	2,3,4	Silver-spotted Skipper

Herbs	Range	TX Regions	Butterfly
Aaron's-rod (*Thermopsis villosa*)	AL,GA,NC, TN		Wild Indigo Duskywing
Abutilon (*Abutilon fruticosum*)	TX	All	Common Streaky Skipper
		3,4	Laviana Skipper
		3,4,5	Texas Powdered Skipper
Abutilon, Yellow (*Abutilon malacum*)	TX	5	Scance Streaky Skipper
Acacia, Fern (*Acacia angustissima*)	TX	3,4,5	Reakirt's Blue
		1,2,3,4	Texas Acacia Skipper
		3,4	Antillean Blue
		3,4,5	Mexican Yellow
		2,3,4,5	Little Yellow
Alfalfa (*Medicago sativa*)	All ext FL	1,2,4,5	Common Sulphur
	All	1,2,4,5	Orange Sulphur
			Dogface Butterfly
			Gray Hairstreak
			Painted Lady
		1,2,4	Northern Hairstreak
		2,4	Northern Cloudywing
	OK,TX	1,2,4,5	Funereal Duskywing
	AL,FL,GA, LA,MS,NC, SC,TX	4	Antillean Blue
	TX	5	Marine Blue
		1,5	Orange-bordered Blue
Alyssum, Sweet (*Lobularia maritima*)	All	All	Checkered White
			Cabbage White
Amaranth (*Amaranthus hypochondriacus*)	All	2,3	Common Sootywing
Amaranth, Redroot (*Amaranthus retroflexus*)	All	All	Common Sootywing
	TX	2,3	Southern Scalloped Sootywing
		5	Mexican Sootywing
Amaranth, Slim (*Amaranthus hybridus*)	All	2,3,4,5	Common Sootywing
Anis-root (*Osmorhiza longistylis*)	All ext FL,LA	2	Eastern Black Swallowtail
Anoda, Crested (*Anoda cristata*)	All	All	Common Checkered Skipper
Antelope-horns (*Ascelpias asperula*)	TX	1,2,4,5	Monarch
			Queen
Aster (*Aster* spp.)	All	All	Pearly Crescentspot
Aster, Flat-top White (*Aster umbellatus*)	All ext LA	2	Silvery Crescentspot
Aster, Heath (*Aster ericoides*)	All ext FL	All	Pearly Crescentspot

Herbs	Range	TX Regions	Butterfly
Beak, Rush (*Rhynchospora inundata*)	FL,GA		Appalachian Eyed Brown
Bean Coral (*Erythrina herbacea*)	All ext OK,TN	2	Spring Azure
Bean, Garden (*Phaseolus vulgaris*)	All	All	Gray Hairstreak
			Painted Lady
		2,4	Silver-spotted Skipper
		2,3,4,5	Long-tailed Skipper
	FL,TX	2,3,4	Cassius Blue
			Lilac-banded Longtail
Bean, Lima (*Phaseolus limensis*)	All	All	Gray Hairstreak
		2,3,4,5	Long-tailed Skipper
	FL,TX	3	Cassius Blue
		2,3,4	Lilac-banded Longtail
Bean, Purple (*Phaseolus atropurpureus*)	TX	3	Lilac-banded Longtail
			White-striped Longtail
Bean, Thicket (*Phaseolus polystachios*)	All	2,4	Silver-spotted Skipper
	AL,FL,GA, LA,MS,SC		Long-tailed Skipper
Beet (*Beta vulgaris*)	All	All	Painted Lady
Begger-ticks (*Bidens pilosa*)	AL,FL,GA, LA,MS,TX	3	Dwarf Yellow
Berula, Stalky (*Berula erecta*)	AR,FL,OK, TX	1,2,4,5	Eastern Black Swallowtail
Bitter-cress (*Cardamine parviflora* var. *arenicola*)	All ext FL	2,4	Falcate Orangetip
Bitter-cress (*Cardamine concatenata*)	GA,TN,NC, SC ·		West Virginia White
	All ext FL	2	Falcate Orangetip
Bitter-cress, Crinkle-root (*Cardamine diphylla*)	GA,TN,NC, SC		West Virginia White
Bitter-cress, Hairy (*Cardamine hirsuta*)	All ext FL	2	Falcate Orangetip
Bluebonnet, Big Bend (*Lupinus harvardii*)	TX	5	Little Yellow
Bluebonnet, Texas (*Lupinus texensis*)	LA,OK,TX	2,3,4	Gray Hairstreak
			Henry's Elfin
		3,4	Little Yellow
	LA,TX	2	Frosted Elfin
Bluegrass, Kentucky (*Poa pratensis*)	All ext FL	2	Pepper-and-Salt Skipper
	All	5	Zabulon Skipper
		2	Tawny-edged Skipper
		1,2,5	Fiery Skipper
		1,2	Roadside Skipper
	AR,GA,NC, SC,TN,TX	1	Yellowpatch Skipper

Herbs	Range	TX Regions	Butterfly
Bluehearts, American (*Buchnera americana*)	All	2,3,4,5	Buckeye
Bluestem, Big (*Andropogon gerardii*)	All	All	Delaware Skipper
		1,2	Dusted Skipper
		2	Bunchgrass Skipper
		2,4	Large Wood Nymph
	All ext FL	2	Cobweb Skipper
	All ext AR,TN	2,4	Beardgrass Skipper
Bluestem, Little (*Schizachyrium scoparium*)	All	1,2	Dusted Skipper
		All	Delaware Skipper
		2	Dixie Skipper
			Crossline Skipper
			Swarthy Skipper
	All ext FL	2	Cobweb Skipper
	All ext AR,TN	2,4	Beardgrass Skipper
Boneset, Late-flowering (*Eupatorium serotinum*)	TX	3,4	Lost Metalmark
Borage (*Borage officinalis*)	All	All	Painted Lady
Broccoli (*Brassica oleraceae* var. *italica*)	All	All	Cabbage White
			Checkered White
	AL,FL,GA, LA,MS,TX	3	Great Southern White
Broomsedge (*Andropogon virginicus*)	All	2	Cobweb Skipper
Brown-eyed Susan (*Rudbeckia hirta*)	TX	2,3,4	Bordered Patch
Brussels Sprout (*Brassica oleraceae* var. *gemmifera*)	All	All	Cabbage White
	AL,FL,GA, LA,MS,TX	3	Great Southern White
	TX	1,2,3	Veined White
Buffelgrass (*Cenchrus ciliaris*)	FL,LA,TX	3	Clouded Skipper
			Eufala Skipper
Bulrush, Wool-grass (*Scirpus cyperinus*)	All	2	Sedge Skipper
Bur-clover (*Medicago polymorpha*)	OK,TX	1,2,4,5	Funereal Duskywing
Bush-bean, Wild (*Macroptilium lathyroides*)	FL		Cassius Blue
Bush clover, Hairy (*Lespedeza hirta*)	All ext OK,TX		Zarucco Duskywing
	All	2	Eastern Tailed Blue
			Gray Hairstreak
			Hoary Edge
			Northern Cloudywing
			Southern Cloudywing

Herbs	Range	TX Regions	Butterfly
Bush clover, Intermediate (*Lespedeza intermedia*)	All	2	Eastern Tailed Blue Northern Cloudywing
Bush clover, Roundhead (*Lespedeza capitata*)	All	2	Eastern Tailed Blue Northern Cloudywing Southern Cloudywing Silver-spotted Skipper
Butter-and-eggs (*Linaria vulgaris*)	All ext AR,SC	2	Buckeye
Butterfly Weed (*Asclepias tuberosa*)	TX TX		Gray Hairstreak Monarch Queen
Butterprint, Velvet-leaf (*Abutilon theophrasti*)	All	1	Common Checkered Skipper
Cabbage (*Brassica oleraceae var. capitata*)	All	All	Checkered White Cabbage White
	AL,FL,GA, MS,LA,TX		Great Southern White
	TX	1	Veined White
Calendula (*Calendula officinalis*)	All	All	Painted Lady
Cane, Giant (*Arundinaria gigantea*)	All	2	Creole Pearly Eye Pearly Eye
	All ext OK,TX		Lace-winged Roadside Skipper
	All ext AR,FL, OK,TX		Carolina Roadside Skipper
Cane, Sugar (*Saccharum officinarum*)	AL,FL,GA, LA,MS,TX	3	Fiery Skipper Long-winged Skipper Obscure Skipper Eufala Skipper
Canna (*Canna × generalis*)	All ext OK	2,3,4	Brazilian Skipper
Canna, Common (*Canna indica*)	All ext OK	2,3,4	Brazilian Skipper
Canary-grass, Reed (*Phalaris arundinacea*)	AL,AR,NC, TN		Northern Pearly Eye
Carex (*Carex hyalinolepis*)	AL,FL,GA, MS,TN		Appalachian Eyed Brown
Carpenter's-square (*Scrophularia marilandica*)	AL,AR,GA, MS,NC,SC, TN		Baltimore
Carrot, Garden (*Daucus hybrida*)	All	All	Eastern Black Swallowtail
Cauliflower (*Brassica oleraceae var. botrytis*)	All	All	Cabbage White Checkered White
	AL,FL,GA, MS,LA,TX	3	Great Southern White
Cloth-of-gold (*Lesquerella gracilis*)	AR,TX	1,2,4	Olympia Marblewing

Herbs	Range	TX Regions	Butterfly
Clover, Alsike (*Trifolium hybridum*)	All ext FL	2	Common Sulphur
	All	All	Eastern Tailed Blue
Clover, Buffalo (*Trifolium reflexum*)	All	2	Orange Sulphur
Clover, Red (*Trifolium pratense*)	All	2	Eastern Tailed Blue Orange Sulphur Southern Cloudywing Northern Cloudywing
Clover, White (*Trifolium repens*)	All ext FL	2,4	Common Sulphur
	All	2,4	Northern Cloudywing Eastern Tailed Blue
		2,3,4	Dogface Butterfly
		2,3,4	Orange Sulphur Gray Hairstreak
	AR,LA,MS, TN,TX	3,4	Reakirt's Blue
	AL,FL,GA, LA,MS,SC, TX	3	Fairy Yellow
Coneflower, Cutleaf (*Rudbeckla laciniata*)	All	2	Silvery Crescentspot
Corn (*Zea Mays*)	All	All	Gray Hairstreak
		1,2,3,4	Least Skipperling
		2,3,4	Clouded Skipper Eufala Skipper
Cotton (*Gossypium hirsutum*)	All	All	Gray Hairstreak Painted Lady
Cowbane, Spotted (*Cicuta maculata*)	All	1,2,4	Eastern Black Swallowtail
Crabgrass (*Digitaria sanguinalis*)	All	1,5	Sachem Fiery Skipper
	All ext OK,TX		Broken Dash
	AR,OK,TX	1,5	Mottled Roadside Skipper
Crabgrass, Slender (*Digitaria filiformus*)	All	2	Tawny-edged Skipper
Crabgrass, Southern (*Digitaria ciliaris*)	All	All	Fiery Skipper
	All ext OK	2,3,4	Broken Dash
Cress, Mouse-ear (*Arabidopsis thaliana*)	All	2	Falcate Orangetip
Crotalaria (*Crotolaria incana*)	FL,TX	3	Cassius Blue
Crotalaria, Arrow (*Crotolaria sagittalis*)	All ext FL,MS, OK	2	Frosted Elfin
	All	2	Wild Indigo Duskywing
Croton, Leatherweed (*Croton pottsii*)	TX	1,3,4,5	Goatweed Butterfly
Croton, Woolly (*Croton Capitatus*)	All	1,2,3,4	Goatweed Butterfly Gray Hairstreak

Herbs	Range	TX Regions	Butterfly
Crownbeard, Golden (*Verbesina enceloides*)	TX	2,3,4,5	Bordered Patch
Crownbeard, Gravel-weed (*Verbesina helianthoides*)	AL,AR,GA, LA,MS,TN, TX	2	Silvery Crescentspot Spring Azure
Crown-vetch, Purple (*Coronilla varia*)	All	All	Wild Indigo Duskywing
Cudweed, Purple (*Gamochaeta purpurea*)	All	2,3,4	American Painted Lady
Cudweed, Wright (*Gnaphalium canescens*)	OK,TX	4,5	American Painted Lady
Cutgrass, Rice (*Leersia oryzoides*)	All	1,2,3,4	Least Skipperling
	AR,GA,NC, SC,TN,TX	1	Yellowpatch Skipper
Cutgrass, Virginia (*Leersia virginica*)	All ext FL,TX		Northern Pearly Eye
Daisy, Ox-eye (*Chrysanthenum leucanthemum*)	All	4	Spring Azure
Deer Vetch (*Lotus purshianus*)	AR,LA,OK, TX	2	Eastern Tailed Blue
Dichanthelium, Deertongue (*Dichanthelium clandsetinum*)	All	2	Tawny-edged Skipper Northern Broken Dash
Dichanthelium, Forked (*Dichanthelium dichotomum*)	All	2	Northern Broken Dash
Dicliptera, Perennial (*Dicliptera brachiata*)	AL,FL,GA, LA,MS,TX	2,3,4	Texan Crescentspot
Dicliptera, Rio Grande (*Dicliptera sexangularis*)	TX	3	Texan Crescentspot
Dill (*Anethum graveolens*)	All	All	Eastern Black Swallowtail
Dock (*Rumex salicifolius*)	TX	5	Gray Hairstreak
Dock, Bitter (*Rumex obtusifolius*)	OK,TX	1	Great Gray Copper
	AR,OK,TN		Bronze Copper
Dock, Curley (*Rumex crispus*)	AR,OK,TN		Bronze Copper
	AR,GA,NC, SC,TN		American Copper
	OK,TX	1	Great Gray Copper
Dogbane, Spreading (*Apocynum androsaemifolium*)	AL,AR,GA, NC,OK,TN, TX	4,5	Monarch
Dutchman's Breetches, Texas (*Thamnosma texana*)	TX	3,4,5	Eastern Black Swallowtail

Herbs	Range	TX Regions	Butterfly
Dutchman's Pipe, Fringed (*Aristolochia fimbriata*)	All	2	Pipevine Swallowtail
Dutchman's Pipe, Texas (*Aristolochia reticulata*)	AR,LA,OK, TX	2	Pipevine Swallowtail
Dutchman's Pipe, Virginia (*Aristolochia serpentaria*)	All	2,4	Pipevine Swallowtail
	FL,TX		Polydamas Swallowtail
Dyssodia, May-weed (*Dyssodia papposa*)	AR,LA,TX	1,5	Dwarf Yellow
Emperor's-Candlesticks (*Senna alata*)	AL,FL,LA, MS,TX	2,3,4	Gray Hairstreak
Erioneuron, Hairy-scaled (*Erioneuron pilosum*)	OK,TX	1	Green Skipper
Eupatorium, Palm-leaf (*Eupatorium greggii*)	TX	4,5	Rawson's Metalmark
Evax, Bighead (*Evax prolifera*)	OK,TX	1,3,4	American Painted Lady
Evax, Silver (*Evax candida*)	LA,TX	2,3	American Painted Lady
Everlasting, Pearly (*Anaphalis margaritacea*)	AR,TN		American Painted Lady
False-abutilon (*Allowissadula holosericea*)	TX	4,5	Common Streaky Skipper
			Texas Powdered Skipper
		5	Scarce Streaky Skipper
False-mallow, Rio Grande (*Malvastrum americana*)	TX	3	Laviana Skipper
False-mallow, Three-lobe (*Malvastrum coromandelianum*)	TX	3,4	Common Checkered Skipper
False-nettle (*Boehmeria cylindrica*)	All	All	Red Admiral
			Question Mark
		2,4	Comma
False Foxglove, Fern-leaf (*Aureolaria pedicularia*)	AR,GA,MS, NC,SC		Baltimore
False Foxglove, Smooth Yellow (*Aureolaria flava*)	AL,AR,GA, MS,NC,SC, TN		Baltimore
Fennel, Common (*Foeniculum vulgare*)	All ext OK	All	Eastern Black Swallowtail
Flamingo Plant (*Jacobinia carnea*)	AL,FL,GA, LA,MS,TX	2,3	Texan Crescentspot
Flax, Blue (*Linum lewisii*)	OK,TX	1,4,5	Variegated Fritillary
Flax, Grooved (*Linum sulcatum*)	AL,AR,FL, GA,NC,OK, TN,TX	1,2,4	Variegated Fritillary

227

Herbs	Range	TX Regions	Butterfly
Flax, Stiff-stem (*Linum berlandieri*)	AL,AR,TX	All	Variegated Fritillary
Flax, Texas (*Linum medium*)	AL,AR,FL, GA,MS,OK, TN,TX	2,3,4	Variegated Fritillary
Flower-of-an-hour (*Hibiscus trionum*)	AR,FL,GA, LA,MS,NC, OK,TN,TX	1,4	Common Checkered Skipper
Fluffgrass (*Dasyochloa pulchella*)	TX	1,4,5 1,5 4	Green Skipper Pahaska Skipper Green Skipper
Fluffgrass, Downy (*Erioneuron pilosum*)	OK,TX	1,4,5 1,5	Green Skipper Pahaska Skipper
Foxglove (*Penstemon cobae*)	TX	1,4	Dotted Checkerspot
Foxglove, White-flowered (*Penstemon albidus*)	TX	1,4,5	Dotted Checkerspot
Frog-fruit, Common (*Phyla nodiflora*)	All ext TN	2,3,4,5	Phaon Crescentspot Buckeye
	AL,GA,SC, TX	3	White Peacock
Frog-fruit, Northern (*Phyla lanceolata*)	All ext TN	2,3,4	Phaon Crescentspot
	FL,GA,SC, TX	3	White Peacock
	TX	2,3,4	Buckeye
Frog-fruit, Texas (*Phyla incisa*)	OK,TX	3 2,3,4,5	White Peacock Buckeye Phaon Crescentspot
Gamagrass, Eastern (*Tripsacum dactyloides*)	All	2	Bunchgrass Skipper
Gerardia, Beach (*Agalinis fasciculata*)	All	2,3	Buckeye
Gerardia, Purple (*Agalinis purpurea*)	All ext OK	2	Buckeye
Gerardia, Slender (*Agalinis tenuifolia*)	All	2,3	Buckeye
Glasswort, Virginia (*Salicornia virginica*)	AL,FL,GA, LA,MS,SC		Eastern Pygmy Blue
	LA,TX	2,3	Western Pygmy Blue
Globe-mallow, Caliche (*Sphaeralcea coccinea*)	OK,TX	1,4,5	Common Checkered Skipper
	TX	5	Small Checkered Skipper
Globe-mallow, Copper (*Sphaeralcea angustifolia*)	OK,TX	1,4,5	Common Checkered Skipper Common Streaky Skipper
	TX	4,5 5	Texas Powdered Skipper Scarce Streaky Skipper
Goldeneye (*Viguiera dentata*)	TX	4,5	Bordered Patch
Goat's-beard (*Aruncus dioicus*)	AR,NC,SC, TN		Dusky Blue

Herbs	Range	TX Regions	Butterfly
Goosefoot, Pit-seed (*Chenopodium berlandieri*)	AL,AR,FL, GA,LA,OK, TN,TX	All	Common Sootywing
	AR,LA,OK, TX	1	Western Pygmy Blue
Goosefoot, Wormseed (*Chenopodium ambrosioides*)	All	2,3,4	Common Sootywing
	TX	2,3	Southern Scalloped Sootywing
Goosegrass (*Eleusine indica*)	All	2,3,4,5	Sachem
Grama, Blue (*Bouteloua gracilis*)	OK,TX	1,4,5	Green Skipper
		1,5	Uncas Skipper
	TX	1,5	Orange Roadside Skipper Pahaska Skipper
Grama, Sideoats (*Bouteloua curtipendula*)	AL,FL,GA, MS,OK,SC, TX	2	Dotted Skipper
	OK,TX	1,4,5	Green Skipper
Grass, Barnyard (*Echinochloa crusgallii*)	All	2,3,4	Eufala Skipper
Grass, Buffalo (*Buchloe dactyloides*)	OK,TX	1,4,5	Green Skipper
Grass, Carpet (*Axonopus compressus*)	AL,AR,FL, GA,LA,TX	2	Hermes Satyr Carolina Satyr
Grass, Centipede (*Eremochloa ophiuroides*)	AL,AR,FL, GA,LA,MS, NC,SC,TX	2	Hermes Satyr Little Wood Satyr
Grass, Common Bermuda (*Cynodon dactylon*)	AL,FL,GA, LA,MS,TX	2,3	Obscure Skipper
	All ext OK,TN	2,3,4	Whirlabout Eufala Skipper
		All	Fiery Skipper
	All	2,3	Gemmed Satyr
		2,3,4	Hermes Satyr
		All	Sachem
		2,3,4	Southern Skipperling
		2	Carolina Satyr
		1,2,4	Roadside Skipper
	TX	1,3,4,5	Orange Skipperling
		2,3,4,5	Julia Skipper
		3	Hermes Satyr
		5	Canyonland Satyr Umber Skipper
	OK,TX	All	Red Satyr
		1,4,5	Green Skipper
Grass, Johnson (*Sorghum halepense*)	All	2,3,4	Clouded Skipper Eufala Skipper

Herbs	Range	TX Regions	Butterfly
Grass, Poverty (*Danthonia spicata*)	AL,AR,GA, NC,OK,SC, TN		Leonardus Skipper
Grass, St. Augustine (*Stenotaphrum secundatum*)	All	2,3,4	Sachem
			Eufala Skipper
			Carolina Satyr
			Little Wood Satyr
			Clouded Skipper
			Hermes Satyr
			Fiery Skipper
			Broken Dash
	AR,OK,TX	2,3,4	Mottled Roadside Skipper
	OK,TX	2,3,4	Red Satyr
	All ext OK,TN	2,3,4	Whirlabout
	TX	3	Roadside Rambler
Grass, Vasey (*Paspalum setaceum*)	All ext OK,TN	2,3,4	Whirlabout
Greenthread (*Thelesperma megapotamicum*)	TX	1,4,5	Dwarf Yellow
Ground Plum (*Astragulus crassicarpus*)	AR,LA,TX	1,2,4,5	Common Sulphur
			Gray Hairstreak
Gypsy-flower (*Cynoglossum officinale*)	AL,AR,GA, NC,TN		Gray Hairstreak
Hammerwort (*Parietaria pensylvanica*)	AL,AR,FL, LA,MS,NC, OK,TN,TX	2,3,4,5	Red Admiral
Hedge-mustard (*Sisymbrium officinale*)	AR,OK,TX	1,2,4	Olympia Marblewing
Hollyhock (*Althaea rosea*)	All	All	Common Checkered Skipper
			Painted Lady
	AL,FL,LA, MS,TX	2,3	Tropical Checkered Skipper
	OK,TX	1,3,4,5	Common Streaky Skipper
Horse-purslane (*Trianthema protulacastrum*)	AR,LA,TX	2,3,4,5	Western Pygmy Blue
Indian Grass, Lopsided (*Sorghastrum secundum*)	AL,GA,LA, MS,SC		Pepper-and-salt Skipper
Indian Grass, Slender (*Sorghastrum elliottii*)	All ext FL	2	Pepper-and-salt Skipper
Indian Grass, Yellow (*Sorghastrum nutans*)	All	2	Pepper-and-salt Skipper
Indian Mallow (*Abutilon fruticosum*)	TX	1,3,4,5	Common Streaky Skipper
		3,4	Laviana Skipper
		3,4,5	Texas Powdered Skipper
Indigo, Lindheimer (*Indigofera lindheimeriana*)	TX	4	Reakirt's Blue

Herbs	Range	TX Regions	Butterfly
Jerusaleum-artichoke (*Helianthus tuberosus*)	All	2	Silvery Crescentspot
Joint Vetch, Sticky (*Aeschynomene viscidula*)	All ext AR,NC, OK,TN	3	Fairy Yellow
Lamb's-quarters (*Chenopodium album*)	AR,LA,OK TX	All	Western Pygmy Blue
	All	1,2,3,5	Painted Lady
			Common Sootywing
		2,4	Scalloped Sootywing
	TX	2,3	Southern Scalloped Sootywing
Lespedza, Roundhead (*Lespedeza capitata*)	All	1,2	Gray Hairstreak
Lettuce, Garden (*Lactuca sativa*)	All	All	Painted Lady
Licorice, Wild (*Glycyrrhiza lepidota*)	AR,OK,TX	5	Silver-spotted Skipper
		1,5	Gray Hairstreak
			Orange Sulpher
	TX	5	Reakirt's Blue
		1,5	Marine Blue
			Orange-bordered Blue
Locoweed, Woolly (*Astragalus mollissimus*)	TX	1,4,5	Gray Hairstreak
		1,5	Orange-bordered Blue
Locoweed, Wooton (*Astragalus wootonii*)	TX	1,5	Acmon Blue
Lousewort, Common (*Pedicularis canadensis*)	All ext FL,LA, OK,TX		Baltimore
Lovegrass, Teal (*Eragrostis hypnoides*)	All	1,2,3,4	Fiery Skipper
Lupine, Slender (*Lupinus perennis*)	All ext AR,OK	2	Wild Indigo Duskywing
			Eastern Tailed Blue
			Common Sulphur
			Orange Sulphur
	AL,GA,LA, NC,SC,TN, TX	2	Frosted Elfin
Mallow, Common (*Malva neglecta*)	AL,AR,GA, NC,OK,TN, TX	1,2,4,5	Common Checkered Skipper
			Gray Hairstreak
			Painted Lady
	TX	5	West Coast Lady
Mallow, High (*Malva sylvestris*)	FL,NC,SC, TN,TX	2,3	Common Checkered Skipper
			Painted Lady
Mallow, Little (*Malva parviflora*)	FL,LA,TX	2,3,4,5	Common Checkered Skipper
			Gray Hairstreak
			Painted Lady
Mallow, Musk (*Malva moschata*)	NC,TN		Common Checkered Skipper

231

Herbs	Range	TX Regions	Butterfly
Marshcress, Bog (*Rorippa palustris*)	TX	1	Veined White
Medic, Black (*Medicago lupulina*)	All	2,4	Eastern Tailed Blue Orange Sulphur
	All ext AR,NC, OK,TN	3	Fairy Yellow
Medic, Toothed (*Medicago polymorpha*)	All ext TN	1,2,4,5	Orange Sulphur
Milfoil (*Achillea millefolium*)	All	All	Painted Lady
Milkvetch, Bent-pod (*Astragalus distortus*)	AR,LA,MS, OK,TX	2,4	Southern Cloudywing
Milkvetch, Canada (*Astragalus canadensis*)	All	2	Wild Indigo Duskywing
Milkvetch, Nuttall (*Astragalus nuttalliana*)	AR,LA,TX	2,4	Northern Cloudywing
Milkweed (*Asclepias* spp.)	All	All	Monarch Queen
Milkweed, Common (*Asclepias syriaca*)	AL,AR,GA, LA,NC,OK, SC,TN,TX	1	Monarch Queen
Milkweed, Mexican (*Asclepias curassavica*)	All	All	Monarch Queen
Milkweed, Swamp (*Asclepias incarnata*)	All	All	Monarch Queen
Mock Bishop's-weed, Nuttall (*Ptilimnium nuttallii*)	AL,AR,LA, MS,NC,OK, TX	2	Eastern Black Swallowtail
Mock Bishop's-weed, Ribbed (*Ptilimnium costatum*)	AL,AR,GA, LA,NC,OK, TN,TX	2	Eastern Black Swallowtail
Mock Bishop's-weed, Thread-leaf (*Ptilimnium capillaceum*)	All	2	Eastern Black Swallowtail
Modiola, Carolina (*Modiola caroliniana*)	All	2,3,4,5	Common Checkered Skipper
Mugwort, Western (*Artemisia ludoviciana*)	AR,GA,LA, MS,NC,OK, SC,TN,TX	All	Painted Lady American Painted Lady
Mullein, Common (*Verbascum thapsus*)	All	All	Gray Hairstreak
Mustard, Black (*Brassica nigra*)	AL,FL,LA, MS,OK,TN, TX	3,5	Cabbage White
Mustard, Hedge (*Sisymbrium officinale*)	All	All	Cabbage White
	All ext FL	1,2,3,4	Falcate Orangetip
	AR,OK,TX	1,2	Olympia Marblewing
	TX	1	Veined White
Mustard, India (*Brassica juncea*)	All	2,3,4	Cabbage White

Herbs	Range	TX Regions	Butterfly
Mustard, Rocket (*Sisymbrium irio*)	FL,LA,TX	All	Cabbage White
	LA,TX	2,3,4	Falcate Orangetip
Mustard, Tumble (*Sisymbrium altissimum*)	AR,FL,GA, NC,OK,TN, TX	1,2	Checkered White Cabbage White
Mustard, White (*Sinapsis alba*)	AL,MS,NC, TX	4	Cabbage White
Nasturtium (*Tropaeolum majus*)	All	All	Cabbage White
	AL,FL,GA, MS,LA,TX	3	Great Southern White
	TX	1	Veined White
Nettle, Burning (*Urtica urens*)	AL,AR,FL, GA,SC,TX	2,3	Painted Lady Red Admiral
Nettle, Low Spring (*Urtica chamaedryoides*)	All ext NC	2,3,4	Red Admiral
Nettle, Tall Wild (*Urtica dioica*)	All ext FL,SC	1,5	Question Mark Painted Lady Red Admiral
	TX	5	West Coast Lady
Nod-violet, Whorled (*Hybranthus verticillatus*)	OK,TX	All	Variegated Fritillary
Noseburn, Catnip (*Tragia ramosa*)	TX	2,3,4,5	Amymone
Oat, Wild (*Avena fatua*)	AL,FL,LA, TX	1,2,4	Large Wood Nymph
Okra (*Hibiscus esculentus*)	All	All	Gray Hairstreak
Paintbrush, Downy (*Castilleja sessiliflora*)	OK,TX	1,4,5	Buckeye
		1,5	Fulvia Checkerspot
Paintbrush, Prairie (*Castilleja purpurea*)	AR,OK,TX	1,2,3,4	Buckeye
	OK,TX	1	Fulvia Checkerspot
Paintbrush, Texas (*Castilleja indivisa*)	LA,OK,TX	2,3,4	Buckeye
Paintbrush, Woolly (*Castilleja lanata*)	TX	5	Fulvia Checkerspot
Pansy, Field (*Viola rafinesquii*)	All	2	Variegated Fritillary
Pansy, Garden (*Viola × wittrockiana*)	All	All	Variegated Fritillary
Parsley (*Petroselinum crispum*)	All	All	Eastern Black Swallowtail
Parsley, Prairie (*Polytaenia nuttallii*)	AL,AR,LA, MS,OK,TN, TX	2	Eastern Black Swallowtail
Parsnip, Garden (*Pastinaca sativa*)	All	All	Eastern Black Swallowtail

Herbs	Range	TX Regions	Butterfly
Paspalum, Thin (*Paspalum setaceum*)	All	2,3,4	Clouded Skipper
	All ext OK,TN	2,3,4	Whirlabout
Pea, Black-eyed (*Vigna unguiculata*)	AL,FL,GA, LA,MS,SC, TX	2,3	Long-tailed Skipper
Pea, Garden (*Pisum sativum*)	All ext FL	All	Common Sulphur
	All	All	Orange Sulphur Gray Hairstreak Painted Lady
		2,3,4,5	Long-tailed Skipper
Pea, Partridge (*Chamaecrista fasciculata*)	All ext AR,NC, OK,TN	2,3,4	Cloudless Giant Sulphur
	All	1,2,3,4	Little Yellow Sleepy Orange Orange Sulphur
Pea, Scarlet (*Indigofera minuata*)	AL,AR,FL, GA,LA,OK,TX	1,2,3,4	Gray Hairstreak
	AR,LA,OK, TX	3,4	Reakirt's Blue
	TX	3	Funereal Duskywing
Pea, Sensitive (*Chamaecrista nictitans*)	AL,FL,GA, LA,MS,SC, TX	2	Cloudless Giant Sulphur
	All	2	Little Yellow
	TX	2	Sleepy Orange
Peanut (*Arachis hypogaea*)	All	1,2,3	Gray Hairstreak
Pellitory (*Parietaria floridana*)	AL,FL,GA, LA,NC,OK, SC,TX	2,3,4,5	Red Admiral
Pencil-flower (*Stylosanthes biflora*)	AL,FL,GA, LA,MS,SC, TX	3	Fairy Yellow
Pennycress, Field (*Thlaspi arvense*)	All	4	Checkered White
Peppergrass, Field (*Lepidium campestre*)	AR,FL,NC, SC,TN		Cabbage White
Peppergrass, Hairy-pod (*Lepidium lasiocarpum*)	LA,TX	1,3,4,5	Checkered White
Peppergrass, Prairie (*Lepidium densiflorum*)	AL,AR,LA, OK,TN,TX	2,3,4	Falcate Orangetip
		All	Cabbage White Checkered White
	AL,FL,GA, MS,LA,TX	3	Great Southern White

Herbs	Range	TX Regions	Butterfly
Peppergrass, Virginia (*Lepidium virginicum*)	All	All	Checkered White Cabbage White
	AL,FL,GA, MS,LA,TX	3	Great Southern White
	TX	1	Veined White
	All ext FL	2,3,4	Falcate Orangetip
Peppergrass, Western (*Lepidium montanum*)	TX	1,4,5	Checkered White
Pigeon-wings (*Clitoria mariana*)	AL,FL,GA, LA,MS,SC, TX	3	Long-tailed Skipper
	All ext OK,TX		Zarucco Duskywing
	AR,LA,OK, TX	2,4	Funereal Duskywing
	All ext OK		Golden-banded Skipper
	FL,TX	2,3	Lilac-banded Longtail
Pimpernel, Yellow (*Taenidia integerrima*)	AL,AR,GA, LA,NC,OK, SC,TN,TX	2	Eastern Black Swallowtail
Plantain, Black-seed (*Plantago rugelii*)	All	2	Buckeye
Plantain, Common (*Plantago major*)	All	2,4,5	Buckeye
Plantain, English (*Plantago lanceolata*)	All ext FL,LA, OK,TX		Baltimore
	All	2,4,5	Buckeye Painted Lady
Plantain, Pale-seeded (*Plantago virginica*)	All	2,4	Buckeye
Plantain, Wright (*Plantago wrightiana*)	OK,TX	2,4,5	Buckeye
Plumbago, Blue (*Plumbago capensis*)	FL		Cassius Blue
Plumbago, Climbing (*Plumbago scandens*)	TX	3	Marine Blue
Plumegrass, Silver (*Erianthus alopecuroides*)	All	2	Clouded Skipper Delaware Skipper
Poppy-mallow, Tall (*Callirhoe leiocarpa*)	OK,TX	2,3	Gray Hairstreak Common Checkered Skipper
Powdery-thalia (*Thalia dealbata*)	AL,AR,GA, LA,MS,OK, SC,TX	2	Brazilian Skipper
Prairie Clover, Purple (*Dalea purpurea*)	AL,AR,FL, LA,OK,TN, TX	1,2,5	Dogface Butterfly
	TX	5	Reakirt's Blue Marine Blue
Prairie Clover, White (*Dalea candida*)	TX	5	Reakirt's Blue
Pussy's Toes (*Antennaria parlinii*)	GA,MS,NC, OK,SC,TX	2	American Painted Lady

Herbs	Range	TX Regions	Butterfly
Queen Anne's Lace (*Daucus carota*)	All	2,3,4	Eastern Black Swallowtail
Radish, Garden (*Raphanus sativus*)	All	All	Cabbage White Checkered White Painted Lady
	AL,FL,GA, MS,LA,TX	3	Great Southern White
	TX	1	Veined White
Radish, Wild (*Raphanus raphanistrum*)	AL,FL,GA, MS,NC,SC, TN		Cabbage White
Ragweed, Giant (*Ambrosia trifida*)	All ext FL	1,2,4	Gorgone Crescentspot
	TX	2,3,4	Bordered Patch
Rattlepod, (*Crotolaria sagittalis*)	AL,AR,GA, LA,NC,SC, TN,TX	2	Frosted Elfin
	All	2	Wild Indigo Duskywing
Rattlesnake-weed (*Daucus pusillus*)	All	All	Eastern Black Swallowtail
Redtop (*Tridens flavus*)	All	2	Crossline Skipper
		1,2,4	Large Wood Nymph
		2	Little Glassywing
Reed, Common (*Phragmites australis*)	AL,AR,FL, GA,LA,MS, NC,TN,TX	2,3	Broad-winged Skipper
Rice (*Oryza sativa*)	AL,FL,GA, LA,MS,OK, SC,TN,TX	2,3	Eufala Skipper Least Skipperling Long-winged Skipper
Rockcress (*Arabis glabra*)	AR,NC,TN		Cabbage White Checkered White Falcate Orangetip
	AR		Olympia Marblewing
Rockcress, Smooth (*Arabis laevigata*)	AR,OK		Olympia Marblewing
	AL,AR,GA, NC,OK,SC, TN		Falcate Orangetip
Rockcress, Green (*Arabis missouriensis*)	AR,OK		Olympia Marblewing
Rockcress, Lyre-Leaf (*Arabis lyrata*)	GA,MS,NC, TN		Falcate Orangetip
Rue (*Ruta chalapensis*)	All	1,3,4,5	Eastern Black Swallowtail Giant Swallowtail
Rue, Common (*Ruta graveolens*)	All	All	Eastern Black Swallowtail Giant Swallowtail
Ruellia (*Ruellia occidentalis*)	TX	3,4	Texan Crescentspot
		3	White Peacock
Ruellia, Carolina (*Ruellia caroliniensis*)	AL,FL,GA, LA,TX	2	Texan Crescentspot

Herbs	Range	TX Regions	Butterfly
Ruellia, Mexican (*Ruellia brittoniana*)	AL,FL,GA, LA,MS,TX	3,4	Texan Crescentspot
Ruellia, Violet (*Ruellia nudiflora*)	TX	2,3,4	Buckeye
		3	White Peacock
Ryegrass (*Lolium perenne*)	OK,TX	4	Green Skipper
Saltbush, Four-wing (*Atrilex canescens*)	TX	1,3,5	Saltbush Sootywing
		1,3,4,5	Western Pygmy Blue
Saltgrass (*Distichlis spicata*)	AL,FL,GA, LA,MS,NA, SC,TX	2,3	Salt Marsh Skipper
Sawgrass (*Cladium jamaicensis*)	AL,FL,GA, MS,NC,SC		Sawgrass Skipper
Scale-seed, Forked (*Spermolepis divaricata*)	AL,AR,FL, GA,LA,MS, NC,SC,TX	2	Eastern Black Swallowtail
Sea Oats, Inland (*Chasmanthium latifolium*)	All ext FL,TX		Northern Pearly Eye
	All ext FL	2	Pepper-and-salt Skipper
	All	1,2,4	Roadside Skipper
	All ext FL,NC	2	Bell's Roadside Skipper
	AR,OK,TN		Arkansas Roadside Skipper
	AR,OK,TX	1,2,4	Bronze Roadside Skipper
Sea-Rocket, American (*Cakile edentula*)	AL,FL,GA, NC,SC		Cabbage White
			Checkered White
	AL,FL,GA		Great Southern White
Sedge, Cedar (*Carex planostachys*)	TX	4	Apache Skipper
Sedge, Giant (*Rhynchospora inundata*)	AL,FL,GA, MS,SC,NC, TN		Appalachian Eyed Brown
Sedge, Thin-scale (*Carex hyalinolepis*)	All	2	Sedge Skipper
	All ext OK	2	Scarce Swamp Skipper
Senna, Coffee (*Cassia occidentalis*)	All	2,3,4	Cloudless Giant Sulphur
			Little Yellow
			Sleepy Orange
Senna, Maryland (*Senna marilandica*)	All ext AR,NC, OK,TN	2	Cloudless Giant Sulphur
	All	2	Little Yellow
			Sleepy Orange
Senna, Sickle-pod (*Cassia obtusifolia*)	All	2,3	Cloudless Giant Sulphur
			Sleepy Orange
Senna, Texas (*Chamaecrista flexuosa*)	TX	3	Tailed Orange
Sesbania (*Sesbania exaltata*)	All ext TX		Orange Sulphur
	All ext OK,TX		Zarucco Duskywing
	OK		Funereal Duskywing

237

Herbs	Range	TX Regions	Butterfly
Sesbania, Drummond (*Sesbania drummondii*)	AR,FL,TX	2,3,4	Gray Hairstreak
	TX	2,3,4	Funereal Duskywing Zarucco Duskywing
Sesbania, Bladder-Pod (*Sesbania vescicaria*)	AL,FL,GA, LA,MS,NC, SC		
Sesuvium, Winged (*Sesuvium verrucosum*)	AR,OK,TX	All	Western Pygmy Blue
Shepherd's Purse (*Capsella bursa-pastoris*)	All	All	Checkered White
	AL,FL,GA, LA,MS,TX	3	Great Southern White
Sickle-pod (*Arabis canadensis*)	AR,OK,TX	2	Olympia Marblewing
	All ext FL	2	Falcate Orangetip
Sida, Arrow-leaf (*Sida rhombifolia*)	AL,AR,FL, GA,LA,MS, NC,SC,TN, TX	2,3	Common Checkered Skipper
	AL,FL,LA, MS,TX	2,3	Tropical Checkered Skipper
Sida, Prickly (*Sida spinosa*)	All	2,3	Common Checkered Skipper
Sida, Spreading (*Sida abutifolia*)	FL,TX	All	Common Checkered Skipper
	TX	3,4,5	Desert Checkered Skipper
Sida, Violet (*Meximalva filipes*)	TX	3,4	Common Streaky Skipper Lavinia Skipper
Sneezeweed (*Helenium autumnale*)	All	1,2,4	Dwarf Yellow
Sneezeweed, Purple (*Helenium flexuosum*)	All	2	Dwarf Yellow
Sorrel, Sheep (*Rumex acetosella*)	AR,GA,NC, SC,TN		American Copper
	All ext FL	4	Mourning Cloak
Sour Clover, Yellow (*Melilotus indicus*)	AR,LA,MS, TX	3,4,5	Reakirt's Blue
	All ext TN	All	Eastern Tailed Blue
Soybean (*Glycine max*)	All ext AR,OK	1,2,3	Orange Sulphur
	All	1,2,3	Dogface Butterfly Painted Lady
Spectacle-pod (*Wislizenia refracta*)	TX	1,5	Checkered White
Speedwell, Water (*Veronica anagallis-aquatica*)	AL,AR,FL, NC,OK,TN, TX	2	Buckeye
Spider Flower (*Cleome hassleriana*)	AL,FL,GA, MS,LA,TX	3	Great Southern White
Spiderling, Erect (*Boerhaavia erecta*)	All	1,2,3,4	Variegated Fritillary
Spiderling, Scarlet (*Boerhaavia diffusa*)	AL,FL,MS, TX	2,3,4,5	Variegated Fritillary

Herbs	Range	TX Regions	Butterfly
Spring-cress (*Cardamine rhomboidea*)	All ext FL	2	Falcate Orangetip
Star-thistle, Barnaby (*Centaurea solstitialis*)	FL,NC, TN,TX	2,4	Painted Lady
Stenandrium (*Stenandrium barbatum*)	TX	5	Definite Patch
Stylisma, Purple (*Stylisma aquatica*)	All ext OK,TN	2	Golden-banded Skipper
Sunflower, Annual (*Helianthus annuus*)	All ext FL	1,2,4	Gorgone Crescentspot
	All	All	Painted Lady
		2,4	Silvery Crescentspot
	TX	2,3,4,5	Bordered Patch
Sunflower, Prairie (*Helianthus petiolaris*)	AR,LA,NC, OK,SC,TX	1,2,4	Gorgone Crescentspot
Sunflower, Stiff (*Helianthus rigidus*)	All ext FL	2	Gorgone Crescentspot
Swan-flower (*Aristolochia erecta*)	TX	2,3,4	Pipevine Swallowtail
Sweet Clover, White (*Melilotus albus*)	All	All	Common Sulphur
			Orange Sulphur
			Gray Hairstreak
		1,2,4,5	Eastern Tailed Blue
	AR,LA,MS, TN,TX	3,4	Reakirt's Blue
	TX	1,5	Acmon Blue
Sweet Clover, Yellow (*Melilotus officinalis*)	All	2	Spring Azure
		1,2,4,5	Eastern Tailed Blue
		4,5	Orange Sulphur
	TX	4,5	Reakirt's Blue
Switchgrass (*Panicum virgatum*)	AL,AR,GA, NC,OK,SC, TN		Leonardus Skipper
	All	All	Delaware Skipper
Tansy-mustard (*Descurainia sophia*)	AL,AR,GA, NC,OK,SC, TX	1,4,5	Cabbage White
			Checkered White
Tansy-mustard, Pinnate (*Descurainia pinnata*)	AR,OK,TX	1,2	Olympia Marblewing
	TX	All	Checkered White
Tephrosia, Lindheimer (*Tephrosia lindheimeri*)	TX	3	White-striped Longtail
Thelesperma (*Thelesperma filifolium*)	AR,MS,OK, TX	All	Dwarf Yellow
Thistle, Bull (*Cirsium vulgare*)	All	4	Painted Lady
Thistle, Canadian (*Cirsium arvense*)	AL,NC,SC, TN		Painted Lady
Thistle, Field (*Cirsium discolor*)	AL,AR,GA, LA,MS,NC, SC,TN		Painted Lady

Herbs	Range	TX Regions	Butterfly
Thistle, Tall *(Cirsium ultissimum)*	AR		Swamp Metalmark
	All	2	Painted Lady
Thistle, Texas *(Cirsium texanum)*	OK,TX	All	Painted Lady
Thistle, Yellow *(Cirsium horridulum)*	All ext AR,OK, TN	2	Little Metalmark
	All	2,3	Painted Lady
Three-awn, Arrowfeather *(Aristida purpurascens)*	All	2	Dixie Skipper
Tick-clover, Hoary *(Desmodium canescens)*	All	2	Eastern Tailed Blue Hoary Edge
	AL,FL,GA, LA,MS,SC		Long-Tailed Skipper
Tick-clover, Large-bract *(Desmodium cuspidatum)*	All	2	Hoary Edge
Tick-clover, Little-leaf *(Desmodium ciliare)*	All	2	Hoary Edge Southern Cloudywing
Tick-clover, Maryland *(Desmodium marilandicum)*	All	2	Eastern Tailed Blue Silver-spotted Skipper
Tick-clover, Prostrate *(Desmodium rotundifolium)*	All	2	Eastern Cloudywing Northern Cloudywing Hoary Edge Silver-spotted Skipper Southern Cloudywing
Tick-clover, Showy *(Desmodium canadense)*	AR,LA,OK, TN		Gray Hairstreak Hoary Edge Northern Cloudywing
Tick-clover, Trailing *(Desmodium glabellum)*	All ext OK	2	Hoary Edge Northern Cloudywing Silver-spotted Skipper
Tick-clover, Twisted stem *(Desmodium tortuosus)*	FL,TX	2	Lilac-banded Longtail
Toadflax *(Linaria canadensis)*	All	All	Buckeye
Tridens, Rough *(Tridens muticus)*	OK,TX	1,4,5	Green Skipper
Tuberose, Texas *(Manfreda maculosa)*	TX	3	Manfreda Giant Skipper
Tube-tongue, Hairy *(Siphonoglossa pilosella)*	TX	3,5 3,4,5	Painted Crescentspot Dymas Checkerspot Elada Checkerspot Texan Crescentspot Vesta Crescentspot
Turtlehead, White *(Chelone glabra)*	AL,AR,GA, MS,NC,SC, TN		Baltimore
Velvet-bur *(Priva lappulacea)*	TX	3	Potrillo Skipper

Herbs	Range	TX Regions	Butterfly
Velvetleaf (*Wissadula amplissima*)	TX	3	Laviana Skipper
			Texas Powdered Skipper
		3,5	Common Streaky Skipper
		5	Scarce Streaky Skipper
Vetch, Carolina (*Vicia caroliniana*)	AL,AR,GA, NC,OK,SC, TN		Silvery Blue
Vetch, Common (*Vicia sativa*)	All	2	Eastern Tailed Blue
			Orange Sulphur
Vetch, Deer Pea (*Vicia ludoviciana*)	AL,AR,FL, LA,MS,OK, TX	2,3,4	Little Yellow
	OK,TX	1,2,3,4	Funereal Duskywing
Vetch, Hairy (*Vicia villosa*)	All	2	Eastern Tailed Blue
Vetch, Leavenworth (*Vicia leavenworthi*)	AR,OK,TX	1,2,3,4	Dogface Butterfly
Vetch, Tufted (*Vicia cracca*)	AR,GA,NC, TN		Eastern Tailed Blue
			Common Sulphur
			Orange Sulphur
Vetchling, Marsh (*Lathyrus palustris*)	GA,NC,TN		Silver-spotted Skipper
Violet (*Viola* spp.)	All	All	Variegated Fritillary
Violet, Arrowleaf (*Viola sagittata*)	All	2	Variegated Fritillary
	AL,GA,NC, SC,TN		Aphrodite Fritillary
Violet, Lanceleaf (*Viola lanceolata*)	AL,GA,NC, SC,TN		Aphrodite Fritillary
	AR,NC,OK,TN		Regal Fritillary
	TX	2	Variegated Fritillary
Violet, Primrose (*Viola primulifolia*)	AL,GA,NC, SC,TN		Aphrodite Fritillary
	All	2	Variegated Fritillary
Violet, Round-leaf (*Viola rotundifolia*)	GA,NC,SC, TN		Great Spangled Fritillary
Violet, Sister (*Viola sororia*)	All	2,4	Variegated Fritillary
	All ext LA,TX		Great Spangled Fritillary
	AL,GA,NC, SC,TN		Aphrodite Fritillary
	AR,NC,OK, TN		Regal Fritillary
	NC,SC,TN		Meadow Fritillary
Violet, Smooth White (*Viola macloskeyi*)	NC,SC,TN		Meadow Fritillary
Water-cress (*Rorippa nasturtium-aquaticum*)	All	1,2,4,5	Cabbage White
Water-hyssop, Coastal (*Bacopa monnieri*)	AL,FL,GA, LA,MS,NC, OK,SC,TX	3	White Peacock

Herbs	Range	TX Regions	Butterfly
Water-parsnip (*Sium suava*)	All ext MS,SC	2	Eastern Black Swallowtail
Water-willow (*Justicia americana*)	AL,FL,GA, LA,MS,TX	3	Texan Crescentspot
Water-willow, Runyon (*Justicia runyonii*)	TX	3	Texan Crescentspot
Wedelia, Hairy (*Wedelia hispida*)	TX	3,4	Bordered Patch
Wheatgrass, Western (*Elytrigia smithii*)	TX	5	Golden Skipper
Wild Buckwheat, Sorrell (*Eriogonum polycladon*)	TX	5	Rita Blue
Wild Indigo (*Baptisia bracteata*)	AL,AR,GA, LA,NC,OK, SC,TX	2,3	Wild Indigo Duskywing
Wild Indigo, Blue (*Baptisia australis*)	AR,GA,NC, OK,TN,TX	2	Frosted Elfin Wild Indigo Duskywing
Wild Indigo, Bushy (*Baptisia tinctoria*)	AR,GA,MS, NC,SC,TN		Common Sulphur
	AL,GA,NC, SC,TN		Frosted Elfin
	AL,FL,GA, MS,SC,TN		Eastern Tailed Blue Wild Indigo Duskywing
Wild Indigo, Nuttall (*Baptisia nuttalliana*)	AR,LA,TX	2	Frosted Elfin
Wild Indigo, White (*Baptisia alba*)	All	2	Wild Indigo Duskywing
	AR,LA,TX	2	Frosted Elfin
Wildrice, Southern (*Zizanopsis miliaceae*)	All ext AR,OK	2,3	Broad-Winged Skipper
	All	2,3,4	Least Skipperling
	GA,NC,SC		Rare Skipper
Wildrye, Canada (*Elymus canadensis*)	AL,AR,GA, MS,NC,OK, TX	2	Zabulon Skipper
Witchgrass, Fall (*Leptoloma cognatum*)	AL,FL,GA, MS,TX	2	Dotted Skipper
Wood-nettle, Canadian (*Laportea canadensis*)	All ext TX		Comma Red Admiral
Wormwood (*Artemisia absinthium*)	All	All	American Painted Lady
Yellow-rocket, Garden (*Barbarea vulgaris*)	AL,AR,GA, NC,SC,TN		Cabbage White Checkered White
	All ext FL,OK, TX		Falcate Orangetip

CHAPTER NINE

Nectar Plants

Here are the best nectar plants for the South. Nectar and the plants which produce it are the material which forms the very foundation of butterfly attracting. A knowledge of good nectar-producing plants is most important, and a few familiar plants known to be good nectar producers are shown and described here; both wild and cultivated plants are included.

See Chapter Eight for explanations of the terms in each description.

In the nectar plant list following the descriptions you will notice that some of our most common plants, such as the Evening Primrose, Coreopsis, and Poppy, are not included. These plants, while they seem to have the characteristics a butterfly wants, evidently lack the thing most important—nectar. Remember, butterflies have to use what is there. So look around before gathering seeds or plants for transplanting: Even though butterflies may be nectaring on a plant, it may not be a preferred nectar source. However, if several other plants are also in flower and butterflies are still coming repeatedly to that particular species, it's a good bet it is a good nectar producer and a preferred choice.

Some of the plants listed here are not desirable garden plants. They are listed to show that in the wild they are heavily used nectar sources. If these plants are already present on or near your property, you might want to let them remain.

Trees

CHASTE TREE (*Vitex agnus-castus*)
Vervain Family (*Verbenaceae*)

Bloom Period: June-September
Range: All except Arkansas, Oklahoma, Tennessee
  Texas: Throughout
Height: 10-20 feet
Class: Escape

Deciduous, long-lived large shrub or small tree, usually with more than one trunk from the base, and broad, spreading, or loose in general outline. The leaves are divided fanlike into three to seven narrow leaflets that are dark green on upper surface, a cool gray beneath. Both twigs and leaves are strongly but pleasantly aromatic when crushed. Numerous small lilac to lavender fragrant flowers form slender spikes terminally as well as in upper leaf axils.

Cultivation: Although not native, the Chaste Tree is widely planted, and in many regions it has escaped and may be found in various "wild" situations. It may even reseed under such situations but never becomes a problem.

The Chaste Tree tolerates a wide variety of soils but requires plenty of summer heat for the most richly colored and profuse bloom, so plant this one in an open spot in full sun. Give it a well-drained site with rather poor soil in your garden and do not overwater. Fertilizing sparingly in the spring with a high-phosphorous fertilizer increases bloom production. Extra-rich soil and too much moisture result in lush foliage but only a few pale-colored flowers low in nectar. New plants may be started from tip cuttings or easily obtained from nurseries or catalogs.

The Chaste Tree is late to put out foliage in the spring and in some areas may be killed to ground level during extremely cold winters. Severe pruning only enhances its shape; if you cut it to within six inches of the ground in late winter or early spring, it quickly resprouts and forms new blossoming stems. New stems easily attain three to five feet the first year before flowering. In this respect the Chaste Tree is quite similar to the Butterfly Bush and can be treated as a herbaceous perennial if the shrub form fits your garden scheme the best. In this form it makes a beautiful hedge or "living fence." It also works well in borders when kept small. If not pruned and in areas where it does not freeze back each year, it may obtain small tree size. The lower branches can be trimmed into a tree form to make a lovely specimen planting. When trimmed this way, the Chaste Tree is especially nice used for shade in a small yard.

Note: A large, healthy potted plant from a nursery should flower the first or second year. In making your selection, you might want to start with only one or two plants to make sure they are good nectar producers before making more final choices. Blue- or purple-flowered plants will probably attract more butterflies than white-flowered ones.

DESERT WILLOW (*Chilopsis linearis*)
Trumper-creeper Family (*Bignoniaceae*)

Bloom Period: April-June
Range: Texas
    Texas: 1, 4, 5, (2, 3)
Height: 6-30 feet
Class: Native

Native shrub or small tree, usually with several trunks from the base, the deciduous leaves long, slender, and willowlike. The large, orchid-like flowers are sweetly fragrant, loosely clustered in large, terminal panicles. Flowers do not last long but appear after each rain. Flowers are replaced by long, slender seed pods, which remain dangling from the branches and aid in identifying this tree long after the flowers are gone.

Cultivation: You can grow the Desert Willow from seed, cuttings, or nursery transplants. If you are trying to raise plants from seed, gather the seed pods as soon as they are dry and brown colored. Remove the seeds from the pods; when they are completely dry, store in the refrigerator until spring. Before planting, soak the seeds in water for a few hours. Semihardwood cuttings can be taken in late summer and should root in two or three weeks. Transplant them to the garden in late fall or carry them over until spring.

Whether from seed or cuttings, the plant grows rapidly and will produce flowers even when very young. This is another shrub which tolerates drought conditions but responds to an occasional watering and a light application of fertilizer. Planted in full sun, the Desert Willow tolerates various soils but prefers limestone soils. It demands good drainage. In the western and northern portions of its range, it may occasionally be broken or damaged by snow or wind, so in these areas it is best to use it in protected places, such as the south side of buildings, fences, or taller growing trees or shrubs.

With its open, somewhat sprawling growth habit, the Desert Willow is at its best when used at the end of a border or as a specimen planting. In areas where it is not bothered by freezing, trim the lower branches for it to eventually form an airy, graceful tree shape. If you desire a more shrubby shape, prune back the plant severely; it actually produces more flowers when so treated.

MIMOSA (*Albizia julibrissin*)
Legume Family (*Fabaceae*)

Bloom Period: April-August
Range: All
    Texas: 1, 2, 3, 4
Height: 15-25 feet
Class: Cultivar/Escape

Hardy to semihardy, tropical-appearing deciduous tree with drooping branches. Leaves large, twice divided into numerous tiny leaflets, and appearing fernlike. The leaves fold at night. Branches tipped with large clusters of delicate, fragrant, fluffy pink flowers. Both the leaves and the flower clusters occur on the upper sides of the branches, giving this tree an exotic look.

Cultivation: This native of Asia is not particularly choosy as to soils but does like adequate moisture. An addition of iron to regular feeding produces more and darker colored flowers. It is at its very best in areas of high summer heat, so it does well practically all over the South. It is one

245

Mimosa

of the few cultivated trees which can tolerate both drought and air pollution quite well.

It is very easy to get the Mimosa started from seed. It also reseeds easily and can often be seen growing as escapes along roadsides or about trash dumps where trimmed limbs and branches have been discarded. Young saplings may be dug either in the spring or fall for planting in the home garden, or potted plants are usually available at local nurseries.

The branches of the Mimosa have a tendency to droop somewhat, so trim off lower limbs at the trunk when planted near a traffic area. The open branching and lacy leaves of this tree allow filtered sunlight through and do not kill lawn grasses as most shade trees do. If you trim the branches high, you may use this as a specimen tree in a bed with low shrubs and perennials planted beneath. Unfortunately, the Mimosa is relatively short-lived and the wood is brittle; sometimes large limbs are lost to storms or high winds. It is also often attacked by a borer which kills the tree if not treated.

The limbs of the Mimosa are sometimes cut

about halfway back, but this totally destroys the natural beauty of this tree and also makes it more susceptible to attack by insects and fungus diseases. If the Mimosa is never trimmed, the growth of the branches naturally slows down, and the tree forms an absolutely beautiful sight with the branches arching almost to the ground and smothered in feathery pink blossoms. The unique, rather flat-topped or gently mounded shape of its branches makes a perfect canopy for a patio. The undulating form and almost solid mat of flowers held above the foliage make this tree espcially nice when viewed from a second-story window, balcony, or deck.

Note: When the Mimosa starts opening its fragrant pink flowers in early spring, butterflies flock to its readily available nectar and continue to work the tree throughout the day. The nectar is so plentiful at times that you will even see Hummingbirds and Orchard Orioles dipping their beaks into the flowers. In late afternoon the fragrance becomes stronger, making this a desirable tree for placing near a porch or patio.

Shrubs

BEE-BRUSH (*Aloysia gratissima*)
Verbena Family (*Verbenaceae*)

Bloom Period: March-December
Range: Texas
  Texas: 3, 4, 5
Height: To 9 feet
Class: Native

A slender, much-branched, usually deciduous shrub, the branches gray, almost square, and noticeably brittle. Leaves are small, opposite, wonderfully aromatic when touched. Leaves often with a bundle of smaller ones in the axils.

Racemes of fragrant, widely spaced, yellow-throated white flowers are borne from the leaf axils, the racemes several and forming bouquetlike panicles.

Cultivation: This plant is easy to transplant from the wild, or you may start it from either seed or cuttings. Within a few years Bee-brush usually forms a nice colony or a small thicket if left unattended. New, unwanted plants can easily be uprooted. In the wild state the shrubs may become a little unruly, but this should present no problem in the garden. If they begin to get out of bounds, simply cut them to the ground, and they will respond by putting forth a multitude of new stems and growing six to eight feet high the first year. Trim periodically anyway for best flower production. By trimming in late winter, Bee-brush can easily be kept to desired height and size in the garden.

Plant in full sun and poor soil, keep it on the dry side, and watch the profusion of flowers which appear after each rain. This is a shrub to use in the driest and poorest soil of the garden; if the soil is gravelly or rocky, the plants will be even happier.

Bee-brush

Note: The flowers of Bee-brush have a strong fragrance similar to vanilla and are a great attractant to many species of butterflies. Bees also find it highly desirable, and in its natural range it is considered one of the best nectar plants for the production of honey.

BIRD-OF-PARADISE (*Caesalpinia gilliesii*)
Legume Family (*Fabaceae*)

Bloom Period: May-September
Range: Oklahoma, Texas
   Texas: Throughout
Height: To 8 feet
Class: Naturalized

Delicate, slender-branched shrub with ferny, blue-green foliage. Leaves twice divided into numerous leaflets. Interestingly shaped yellow flowers numerous, in large terminal clusters. Long, red stamens protrude conspicuously, curving upward from the base of the petals. Both the foliage and the flowers of this plant are rather unpleasantly scented.

Cultivation: An almost perfect small shrub for the garden, the Bird-of-paradise should be one of the first considered for your butterfly plantings. A native of Argentina, it has escaped cultivation and is often found growing along with the native species, especially in the western and southwestern portions of Texas. It is a very common plant in Mexico.

Easy to grow and hardy, it is now being offered by most nurseries which carry native plants. It is also easy to propagate from seed. Seeds are usually produced in abundance, with

247

the pods maturing in the lower portion of the raceme as flowers continue to open at the tip.

If you plant seeds indoors in early spring and transplant the seedlings to your garden after the last frost, it would not be unusual to have flowers by fall. By the second year the plant should produce a wealth of exotic blooms, with flowering increasing each year. Place the young plant in full sun in a well-drained location, watering in with a mild solution of root stimulator. Fertilize sparingly a couple of times during the growing season for added growth and bloom. Many of the seeds which fall to the ground will germinate, and there will usually be a number of young seedlings around the mother plant each year.

Bird-of-paradise is very hardy and not generally bothered by insects or diseases. Its worst enemy is too much moisture or shade, which can cause it to become weak and spindly and with few or no flowers. Under such adverse conditions, it may also become infested with red spider mites. The best solution is to move the plant to an open, sunny, well-drained spot in the garden.

BUTTERFLY BUSH (*Buddleia davidii* cultivar "Charming Summer") Vervain Family (*Verbenaceae*)

Bloom Period: May-Frost
Range: All
   Texas: Throughout
Height: To 12 feet
Class: Cultivar

Deciduous or semi-evergreen, widely spreading shrub with slender, arching branches. Thick, felty leaves dull green on upper surface, dull silvery beneath. Numerous small, fragrant flowers are densely compacted into large, thick, terminal, often drooping racemes.

Cultivation: A native of China, the Butterfly Bush is an exceptionally hardy, easily cultivated shrub blooming the first year after planting. It requires little care after becoming established. Plant in soil liberally enriched with peat moss, leaf mold, or compost. The plants do not like to be crowded, so place them at least six to ten feet apart to allow them plenty of room to spread out. The plants will remain healthy and blooming with a light fertilizing in early spring with 5-10-10 to encourage blooms and adequate moisture during the hot, dry summer months. The Butterfly Bush blooms best on new wood and should be cut back to three or four buds from the base of the old wood (approximately ten inches above the ground) in early February or at least before spring growth begins. However, unpruned shrubs begin flowering earlier in the spring, so if you have several, you might want to leave at least one unpruned, rotating the pruning each year. Pruning keeps the plant at a lower height and spread of around six feet. It does not put forth new growth until late spring, but once started, it grows rapidly.

This plant can be grown in almost any soil, but it needs good drainage and full sun. A regular addition of iron may be necessary to prevent iron chlorosis if the water in your area is alkaline. In the hotter, drier regions, the Butterfly Bush may occasionally be bothered by red spider mites. Treat with one of the organic methods discussed in this book.

New plants are easy to obtain from semihardwood cuttings taken anytime from late summer to late fall using normal rooting methods. Root the cuttings directly in your garden in a sheltered area or in a coldframe.

Note: I know of no better cultivated shrubs for attracting butterflies to the home garden than the Butterfly Bushes. They are usually prolific bloomers, producing masses of flowers throughout the season. Butterflies will not leave them. There will be from one to several species feeding almost constantly. The racemes are sturdy enough to hold the weight of the larger butterflies, such as the Fritillaries and the Swallowtails, which often perch, nectaring at length. At times there will be so many butter-flies feeding around these plants that they will actually jostle one another for the best nectar spots. The wonderful honeylike fragrance is very strong, especially in late evening and early night, so the Butterfly Bush is especially nice planted near a window, porch, or patio.

There are may cultivars of *B. davidii*, with flower colors ranging from white through pinks, blues, and purples. Butterflies generally seem to like the lavender or purple shades the best.

BUTTON-BUSH (*Cephalanthus occidentalis*)
Madder Family (*Rubiaceae*)

Bloom Period: June-September
Range: All
    Texas: Throughout
Height: 3-15 feet
Class: Native

Medium to large deciduous shrub, often with few to several trunks from the base. Long, shiny, dark green leaves may be solitary, opposite, or in whorls of three or four along slender branches. The numerous fragrant, creamy white to pinkish flowers with conspicuously protruding stamens form perfect spheres.

Cultivation: In the wild, Button-bush is always found in areas of plentiful moisture or even actually growing in shallow water, but it tolerates much drier conditions under cultivation. For best flower production, it still needs more water than the other shrubs in your garden, so plant it near a dripping water faucet or where extra water can be provided with no problem. It is a hardy shrub and grows in almost any soil. Plant the Button-bush in sun or semishade, but it produces more flowers in the sun. It is ideal when used in front of taller shrubs or trees to form an "edge" effect.

Plants may be obtained from cuttings or may occasionally be offered by nurseries. Extract ripe seeds from the dried balls in late fall and sow them immediately in a moist, sandy site. You can later transfer young seedlings to permanent locations in your garden. If you dig from the wild, it is best to dig very small plants in order to get good root systems. Unless you have a very large space, only one or two plants are needed be-cause these shrubs become quite wide and require a lot of growing space. Also, they eventually root-sprout, providing more plants for your use. Under normal growing conditions, the Button-bush remains a large shrub six to eight feet high and wide, but it can become treelike with age. As it gets older, the trunks become dark, gnarled, and very picturesque.

If you decide you would like a tree form, select one, two, or three of the strongest, straightest trunks, trim all the other trunks to ground level, then trim the lower branches to the height you want. This will never become a real tree, so do not trim the branches too high.

Note: When this plant is in flower, the fragrant balls are absolutely covered with butterflies and other insects. The butterflies become so engrossed in feeding that you can sometimes pick them up by their wings. It seems to be a favorite with all species but especially Hairstreaks, Skippers, and Swallowtails.

FALSE INDIGO (*Amorpha fruticosa*)
Legume Family (*Fabaceae*)

Bloom Period: April-June
Range: All
   Texas: Throughout
Height: 2-15 feet
Class: Native

An upright, slender-stemmed shrub or small tree, often with several stems and forming a clump. Many small, opposite leaflets form interesting ferny leaves up to nine inches long. Numerous small, dark purple flowers with protruding, bright orange anthers are densely compacted into long, gracefully tapering racemes.

Cultivation: The False Indigo may be propagated by either seed, cuttings, or transplanting. Obtain the dark brown, shiny seeds by gathering the pods in late summer or early fall or as soon as they turn yellowish brown. Remove the seeds and place them on an open tray or in an open paper bag for a few days. Store them in the refrigerator until ready to plant.

Plant the seeds in either fall or early spring. For spring planting, first soak the seeds in hot water for ten or fifteen minutes. Sow where the plants are to remain, covering the seeds to a depth of one-half inch. After seedlings are up and growing well, you may transplant them if necessary, but do so as soon as possible, for this plant quickly develops a very long taproot. Seeds germinate better if sown after the ground has become thoroughly warm.

Take softwood cuttings anytime from late spring through summer. Make the cut just below a node, and root in sand. Plants from cuttings grow rapidly, often attaining a height of six to eight feet the first year from fall-rooted cuttings.

Mature stands of False Indigo usually have numerous stems, which can usually be separated for transplanting in either spring, fall, or winter. After planting, trim the stems back two thirds and water in with a root stimulator. Keep moist but not soggy until new growth appears, and then give them a mild solution of soluble fertilizer. Once the plants start growing well, thin the clumps by trimming, leaving five or six stems for a more shaply grouping.

Found naturally in very mesic habitats, such as along stream banks, edges of wet meadows or marshes, or along roadside ditches, the False Indigo does quite well in a garden if given just a bit of extra moisture. It thrives better and requires less care and attention if used with other moisture-demanding plants in a special area or bed of its own. It is not too choosy as to soil, but good garden loam produces more and better growth and flowering. False Indigo also produces more and darker colored flowers in full sun, so use this plant in open, exposed areas, such as at the back of perennial borders, along moist woodland edges, or as a specimen planting. False Indigo should be placed somewhat away from perennials as it is a rather aggressive surface feeder.

False Indigo has become such a favorite for the home garden that it is now often available as a container-grown plant at nurseries offering native stock.

Note: False Indigo is also the larval food plant for the Dogface Buttterfly, Hoary Edge, Silver-spotted Skipper, and Gray Hairstreak.

GLOSSY ABELIA (*Abelia × grandiflora*)
Honeysuckle Family (*Caprifoliaceae*)

Bloom Period: June-October
Range: All
  Texas: Throughout
Height: To 8 feet
Class: Cultivar

Hardy, evergreen to semideciduous shrub with graceful, arching branches. Leaves small, conspicuously shiny, bronze when young and again in the fall. The white to pale pink flowers are tubular or bell-shaped, fragrant, occurring in terminal clusters and from the leaf axils along the branches.

Cultivation: The shrub we know as Glossy Abelia is a cross between two species, *chinensis* and *uniflora*. It is a very hardy, fast-growing shrub with no significant insect or disease problems. It tolerates neglect and grows in shade, but for the healthiest plant producing the most flowers, give it a moist but well-drained, humus-enriched soil in full sun. It takes some drought but grows much more vigorously with adequate but normal watering. This shrub does not like wind; in western and northern areas it grows and blooms better if planted where protection is offered by a building or a fence of some solid material. Flowers appear on both old and new wood, so prune at any time, although spring is generally best. New plants may be started from the trimmed branches. This is a plant commonly offered by nurseries and mail-order catalogs, so getting nice, well-developed plants is no problem.

Glossy Abelia is often used as hedges and screens, where it is severely trimmed, but it is much more impressive as a specimen plant. When used as such and left unpruned, it forms a beautiful, large mound, with slender drooping or "weeping" branches covered with dense, lush foliage and a wealth of flowers. A long hedge of unpruned or moderately trimmed plants being avidly used by butterflies is truly a wonderous sight.

Note: The nectar-rich flowers of Glossy Abelia are especially liked by Swallowtails, who spend much time flying lazily about the bush, then periodically sailing in to nectar long and contentedly on some choice cluster.

HOARY AZALEA (*Rhododendron canescens*)
Heath Family (*Ericaceae*)

Bloom Period: March-May
Range: All
  Texas: 2
Height: To 10 feet
Class: Native

Upright, many-branched but open, deciduous perennial shrub, flowering before or just as first leaves put forth. The pale pink to dark rose, trumpet-shaped flowers grow in loose clusters at the ends of the branches, often in great profusion. The flowers are richly fragrant, and the scent from a few plants in bloom is almost intoxicating.

Cultivation: Hoary Azaleas may be started from seed but are a little difficult and require more care than most plants. The easiest and fastest method of propagation is by taking four-to six-inch cuttings from new growth in the spring. Crush the cut ends of the cuttings, dip in rooting hormone, and pot in a peat and per-

251

Hoary Azalea

lite mixture. Place cuttings under a glass jar or a plastic tent and mist occasionally until rooted. Remove the covering often to give the cuttings fresh air.

Simple rooting of the cuttings is not sufficient for survival. The cuttings would die the following spring unless new top growth has been forced by frequent additions of a weak-strength fertilizer throughout the past season.

Healthy, well-established plants of Hoary Azalea are offered by some nurseries, and this is by far the best means of obtaining plants. Do not try digging these plants from the wild—they are much too uncommon now due to extensive local habitat destruction. Even if they were plentiful, they simply do not transplant well.

To keep your plants happy and growing well, place them in open semishade—ideally beneath tall pines and high-branched hardwoods. Place them in a raised bed to ensure the good drainage they require, and work plenty of humus-rich organic matter into the soil. Half-rotted pine needles are excellent for this, for these plants thrive best in an acid soil. If pine needles are not available, use leaf mold, rotten sawdust (from pines if possible), or peat moss. Peat moss is the best to use in a new planting as it absorbs and retains the moisture which is so essential to Azaleas. Add plenty of sharp sand if the soil is not naturally sandy. Another method is to spread a layer of sand one or two inches deep on top of a

prepared bed, placing the plants on top of the sand and filling around the roots with a mixture of sand, bark, and peat. Azaleas are very shallow rooted, so good mulching is mandatory for their survival. After planting, spread a four- or five-inch layer of pine needles, pine bark, or coarsely shredded cedar bark around the shrub and well beyond its branches. A mixture of materials is preferable since the mulch naturally decays and continually adds food to the soil.

If using Hoary Azaleas against a house or another building with a brick or concrete foundation, take care to prevent lime seepage from the concrete. Line the back of the bed and at least partway under the bed with plastic before adding the soil. Do not use bone meal or wood ashes near Azaleas, for both of these contain lime. To retain the high acidity necessary for Azaleas, add a new layer of mulch each year. Azaleas also benefit from specially formulated Azalea food, which should be applied each spring after flowering, at midsummer, and again in early fall. Manure is not recommended for Azaleas due to the high alkaline reaction.

Azaleas require consistent moisture year round, with extra waterings during the hot summer months. It is especially critical to the plants the first two or three years after planting. Keep a close watch on the plants; do not let the soil become so dry the plants begin to wilt. After permanent wilt, no amount of water will save them, so continually check the soil to be sure it is thoroughly soaked at least two inches deep.

In the garden, Hoary Azaleas are especially lovely when used in a shrubby border or at the edge of woodlands and mingled with such other natives as Dwarf Pawpaw (*Asimina parviflora*), Flowering Dogwood (*Cornus florida*), and Parsley Hawthorn. In the foreground use great drifts of some of the lower growing perennials, such as Moss Phlox (*Phlox subulata*), Prairie Phlox (*Phlox pilosa*), Rose Vervain, and the vine Carolina-jessamine. All of these bloom simultaneously with the Azaleas, and in the wild they form spectacular displays.

Note: All Azaleas, both native and cultivated, are much liked by butterflies, especially the large ones such as Swallowtails, Gulf Fritillaries, and migrating Monarchs. Hairstreaks and Skippers crawl into the large blossoms in order to reach the nectar with their shorter proboscises.

TEXAS SNAKEWOOD (*Colubrina texensis*)
Buckthorn Family (*Rhamnaceae*)

Bloom Period: March-May
Range: Texas
   Texas: 1, 3, 4, 5
Height: 3-6 feet
Class: Native

Densely branched, low-growing deciduous shrub, with numerous silvery-barked, zigzag, twiggy branches bearing small, solitary or clustered grayish green leaves. Clusters of small greenish yellow, oddly shaped flowers are borne in abundance in early spring, followed by hard, dry fruits if more than one shrub is planted, providing cross-fertilization.

Cultivation: In its natural habitat Texas Snakewood is usually common but not intrusive. Since it does not bear thorns, it is one of the more desirable native shrubs. Whether plants are started from seeds or by cuttings, Texas Snakewood is one of the more difficult ones to propagate. Unless eaten by wildlife, the hard, dry seed capsules remain on the plants for several months after ripening. Gather the mature fruit and plant either in fall or spring, although fall planting seems to result in better germination.

Make cuttings by taking six-inch-long semihardwood tips, dipping in a rooting powder, and potting individually in a good rooting medium.

Texas Snakewood is not too difficult to transplant from the wild with fair success. Take the youngest plants with as much surrounding soil as possible. Cut the branches back at least two thirds and water thoroughly after planting. Fertilize two or three times a year with a very mild water-soluble fertilizer the first year or two. This helps the plants become established but will not be necessary later on. After the plants are two or three years old, occasional trimming in the fall produces thicker, more compact growth.

This is a wonderful plant to use in the driest, rockiest portion of your garden and worth the trouble of establishing it. If your soil is not already sandy or rocky, some gravel from the area where you dug the plants, or pea gravel bought at a cement-mixing place and combined with the soil in the planting hole, would be beneficial. Texas Snakewood likes good drainage, although it grows in some western clays.

Use Texas Snakewood at the back of a flower border, or mix it with other native shrubs to form a woodland edge. It also makes striking specimen plants or solid borders.

Note: Scientific studies have shown that the Texas Snakewood is avidly visited by several species of butterflies, whose objective, however, is not a sugar-rich nectar. Instead, the butterflies work the central disks of the flowers, possibly obtaining various amino acids.

THOROUGHWORT (*Eupatorium havanense*)
Sunflower Family (*Asteraceae*)

Bloom Period: September-November
Range: Texas only
   Texas: 4
Height: 1-15 feet
Class: Native

An open, semiwoody, many-stemmed shrub forming a loose, rounded clump or becoming scandent and clambering into nearby shrubs and trees. Numerous scented white flowers form showy terminal clusters. Stamens of the

253

Thoroughwort

flowers protrude far beyond the corolla and give the flowers an airy, frothy look.

Cultivation: New plants of Thoroughwort can be obtained easily by seeds or cuttings. For seeds, gather the entire flower cluster after it has become brown, dry, and fluffy. Place the clusters in an open paper bag to air-dry for a few days, then store in the refrigerator until you are ready to plant. In late winter, plant the seeds in flats in loose, well-drained soil and at medium temperatures until up and growing well. Transplant to the garden in early spring for autumn-flowering plants. They are very hardy and are not usually bothered by pests or diseases.

To start plants by cuttings, take a four- to six-inch portion of a well-developed branch showing new growth, remove the bottom leaves, dip in rooting powder, and place in flats or individual pots. Once rooted, plant in a permanent position in your garden.

Thoroughwort is easily transplanted at any time of the year. Trim foliage to a few inches above the ground before digging. Keep the plants watered thoroughly until well established. Container plants are commonly offered by nurseries and are usually strong and healthy stock, ensuring much larger and bushier plants for first-year flowering.

This is a plant for the less fertile and more arid sites in your garden, performing beautifully with practically no attention. Fertilizing is beneficial if done sparingly, and an occasional extra watering during the hottest months ensures better growth and more flowers in the fall. For really bushy plants with the most flowers, trim them severely in late winter. If not trimmed, the plants eventually become scandent, climbing into nearby shrubbery or low trees.

For spectacular fall displays in the garden, combine Thoroughwort with one or two other species, such as Cherry Sage, purple-flowered Garden Lantana, Lindeheimer's Morning Glory (*Ipomoea lindheimeri*), Sharp-pod Morning Glory (*Ipomoea trichocarpa*), Bush Sunflower (*Simsia calva*), Maximilian Sunflower (*Helianthus maximiliani*), Cardinal Flower, Pineapple Sage, or any of the Asters, Gerardias (*Agalinis* spp.), or Verbenas.

Note: This is one of the few white-flowered plants used extensively by butterflies, but it is one of the best natives for drawing them into your garden. The fragrance is very strong and may not be pleasing to some folks, but butterflies apparently love it.

WEEPING LANTANA (*Lantana montevidensis*)
Vervain Family (*Verbenaceae*)

Bloom Period: February-September
Range: Alabama, Florida, Georgia, Louisiana, Texas
   Texas: 3, 4 (2, 5)
Height: To 10 feet
Class: Exotic/Naturalized

Woody perennial forming large, many-stemmed clumps with spreading or weeping, vinelike branches. The coarsely toothed leaves are opposite. The entire plant is very aromatic.

Flowers pale lilac to magenta or purple, numerous, and forming rather flat or somewhat rounded showy clusters.

Cultivation: Weeping Lantana is a hardy shrub which does best in the garden if cut back to about four to six inches from the ground in late fall after flowering or the first hard freeze. The roots are strong, and many shoots put forth each spring from healthy plants. When planting, give Weeping Lantanas plenty of

Weeping
Lantana

room to spread, placing the plants at least eight feet apart and in full sun. By the middle of the growing season, they will have formed lush, solid masses, spreading equally as far forward and backward as well as upward. As new growth starts, the long, slender branches begin extending upward; if there are nearby shrubs or trees, the Lantana will lean on or climb into the branches. If no support is near, the branches of the Lantana eventually fall back to the ground in a weeping effect, sprawling gracefully into large, beautiful clumps or mounds.

Weeping Lantana makes almost unbelievable growth if a little extra fertilizing and moisture are available. Light top-dressings of horse manure in the spring and fall are excellent. Most Lantanas grow quite well in various garden soils, but if you take plants from the wild, try to duplicate the wild soil as closely as possible. Lantanas are usually exceptionally drought tolerant, but adequate moisture ensures the most bloom over the longest period. Good drainage is necessary; otherwise, mildew will be a problem. With overwatering, blooming slows down until the soil moisture has become balanced enough for it to put forth new blooming shoots. In the garden, Lantanas are sometimes infested with white flies (especially if crowded), but frequent and forceful spraying with the water hose to the underside of the leaves in early morning usually keeps the pest under control.

A corner or bed filled with several plants of Weeping Lantana is well worth considering if space allows. Butterflies will readily repay you. If not disturbed, the insects stay on the bushes all day long, flying from one cluster of flowers to another. During the middle of the day at the height of nectar production, there will often be dozens of butterflies around the plants. Certainly the number of butterflies will be in direct proportion to the number of plants you have, so try to include as many plants as your garden will bear. Even if there is room for only one, plant it. To prolong the flowering period and ensure the greatest flower productivity, keep the clusters of violet-black berries trimmed off.

Weeping Lantana is propagated by seeds, cuttings, or divisions. Four- to eight-inch cuttings— taken in late spring, dipped in a rooting hormone, and inserted in a peat and perlite mixture—should root in three to four weeks. Place a clear plastic bag over the rooting container and keep the plants and rooting mixture moist but not soggy. The Weeping Lantana also roots readily at each node; new plants are easy to obtain by cutting on each side of the rooted node and gently lifting from the soil. Replant immediately. Plant the berries in either the fall or the spring.

Note: The foliage of all the *Lantanas* has a strong, pungent scent when disturbed, which some people find unpleasant. Butterflies also have a dislike for the smell and usually fly to another part of the garden until the scent has dissipated.

Related Species: Many color and growth forms of *Lantana* are available at nurseries as cultivars (but usually of more dwarf form and with smoother foliage). All of them are readily used by butterflies.

255

Vines

CORAL VINE (*Antigon leptopus*)
Knotweed Family (*Polygonaceae*)

Bloom Period: August-December
Range: Alabama, Georgia, Florida, Mississippi, South Carolina, Texas
   Texas: 2, 3, 4
Height: To 40 feet
Class: Cultivar

Rampantly climbing or sprawling deciduous vine from large, tuberlike root, climbing by tendrils. Leaves large, thin, pale green, deeply indented at base, conspicuously veined. Flowers white to rose-pink, hanging from slender, wiry stems in branched, terminal clusters.

Cultivation: A native of Mexico and Central America, where it is known as Chain-of-love, the Coral Vine makes a spectacular late summer and autumn display. This vine loses its leaves each winter in the northernmost limits of its range, and in cold winters most of the top growth may die to the ground, but it recovers quickly. Where the temperature drops below 25, protect the roots with a deep, loose straw mulch. In the Rio Grande Valley and Florida area, the Coral Vine often remains evergreen and hardly stops flowering.

Coral Vine is offered in pots by many nurseries, or you can take rooted sections from a mother plant. Either way, plant in loose, well-drained soil and keep moist until new growth begins to show. Fertilize twice yearly with a good, all-around fertilizer such as 20-20-20. Give this plant the hottest spot in your garden and full sun. It revels in the high summer heat but appreciates regular and thorough waterings.

The Coral Vine is at its very best when shading a patio or terrace or draping its foliage and long, trailing sprays of blossoms over a fence or garden wall. If using it as a climber, at its base use a blue-flowered Butterfly Bush, Thoroughwort, Blue Plumbago, Gayfeather, Globe Amaranth, Mist-flower, or New England Aster.

Herbs

BABY-WHITE ASTER (*Chaetopappa ericoides*)
Sunflower Family (*Asteraceae*)

Bloom Period: March-October
Range: Texas
    Texas: 1, 4, 5
Height: 3-6 inches
Class: Native

A low, many-branched perennial forming mounds or clumps. Leaves very small, usually pressed against the stem and densely hairy. Flowers are large for size of plant, numerous, and almost covering foliage. A single inflorescence, or flower head, bears narrow, white ray flowers and a center of small, yellow disk flowers.

Cultivation: The Baby-white Aster has not been well known among wildflower gardeners in the past, but butterflies know it well and use it heavily for its rich nectar. Besides being liked by the insects, this plant also has a number of very desirable qualities in the home landscape. It is especially strong and durable once established, requiring little attention, and attractive even when not in flower. At first glance this species, with its numerous flowering heads and narrow ray flowers or petals is reminiscent of a dwarf Fleabane, but it is much more sturdy. The Baby-white Aster branches at the base, with as many as a hundred branches forming lovely, compact clumps and bearing many individual flower heads. It has two major flowering periods, one in the spring and another one in the fall. After the first flowering has ended, clip the dried seed heads and gather the seeds for starting new plants. Otherwise, leave the seed heads on the plant: They dry to an attractive warm straw color.

If you want more plants, gather the seeds as soon as mature and let air-dry in a paper bag or spread on paper towels for a few days. Then place them in a sealed jar with a small piece of insect strip for two weeks. Many of the seeds will not be viable, and germination is not very good even when they are, so plant about four times as many seeds as the number of plants you need. Little is known about the propagation of this native, so experiment. Plant some of the

seeds as soon as fully dry, scattering in a lightly raked soil. In the spring after the soil has warmed, scatter refrigerated seeds about and cover lightly. Do any needed transplanting while the plants are still young, for they form deep roots. They also spread by deep rhizomes, so do not disturb mature, well-established plants. These are plants of dry, calcareous soils, and they also like an open growing space, so do not crowd. Once established, they should need only an occasional extra watering during the driest periods of summer. With the exception of a couple of weak applications of liquid fertilizer to get the seedlings going, extra nutrients should not be needed.

The Baby-white Aster is an excellent low, dense groundcover, or use it in a solid border or intermixed with Blue Flax (*Linum lewisii*), Stiff-stem Flax (*L. berlandieri*), Dakota Vervain, Tuber Vervain, Drummond Wild Onion (*Allium drummondii*), Dwarf Crownbeard, Huisache Daisy, Tansy Aster, and Woolly Paper-flower.

257

BUTTERFLY WEED (*Asclepias tuberosa*)
Milkweed Family (*Asclepiadaceae*)

Bloom Period: June-August
Range: All
   Texas: Throughout
Height: 1-3 feet
Class: Native

A hardy, long-lived perennial from a stout root, sending up many flowering stems from a central axis. The milky sap typical of other members of this genus is absent in this species. Large, flat clusters of small, uniquely shaped blossoms—ranging from yellow to red, but most commonly a brilliant orange—are borne in the terminal portions of slender stems.

Cultivation: The Butterfly Weed is easy to raise from seed. Gather the pods six to eight weeks after flowering or just as they begin to split open. Strip the silken down from the seeds and sow outside immediately, preferably where the plants are to remain. Seed germination is rather erratic, but it is possible for seeds sown in late summer or fall to produce blooming plants the following season. Flowering is most abundant if the plants receive full sun.

Butterfly Weed can be transplanted from the wild, but the taproot is both brittle and extremely deep and must not be broken or cut off in the moving. Transplanting young, smaller-sized plants gives the best results. Healthy, well-established plants are commonly offered by nurseries and through catalogs; this is the best method to obtain starter plants. You can easily obtain more Butterfly Weeds by planting seeds from your own plants each year. Slow to show growth in the spring, permanently mark these plants to prevent their being stepped on or dug up by mistake.

In the wild, Butterfly Weed commonly grows in thin, dry soil. In the garden with somewhat richer soil and more moisture, the plant forms lush clumps and produces an abundance of flower clusters. Take caution, however, for in a too-rich, moisture-retaining soil, the roots will rot. Good drainage is absolutely essential for this plant. If your soil is not naturally sandy, work in a couple of shovelfuls of sand or small pea gravel per plant to guarantee good drainage. This plant is perfectly hardy once established and within two or three years will have formed a spectacular barrel-sized clump under good garden conditions. To get the most from your Butterfly Weed, after the first flowering is over, trim back a healthy thriving clump to about four inches from the ground. The plant will resprout and bloom again two or three months later.

Note: Well named, Butterfly Weed is an excellent nectar producer and attracts multitudes of butterflies of many different species throughout the flowering period. Butterfly Weed may occasionally be used as a larval food plant by the Monarch and the Queen, but it is not preferred because of the toughness and hairiness of the leaves and its low concentration of poisonous chemicals.

Related Species: Almost all of the *Asclepias* produce showy clusters of flowers and are attractive to butterflies. Some others excellent for garden use as nectar sources include pale pink-to dark rose-colored Common Milkweed (*Asclepias syriaca*), Purple Milkweed (*A. purpurascens*), and Swamp Milkweed (*A. incarnata*), and the snowy blossomed White-flowered Milkweed (*A. variegata*). The cultivated Mexican Milkweed (*A. curassavica*), with two-toned red and orange flowers, is easy to raise from seed, forming nice plants and producing flowers about five months after early spring sowing. It is root-hardy only in the extreme southern climes, but it is easy to be grow in pots or tubs to be brought inside during the freezing months elsewhere. If kept over winter, it will begin producing flowers earlier in the year. It is an especially good nectar producer.

ENGELMANN DAISY (*Engelmannia pinnatifida*)
Sunflower Family (*Asteraceae*)

Bloom Period: February-November
Range: Oklahoma, Texas
    Texas: Throughout
Height: To 3 feet
Class: Native

An upright to somewhat sprawling perennial, with one to many stems forming a rounded clump. Large, dark green, deeply lobed leaves form a flattish basal rosette and extend upward along lower portion of stem. Terminal clusters of yellow flowers open in late afternoon, remain open during the night, then close during the hottest part of the day.

Cultivation: If you give the proper growing conditions to this plant, it will be a joy in your garden for many years. Once established, it is long-lived, becoming more robust and producing more flowering stalks each season.

To establish Engelmann Daisy, collect seeds as soon as they ripen and store them in a cool, dry place. In the fall, plant a couple of seeds in each spot where the plants are to remain. A very young plant can be moved without too much difficulty, but an older, well-established plant develops a long, tough taproot, which makes transplanting very difficult. When digging, get a ball of soil with the root if possible. This requires a large, deep hole, so be prepared for work when digging from the wild or even transplanting in the garden.

Englemann Daisy needs little care in the garden, growing in just about any soil with or without much water. Give it rich garden soil and a little fertilizer and moisture, and it becomes a prize specimen. Clip the flowering heads for a longer bloom period. If the entire flowering spikes are sheared off to the foliage in late June or July, the plant will flower again in the fall.

Use Engelmann Daisies in groups of three to five plants scattered through the border, making a continuous ribbon of color. They also natural-

ize beautifully when scattered either randomly throughout an area or concentrated in one spot. They will reseed under good growing conditions but rarely become obnoxious. Simply transplant new seedlings into other areas or share them with friends.

If extra watering is not continued after the first heavy flowering, the plants normally become dormant during the summer months. Under these conditions, it is good to have them planted near other plants which become their largest size late in the season, such as Indian Blanket, Phacelia, Mexican Sunflower, Tansy Aster, various Salvias, and Zinnias.

259

GOLDEN-EYE (*Viguiera dentata*)
Sunflower Family (*Asteraceae*)

Bloom Period: September-Frost
Range: Texas
   Texas: 4, 5
Height: To 6 feet
Class: Native

A tall, robust perennial forming colonies. The sunflowerlike leaves occur opposite on the lower portion of the stalk, becoming alternate in the upper portion. Numerous golden yellow flower heads form loose clusters at tips of long, slender branches.

Cultivation: The best method for obtaining Golden-eye for your garden is by seed. Gather the seeds when mature and place in an open paper bag for a few days until completely dry. Plant in prepared beds in late September or when good fall rains begin. Seeds can be held over and planted in the spring, but more robust plants producing the most flowers come from fall-planted seeds.

The Golden-Eye grows beautifully in its native limestone soil of Central and West Texas but will grow admirably in good garden soil past its normal range. In more northern areas give it a protective loose straw mulch for the winter; to the south, give some semishade; to the east, provide sandy soil with extra drainage, and add a bit of lime from time to time.

Because of its height, use Golden-eye toward the back of the border, against a fence, or as accent clumps. They are wonderful for hiding compost heaps, trash receptacles, brushpiles, small storage buildings, or any other unsightly object. As these plants form large colonies, they are also useful on slopes to help control erosion. If you are using Golden-eye in a naturalizing planting, sow the seeds toward the outer fringes of the planting, as their height and natural tendency to multiply may shade or crowd out lower growing and less robust wildings.

Note: This is one of our best western native fall wildflowers for attracting butterflies. Some of the most frequent visitors are Bordered Patch, Gray Hairstreak, Pearly Crescentspot, Texan Crescentspot, Sachem and Fiery Skipper. The Gulf Fritillary, Great Purple Hairstreak, Julia, Monarch, Orange Sulphur, and Sleepy Orange are also commonly seen nectaring on the flowers.

HUISACHE DAISY (*Amblyolepis setigera*)
Sunflower Family (*Asteraceae*)

Bloom Period: February-June
Range: Texas
   Texas: Throughout
Height: 4-20 inches
Class: Native

Low, mounded or sprawling annual. Leaves mostly in basal portion of plant, becoming smaller and clasping in upper portion of the stem. Fragrant, yellow flower heads are solitary and terminal on long, slender stalks. Outer ray flowers conspicuously square and notched at tips.

Cultivation: Huisache Daisy is an excellent plant for drier sites, growing its best in sandy, limestone, or chalk soil. It grows great in rocky soil and disturbed habitats. This plant will not be found in nurseries but readily comes up from seed. Gather seeds from a choice plant and sow in raked soil in late fall for flowering plants the following season. Place young plants one to two feet apart and do not fertilize. Keep moist until they are growing well, then water only occasionally for best growth and bloom. When so treated, the plants stay mounded until late summer, when they begin to sprawl. Keep all seed heads clipped or pinched off until late fall for the plants to keep producing flowers. These plants reseed very well, and a plentiful supply of plants for the garden should be available if you allow the September flowers to make seeds.

Use these plants in groupings scattered throughout the beds or as an edging. They are especially attractive among rocks or pieces of weathered wood. They are also a good choice for hillsides, slopes, or natural areas, alone or in combination with other natives.

Note: In the wild, Huisache Daisy grows in colonies; when the plants are in flower, the

Huisache Daisy

entire area becomes almost intoxicating in its delightful fragrance. Many species of butterflies are attracted to the plants by the scent and stay around to sample the nectar.

INDIAN BLANKET (*Gaillardia pulchella*)
Sunflower Family (*Asteraceae*)

Bloom Period: February-December
Range: All
   Texas: Throughout
Height: To 2 feet
Class: Native

Upright to sprawling, many-branched annual usually forming a mound. Large flower heads are displayed at tips of long stems held well above the foliage. Usually the flower heads bear brilliant red and yellow ray flowers, but occasionally plants with ray flowers of various other colors are found.

Cultivation: Getting Indian Blanket started in your garden or in naturalized areas is no problem at all. It is a hardy, vigorous plant easily propagated from seed and, once started, readily reseeds each year. To start your own colony, choose flowers you especially like as to size and color, then tag the plants for later harvesting. Once the seed head has become grayish white and obviously dry, clip and place in a paper bag. Store in the refrigerator until ready to sow. Each seed head yields three or four dozen seeds. In late fall, tear the seed heads apart or loosen

the seeds by shaking the heads vigorously. Plant in prepared beds, covering the seeds with a thin layer of soil and watering well.

Seedlings should be up and growing well within six to eight weeks. In the warmer portion of its range, you may transplant seedlings anytime during winter or early spring. Spring is the best time for other areas. Space seedlings

261

twelve to sixteen inches apart when transplanting. Where plants have reseeded, simply thin to the appropriate growing distance by taking out the extra plants for transplanting to other areas.

Use Indian Blanket in full sun in any kind of soil. It does especially well in light, open, well-drained soils exposed to full sunlight and air. Good drainage is essential. In normal garden soils it needs no fertilizing. If kept moist, the plants continue flowering long after the wildings of the fields are gone. Clipping the spent blossoms also prolongs flowering, but since this plant is so floriferous, this may become drudgery. If you have many plants, the best thing to do is to trim some of the plants, cutting back the entire plants about halfway to the ground. These will form new growth and flowers, yet you will have left some untrimmed plants to continue flowering. If reseeding is desired, do not mulch around the plants. Occasional weeding may be needed early in the season, but the plant will soon become a solid mass, forming its own "mulch."

Because Indian Blanket continues to spread and sprawl as the season advances, it is best in combination with earlier flowering plants, such as Bluebonnets, Drummond Phlox, Larkspur, Phacelia, and Wild Onion. These plants will have bloomed earlier and are gone by the time the Indian Blanket needs the space.

Indian Blanket makes a most striking display when used alone to form a low border along a walk, drive, or fence or to fill the area between sidewalk and street. In the far South the plants may not winterkill, continuing to flower sporadically between the cold spells.

JOE-PYE-WEED (*Eupatorium fistulosum*)
Sunflower Family (*Asteraceae*)

Bloom Period: July-August
Range: All except Arkansas
   Texas: 2
Height: 3-10 feet
Class: Native

Stiffly upright, robust perennial often forming large colonies. Thick, conspicuously veined leaves are arranged in a whorl about the purplish or reddish stem, which is usually hollow. Large masses of bright lilac-pink to purple or brownish-lavender flowers are held in broadly rounded or dome-shaped terminal clusters.

Cultivation: You may easily obtain bedding plants of Joe-Pye-weed from seed. Best results are from seeds gathered in late August or as soon as mature and sown immediately or no later than mid-September for germination the following spring. Plants from seeds sown in flats indoors in late winter will be ready to transplant into the garden after the last frost.

Normally growing in well-drained marshy or boggy areas, Joe-Pye-weed grows quite well in rich loamy garden soil but needs a bit of extra moisture. If allowed to dry out, especially during the hot, dry summer months, the plant quickly dies. Place near a dripping faucet or, better yet, combine with other moisture lovers, such as Blue Waterleaf (*Hydrolea ovata*), Cardinal Flower, Mist-flower, New England Aster, Purple Loosestrife, Salt Marsh-mallow (*Kosteletzkya virginica*), Swamp Milkweed, Swamp Sunflower (*Helianthus angustifolius*), and the vine Climbing Hemp-weed. Use two or three species in a bed of their own, working in lots of well-rotted humus, mulch deeply, and give them a separate soaker hose which can be run more often than the rest of the ones in the garden.

Joe-Pye-weed eventually forms a nice clump of several stems. Once the plant has become well established, you can lift and divide this clump either in the fall or in early spring just as new growth appears. Dig the clump and cut or separate with a large, sharp knife, leaving one old stem and a portion of the fibrous roots in each section. Replant immediately and water well.

Use these majestic plants at the back of the border, allowing at least three feet between plants. If the bed is in the open, plant in the middle, using lower growing plants on either side. If in an excessively windy or exposed site, staking may be necessary. Naturally adapted to filtered sunlight, if given plenty of moisture, Joe-Pye-weed grows even better in full sun and does not become quite as tall.

Note: Almost all of the larger butterflies, such as the Buckeye, Gulf Fritillary, Monarch, Painted Lady, Red Admiral, Sulphurs, and Swallowtails commonly nectar on Joe-Pye-weed.

KANSAS GAYFEATHER (*Liatris pycnostachya*)
Sunflower Family (*Asteraceae*)

Bloom Period: June-October
Range: Arkansas, Louisiana, Oklahoma, Texas
    Texas: 2
Height: 3-5 feet
Class: Native

Stiffly upright, unbranched perennial somewhat rough to the touch, growing from a woody corm or rootstock. Leaves narrow, in a dense grasslike basal clump and along stem, becoming smaller toward the flowering spike. Lavender to dark purple flowers in small heads, the heads numerous and densely crowded in a long, slender, wandlike spike. The flowers open from the tip downward, the flowering period lasting for a month or more.

Cultivation: You may acquire the Kansas Gayfeather either from seeds, corms, or as potted nursery plants. Seeds from wildings need to be gathered late in the season. After flowering, the spikes normally remain green until after the first frost or two; then you can see the purplish pappus hairs on the seeds changing to a grayish white as they become dry and fluffy. After the entire stalk has taken on this fluffy appearance, clip the entire seed portion and place it in an open paper bag. Let this stay in a dry, warm place for a few days to become completely dry. The seeds should then be easy to remove by shaking or hitting the spike against the side of the sack. Removing the fluff or other debris is not necessary unless desired. Place all the mass in a dry container and store in the refrigerator. Seeds may be planted in flats in the house or the greenhouse in late winter, then transplanted to pots after three or four leaves have developed. Transplant to the garden in May or early June. Better germination may come from seeds a year or two old.

A simpler planting method is to clip the dried seed spike, lay the entire stalk on the ground, cover with soil, and mark the spot well. Seedlings (which resemble grass or onions) should come up the following spring. After the seedlings have developed true leaves, transplant them to their permanent places in the garden, spacing them at least two feet apart. Plant in groups of five to seven or even more for best show of flowers. Give them good to moderately rich, well-drained soils and plant in full sun. They like a bit of moisture now and then, but soggy winter soils cause the corms to rot. Depending on growing conditions, the plants may possibly become so tall and top-heavy that they need staking. Do this early because the spikes bend and twist; once twisted, the spikes will not straighten even if staked.

The purple flowers of the Kansas Gayfeather plants are absolutely spectacular in late summer when combined with pink-flowered Butterfly Bush, Confetti Lantana, Thoroughwort, Bush Sunflower, Frostweed, Golden-eye, Goldenrod, Golden Crownbeard, Hairy Wedelia, Late-flowering Boneset, Mist-flower, or Two-leaved Senna (*Senna roemeriana*).

Note: Use Gayfeathers lavishly, for they take only a small amount of space in the garden and butterflies absolutely flock to them during the entire time of blooming. The flowering period is somewhat variable, depending on climatic and garden conditions.

MEXICAN SUNFLOWER (*Tithonia rotundifolia* cultivar "Torch")
Sunflower Family (*Asteraceae*)

Bloom Period: June-Frost
Range: All
   Texas: Throughout
Height: To 6 feet
Class: Cultivar

Upright, widely branched, robust annual with velvety leaves. The large, vivid, orange-scarlet flowers are terminal on long, hollow branches.

Cultivation: The Mexican Sunflower is very easy to grow from seed. Although fast growing, this plant takes three or four months to begin flowering, so it is best to start the seed as early as possible. Plant in flats or individually sectioned cartons indoors in late February for transplanting to the garden after the last frost or freeze date. In the garden, place the Mexican Sunflower in full sun. Water well with a root stimulator when setting into the beds, and fertilize periodically with a good all-around fertilizer during the entire growing season. Do not let the plant wilt from lack of water, but be careful not to give either too much moisture or fertilizer, for this will cause lush, weak growth and the plant will fall or break. Staking is recommended for this plant, for strong winds can easily topple it over. Also, the branches are hollow, easily bent and broken by the wind. Despite its few drawbacks, the Mexican Sunflower is an easily grown plant which makes a spectacular splash in the garden. Use it at the back of the border, allowing plenty of room to expand. Crowding will cause it to drop the lower leaves and be rather unsightly. It works equally well in a solid border, as a screen, or as a hedge. The plant is very floriferous, producing over a long period.

You need to order seeds the first time around,

as they are not generally offered over the counter. Also, due to the plant's popularity, some years the seed companies exhaust their supplies early in the year. Once growing in the garden, leave a few choice flowers to mature their seed for the following year. Otherwise, keep the seed heads clipped for more abundant flowering. In some areas this plant readily reseeds, but do not depend on this in your garden.

Note: As far as butterflies are concerned, you cannot have too many Mexican Sunflowers.

They are an excellent attractant, and butterflies literally swarm around them continuously. All of the Swallowtails, the Gulf Fritillary, Julia, Monarch, and Queen seem especially attracted.

Related Species: The cultivars "Sundance," a three-foot form; "Goldfinger," a twenty-four- to thirty-inch form; and "Yellow Torch," a three- to four-foot yellow-flowered version of the original "Torch," have recently been offered by the trade. Any or all of these are excellent for attracting butterflies.

PENTAS (*Pentas lanceolata*)
Madder Family (*Rubiaceae*)

Bloom Period: April-Frost
Range: All
   Texas: 2, 3, 4 (1, 5)
Height: 1-2 ½ feet
Class: Cultivar

Upright to somewhat sprawling, many-branched herb, woody near the base, with opposite, conspicuously veined, dark green leaves. Flowers five-lobed, trumpet-shaped, numerous, and borne in rounded terminal clusters from upper portion of the stem.

Cultivation: Originally a native of tropical Africa, Pentas has numerous clusters of starlike flowers, adding wonderful drifts of bright color to gardens all year long in some areas and from early spring until hard freezes in others.

You may plant Pentas in full sun if you give it plenty of moisture, but it also grows lush and produces loads of flowers in beds with open, evening shade. Ideally, it should receive morning sun and open, dappled shade during the hottest part of the day. Its flowers are such favorites that butterflies continuously nectar from even the lightly shaded plants, feeding from them until almost dark every day.

Although tolerant of a fairly wide range of growing conditions, Pentas likes a deep, rich garden loam with excellent drainage, and it likes moisture when the ground dries out. It also likes occasional spraying of the foliage in early morning, especially during the hot, driest parts of summer. Well-rotted barnyard manure is an excellent fertilizer when applied in moderation.

In the extreme southern zones, Pentas may be evergreen, eventually becoming almost

shrublike. In other areas, you can purchase new plants each spring and treat them as annuals. Often Pentas is listed and sold as a greenhouse or indoor plant, and it is a wonderful subject when used this way. If you want to carry your garden plants over the winter instead of purchasing anew each spring, lift them from the garden in early fall, trim them back severely, pot them, and bring them inside to be placed in a sunny window. Fertilize lightly during the winter months.

You may also obtain new plants for potting by taking tip cuttings in early fall and rooting in either water or a peat and soil mix. Repot in a mixture of loam, sand, and peat after it is well rooted. Set winter plants in the garden after the soil becomes thoroughly warm in the spring, or

265

gradually expose them to outside conditions and leave them in the pots for patio or porch use. Whether indoors or out, after the plants have begun to show good growth, pinch out all growing tips for low, bushier plants which will produce even more flowering clusters.

In the garden, massed plantings of Pentas produce the most striking effects and of course attract the most butterflies. Cluster them in groupings of six to ten plants intermittently throughout the border, edge a walk or drive-way, or use extravagantly along the edge of a wooded area—or use in a solid bed of their own. The flower color is usually vibrant pink, rose, magenta, or red, so use Pentas with the more subtle colors of Blue Lobelia, Columbine (*Aquilegia* spp.), pink-flowered Sweet Alyssum (*Lobularia maritima*), one of the Plumbagos, Mist-flower, Salt Marsh-mallow, Stokes Aster (*Stokesia laevis*), or the cream-colored Garden Lantana.

PHACELIA (*Phacelia congesta*)
Waterleaf Family (*Hydrophyllaceae*)

Bloom Period: March-June
Range: Texas
   Texas: 1, 3, 4, 5
Height: To 3 feet
Class: Native

An upright, leafy, several-stemmed annual or biennial with soft, sticky foliage. Numerous small, blue to purplish flowers are borne in conspicuously coiled terminal clusters, which uncurl as the flowers open.

Cultivation: As Phacelia is not commonly available either from nurseries or seed dealers, you will almost surely have to gather the seeds yourself. Since Phacelia begins opening flowers at the base of the curled racemes and continues for some time, seeds will be mature in the basal capsules of the spike while the tip is still in tightly coiled buds. The best time to collect seeds is when the first basal capsules have begun to split open. The upper capsules will still be immature, but the ones in the middle should be ripe, and some of the upper ones will continue to mature.

To collect the seeds, clip only the most mature racemes, and only one from each plant. Keep them in an open paper bag a few days for the seeds to continue maturing and drying. Most viable capsules open within a week. Shake the plant against the bag to loosen all the seeds, then store the seeds in the refrigerator until time to plant. After all danger of frost is past, plant in prepared beds where plants are to remain. Thin as soon as the plants are three or four inches high, but do not wait long to transplant, as older plants do not like being moved.

Phacelia grows well in many soil types but does best in a loose, rich soil. Plant it to receive the morning or late afternoon sun, but do not expose it to the hot midday sun. Keep it moist and fertilize occasionally. A good mulch helps keep the roots cool and retains moisture.

Phacelia readily reseeds itself each year, so once plants are established, yearly seed collecting and sowing should not be necessary. Simply transplant the new seedlings to the desired sites each spring. Germination is much better in disturbed ground, so each fall scratch or rake the ground thoroughly around the plants.

Phacelia is most effective when displayed in groups of several plants and forming large masses. It is lovely combined with Columbine, Dakota Vervain, Engelmann Daisy, Huisache Daisy, Indian Blanket, pink or yellow Milfoil,

266

Plains Black-foot, Purple Coneflower, Sand-verbena, Scarlet Musk-flower (*Nyctaginia capitata*), and Western Peppergrass. Clumps of Phacelia in front of shrubs such as Cherry Sage, Bee-brush, Texas Kidneywood, and Agarita make an impressive showing.

PLAINS BLACK-FOOT (*Melampodium leucanthum*)
Sunflower Family (*Asteraceae*)

Bloom Period: March-November
Range: Oklahoma, Texas
    Texas: 1, 4, 5
Height: 8-12 inches
Class: Native

A low, bushy or mounded perennial, with one or several many-branched stems woody at the base. Leaves opposite, long, very narrow, gray-green, and rough to the touch, mostly ever-green. Flower heads numerous, solitary, and terminal on long, slender stalks. Outer ray flowers white, with the inner disk flowers yellow.

Cultivation: Hardly enough can be said about the ease of culture, prolific flowering, and general attractiveness of this plant for the perennial border. Its main drawback is that in some areas it is very short-lived, usually only about two years. Plains Black-foot seems to absolutely revel in the hot, dry summers of the western half of Texas and Oklahoma and continues to bloom rain or no rain. It is absolutely one of the best plants to use in dry, rocky, calcareous soils. It grows in a richer, more loamy garden soil but tends to become a little more leggy or sprawly. Late in the season, or as the plant becomes older, it may sprawl somewhat anyway from the simple weight and mass of flowers. To some, this informality appears natural and attractive, but if not desired, the plant can be kept more compact by occasional trimming.

As the Plains Black-foot is a taprooted perennial from a central crown, it does not transplant well, nor can it be divided. More plants are best obtained from seeds or cuttings. Collect seeds as soon as they become fully mature, or black in color. The seeds are enclosed in a black, foot-shaped, papery husk, which gives the plant its common name. Germination is much better in warm soil, so plant the seeds immediately after collecting. To start plants from cuttings, in August through September take semisoft or almost woody stem portions, dip in rooting powder, and place the cuttings in sand. Some should be rooted in seven to ten days, although there is usually poor success with this method. Happily, some native plant nurseries are now offering the Plains Black-foot and this is the best method of obtaining stock which will do well in the garden.

As this is a plant naturally adapted to rather adverse conditions, understand it and do not love it to death through indulgence. Except for an occasional deep watering during the driest periods of summer, basically leave it alone. Overwatering, especially during early spring or winter or in loamy soils, will cause the plant to rot at the base. As a general rule, the more moisture it receives, the sooner it dies out. Except for one or two very weak applications of liquid fertilizer right after growth has started in spring, it will need no more extra nutrients.

When placing Plains Black-foot in flower beds, do not crowd overly close but give each plant a bit of space to breathe. If you are using it in the western part of its range, the plants will naturally form wonderful mounds of compact foliage almost completely covered with flowers, and no trimming will be necessary.

267

Because of its white flowers and low, compact growth, this native daisy can be used in a number of situations, blending beautifully with almost everything. Use it in massed groupings toward the front of the border, to line walks, or as a groundcover. It is also lovely when used in small cracks or crevices of a dry-stacked stone wall or natural rock outcropping.

WOOLLY PAPER-FLOWER (*Psilostrophe tagetina*)
Sunflower Family (*Asteraceae*)

Bloom Period: March-October
Range: Oklahoma, Texas
    Texas: 1, 3, 4, 5
Height: 4-24 inches
Class: Native

A low, upright or sprawling, many-stemmed biennial or perennial from a woody taproot. Stems usually much branched, with the plant forming clumps or mounds. Flower heads yellow, several, and closely congested in terminal clusters.

Cultivation: The Woolly Paper-flower is commonly found throughout the northern, western, and occasionally southern portions of Oklahoma and Texas, usually in gypsum or sandy soils. It is very drought resistant and is most conspicuous when in flower. In the wild it often forms extensive and showy masses along roadsides or in fields and meadows. When introduced into the garden, the plant's appearance becomes even more dramatic. After flowering, the numerous dried flowers become papery and remain on the plant for months, gradually fading to beautiful browns and tans.

The best method for propagating this plant is by seed. The best time for collecting the seeds is in late summer or early fall, after they have become fully mature. Cut the stems below a few heads and hang them upside down for a few days to air-dry. Plant in late fall for flowering plants the following season. In early spring you can move young plants to the desired location in your garden.

The Woolly Paper-flower is ideal as an edging for the front of the sunny perennial border, or use it in small staggered groupings. It is also good in masses as filler plants when other plants finish flowering and are removed. Try using it as an edging plant along a path, in large containers, and in natural plantings. It is especially lovely placed close to rocks and in the company of Cenizo, Snapdragon Vine (*Maurandya antirrhiniflora*), Baby-white Aster (*Chaetopappa ericoides*), Downy Paintbrush (*Castilleja sessiliflora*), Fine-leaf Woolly-white (*Hymenopappus flavescens*), Heath Aster, Huisache Daisy, Phacelia, Plains Black-foot, and Verbenas.

The dense, woolly coating of soft hairs on the foliage of the Woolly Paper-flower enables it to stand long periods of drought by reducing moisture lost by the leaves through evaporation. This ability to retain moisture could be fatal if the plant were kept continually moist. Let the ground become completely dry between waterings and add sand to the soil for good drainage when planting. Use only very light applications of fertilizer, if any at all. After a plant is growing well, you can trim it back to encourage even lusher growth, but this is usually not necessary.

PURPLE CONEFLOWER (*Echinacea purpurea*)
Sunflower Family (*Asteraceae*)

Bloom Period: June-October
Range: All
   Texas: Throughout
Height: 1-3 feet
Class: Native/Cultivar

A hardy, stocky, long-lived perennial with long, dark green, rough leaves mostly in a basal clump. Large, four-inch, sunflowerlike blossoms of pink to dark rose are borne in abundance atop slender stems. The central disk or cone consists of numerous small, bright golden bronze flowers surrounded by numerous drooping ray flowers. The flower heads are particularly long lasting, often remaining in good condition a month or more.

Cultivation: The Purple Coneflower offered by nurseries and through catalogs is simply an "improved" form of one of the wild species from the northeastern states. The most common cultivar is called Bright Star, with dark pink flowers, but white-, red-, and purple-flowered forms are also available.

If you want the cultivars, purchase them as small potted seedlings for spring planting. The plants will flower the first year. More plants can be obtained by digging a two- or three-year-old clump in the fall and dividing. After digging, shake the dirt loose and gently separate the multiple crowns into separate sections, making sure each section includes several well-developed roots. Replant the divisions with the tips about one inch below the soil surface. Water thoroughly. For best growth and flowering effect, space plants eighteen to twenty-four inches apart and divide every three or four years. These plants die back to ground level each winter and are late to leaf out in the spring.

It is always best to start the native species from seed. Tag a flowering plant and return four or five weeks later. Give the cones plenty of time to mature and to loosen the seed, for the cones are prickly when dry and not pleasant to work with. Bend the ripe seed heads over an open paper bag and knock them against the sides to loosen the seeds, or clip the cone from the plant and shake it vigorously in the bag. Some seeds will remain in the seed head, so scatter the heads around the mother plant for natural propagation. Immediately after harvesting, sow the gathered seeds in a prepared seed bed and mark well. Seedlings should appear the following spring. Move them to permanent places in your garden when four true leaves appear. You can also hold over seeds for planting in the spring. If started after the last frost, plants should bloom by fall.

Although the flowering stalks of the Purple Coneflower are tall and slender, wind does not seem to bother them. This plant can survive in dry, droughty soil but thrives best in well-drained, fertile, somewhat limey soil, so work a handful of limestone amendments around each plant in the spring. Plant in full sun. Purple Coneflower tolerates some light shade, but will become somewhat taller growing and scraggly, and the color will be lighter. If not given good drainage, the plant will simply rot away, so if there is any doubt, add a shovelful of sand to each planting hole.

Scatter Purple Coneflowers in small groups throughout the middle of a bed or border. For a truly stunning effect, try planting the taller native ones at the back of a group of the cultivars and border with Plains Black-foot, Sweet Alyssum, or Verbena. The natives are also very drought tolerant and are wonderful used in naturalized plantings.

269

PURPLE LOOSESTRIFE (*Lythrum salicaria*)
Loosestrife Family (*Lythraceae*)

Bloom Period: June-September
Range: All
   Texas: 2, 3, 4 (1, 5)
Height: 3-6 feet
Class: Cultivar/Escape

A tall, stately, woody, almost shrubby perennial of regal appearance, usually many-stemmed and forming large clumps. Numerous rose-purple flowers form exquisite spikes more than a foot long, rising high above the dark green, willowlike foliage.

Cultivation: Occasionally Purple Loosestrife grows wild where unwanted plants were dumped and later became rooted. You may obtain plants from such areas, from nurseries, or through almost any mail-order catalog. Cultivation is not difficult if certain requirements are met. It grows in just about any soil but prefers a rich loam with lots of humus. If your soil is not of this type, work lots of half-rotted leaves, straw, horse manure, old peat moss, compost, or deteriorated hardwood bark into the spots where you will place the plant. Work this hole three or four times wider than the plant needs at the present, as each plant eventually spreads into a three- or four-foot-wide clump.

The one thing Purple Loosestrife demands is water, and a constant supply of it. If you place them around a dripping faucet or in a bed with a soaker hose all their own which can be turned on frequently, they grow their loveliest. A good, moisture-retaining mulch helps. Even though Purple Loosestrife needs a lot of water, good drainage is very important. It also likes full sun. Extend the flowering period by removing spent flowering spikes.

For new plants, dig and divide old clumps after about three years. Do this in either early spring or late fall. Sow seeds outdoors in early spring; germination takes about fifteen to twenty days. Move young seedlings to permanent places in the border for flowering plants the next year.

There are lower growing forms of Purple Loosestrife available, with colors ranging from carmine to various shades of rose to pink. All of them are beautiful in a border or when planted in a large bed of their own. They are very striking when used in a semiwild situation along a stream or the edge of a pond.

Some companion plants for Purple Loosestrife which tolerate the extra-moist soils include Button-bush, Blue Waterleaf, Cardinal Flower, Joe-Pye-weed, Mist-flower, Salt Marsh-mallow, Showy Bergamot (*Monarda didyma*), and Swamp Milkweed. The fall-flowering vine Climbing Hemp-weed, either clambering on a fence or left to sprawl on the ground, is quite showy in a mixed planting.

SALT MARSH-MALLOW (*Kosteletzkya virginica*)
Mallow Family (*Malvaceae*)

Bloom Period: June-October
Range: All except Arkansas, Oklahoma, Tennessee
   Texas: 2, 3

Height: 3-6 feet
Class: Native

Robust, upright, almost shrublike herbaceous perennial from tough roots. Stems usually sev-

Salt
Marsh-
mallow

eral, much branched, and forming a large clump. Leaves large, gray-green, somewhat rough to the touch. Large, cupped flowers of shell pink to soft rose are borne in the terminal portion of the leafy stems and branches.

Cultivation: Blooming from late spring to early fall, the softly colored and attractive blossoms of this little-known native perennial are a welcome contrast to the usual reds and yellows of the garden. Naturally occurring in saline soils along brackish coastal marshes, the Salt Marshmallow performs admirably under ordinary garden conditions throughout the southern halves of the coastal states. The tough roots go deep, so the plant usually requires no additional watering except during really dry periods. Plant in good garden soil; if the soil is not already sandy, add a couple of shovelfuls to each planting hole. Yearly additions of compost (along with the natural deterioration of the mulch) provide all the added nutrients needed. Mulching is very important, so apply fresh material as often as needed to help keep the roots cool. If you fertilize, do so sparingly, as the plant can be burned, and can also be caused to produce foliage instead of flowers. An exposure of full sun is ideal; plants in the shade will be weak, leggy, and with only a few, pale flowers. Place the plants at least four feet apart, allowing plenty of room to spread.

Potted plants of Salt Marsh-mallow are occasionally sold by nurseries offering native plants. New plants are easy to grow from seed. Each section of the five-part, brown capsule contains a dark brown seed. Collect the capsules after they begin to split open. These seeds are frequently attacked by weevils, so put the seeds in a glass or plastic container along with a portion of insect strip, seal, and store in a dark closet for a couple of weeks. At the end of the two weeks, remove the strip and store the seeds in the refrigerator until spring. Plant the seeds in a marked location in the garden after the soil has become thoroughly warm. Seedlings should be well rooted and large enough to transplant to permanent locations in your garden six to eight weeks later. Weekly applications of a weak, all-purpose liquid fertilizer hasten seedling growth. You can also start new plants by taking tip cuttings before flowering begins and rooting them in a sand and perlite medium. Even first-year plants, whether from seed or cuttings, can be expected to flower modestly. Once the root system is well developed, vegetative growth is vigorous and flowering profuse.

Use Salt Marsh-mallow in liberal masses in the border, where its lovely pink blossoms will be easily found by the butterflies. A single large grouping against a fence draped in Autumn Clematis (*Clematis paniculata*), Climbing Hemp-weed, or Coral Vine can be spectacular. It is late to break dormancy, so it can be interplanted with shallow-rooted spring- and early summer-flowering plants.

For complementary fall companions, try Confetti Lantana, Thoroughwort, Goldenrod, Kansas Gayfeather, Mist-flower, New England Aster, Purple Loosestrife, Summer Phlox, or some of the blue-colored *Salvias*.

271

SAND-VERBENA (*Abronia ameliae*)
Four-o'clock Family (*Nyctaginaceae*)

Bloom Period: December-July
Range: Oklahoma, Texas
   Texas: 1, 2, 3
Height: To 24 inches
Class: Native

An upright to widely sprawling, usually many-branched perennial. Leaves opposite, thick. Flowers trumpet-shaped, fragrant, lavender to violet-purple, numerous, and forming almost spherical terminal clusters. Almost the entire plant is covered with glandular hairs, making it sticky to the touch.

Cultivation: Throughout its range, this is an absolutely fabulous plant to use in the garden for attracting butterflies. It is extremely rich in nectar, and butterflies of many species find it much to their liking. Beginning to flower as early as December in south Texas, it continues on until the extreme heat of summer does it in. About the end of June or July, it stops flowering, and the aboveground portion of the plant just withers away.

The *Abronias* are not easy, but some, such as this one, are so well liked by butterflies that they are worth the special effort necessary to get them to grow. They absolutely demand deep, well-drained sand for growing, and we are talking almost dune-type here. Unless you live where these plants grow naturally, it is best to prepare a bed specially for them where they will have the best chance of surviving and doing well. Either build a raised bed and fill it with loose sand, or dig out the soil to a depth of one-and-a-half feet and fill the bedding space with the sand. In most cases, the raised bed will probably work better and be easier to prepare.

The foliage of Sand-verbena is very tender and fragile and breaks easily, especially when young, so try not to work the beds any more than absolutely necessary. Once the plants have started growing, they require very little water and usually do best with no fertilizer being applied. Do not mulch, for this will cause the plants to rot at ground level and die.

It is virtually impossible to transplant any of the Sand-verbenas, but they normally reseed themselves, producing young seedlings around the mother plant. However, there are always adverse years when natural conditions are not the best for germination, so it does not hurt to lend a hand. Gather seeds as soon as ripe, let them air-dry for a few days, and store them in the refrigerator until time to plant. Planting time is very critical for best germination: Seeds should be put into the ground sometime during October. For best results, make two to four plantings during the month. Scatter the seeds about on an area which you have lightly raked, then tamp the soil down lightly with a board or the back of a hoe. Sprinkle the planted area until thoroughly moist but not soggy.

After the first flush of flowering, trim back the plants if they have become sprawly, and they will respond with another burst of bloom.

Because of the Sand-verbenas' demand for deep, dry, sandy soil, companion plants for the garden are rather limited. Use them with Huisache Daisy, Plains Black-foot, Rose Palafoxia (*Palafoxia rosea*), or Western Peppergrass or fill the bed solid with the Sand-verbenas for a spectacular sight and an area which will be much appreciated by butterflies. After the plants have faded in midsummer, replace them with nursery-purchased Moss Rose and Globe Amaranth.

SEDUM (*Sedum spectabile* cultivar "Meteor")
Orpine Family (*Crassulaceae*)

Bloom Period: August-November
Range: All
    Texas: Throughout
Height: 12-24 inches
Class: Cultivar

Strong, stocky, succulent perennial with thick, leathery, silvery-green leaves. Numerous small, glowing-pink flowers are tightly compacted into large, flattish, terminal clusters. As flowers age, they deepen into darker hues.

Cultivation: Sedum is not readily propagated from seed, but the plants are available from almost all local nurseries and through catalogs. Many different growth forms and colors are available, but for butterflies the taller ones are the best. Also, butterflies do not seem to be very fond of the spring-flowering yellow one or the red-flowered form "Autumn Joy." For best results, stick to the tall-growing, mass-flowering, pink-flowered Sedums.

Sedum is exceptionally easy to grow, requiring little or no attention, and the plants may be left undisturbed for years. They do best when planted in infertile, gravelly soils with excellent drainage. Under ideal conditions the flower clusters reach dinner-plate size. Be careful not to overfertilize or overwater these plants, or the growth will become too lush and succulent, the plants will sprawl and break, and only a few flowers will be produced, if any at all. Sedum is normally hardy, pratically insect- and disease-free, and, once well established, actually quite drought tolerant.

Flower color is the brightest when Sedum grows in full sun. Sedum tolerates some light shade, but the flowers will usually be lighter in color and fewer in number, and the plants will be weaker.

To increase the number of plants for your garden, lift and divide clumps in the spring. Plant new divisions in small groups, spacing the divisions eighteen to twenty inches apart. You can also take stem cuttings in the summer. As soon as they are rooted, place the cuttings in the garden in permanent locations. They will bloom the following year. Once established, Sedum does not like to be moved, so unless you desire new plants, leave clumps undisturbed.

In the border, Sedum blends beautifully with Hairy Wedelia, Gayfeather, Golden-eye, Goldenrod, Lindheimer Senna (*Senna lindheimeri*), Mist-flower, New England Aster, Plains Blackfoot, Tansy Aster, Texas Aster (*Aster drummondii*), Verbena, or Wishbone Flower (*Torenia fournieri*). It is especially lovely planted in great masses in front of shrubs such as Bee-brush, Blue Mist Shrub (*Caryopteris incana*), Butterfly Bush, Texas Snakewood, and Thoroughwort.

Note: This Sedum is one of the best cultivated late-fall-flowering plants for attracting butterflies. It draws in just about every species still flying at the time of its flowering. The insects frequently use the large, flat flower clusters for basking as well as nectaring.

273

SHOWY BERGAMOT (*Monarda didyma* cultivar "Crofway Pink")
Mint Family (*Lamiaceae*)

Bloom Period: June-August
Range: All
   Texas: Throughout
Height: To 4 feet
Class: Native/Cultivar

Lush, robust, evergreen, square-stemmed perennial forming colonies. The large, opposite leaves emit a strong minty fragrance when crushed. Numerous lavender to rose-pink tubular flowers form flat, terminal clusters, with each cluster surrounded by several green, leaflike bracts.

Cultivation: If given the proper growing conditions, Showy Bergamot can be a spectacular plant for the garden. And considering its attractiveness to butterflies, it is well worth whatever extra effort is necessary. Well-established plants or dormant roots are readily obtained from nurseries or from catalogs, and this is the best method for obtaining a start of Showy Bergamot. Many different color forms are available in the cultivars, ranging from pure white to darkest purple to the scarlet of the wild form.

Propagation can be by seed, cuttings, or root division. Seeds are normally mature three or four weeks after the flowers fall. Sow seeds indoors in January, using a good potting mixture and barely covering the seeds with soil. Seedlings are slow growing and benefit from occasional applications of a starter solution. Transfer the plants to your garden as soon as all danger of frost has passed and they have three or four true leaves. You may also sow seeds directly in the garden in spring or early summer for flowering plants the following year.

When well-established clumps have obtained a growth of six to eight inches in the spring, pinch or clip each new shoot back to three or four inches. This will cause the plants to form several new branches and will ensure a lower growing and bushier plant. This also provides cuttings for new plants. Strip the lower leaves from the pinched tips, dip the stems in rooting powder, and place in clay pots filled with a good rooting mixture. Sink the pots in the ground where they can be watered frequently and will receive humidity. The cuttings should be rooted in four or five weeks and can then be transferred to the garden.

Showy Bergamot spreads by shallow underground runners, and you can obtain new plants by simply lifting one of the young plants along with a good ball of soil. You can divide mature clumps in early spring before new shoots appear. If your Showy Bergamots spread more than you desire, when replanting, place three or four plants in a large fifteen- or twenty-gallon plastic pot with the bottom removed and sink to ground level.

These hardy plants like continually moist soils during the growing season, and their lushness of foliage and amount of flowering depend on how much moisture they get. Try using them in a raised bed with rich, loamy soil, well-drained and full of organic matter such as peat moss or leaf mold. Add sand for drainage if necessary. Mulch heavily and use a soaker hose. With extra watering, Showy Bergamot becomes spectacular even in full sun instead of the normally recommended semishade. Keep faded flowers clipped to prolong flowering.

SKELETON PLANT (*Lygodesmia texana*)
Sunflower Family (*Asteraceae*)

Bloom Period: April-October
Range: Oklahoma, Texas
    Texas: 1, 3, 4, 5
Height: To 2 feet
Class: Native

Perennial from large, deep, woody root, often forming thin clumps. Stem tough, slender, rather stiff, pale green or blue-gray. Larger leaves few, grasslike, mostly near base of plant, and withered away before flowering begins. Stem leaves few, very small or practically nonexistent. Flower heads pink to lavender, solitary, terminal, appearing large for the delicate stems. Several raylike flowers in single row around the conspicuously erect purple-striped anther tubes and two-parted styles.

Cultivation: Not offered by nurseries, Skeleton Plant must be started from wild stock. This plant may be transplanted if you take care to dig deeply in order to obtain the root, but this is very difficult. Young plants are easier to dig and are better able to bear the shock of transplanting. Seeds can be gathered as soon as they are ripe and sown later in the fall for plants the following spring. One method to obtain more plants is by digging a large clump and dividing the numerous large roots into sections. Replant immediately, water with a root stimulator, and keep the soil moist until new growth is well started.

Skeleton Plant grows in many diverse habitats throughout the drier three-fourths of Oklahoma and Texas, so you need not pay any particular attention to soil. In the garden keep it on the dry side after it has become well established, and do not fertilize or do so very sparingly. In a sunny garden planting with less vegetative competition, Skeleton Plant appears more vigorous and produces an abundance of flowers. Use these plants in great bunches, because one plant quickly becomes lost due to its slender stems and absence of foliage. Also, place them in open areas in the border as they do not survive crowding, shading, or severe root competition.

STOKES ASTER (*Stokesia laevis* cultivar "Blue Star")
Sunflower Family (*Asteraceae*)

Bloom Period: May-November
Range: All
    Texas: 2, 3, 4 (1, 5)
Height: 12-18 inches
Class: Native/Cultivar

Strong, clump-forming perennial with a dense rosette of dark green, leathery leaves. Tight clusters of large, four- to five-inch lavender or blue-violet flowers top long, leafy stems, with one flower head opening at a time, the flower heads surrounded by numerous, stiff, leaflike bracts.

Cultivation: The Stokes Aster is a very hardy, easily grown plant which remains evergreen in many areas. It is another of the wildings which has been taken and "improved" for lower growth, longer flowering, and a generally darker flower color. It is a common native in the southeastern states, ranging naturally as far west as eastern Louisiana.

Whether you gather seed from the wild or purchase a cultivar from catalogs or nurseries, the growing methods are the same. Do not be

275

Stokes Aster

Stokes Aster generally grows best and produces the most flowers with afternoon shade and morning sun. It is not particular as to soil but must have excellent drainage. If your soil is extra heavy, add a shovelful of coarse sand when planting. This plant is tolerant of heat, drought, and abuse, but it responds with lusher foliage and more and larger flowers if you provide a little tender, loving care. If you do not want seeds, keep all spent flowers clipped for longer flowering. Once flowering has slowed down, usually in early summer, trim the plant back and it will bloom again in the fall.

This is a wonderful, low-maintenance plant that makes a beautiful addition to the perennial border, providing a wealth of remarkably long-lasting blooms. Place it toward the front of the border, interplanted with other sun-loving species, such as Butterfly Weed, Cherry Sage, Indian Blanket, Purple Coneflower, or Speedwell (*Veronica* spp.). Or use this versatile plant in large containers for patio or deck gardening, maybe with an edging of "Royal Robe" Sweet Alyssum or the white-flowered Plains Black-foot.

in a hurry to collect the seeds, for it will probably be at least two months after the petals fall before they are mature. Once the bracts curl away from the head, clip the fruiting spikes and hang them head-down in a paper bag. Let them air-dry for several days. Shake vigorously and crush the heads if necessary. You may sow the seeds directly in the garden in late spring, then move the plants to permanent locations in the fall.

Once a few plants are established, new plants are easily obtained by divisions since you need to divide the clumps every three or four years anyway to maintain vigor. In the spring or fall, take up the clump and with a sharp knife divide it into sections, leaving plenty of roots with each section. Replant immediately, watering in well.

Note: Colors of the cultivars range from white to pink and various blues and lavenders. Butterflies prefer the darker lavenders and pinks, but for fun you might try some of the lighter blues. If any of the cultivars are advertised as being fragrant, try those.

SUMMER PHLOX (*Phlox paniculata*)
Phlox Family (*Polemoniaceae*)

Bloom Period: June-October
Range: All
  Texas: Throughout
Height: 3-6 feet
Class: Native/Cultivar

A robust, upright, clump-forming and long-lived perennial with pale to dark green opposite leaves. Large pink to magenta, trumpet-shaped flowers numerous and borne in large, somewhat elongated or dome-shaped terminal clusters.

Cultivation: Summer Phlox is a common native wildflower of the southeastern states. It is used frequently in cultivation, and the spectacular clusters of rich color add greatly to the summer border. The flowers are strongly and sweetly scented and lure butterflies like magnets. At any one time, there will usually be a multitude of the insects, of all colors and sizes, for this Phlox is well liked by just about every nectar-using butterfly.

Give Summer Phlox an extra-sandy soil, good drainage, full sun, and adequate moisture, and you will have absolutely spectacular plants. Where the soil is more compacted, such as with a lot of clay, flowering and foliage are still excellent, but the plants are much shorter. There seems to be a direct relation between sandy soil producing the tallest growth and compacted soil producing shorter plants.

You can occasionally find these plants in local nurseries, but not often. You can start new plants from seeds, but the colors rarely come true and are often muddy or generally undesirable. For new plants it is much better to take cuttings or divisions. Start four- to six-inch cuttings in May or June and place them in the garden in the fall for flowering plants the following year. As there are large clumps of Summer Phlox wherever it grows, the gardener possessing these plants is usually happy to share a sprout or two. The young offshoots are easily separated from the mother plant and, with good care, will bloom the first year. Space new plants at least two feet apart and leave them uncrowded. These plants are susceptible to mildew if not given good air circulation. Use a soaker hose for watering or lay a regular hose on the ground, keeping the foliage as dry as possible.

The plants thrive in soil enriched with regular, generous amounts of organic matter. To maintain attractive plants with continuous flowering throughout the growing season, deep, regular watering is essential during excessively dry periods. Keep old flowering heads trimmed to prevent seed-set and ensure continued bloom. A deep, loose mulching conserves moisture and prevents dirt from splashing on the leaves, which can cause mildew. Lift and divide the clumps every two or three years.

Summer Phlox is the perfect border plant, with its strong, upright growth form and long blooming period. Place them in groups toward the back of the border if the soil is sandy or in the middle if the soil is heavier with clay. Combine with other summer- and fall-flowering species, such as Butterfly Bush, Thoroughwort, Climbing Hemp-weed, Coral Vine, Blue Plumbago, Globe Thistle (*Echinops banaticus*), single-flowered Hollyhocks (*Althea* spp.), Mistflower, New England Aster, Purple Loosestrife, Salt Marsh-mallow, and Mexican Sunflower.

TANSY ASTER (*Machaeranthera tanacetifolia*)
Sunflower Family (*Asteraceae*)

Bloom Period: May-Frost
Range: Texas
   Texas: 1, 4, 5
Height: To 16 inches
Class: Native

Low annuals, somewhat sprawling or more often forming well-rounded mounds. Leaves pale green, deeply divided, and fernlike, overtopped by masses of large purple and yellow flower heads.

Cultivation: Tansy Aster is one of the most showy of the western annuals and is easily cultivated. It is easy to raise from seeds and is also now being commonly offered as a container plant in the nursery trade under the name Tahoka Daisy. In the wild this plant generally grows in large colonies or masses, and this is

how to use it in your garden to attract butterflies. Plant as many as you can possibly allow space for, placing no less than five or six in a group—a dozen or more is even better. Plant them fourteen to sixteen inches apart for a wonderful solid mass of color. They are excellent in several large containers for patio, deck, or porch plantings. Plant in full sun in any good garden soil, hold the fertilizer and water, keeping them on the light and dry side, and they should perform beautifully. If your garden soil is extra-heavy with clays, add a generous amount of sand and coarse compost when planting. If an excessive amount of water is given these plants, they will eventually "grow" themselves to death, producing a lot of foliage and no flowers.

First peak bloom is usually in May, but if you regularly clip or pinch off the spent flower heads, a good showing will continue through the summer until another peak period in the fall. If the flowers are not cut, the plants still continue flowering, but not as heavily. For a natural effect, scatter seeds in early fall in undisturbed beds, watch for the ferny rosettes in early spring, and thin as needed. You may transplant extra plants to other areas. If seeds are to be sown in the spring, place them between paper towels, put the towel layers between two layers of very wet peat moss in a plastic bag, and chill in the refrigerator at least two weeks before planting. As these plants vary in flower color, ranging from a dark royal purple all the way through pinkish to pure white, choose the plants whose seeds you want while the plants are in flower.

Note: While used by many species of butterflies, Tansy Aster seems to be especially favored by Skippers and Hairstreaks.

THREADLEAF GROUNDSEL (*Senecio douglasii*)
Sunflower Family (*Asteraceae*)

Bloom Period: April-September
Range: Texas
 Texas: 1, 3, 4, 5
Height: To 2 1/2 feet
Class: Native

An erect to somewhat spreading or bushy perennial, usually with several woody-based stems. Leaves numerous, crowded, finely lobed near base. Flower heads yellow, numerous, in branched terminal clusters. Plant covered with silvery hairs.

Cultivation: Threadleaf Groundsel may be used in the poorest, hottest, and driest portion of your garden. You may grow it from either seed or root cuttings. The easiest method is to gather seed you want as soon as they are mature and scatter them in late fall in prepared beds where you want the plants. Thin the seedlings to at least three feet apart, transplanting the extras to other locations. Do not crowd this plant, for it likes breathing room. It is not particular to soil but definitely requires good drainage. Rocky or gravelly soil where there is no problem with water retention is ideal. Do not overwater, but occasional extra waterings

between rains in the middle of summer keeps the plant in vigorous flower. It ordinarily performs admirably without fertilizing.

Use Threadleaf Groundsel in groups toward the back of the border or as specimen plantings, maybe in a grouping with rocks or silvery, weathered wood. The plants are extremely hardy under the most trying conditions, and when well grown they form beautiful mounds of true yellow throughout the year. Peak bloom is about mid-April or early May, then again in

September, but if you keep the spent flower clusters clipped, there will be continuous color all summer. In protected areas the plants may be evergreen, with scattered flowers occuring even during the winter months.

TUBER VERVAIN (*Verbena rigida*)
Vervain Family (*Verbenaceae*)

Bloom Period: April-Frost
Range: All except Arkansas, Oklahoma, Tennessee
    Texas: 2, 3
Height: 8-24 inches
Class: Naturalized

An upright perennial from elongated rhizomes and forming large colonies. Leaves opposite, dark green, somewhat rough to the touch. The inflorescence is composed of several vivid purple to magenta, trumpet-shaped flowers in terminal clusters.

Cultivation: Perhaps because it is generally considered a roadside weed and persists in poor growing conditions, Tuber Verain has been neglected by gardeners, but not by butterflies. From the opening of the first brilliant flower cluster to the withering of the last one by frost, butterflies flock to the plants, hardly leaving them unless other extra favorites are in flower.

Like many other common roadside species, Tuber Vervain excels in cultivation and is a real show-stopper wherever used. In truth, this is a South American plant that was once cultivated and has now escaped in some areas to become one of our showiest naturalized wildings. It spreads by rooting at the nodes, with each clump multiplying rapidly and quickly, forming large mats or colonies. Tuber Vervain readily adapts to a wide range of growing conditions, in a sunny area blooming prolifically from early spring to fall.

This is not an easy plant to grow from seed, being best started from rooted divisions or cuttings. To divide, in early spring simply lift a healthy plant from your garden, shake the soil loose, then separate the rooted sections, clipping betweeen the nodes. Cut all the old stems back, replant, and water thoroughly. Cuttings can be taken almost anytime during the growing season. Also, potted plants, recently offered

Note: Each time I have observed this plant in the wild it was being used by several species of butterlies.

by nurseries dealing in native plants, are the perfect way to get a "start."

Tuber Vervain can endure dry, impoverished soil and survive with little, if any, garden care. With adequate moisture and a light application of fertilizer once or twice a year, the plant grows dramatically, producing extra-lush foliage and flowers. Tuber Vervain, as well as all other *Verbenas*, likes good air circulation. Water carefully (avoiding late evenings) to avoid powdery mildew disease.

For continuous flowering, keep spent flower heads clipped. Under good garden conditions, these plants are more agressive than in the wild and may require some control, for they tend to crowd out less hardy species. You can gain some control by mulching deeply to the edge of the clump. Do not mulch over the clump, however, or the center will die out. If you do not want to lift and divide the clump, simply cut the outside plants away with a sharp knife or hoe.

Note: There are many native members of the genus *Verbena* which are quite showy. There

279

are also two quite distinct forms. Plants with flowers crowded into flat or somewhat mounded clusters are generally referred to as either *Verbenas* or *Vervains*, while the ones with their flowers spread out into elongated spikes are almost always referred to as *Vervains*.

YELLOW SHRUB DAISY (*Euryops pectinatus*)
Sunflower Family (*Asteraceae*)

Bloom Period: February-December
Range: All
   Texas: 1, 2, 3, 4
Height: 1-3 feet
Class: Cultivar

A low, shrubby, evergreen perennial becoming clumped or mounded. Leaves green to grayish green, finely divided, and almost fernlike. Flower heads yellow, terminal on long stems held just above the foliage.

Cultivation: A native of South Africa, the Yellow Shrub Daisy is a wonderful plant both for the low-maintenance garden and for attracting butterflies. It is an extremely tough plant once established and needs little care. Healthy, well-established plants are hardly out of flower unless the temperature gets to 20° or below. It is tolerant of a wide range of soils, doing as well in dry limestone or alkaline soils as in sands and heavier clays. This plant can tolerate droughty conditions but blooms better if watered during periods of stress. Flowering the best in full sun, Yellow Shrub Daisy will produce some flowers even in shade. A regular, sensible application of a good fertilizer is appreciated, but as with most other plants, a fertilizer high in nitrogen will burn the plant. These are wonderful plants to use in containers, but they may be somewhat salt sensitive in the summer. If using in containers, water mostly with rainwater or purchased drinking water. These plants form wonderful sprawly mounds and should never need trimming, but if they should get out of bounds, trim them back in late spring after the first heavy flowering is finished. They are fast-growing in full sun and will quickly be back in flower.

Yellow Shrub Daisy is offered by most nurseries, so getting a start of the plant is no problem. To obtain more plants, lift a plant and, with a sharp knife, divide it into many smaller pieces, leaving some roots with each piece.

Use masses of Yellow Shrub Daisy to cascade down a rock wall or to sprawl over into a walkway. Intermingle it with Tansy Aster, low-growing Lantanas, Thoroughwort, Gayfeather, Golden-eye, Mist-flower, New England Aster, Plains Black-foot, Purple Coneflower, Tuber Vervain, or Verbenas. Back the plants with low shrubs, such as Bee-brush, Bird-of-paradise, Black Dalea, Cenizo, Flame Acanthus, Pink Mimosa (*Mimosa borealis*), or Texas Kidneywood.

Nectar Plant List

Bloom periods given here are only approximate.

CULTIVATED TREES

Tree	Height	Color	Blooms
Apple (*Malus pumila*)	15-50 feet	white or pink	April and May
China-berry (*Melia azedarach*)	to 45 feet	purplish	March through May
Grapefruit (*Citrus maxima*)	to 20 feet	white	throughout year
Lemon (*Citrus limon*)	to 15 feet	white and purplish	throughout year
Lime (*Citrus aurantifolia*)	to 15 feet	white	throughout year
Mimosa (*Albizia julibrissin*)	15-25 feet	pale pink to dark rose	April through August
Orange, Sweet (*Citrus sinensis*)	to 20 feet	white	throughout year
Peach (*Prunus persica*)	to 24 feet	pink	March through May
Plum (*Prunus americana*)	to 35 feet	white	March through May

NATIVE/NATURALIZED TREES

Tree	Height	Color	Blooms
Basswood, American (*Tilia americana*)	to 120 feet	white or yellowish	May through June
Black-haw, Rusty (*Viburnum rufidulum*)	to 30 feet	whitish	March through May
Caesalpinia, Mexican (*Caesalpinia mexicana*)	to 30 feet	yellow and red	February through July
Catalpa (*Catalpa bignonioides*)	to 60 feet	white to cream to pale pinkish	May and June
Cedar, Salt (*Tamarix* spp.)	to 30 feet	whitish to pinkish or rose	throughout year
Chaste Tree (*Vitex agnus-castus*)	10-20 feet	lilac to lavender	June through September
Cherry, Black (*Prunus serotina*)	to 100 feet	white	March and April
Chinquapin (*Castania* spp.)	to 50 feet	cream to yellowish green	March to June
Dogwood, Flowering (*Cornus florida*)	to 36 feet	greenish yellow and white	March and April
Ebony, Texas (*Pithecellobium flexicaule*)	to 40 feet	white	April to July

Tree	Height	Color	Blooms
Gum Elastic (*Bumelia lanuginosa*)	to 45 feet	greenish yellow	May to July
Huisache (*Acacia smallii*)	to 30 feet	golden yellow	February and March
La Coma (*Bumelia celastrina*)	6-26 feet	whitish to yellowish or greenish	May to November
Lead-tree, Golden-ball (*Leucaena retusa*)	to 25 feet	bright yellow	May and June
Locust, Black (*Robina pseudo-acacia*)	to 45 feet	white	May and June
Mesquite, Honey (*Prosopis glandulosa*)	to 30 feet	yellowish green	May to September
Mock-orange (*Styrax americana*)	to 18 feet	white	April and May
Olive, Wild (*Cordia boissieri*)	24-30 feet	white	April to June
Palo Verde, Border (*Parkinsonia texana*)	to 25 feet	bright yellow	spring and summer
Plum, Mexican (*Prunus mexicana*)	to 25 feet	white	March
Redbud (*Cercis canadensis*)	to 35 feet	pink-purplish to dark rose	March and April
Retama (*Parkinsonia aculeata*)	to 36 feet	bright yellow	spring through summer
Serviceberry, Downy (*Amelanchier arborea*)	15–30 feet	white	March through May
Serviceberry, Smooth (*Amelanchier laevis*)	to 30 feet	white	April and May
Silver-bells, Carolina (*Halesia carolina*)	to 36 feet	snowy white	April and May
Snowdrop-tree (*Halesia diptera*)	to 24 feet	snowy white	March through May
Sourwood (*Oxydendrum arboreum*)	to 70 feet	white	June and July
Tenaza (*Pithecellobium pallens*)	to 30 feet	white	May through August
Tulip-tree (*Liriodendron tulipifera*)	to 100 feet	yellow	April and May
Willow, Desert (*Chilopsis linearis*)	6-30 feet	white to dark rosy-pink or violet-purple	April through June

CULTIVATED SHRUBS

Shrub	Height	Color	Blooms
Abelia, Glossy (*Abelia × grandiflora*)	to 8 feet	white to pale pink	June through October
Azalea (*Rhododendron* spp.)	to 6 feet	white, pink to magenta, salmon to yellow or orange	April through June
Blue Mist Shrub (*Caryopteris incana*)	18-24 inches	white or blue	late summer through fall
Butterfly Bush (*Buddleia davidii*)	to 12 feet	white, pink, blue, lavender to purple	May to frost
Butterfly Bush, Lindley (*Buddleia lindleyana*)	to 6 feet	reddish to purplish or violet	summer through fall
Clematis, Bush (*Clematis heracleifolia* cultivar "Davidiana")	2-3 feet	lilac	summer through fall
Daisy, Bush (*Olearia* spp.) evergreen	to 6 feet	white, pink, lavender	summer through fall
Daphne (*Daphne* spp.)	to 5 feet	white to rose	March to June
Eupatorium, Mexican (*Eupatorium ligustrinum*)	5-8 feet	white	summer through fall
Genista (*Genista pilosa*) evergreen groundcover	4-6 inches	golden yellow	April through June
Golden-dewdrop, Lilac-flowered (*Duranta repens*)	to 18 feet	white, blue to lavender	February through August
Hibiscus, Garden (*Hibiscus* spp.)	2-6 feet	white, pink to red, salmon	spring through fall
Lantana, Confetti (*Lantana camara forma confetti*)	to 6 feet	cream and pink	May to frost
Lantana, Garden (*Lantana hybrida*)	to 4 feet	white to yellow, pink to maroon or magenta	May to frost
Lantana, Weeping (*Lantana montevidensis*)	to 10 feet	pale lilac to magenta or purple	February through September
Lilac, Common (*Syringa* spp.)	4-15 feet	white, rose to purple	early spring
Mock-orange, Philadelphia (*Philadelphus* spp.)	to 6 feet	white to pink	April through May
Poinsettia, Common (*Poinsettia pulcherrima*)	to 6 feet	greenish yellow and creamy-white, pink or brilliant red	winter or all year
Privit, Chinese (*Ligustrum sinense*)	to 20 feet	white	March to May

283

Shrub	Height	Color	Blooms
Snowbell, Fragrant (*Styrax* spp.)	to 20 feet	white	April to June
Spiraea (*Spiraea japonica*)	2-3 feet	white, rose and pink	summer through fall
Summersweet (*Clethra alnifolia*)	4-5 feet	pink	July and August
Sweet Broom (*Genista racemosa*) evergreen	to 2½ feet	yellow	spring
Sweet-spire, Virginia (*Itea virginica*)	to 6 feet	white	spring to early summer
Tamarix (*Tamarix pentandra*)	to 8 feet	rose-pink	summer

NATIVE/NATURALIZED SHRUBS

Shrub	Height	Color	Blooms
Acacia, Catclaw (*Acacia greggii*)	to 30 feet	creamy white to yellowish	April through October
Acacia, Twisted (*Acacia schaffneri*)	to 5 feet	bright yellow	spring
Acanthus, Chinati (*Anisacanthus puberulus*)	to 6 feet	white to dark pink or purple	April through June (after rains)
Acanthus, Dwarf (*Anisacanthus linearis*)	to 5 feet	golden yellow, orange to brick red	summer (after rains)
Acanthus, Flame (*Anisacanthus quadrifidus*)	2-4 feet	deep orange to orangy-red	June to frost
Agarita (*Mahonia trifoliolata*)	to 6 feet	yellow	February through April
Azalea, Hoary (*Rhododendron canescens*)	to 10 feet	pale pink to dark rose	March to May
Baccharis, Willow (*Baccharis salicina*)	3-6 feet	greenish yellow	May to July
Bee-brush (*Aloysia gratissima*)	to 9 feet	white	March to December
Bee-brush, Woolly (*Aloysia macrostachya*)	to 3 feet	pink to red or lavender	January through October
Bee-brush, Wright (*Aloysia wrightii*)	to 6 feet	white	April and May
Bird-of-paradise (*Caesalpinia gilliesii*)	to 8 feet	yellow and red	May to September

Shrub	Height	Color	Blooms
Black-mangrove (*Avicennia germinans*)	to 3 feet	white	May through July
Blueberry, Highbush (*Vaccinium corymbosum*)	4-15 feet	white	February through May
Boneset, Blue (*Eupatorium azureum*)	6-9 feet	bluish to blue-lavender	February through May
Bouvardia, Scarlet (*Bouvardia ternifolia*)	to 3 feet	red	May through November
Buckeye, Mexican (*Ungnadia speciosa*)	to 15 feet	pink to lavender	March to June
Buckeye, Red (*Aesculus pavia*)	5-15 feet	red or yellow	March and April
Buckeye, Texas (*Aesculus glabra*)	10-20 feet	greenish yellow to yellow	March and April
Butterfly-bush, Woolly (*Buddleia marrubiifolia*)	to 3 feet	golden yellow to orange-red	March through August
Button-bush (*Cephalanthus occidentalis*)	3-15 feet	creamy white to pinkish	June through September
Cactus, Desert Christmas (*Opuntia leptocaulis*)	to 5 feet	green, yellow, or bronze	May and June
Ceanothus, Desert (*Ceanothus greggii*)	3-6 feet	white	spring
Ceanothus, Fendler (*Ceanothus fendleri*)	to 3 feet	white	June through August
Cenizo (*Leucophyllum frutescens*)	to 8 feet	pink to lavender or purple	throughout year
Century Plant (*Agave americana*)	to 6 feet	greenish yellow	May through July
Cherry, Barbados (*Malpighia glabra*)	to 8 feet	pink to reddish or purplish	March through October
Chokeberry, Red (*Aronia arbutifolia*)	3-12 feet	white to pale pink	March to July
Cholla (*Opuntia imbricata*)	3-6 feet	rose to lavender or reddish purple	spring
Cliff Rose, Heath (*Purshia ericifolia*) evergreen	to 3 feet	white to yellowish	July through October
Condalia (*Condalia* spp.)	to 15 feet	yellowish to greenish	spring and summer
Dewberry (*Rubus* spp.)	to 3 feet	white	February through April
Dogwood, Rough-leaf (*Cornus drummondii*)	to 15 feet	creamy white	April and May

Shrub	Height	Color	Blooms
Eupatorium, Fragrant (*Eupatorium odoratum*)	3-6 feet	lilac to purplish blue	late summer and fall
Fendler Bush, Cliff (*Fendlera rupicola*)	to 6 feet	white to pinkish	May and June
Forestiera (*Forestiera ligustrina*)	6-12 feet	greenish yellow	August through November
Golden-eye, Skeleton-leaf (*Viguiera stenoloba*)	to 4 feet	yellow	May through August
Guajillo (*Acacia berlandieri*)	3-6 feet	creamy white	November through March
Hawthorn, Parsley (*Crataegus marshallii*)	to 25 feet	white	March and April
Honeysuckle, Bush (*Diervilla sessiolia*)	4-5 feet	yellow	June through August
Honeysuckle, Fly (*Lonicera fragrantissima*)	3-9 feet	white to yellowish and pink	February through May
Honeysuckle, White (*Lonicera albiflora*)	3-6 feet	white to creamy	April
Hop-tree (*Ptelea trifoliata*)	2-25 feet	greenish white	March through July
Indigo, False (*Amphora fruticosa*)	2-15 feet	dark purple	April through June
Juneberry, Low (*Amelanchier humilis*)	1-6 feet	white	May
Juneberry, Roundleaf (*Amelanchier sanguinea*)	3-7 feet	white	May
Kidneywood, Texas (*Eysenhardtia texana*)	4-10 feet	white to creamy	April through October
Lantana, Desert (*Lantana macropoda*)	to 5 feet	pink or lavender to purple and yellow	February through November
Lantana, Texas (*Lantana horrida*)	to 6 feet	yellow to orange or red	May to frost
Lantana, West Indian (*Lantana camara*)	to 6 feet	yellow to orange or red	May to frost
Lechuguilla (*Agave lechuguilla*)	3-12 feet	yellow to red or purplish	May to July
Lippia, Bushy (*Lippia alba*)	to 6 feet	white, pink, violet to purple	March through October
Lippia, Scented (*Lippia graveolens*)	to 9 feet	yellowish or white and yellow	March through December
Meadowsweet (*Spiraea alba*)	to 6 feet	white to pale pink	June through October

286

Shrub	Height	Color	Blooms
Meadowsweet, Broadleaf (*Spiraea latifolia*)	to 5 feet	white to pale pink	June through August
Mimosa, Cat's-claw (*Mimosa biuncifera*)	3-8 feet	whitish to pink	April through September
Mimosa, Pink (*Mimosa borealis*)	3-6 feet	white to pink	March through May
Mimosa, Velvet-pod (*Mimosa dysocarpa*)	to 6 feet	purplish-pink	June and July
Mist-flower, Fragrant (*Eupatorium odoratum*)	3-6 feet	lilac to purplish blue	late summer through fall
Morning Glory, Shrubby (*Ipomoea carnea*)	to 10 feet	pink	June through September
New Jersey Tea (*Ceanothus americanus*)	1-4 feet	white	May and July
Ninebark, Common (*Physocarpus opulifolius*)	3-10 feet	white to pinkish	May through July
Ocotillo (*Fouquieria splendens*)	6-21 feet	red	April through June
Orange, Mexican (*Choisya dumosa*)	2-3 feet	white	June through November
Pavonia, Rose (*Pavonia lasiopetala*)	1-3 feet	pink to rose	throughout year
Pepper-bush, Sweet (*Clethra alnifolia*)	3-9 feet	white	July to September
Plum, Chickasaw (*Prunus angustifolia*)	to 14 feet	creamy white	March and April
Plum, Creek (*Prunus rivularis*)	3-8 feet	white	March
Plum, Oklahoma (*Prunus gracilis*)	to 5 feet	creamy white	March and April
Poliomintha (*Poliomintha longiflora*)	to 3 feet	lavender-pink	spring through fall
Prickly Pear (*Opuntia humifusa*)	to 2 feet	yellow to reddish or bronze	April through June
Queen's Delight (*Stillingia sylvatica*)	to 3 feet	greenish yellow	April through June
Queen's Delight, Texas (*Stillingia texana*)	8-16 inches	greenish yellow	April through June
Rabbit-brush, Southwest (*Chrysothamnus pulchellus*)	2-3½ feet	golden yellow	August through October

Shrub	Height	Color	Blooms
Redroot (*Ceanothus herbaceus*)	1-2½ feet	white	March to July
Rose, Carolina (*Rosa carolina*)	to 3 feet	pink	May through July
Rose, Prairie (*Rosa setigera*)	6-15 feet	white to rose-pink	May to July
Rose-mallow, Desert (*Hibiscus coulteri*)	to 3 feet	pale to dark yellow	April to August
Rose-mallow, Swamp (*Hibiscus moscheutos*)	2-6 feet	white to creamy and crimson-purple	June through October
Rosemary-mint, Hoary (*Poliomintha incana*)	1½-3 feet	white, pale purple to bluish	April through June
Roosevelt Weed (*Baccharis neglecta*)	3-9 feet	yellowish white to creamy	September and October
Sage, Cherry (*Salvia greggii*)	to 3 feet	white to red	April to frost
Sage, Shrubby Blue (*Salvia ballotiflora*)	to 6 feet	bluish or purple	January through October
Salt Cedar (*Tamarisk* spp.)	to 15 feet	pale pink to rose	throughout year
Sand-myrtle (*Leiophyllum buxifolium*) evergreen	1-6 feet	white to pinkish	March through May
Screwbean (*Prosopis pubescens*)	to 20 feet	pale yellowish	throughout year
Seep-willow (*Baccharis salicifolia*)	3-10 feet	yellowish white or cream	summer through fall
Senna, Wislizenus (*Senna wislizenii*)	5-9 feet	yellow	May through July
Silver-bell (*Halesia diptera*)	to 4 feet	snowy white	April and May
Snakewood, Texas (*Colubrina texensis*)	3-6 feet	greenish yellow	March through May
Snow-bell, Sycamore-leaf (*Styrax platanifolia*)	to 12 feet	white	April and May
Spiraea, Corymbed (*Spiraea corymbosa*)	to 3 feet	white	May and June
Spiraea, Japanese (*Spiraea japonica*)	to 6 feet	pink	June through August
Steeplebush (*Spiraea tomentosa*)	to 6 feet	pink	July through September
Sumac, Stag-horn (*Rhus typhina*)	to 30 feet	white to greenish-yellow	May and June

Shrub	Height	Color	Blooms
Sweetspire, Virginia (*Itea virginica*)	to 6 feet	white	April to June
Thoroughwort (*Eupatorium havanense*)	1-15 feet	white	September through November
Thoroughwort, Wright (*Eupatorium wrightii*)	1-2 feet	whitish	October and November
Wax-mallow, Drummond (*Malvaviscus arboreus*)	2-4 feet	red	June to November or throughout year
Yellow-bells (*Tecoma stans*)	to 9 feet	yellow	April through November

CULTIVATED VINES

Vine	Annual, Perennial, Evergreen	Color	Blooms
Bean, Scarlet Runner (*Phaseolus coccineus*)	annual	red	summer to frost
Bougainvillea (*Bougainvillea spectabilis*)	perennial	white to mauve or purple, red to salmon	March to frost or all year
Clematis, Autumn (*Clematis paniculata*)	perennial	white	August and September
Coral Vine (*Antigon leptopus*)	perennial	white to rose-pink	August through December or almost all year
Flame Vine, Mexican (*Senecio confusus*)	perennial	orange	June through September
Honeysuckle (*Lonicera* spp.)	perennial	white to red or yellow	spring to fall
Jasmine, Star (*Trachelospermum jasminoides*)	evergreen	white to creamy	May and June
Morning Glory, Common (*Ipomoea purpurea*)	annual	white, blue, rose to red	spring through fall
Silver Lace Vine (*Polygonum aubertii*)	perennial	white	summer
Sweet Pea, Annual (*Lathyrus odoratus*)	annual	white, pink to red or purple	spring or fall
Sweet Pea, Perennial (*Lathyrus latifolius*)	perennial	white, pink to red or purple	June through September
Wisteria, Chinese (*Wisteria sinensis*)	perennial	white, blue to blue-purple	April and May

289

NATIVE/NATURALIZED VINES

Vine	Color	Blooms
Alamo Vine (*Ipomoea sinuata*)	white and red	May through October
Bindweed (*Convolvulus arvensis*)	white or pink	April through October
Bindweed, Texas (*Convolvulus equitans*)	white and red	April through October
Carolina-jessamine (*Gelsemium sempervirens*)	yellow	January to April
Grape, Fox (*Vitis vulpina*)	creamy to greenish	May to June
Hemp-weed, Climbing (*Mikania scandens*)	whitish to pinkish	June to frost
Honeysuckle, Trumpet (*Lonicera sempervirens*)	red or yellow	March to June
Honeysuckle, Yellow (*Lonicera flava*)	yellow	April and May
Milkweed-vine, Climbing (*Sarcostemma cynanchoides*)	white to pinkish or purplish	May through September
Morning Glory, Ivy-leaf (*Ipomoea hederacea*)	blue to lavender, red to purple	July to frost
Morning Glory, Lindheimer (*Ipomoea lindheimeri*)	pale blue to lavender	April through October
Morning Glory, Salt-marsh (*Ipomoea sagittata*)	dark pink to red-purple	April through October
Morning Glory, Sharp-pod (*Ipomoea trichocarpa*)	lavender to rose-purple	April to frost
Passionflower (*Passiflora incarnata*)	lavender to purplish	April through September
Pepper-vine (*Ampelopsis arborea*)	greenish	June through August
Potato, Wild (*Ipomoea pandurata*)	white and wine red	June through September

CULTIVATED HERBS

Herb	Height	Color	Blooms
Allium (*Allium* spp.) perennial	to 4 feet	white through reds and purples	spring through summer
Allium, Giant (*Allium giganteum*) perennial	3-5 feet	purple	June
Alyssum (*Lobularia saxatile*) perennial	to 12 inches	yellow	spring
Alyssum, Sweet (*Lobularia maritima*) annual/perennial	3-10 inches	white, pink to purple	spring to frost
Amaranth, Globe (*Gomphrena globosa*) annual	6-18 inches	white, pink to apricot, wine or maroon to purple	April to frost

Herb	Height	Color	Blooms
Asperula (*Asperula azurea*) annual	to 12 inches	lavender-blue	midsummer
Aster, Monk (*Aster frikartii*) perennial	to 2 feet	lavender-blue	June to frost
Aster, New England (*Aster novae-angliae*) perennial	3-4 feet	pale blue to deep purple	late summer through fall
Aster, New York (*Aster novae-belgii*) perennial	3-4 feet	blue to purple	fall
Aster, Stokes (*Stokesia laevis*) perennial	12-18 inches	lavender to blue-violet	May through November
Balsam, Himalayan (*Impatiens glandulifera*) annual	3-5 feet	pink and white	spring to fall
Balsam-root (*Balsamorrhiza sagittata*) perennial	24-30 inches	yellow	summer
Bergamot, Showy (*Monarda didyma*) perennial	to 4 feet	white to scarlet	June through August
Boltonia (*Boltonia asteroides*) perennial	to 4 feet	white, pink, violet	midsummer to fall
Borage (*Borage officinalis*) perennial	1-3 feet	blue	spring to late fall
Butterfly Weed (*Asclepias tuberosa* cultivar 'Gay Butterflies') perennial	to 2 feet	pink to scarlet, yellow to gold	midsummer through fall
Calendula (*Calendula officinalis*) annual	to 2 feet	orange	summer to frost
Camassia (*Camassia leichtlinii*) perennial	2-3 feet	lavender-violet	March through May
Candytuft (*Iberia umbellata*) perennial	12-18 inches	white, pink to lilac	June through September
Catmint (*Nepeta mussinii*) perennial	to 12 inches	white to lavender-blue	May through September

Herb	Height	Color	Blooms
Catnip (*Nepeta cataria*) perennial	24-36 inches	white	spring through summer
Chives (*Allium schoenoprasum*) perennial	8-12 inches	lavender	May and June
Chrysanthemum, Single (*Chrysanthemun* spp.) perennial	6-26 inches	yellow, white to red to purple	late summer through fall
Cigar Plant (*Cuphea micropetala*) perennial	to 2 feet	orange-yellow	fall
Coneflower, Purple (*Echinacea purpurea*) perennial	2-3 feet	dark pink to rose	July through September
Coneflower, Sweet (*Rudbeckia subtomentosa*) perennial	30-60 inches	yellow	summer to frost
Cornflower (*Centaures cyanus*) annual or perennial	1-2 ½ feet	white, pink, blue	spring to fall
Cosmos (*Cosmos bipinnatus*) annual	to 4 feet	white to pink or rose, yellow to red	spring to frost
Cupid's Dart (*Catananche caerulea*) perennial	to 24 inches	sky blue	June through October
Daisy, Yellow Shrub (*Euryops pectinatus*) perennial	1-3 feet	yellow	almost all year
Daylily (*Hemerocallis* spp.) perennial	to 3 feet	yellow, orange, pink to maroon	spring to fall
Daylily (*Hemerocallis x* cultivar "Stella de Oro") perennial	to 2 feet	golden-yellow	summer
Garlic, Society (*Tulbaghia violacea*) perennial	to 2 feet	lilac	summer
Geranium (*Pelargonium* spp.) perennial	12-36 inches	white to pink, red	spring through fall
Goldenrod (*Solidago canadensis*) perennial	to 3 feet	yellow	summer and fall

Herb	Height	Color	Blooms
Heliopsis (*Heliopsis helianthoides*) perennial	2-3 feet	soft yellow	August and September
Heliotrope, Common (*Heliotropium arborescens*) perennial	to 16 inches	lavender to purple	summer and fall
Hollyhock, Single (*Althea* spp.) annual or perennial	to 5 feet	white to red, yellow	summer and fall
Honesty (*Lunaria annua*) biennial	to 2 feet	purple	June and July
Horehound, Common (*Marrubium vulgare*) perennial	to 3 feet	white	May to frost
Hyacinth, Wild (*Camassia scilloides*) perennial	to 24 inches	pale blue to violet	March through May
Hyssop, Anise (*Agastache foeniculum*) annual	to 3 feet	pale lavender to bluish	spring through fall
Impatiens (*Impatiens balsamina*) annual/perennial	4-24 inches	white to red, salmon	June to frost
Iris, Yellow (*Iris pseudacorus*) perennial	to 3 feet	yellow	April and May
Jupiter's Beard (*Centranthus rubra*) perennial	2-3 feet	white, pink, red	June to frost
Kalanchoe (*Kalanchoe* spp.) perennial	9-24 inches	pink to red, salmon	fall to spring or all year
Lace-flower, Blue (*Trachymene coeruleus*) annual	to 2½ feet	lavender	summer to fall
Lavender (*Lavandula latifolia*) perennial	to 12 inches	lavender to purple	summer through fall
Lily (*Lilium* spp.) perennial	to 6 feet	white, yellow, pink to red	spring to fall
Loosestrife, Purple (*Lythrum salicaria*) perennial	3-6 feet	pink to rose-purple	June through September
Maltese Cross (*Lychnis chalcedonica*) perennial	to 3 feet	vivid scarlet	June and July

293

Herb	Height	Color	Blooms
Marigold, Single (*Tagetes* spp.) annual	6-18 inches	yellow to scarlet	spring to frost
Marjoram (*Origanum vulgare*) annual	to 15 inches	white	summer
Milfoil (*Achillea millefolium*) perennial	to 18 inches	pink to red or yellow	July through October
Milkweed (*Asclepias physocarpa*) perennial	to 30 inches	creamy white	summer to fall
Milkweed, Mexican (*Asclepias curassavica*) annual or perennial	24-36 inches	yellow and orange	spring to frost
Mint, Field (*Mentha arvensis*) perennial	to 2 feet	white to pink or lavender	May through October
Moss Rose (*Portulaca* spp.) annual or perennial	to 10 inches	white, pink to red, yellow to orange	spring to frost
Pansy (*Viola* spp.) winter annual	to 12 inches	white to orange, red to maroon, blue to purple	September to late June
Pentas (*Pentas lanceolata*) annual or perennial	1-2 ½ feet	pink to rose, magenta to red	April to frost or all year
Periwinkle, Madagascar (*Catharanthus roseus*) annual	6-18 inches	white, pink to rose, purple	spring through fall
Petunia (*Petunia axillaris x violacea*) annual	to 2 feet	white to red, blue to purple	spring to frost
Phlox, Moss (*Phlox subulata*) perennial	to 6 inches	white, pink, red, or blue	February to May
Plumbago (*Plumbago auriculata*) perennial	to 4 feet or more	white to pale blue	March to frost
Plumbago, Blue (*Plumbago capensis*) perennial	to 3 feet	pale blue	May to frost
Purslane (*Portulaca oleracea* var. *sativa*) annual	to 12 inches	white or orange, pink to red	March to frost

Herb	Height	Color	Blooms
Radish, Garden (*Raphanus sativus*) annual	to 12 inches	white	spring
Red-hot Poker (*Kniphofia uvaria*) perennial	2½-3½ feet	white, pink to red and yellow to orange	May through September
Rocket, Sweet (*Hesperis matronalis*) annual or perennial	1-2 feet	white, lilac to purple	April through June
Rose Mallow (*Lavatera trimestris*) annual	3-5 feet	pink to rose	June through September
Sage, Mexican Bush (*Salvia leucantha*) perennial	to 4 feet	royal blue	summer through fall
Sage, Pineapple (*Salvia elegans*) perennial	to 3½ feet	red	May to frost
Scabiosa (*Scabiosa lyrophylla*) annual	to 2 feet	white to rose or lavender	summer
Scilla (*Scilla siberica*) perennial	4-6 inches	blue	April
Sedum (*Sedum spectabile*) perennial	12-24 inches	pink	August through November
Shrimp Plant (*Beloperone guttata*) perennial	2-3 feet	white, pink to salmon and reddish-brown	April through November
Spearmint (*Mentha spicata*) perennial	1-2 feet	pale lavender	June through September
Speedwell (*Veronica* spp.) perennial	10-18 inches	white, pink to reddish, blue	June through September
Stocks (*Matthiola incana*) annual or biennial	8-30 inches	white, pink, rose to purple	January to frost
Sunflower, Mexican (*Tithonia rotundifolia*) annual	to 6 feet	yellow or orange	June to frost
Swan Plant (*Asclepias physocarpa*) perennial	to 30 inches	creamy white	summer
Sweet Sultan (*Centaurea imperialis*) annual or perennial	2-3 feet	white, rose to lavender	April to July

295

Herb	Height	Color	Blooms
Thistle, Globe (*Echinops banaticus*) perennial	5-6 feet	powdery blue	July to September
Tidy Tips (*Layia platyglossa*) annual	12-14 inches	yellow and white	March through May
Tweedia (*Oxypetalum cruella*) evergreen perennial	to 12 inches	blue	April to frost or throughout year
Verbena, Garden (*Verbena hybrida*) annual or perennial	6–12 inches	white, pink, red to maroon, lavender to purple	March to frost or throughout year
Wallflower (*Cheiranthus cheiri*) annual	to 18 inches	cream to gold, pink to purple	May to June
Wishbone Flower (*Torenia fournieri*) annual	to 8 inches	blue with purple and yellow	spring through fall
Zinnia (*Zinnia angustifolia*) annual	to 8 inches	golden orange	spring to frost
Zinnia, Classic (*Zinnia linearis*) annual	to 15 inches	orange	spring to frost
Zinnia, Mexican (*Zinnia* spp.) annual	to 10 inches	yellow, gold and red	spring to frost
Zinnia, Rose Pinwheel (*Zinnia angustifolia* × *elegans*) annual	to 12 inches	pink	spring to frost

NATIVE/NATURALIZED HERBS

Herb	Height	Color	Blooms
Anemone, Carolina (*Anemone caroliniana*) perennial	to 12 inches	white, pink, pale to dark blue	February through April
Anemone, Ten-petal (*Anemone berlandieri*) perennial	6-15 inches	white, pink, lavender, pale blue to dark blue	February through April
Antelope-horns (*Asclepias asperula*) perennial	8-24 inches	greenish yellow	March through November
Aster, Baby White (*Chaetopappa ericoides*) perennial	3-6 inches	white and yellow	March through October
Aster, Heath (*Aster ericoides*) perennial	to 3 feet	white and yellow	October to frost

Herb	Height	Color	Blooms
Aster, Tansy (*Machaeranthera tanacetifolia*) annual	4-16 inches	white, lavender, red-violet to purple and yellow	May through October
Aster, Tall (*Aster praealtus*) perennial	1-4 feet	purple and yellow	October and November
Aster, Texas (*Aster drummondii*) perennial	1-3 feet	lavender to purple and yellow	September to frost
Barbara's-buttons, White (*Marshallia caespitosa*) perennial	to 18 inches	white	April and May
Bee Plant, Rocky Mountain (*Cleome serrulata*) annual	8-60 inches	pink to purplish	May through September
Beebalm, Basil (*Monarda clinopodioides*) annual	8-15 inches	white to pale pink	April to July
Beebalm, Spotted (*Monarda punctata*) perennial	1-3 feet	yellowish, pinkish to pale purple	May through August
Bergamot, Lindheimer (*Monarda lindheimeri*)	1-2 feet	creamy white	April to August
Bergamot, Scarlet (*Monarda didyma*) perennial	to 5 feet	scarlet	July through September
Bergamot, Wild (*Monarda fistulosa*) perennial	to 5 feet	dark pink to lavender	May to July
Bitter-cress, Hairy (*Cardamine hirsuta*) annual	4-16 inches	white	March through April
Black-foot, Plains (*Melampodium leucanthum*) perennial	8-12 inches	white and yellow	March through November
Bladder-pod, Scaley (*Lesquerella gracilis*) annual	to 20 inches	yellow	March through May
Blue-eyed Grass (*Sisyrinchium ensigerum*) perennial	6-18 inches	blue	March and April
Blue-eyed Grass, Bray (*Sisyrinchium dimorphum*) perennial	to 12 inches	white to dark blue	April to July

297

Herb	Height	Color	Blooms
Blue-eyed Grass, Dotted (*Sisyrinchium pruinosum*) perennial	to 12 inches	blue, blue-purple to purple-violet	April and May
Bluebells (*Campanula rotundifolia*) perennial	12-18 inches	violet-blue	June through October
Bluebonnet (*Lupinus* spp.) winter annual	to 16 inches	blue	January to June
Bluets (*Hedyotis* spp.) annual	1-5 inches	white, pink, lavender, or purple	January through April
Bluets, Fine-leaf (*Hedyotis nigricans*) perennial	2-20 inches	white, pink to purplish	April through November
Bluets, Perennial (*Hedyotis caerulea*) perennial	2-8 inches	white to lilac, but usually clear, pale blue with yellow eye	April through June
Bluets, Summer (*Hedyotis purpurea*) perennial	4-12 inches	white to dark lavender	May through August
Boneset, Late-flowering (*Eupatorium serotinum*) perennial	3-6 feet	whitish	August through November
Boneset, Round-leaf (*Eupatorium rotundifolium*) perennial	1-5 feet	white	July through October
Brown-eyed Susan (*Rudbeckia hirta*) winter annual	1-3 feet	yellow and brown	May through November
Buckwheat (*Fagopyrum esculentum*) annual	4-20 inches	white	June to frost
Bull Nettle (*Cnidoscolus texanus*) perennial	to 40 inches	white	March through September
Bur-clover (*Medicago polymorpha*) annual	1½-10 feet	yellow	spring
Butterfly Weed (*Asclepias tuberosa*)	1-3 feet	yellow to orange or red	June through August
Cardinal Flower (*Lobelia cardinalis*) perennial	1-6 feet	scarlet-red	August through December
Catchfly (*Silene* spp.) annual or perennial	4-24 inches	white, pink to red	May through September

Herb	Height	Color	Blooms
Celestials (*Nemastylis geminiflora*) perennial	5-18 inches	white or blue	March through May
Chicory (*Cichorium intybus*) perennial	8-40 inches	blue	June through October
Clover, White (*Trifolium repens*) perennial	to 10 inches	white to pinkish	April through September
Columbine (*Aquilegia* spp.) perennial	1-2 feet	cream to yellow, pink to red, blue to purple	March through May
Coneflower, Purple (*Echinacea purpurea*) perennial	1-3 feet	pink to dark rose	June through October
Corydalis, Golden (*Corydalis aurea*) annual or biennial	to 24 inches	pale to bright yellow	February through April
Corydalis, Southern (*Corydalis micrantha*) winter annual	to 24 inches	pale yellow	February through April
Crownbeard, Dwarf (*Verbesina nana*) perennial	4-8 inches	orangish	June through October
Crownbeard, Golden (*Verbesina encelioides*) annual or perennial	to 3 feet	yellow	almost all year
Daisy, Engelmann (*Engelmannia pinnatifida*) perennial	to 3 feet	yellow	February through November
Daisy, Huisache (*Amblyolepis setigera*) annual	4-20 inches	yellow	February through June
Daisy, Plains Yellow (*Tetraneuris scaposa*) perennial	to 16 inches	yellow	February through October
Dalea, Woolly (*Dalea lanata*) perennial	12-20 inches	white to blood red or purple	June through October
Dalea, Wright (*Dalea wrightii*) perennial	to 6 inches	yellow	April through September
Dandelion, Common (*Taraxacum officinal*) annual or perennial	to 10 inches	yellow	throughout year

Herb	Height	Color	Blooms
Dandelion, Texas (*Pyrrhopappus multicaulis*) annual	8-20 inches	yellow	February through June
Dandelion, White (*Pinaropappus roseus*)	6-18 inches	white to yellowish and pink to dark	March through May
Dogbane, Spreading (*Apocynum androsaemifolium*) perennial	to 20 inches	white to pink	April through July
Dogweed, Prickle-leaf (*Thymophylla acerosa*) perennial	to 6 inches	lemon yellow	March through November
Encelia, One-head (*Encelia scaposa*) perennial	12-20 inches	yellow	March and April
Eupatorium, Betony-leaf (*Eupatorium betonicifolium*) perennial	to 3 feet	bluish	summer through fall
Eupatorium, Palm-leaf (*Eupatorium greggii*) perennial	2-3 feet	blue to purplish blue	spring through fall
Flame-flower, Orange (*Talinum aurantiacum*) perennial	8-14 inches	orange to reddish	June through October
Flax, Blue (*Linum lewisii*) perennial	8-32 inches	white to dark blue	April through October
Flax, Stiff-stem (*Linum berlandieri*) annual	8-20 inches	golden-yellow to copper and reddish	February through September
Fleabane (*Erigeron* spp.) perennial	4-24 inches	white	early spring to summer
Frog-fruit (*Phyla* spp.) perennial	2-10 inches	white	spring through fall
Frostweed (*Verbesina virginica*) perennial	3-7 feet	white	August to frost
Funnel Flower (*Androstephium coeruleum*) perennial	3-10 inches	white to blue or lavender	March and April
Gaillardia, Fragrant (*Gaillardia suavis*) perennial	to 24 inches	yellow to red and brown	March through May

Herb	Height	Color	Blooms
Gaillardia, Red (*Gaillardia amblyodon*) annual	12-20 inches	dark red	April through October
Garlic, False (*Nothoscordum bivalve*) perennial	6-22 inches	white to creamy yellow	throughout year
Gayfeather, Dense (*Liatris spicata*) perennial	1-6 feet	rose-purple	July through September
Gayfeather, Kansas (*Liatris pycnostachya*) perennial	3-5 feet	lavender to dark purple	June through October
Gayfeather, Large (*Liatris scariosa*) perennial	1-5 feet	pink to lavender	August through October
Gayfeather, Narrow-leaf (*Liatris mucronata*) perennial	1-3 feet	purple	August through December
Gayfeather, Rough (*Liatris aspera*) perennial	16-48 inches	lavender	July through October
Gerardia, Plateau (*Agalinis edwardsiana*) annual	1-3 feet	pink to lavender	September through November
Gerardia, Prairie (*Agalinis heterophylla*) annual	1-2 feet	white to pink or lavender	September and October
Gerardia, Purple (*Agalinis purpurea*) annual	to 4 feet	light pink to purplish	August through November
Gilia, Blue (*Gilia rigidula*) perennial	4-12 inches	blue to blue-violet	March through October
Golden-aster (*Heterotheca subaxillaris*) annual	to 6 feet	yellow	almost all year
Golden-eye (*Viguiera dentata*) perennial	3-6 feet	yellow	September to frost
Goldenrod (*Solidago* spp.) perennial	2-6 feet	yellow	summer through fall
Greenthread, Long-stalk (*Thelesperma longipes*) perennial	10-20 inches	yellow	summer to midfall
Greggia, Narrow-leaf (*Nerisyrenia linearifolium*) perennial	4-12 inches	white	April through August

301

Herb	Height	Color	Blooms
Groundsel, Broom (*Senecio riddellii*) perennial	1½-3½ feet	yellow	July through October
Groundsel, Threadleaf (*Senecio douglasii*) perennial	to 2½ feet	yellow	April through September
Hedge-parsley (*Torilis arvensis*) annual	to 2 feet	white	April through June
Heliotrope, Seaside (*Heliotropium curassavicum*) perennial	to 16 inches	white	March through November
Hemp, Indian (*Apocynum cannabinum*) perennial	to 3 feet	white to greenish	April through August
Henbit (*Lamium amplexicaule*) annual or biennial	6-16 inches	purple and pale lavender	December through May
Herbertia (*Herbertia lahue*) perennial	to 12 inches	pale to dark lavender	March through May
Holly, Desert (*Acourtia nana*) perennial	to 6 inches	pink to lavender-pink	April through December
Horehound, Common (*Marrubium vulgare*) perennial	to 3 feet	white	spring through summer
Hyacinth, Wild (*Camassia scilloides*) perennial	6-24 inches	pale blue to lavender	March through May
Hymenoxys, Slender-leaf (*Tetraneuris linearfolia*) annual	to 16 inches	yellow	March through June
Indian Blanket (*Gaillardia pulchella*) annual	1-2 feet	red and yellow	February through December or all year
Iris, Yellow (*Iris pseudacorus*) perennial	to 3 feet	yellow	April and May
Ironweed, Barestem (*Vernonia acaulis*) perennial	1-4 feet	purple	June through September
Ironweed, Powdery (*Vernonia glauca*) perennial	2-5 feet	purple	June through September
Ironweed, Missouri (*Vernonia missurica*) perennial	3-5 feet	dark rose to purple	July to October

Herb	Height	Color	Blooms
Ironweed, New York (*Vernonia noveboracensis*) perennial	3-7 feet	dark lavender to violet or purple	July through October
Ironweed, Western (*Vernonia baldwinii*) perennial	2-5 feet	purple to rose-purple	July to October
Ironweed, Woolly (*Vernonia lindheimeri*) perennial	8-32 inches	purplish	May to August
Joe-Pye-weed (*Eupatorium fistulosum*) perennial	3-10 feet	lilac-pink to purple or brownish-lavender	July and August
Joe-Pye-weed, Sweet (*Eupatorium purpureum*) perennial	to 7 feet	pink to rose	July through October
Knapweed, Spotted (*Centaurea maculosa*) perennial	2-3 feet	pink to lavender	June to frost
Larkspur, Prairie (*Delphinium virescens*) perennial	to 60 inches	whitish or pale bluish	April through July
Leek (*Allium ampeloprasum*) perennial	3-4½ feet	lavender	May through August
Lemon-mint (*Monarda citriodora*) annual or biennial	to 32 inches	white to rosy-pink or purple	April through October
Lily, Copper (*Habranthus tubis pathus*) perennial	6-12 inches	golden or orange-yellow	August through October
Lobelia, Blue (*Lobelia siphilitica*) perennial	2-5 feet	blue	spring through fall
Loosestrife, Purple (*Lythrum salicaria*) perennial	3-6 feet	rose-purple	June through September
Marigold, Desert (*Baileya multiradiata*) perennial	8-12 inches	bright yellow	throughout year
Marsh-mallow, Salt (*Kosteletzkya virginica*)	to 6 feet	pale pink to rose-pink	June to October
Mexican Hat (*Ratibida columnifera*) perennial	to 2½ feet	yellow, brown, or yellow and brown	March to frost

303

Herb	Height	Color	Blooms
Milfoil (*Achillea millefolium*) perennial	8-40 inches	white or pink	April through June
Milkweed, Common (*Asclepias syriaca*) perennial	3-7 feet	greenish purple to rose-purple	June through August
Milkweed, Mexican (*Asclepias curassavica*) perennial	1-3 feet	yellow and orange	April to frost or all year
Milkweed, Purple (*Asclepias purpurascens*) perennial	16-40 inches	dark rose	April through July
Milkweed, Swamp (*Asclepias incarnata*) perennial	16-60 inches	pale to dark pink	June through October
Milkweed, White-flowered (*Asclepias variegata*) perennial	to 3½ feet	white	April through July
Mint, Wild (*Mentha arvensis*) perennial	6-24 inches	white to lilac	July through September
Mist-flower, Blue (*Eupatorium coelestinum*) perennial	to 6 feet	blue to purplish blue	July to frost
Mist-flower, Pink (*Eupatorium incarnatum*) perennial	to 6 feet	whitish, pink, or lilac	October through February to first freeze
Mock Pennyroyal (*Hedeoma molle*) perennial	6-26 inches	pink to lavender	July through November
Morning Glory, Bush (*Ipomoea leptophylla*) perennial	to 4½ feet	lavender-pink to purple-red	May through July
Mountain-mint (*Pycnanthemum* spp.) perennial	16 inches to 6 feet	white to creamy, pinkish or lavender, often spotted with purple	June through October
Mountain Pink (*Centaurium beyrichii*) annual	4-12 inches	white to pink or rose	May through July
Musk-flower, Scarlet (*Nyctaginia capitata*) perennial	6-18 inches	pink to dark red	March through November
Oyster Plant (*Tragopogon porrifolius*) biennial	1-2 feet	blue to dark violet	May and June

Herb	Height	Color	Blooms
Paintbrush, Downy (*Castilleja sessiliflora*) perennial	6-12 inches	yellowish green and pink to mauve	May through October
Paintbrush, Texas (*Castilleja indivisa*) annual or biennial	to 16 inches	whitish or greenish and orangy-red	May and June
Palafoxia, Hooker (*Palafoxia hookeriana*) annual	2-4 feet	pale to dark rose	July through November
Palafoxia, Rose (*Palafoxia rosea*) annual	1-2 feet	pink to rose	June through October
Paper-flower, Woolly (*Psilostrophe tagetina*) perennial	4-24 inches	yellow	March through October
Parsley, Prairie (*Polytaenia nuttallii*) perennial	to 3 feet	yellow	April through June
Parsley, Texas (*Polytaenia texana*) perennial	20-32 inches	yellow	April through July
Penstemon, Pink Plains (*Penstemon ambiguus*) perennial	to 20 inches	white to dark pink	May through August
Peppergrass, Western (*Lepidium montanum*) perennial	to 28 inches	white	February through August
Peppermint (*Mentha piperita*) perennial	1-3 feet	lavender	July through October
Phacelia (*Phacelia congesta*) annual or biennial	to 3 feet	blue to purplish	March through June
Phlox, Drummond (*Phlox drummondii*) annual	4-20 inches	white to scarlet-red	February through June
Phlox, Prairie (*Phlox pilosa*) perennial	to 2 feet	pale pink to purple	April and May
Phlox, Smooth (*Phlox glaberrima*) perennial	1-5 feet	white to pink, lavender to red-purple	April through July
Phlox, Summer (*Phlox panaculata*) perennial	3-6 feet	pink to magenta	June through October

Herb	Height	Color	Blooms
Phlox, Thick-leaf (*Phlox carolina*) perennial	to 3½ feet	white to pink or purple	May through July
Phlox, White-eye (*Phlox mesoleuca*) perennial	to 24 inches	rose	May through October
Pickerelweed (*Pontederia cordata*) perennial	1-2 feet	violet-blue	June through September
Prairie Clover, Purple (*Dalea purpurea*) perennial	1-3 feet	rose-purple	June and July
Prairie Clover, White (*Dalea candida*) perennial	1-3½ feet	white	May through September
Puccoon, Fringed (*Lithospermum incisum*) perennial	to 12 inches	yellow	November through June
Queen-of-the-prairie (*Filipendula rubra*) perennial	3-6 feet	pink	June through August
Rain-lily (*Cooperia pedunculata*) perennial	to 8 inches	white	March through August
Rain-lily, Evening-star (*Cooperia drummondii*) perennial	to 12 inches	white	May through September
Ramp (*Allium tricoccum*) perennial	6-24 inches	cream to pale yellow	June through September
Rush-pea, Indian (*Hoffmanseggia glauca*) perennial	4-12 inches	bright yellow	March through September
Sage, Blue (*Salvia azurea*) perennial	to 5 feet	white, pale blue to dark blue	May through November
Sage, Cedar (*Salvia roemeriana*) perennial	1-2 feet	brilliant red	March through July
Sage, Lyre-leaf (*Salvia lyrata*) perennial	1-2 feet	pale blue to violet	April through June
Sage, Mealy (*Salvia farinacea*) perennial	to 3 feet	blue	March through November
Sage, Tropical (*Salvia coccinea*) perennial	1-3 feet	bright red to dark scarlet or rarely white to pink	March through December or all year

Herb	Height	Color	Blooms
Sand-verbena (*Abronia* spp.) annual or perennial	8-30 inches	white to pink, lavender to violet-purple or reddish	spring through fall
Sand-verbena, Amelia's (*Abronia ameliae*) perennial	to 2 feet	lavender to violet-purple	December to July
Sand-verbena, Sweet (*Abronia fragrans*) perennial	to 2 feet	white tinged with pink or lavender	December through July
Sea Lavender (*Limonium carolinianum*) perennial	8-34 inches	violet to lavender-blue	May through November
Self-heal (*Prunella vulgaris*) perennial	to 2 feet	purple or violet and lavender	April through June
Senna, Lindheimer (*Senna lindheimeriana*) perennial	3-6 feet	yellow	June through October
Senna, Two-leaved (*Senna roemeriana*) perennial	to 2 feet	yellow	April through September
Shell-flower, Slender (*Nemastylis tenuis*) perennial	10-12 inches	pale blue	May and June
Shepherd's-needle (*Bidens pilosa*) annual or perennial	1-3 feet	white and yellow	March to frost
Sida, Spreading (*Sida abutifolia*) perennial	to 6 inches	yellow to orange-yellow	March through September
Skeleton Plant (*Lygodesmia texana*) perennial	to 2 feet	pink to rose or lavender to pale blue	April through October
Snakeroot, White (*Eupatorium rugosum*) perennial	20-32 inches	white	September through November
Spectacle-pod (*Dimorphocarpha wislizenii*) biennial or perennial	to 2 feet	white	February through May
Spring Beauty (*Claytonia virginica*) perennial	to 12 inches	white to rose	January through April
Squaw-weed, Texas (*Senecio ampullaceus*) annual	1-3 feet	yellow	February to April

307

Herb	Height	Color	Blooms
Star-grass, Yellow (*Hypoxis hirsuta*) perennial	2-8 inches	yellow	March through May
Stenandrium, Shaggy (*Stenandrium barbatum*) perennial	to 2½ inches	reddish to purple	March through June
Sunflower, Annual (*Helianthus annuus*) annual	to 6 feet	yellow and red or purple	March through December or first frost
Sunflower, Bush (*Simsia calva*) perennial	2-3 feet	yellow	April through October
Sunflower, Maximilian (*Helianthus maximiliani*) perennial	3-10 feet	bright yellow	July through November or until frost
Sunflower, Swamp (*Helianthus angustifolius*) perennial	3-6 feet	yellow and purplish red	August through November
Sweet Clover, White (*Melilotus albus*) annual or biennial	3-8 feet	white	May through October
Sweet Clover, Yellow (*Melilotus officinalis*) biennial or rarely annual	2-5 feet	yellow	May through October
Teasel (*Dipsacaceae sylvestris*) biennial	3-9 feet	pink to lavender	July through September
Thistle, Carolina (*Cirsium carolinianum*) biennial or weak perennial	2-6 feet	pink, lavender to purple	May through July
Thistle, Leconte (*Cirsium lecontei*) biennial	1-4 feet	purple	June through August
Thistle, Nodding (*Carduus nutans*) biennial	16-80 inches	pink to rose-purple	May through July
Thistle, Purple (*Cirsium discolor*) biennial	3-10 feet	lavender to purple	July to frost
Thistle, Tall (*Cirsium altissimum*) biennial	3-13 feet	lavender to purple	July to frost

Herb	Height	Color	Blooms
Thistle, Texas (*Cirsium texanum*) biennial or perennial	2-6 feet	pink to rose-purple	May through August
Thistle, Virginia (*Cirsium virginianum*) biennial	1-5 feet	lilac to purple	August to frost
Toadflax, Texas (*Linaria canadensis*) annual or biennial	to 28 inches	pale blue to violet	March through May
Tulipan del Monte (*Hibiscus martianus*) perennial	to 3 feet	dark rose-red to crimson	throughout year
Twin-pod, Rough (*Mendora scabra*) perennial	to 12 inches	yellow	March through October
Verbena, Desert (*Verbena wrightii*) annual	to 2 feet	pink, rose, magenta to purple	February through November
Verbena, Moss (*Verbena tenuisecta*) perennial	6-24 inches	white, pink to purple	March to July
Vervain, Dakota (*Verbena bipinnatifida*) perennial	6-18 inches	pink to lavender or purple	throughout year
Vervain, Hoary (*Verbena striata*) perennial	to 6 feet	blue or purple	June through September
Vervain, Gulf (*Verbena xutha*) perennial	to 6 feet	blue to purple	March through October
Vervain, Hoary (*Verbena stricta*) perennial	to 3½ feet	blue to violet	June through September
Vervain, Rose (*Verbena canadensis*) perennial	to 16 inches	pink to rose or lavender to purple	February through June
Vervain, Tuber (*Verbena rigida*) perennial	to 2 feet	dark purple to magenta	April to frost
Violet (*Viola* spp.) annual or perennial	to 8 inches	white, rose, blue to purple or yellow	February through May
Viper's Bugloss (*Echium vulgare*) biennial	1-2½ feet	blue-violet	June through October

Herb	Height	Color	Blooms
Wallflower, Plains (*Erysimum asperum*) biennial or perennial	6-24 inches	yellow to orange-red	April through July
Wallflower, Western (*Erysimum capitatum*) biennial or perennial	16-40 inches	yellow to orange-red	March through July
Waterleaf, Blue (*Hydrolea ovata*) perennial	to 30 inches	blue	September through October
Wedelia, Hairy (*Wedelia hispida*) perennial	20-40 inches	yellow-orange	March through November
Wild Onion (*Allium canadense*) perennial	8-24 inches	pale to dark pink	April and May
Wild Onion, Drummond (*Allium drummondii*) perennial	4-12 inches	white, pink to reddish	March through May
Wild Onion, Fragrant (*Allium perdulce*) perennial	4-8 inches	white to pink	March
Wild Onion, Nodding (*Allium cernuum*) perennial	4-20 inches	white or pink	late summer
Wild Onion, Yellow-flowered (*Allium coryi*) perennial	to 8 inches	yellow	April and May
Winter-cress, Garden (*Barbarea vulgaris*) biennial	to 12 inches	yellow	April through June
Wood-sorrel, Yellow (*Oxalis dillenii*)	to 16 inches	yellow	February to November or frost
Woolly-white, Fine-leaf (*Hymenopappus flavescens*) perennial	1½-3 feet	yellow	May through September
Woolly-white, Flat-top (*Hymenopappus scabiosaeus*) biennial	1½-3½ feet	white	March through July
Yellow Star, Texas (*Lindheimera texana*) annual	to 20 inches	yellow	March through June
Zephyr-lily, Copper (*Zephyranthes longifolia*) perennial	to 10 inches	bright yellow	April through July

Herb	Height	Color	Blooms
Zinnia, Dwarf (*Zinnia acerosa*) perennial	to 10 inches	white and yellow	June through October
Zinnia, Plains (*Zinnia grandiflora*) perennial	3-9 inches	yellow	June through October

Tiger Swallowtail

APPENDICES

How to Photograph Butterflies

Having enticed butterflies into your garden, you may now be interested in photographing them. After you attempt it once or twice, however, you may feel like giving up butterfly photography as being too frustrating. Butterflies just don't ordinarily stay still long enough to have their pictures taken.

Patience and persistence, year in and year out, are the first and most basic requirements in good butterfly photography. Following are some tips which may help—even with your first efforts. I have tried to concentrate on the equipment and techniques which I have found to work the best in photographing butterflies. The information given here is for photographing in the field, for it is here, in the butterflies' natural habitat, that you will often be presented with exciting opportunities for recording their natural behavioral activities and beauty.

Equipment

My first choice in cameras for butterfly photography is a 35mm single-lens reflex (SLR). Versatility, small size, light weight, and ease of handling make it unrivaled for this type of work. Top-quality 35s are within an affordable price range.

Almost all of today's cameras offer through-the-lens metering. This allows for more rapid adjustment of the light than if a separate light meter is used, and it is almost mandatory in butterfly photography.

The lenses you choose are most important. Even modestly priced lenses provide good resolution when stopped down three or four f-stops, while the more expensive lenses "show their stuff" by featuring wider apertures and having flatter fields. The best results are *usually* obtained by using the lenses made for the camera body you choose—Nikkor lenses for Nikon, Canon lenses for Canon. Put a little time and effort in becoming acquainted with various lenses and their features, always keeping in mind the type of photography you will be doing the most of, before making your final choice. It pays to shop around.

The standard 50mm lens usually sold with the camera can be used for insect photography, but to even come close to filling the frame (the actual portion of the slide or print), you'll have to add some sort of extension, such as a close-up lens, extension tube, or bellows. When you do this, though, the distance between lens and subject has been drastically reduced, and, in most cases, butterflies do not allow such close encounters. Such extensions are best when you can place the camera on a tripod and move it in close, with a butterfly made immobile with dew or on a cool autumn morning.

Long telephoto lenses, those 300mm or longer, sometimes have a macro mode which allows you to move in semiclose. However, in actual use, they generally do not work out very well in photographing butterflies. Their biggest drawbacks are shallow depth of field and unwieldiness in bulk and weight. They are almost impossible to hand-hold without movement and are best left to the photographer after much bigger game and using a tripod or shoulder stock.

Some of the zoom lenses on the market are advertised as "macro-focusing," but they would probably be more accurately referred to as close-focusing lenses. While some of them can focus to a subject area of four by six inches, they cannot fill the frame with a small butterfly as a true macro lens can. The main problem with lenses of this type is that they are usually "slow" lenses to start with, and after stopping down two or three stops to obtain some depth of field, the shutter speed will be so slow as to not freeze action or stop camera shake.

If you really feel you want to try a zoom, it is important to pay attention to the focal length. Some zoom lenses, in order to get the largest magnification, put you within inches of your subject—definitely not the lens for butterfly photography. Try focusing on a butterfly-sized object in the camera shop before purchasing, being sure to measure the distance from the edge of the lens to the subject when filling the frame. If the distance is closer than two feet, you haven't got much of a chance.

Autofocus cameras may seem like the answer to a butterfly photographer's dream, but in actuality they are just that—a dream. The main problem is their point of focus. Autofocus cameras or lenses are designed to focus on whatever is in the center of the screen and the center only. For good composition, however, the butterfly you are photographing will most often not be situated in the exact center of the screen. Another drawback is that most autofocus cameras do not allow the shutter to move until the subject is in focus. Working close to butter-

Zebra Swallowtail

flies, with their fast-moving bodies and rapidly beating wings, the camera rarely gets in focus long enough to allow release of the shutter. It is true that most autofocus cameras have a focus-lock, where you can focus on the subject, push the focus-lock button, then recompose and shoot. This works with a basking butterfly or one stilled by cold or dew, but it will rarely work well in trying to shoot rapidly moving insects. Some cameras with automatic focusing do have manual focusing controls, which of course work the same as nonautomatic focusing cameras.

By far the best lenses for butterfly photography are the true macro (or in some instances sold as "micro") lenses in the "medium" 100mm, 105mm, or 200mm range. These are lenses with finely ground optics and exceptional focusing quality. With their precision built-in extension mechanisms, they give the photographer adequate working distance while still focusing close enough for good shots of the butterfly, often without the necessity of adding extra extensions. And their weight is such that, with practice, you can hand-hold them without exceptional shake or movement.

314

Using the 200mm macro lens, you can fill the frame with a basking Giant Swallowtail, wings spread out flat and approximately five-and-a-half inches across, with the front of the lens approximately three feet away. For the smaller butterflies, such as Skippers and Hairstreaks, you can attach one or more close-up tubes between the camera and the lens, giving more magnification yet still allowing more working distance than if working with a shorter focal length lens plus extensions. One thing to keep in mind is that when a close-up tube or lens is attached, different measurements apply and the ones shown on the lens are no longer useful. The new distances are easily memorized, or, after a little practice, you will develop a feel for which size extension you will need for each size subject.

There is an added bonus in using the longer focal length lens. The angle of coverage is much narrower, thereby cutting out many distracting objects to the sides and in the background.

The simplest way to get more magnification for your lens and retain best image quality is to add extension tubes. Extension tubes are rigid and hollow and come in different lengths. These tubes, by adding space between the camera lens and body, allow a lens to focus closer by moving it away from the film plane. Once having added an extension tube, you will be limited to close focusing. This may not be bad, however, if you are out for an extended period of only butterfly photography.

The next thing to consider when photographing butterflies is film. You have choices of film which give slides or film which produce prints. If you want to make slides, the next thing to consider is the speed of the film. For the inexperienced and impatient photographer, really slow films (such as Kodachrome 25) are definitely out. Also, if you desire a good-quality slide, do not use the really fast (200 or more) films. Medium-speed Kodachrome 64 and Ektachrome 64 and 100 are excellent choices, giving good color and grain in the finished slide and a speed and depth of field the photographer can work with. With or without using flash, Fujichrome 100 gives an extra crispness and deeper color saturation, especially for greens, reds, and yellows. It is always best to use the film with the lowest ISO rating (film speed) possible, thereby obtaining the truest color rendition and the finest grain. Decide on your optimum film speed and brand after you shoot a few rolls and compare the results to carefully kept notes.

If you want to produce good-quality prints, again stick to the lowest speed films possible. Kodacolor 100 and 200 and Fujicolor 100 and 200 allow relatively fast shutter speed with good depth of field. For the sharpest printing and truest color, have all your film developed by Kodak, the maker of your film, or a good custom lab.

Until you learn all the idiosyncrasies of your camera as well as what is most pleasing to your eye, try taking shots using slide film with your exposure dial set at 0 or normal. Then shoot the same subject under the exact conditions but underexposing in one-half increments for at least one-and-a-half increments. For print film, do the exact opposite. First expose at 0 or normal exposure, then overexpose in one-half increments for at least three shots. Keep notes and compare the results. It may be that you will choose to leave your exposure dial set on one of the under- or overexposure settings.

Shutter speed is of the utmost importance when photographing butterflies, for almost without exception the camera has to be hand-held. In order to get a good shot, you have to constantly and quickly be changing position, and only if you happen upon a butterfly basking will you have time to set up a tripod. When hand-holding a camera, there is a general rule which states that you use the closest (or next fastest) shutter speed to the focal length of the lens being used. You need to use a shutter speed of at least 1/125 second if using the 105mm lens, 1/250 second if using the 200mm lens, and so on. These are general setting guidelines for stopping hand shake and other movements of a hand-held camera as well as the motion of the insect's wings. These shutter speed settings are the absolute minimum; for the inexperienced or those new to butterfly photography, I would suggest *doubling* these settings: 1/250 second for the 105mm, 1/500 second for the 200mm lens, and so on. In some instances, as with the Swallow-tails, even the 1/500 second may not be enough to completely stop motion. A Swallowtail lightly clasps the flower with its feet while feeding and continues to flutter its wings rapidly, making a fast shutter speed mandatory. The wing movement is sometimes not detrimental to the overall appeal of the photo, however, adding a spark of life and ethereal beauty not obtained in a sharp but perfectly still photograph.

An electronic flash helps ensure sharpness when you are having to hand-hold your camera. Different cameras synchronize at different shutter speeds, and a model that synchronizes at 1/125 second or 1/250 second is preferable to one that synchronizes at 1/60 second, for the shorter the flash duration, the more effective the stopping of movement. A flash which can be used off the camera works best when photographing butterflies and other small creatures. Properly designed brackets for the flash are not easy to find, so you may want to design your own.

Either one or two flashes can be used. More flashes than this become somewhat unwieldy and really should not be needed in field photography. If using two flashes, mount one somewhat above the other and on the opposite side of the camera. Better modeling is obtained if the lower flash is less powerful and is used as a fill-in for the shadow area.

When using two flashes, the more distant parts of the background tend to become darker, sometimes losing the natural look of the photo. Also, as the f-stop gets larger, the background gets darker. For instance, at f 5.6 the background is very light with practically no shadows, at f 8 it is almost at natural conditions, but at f 32 the background is almost black.

Another way of using flash which retains a more natural look involves only one flash. This single flash is used as a supplement to sunshine to stop action and to fill in shadow areas only. This is known as fill-flash or synchro-sunlight photography. Again, the flash is mounted off-camera on a manufactured bracket or one you make yourself.

Always use a cable release. Being able to release the shutter with your thumb behind the camera eliminates both movement of the finger in sight of the butterfly and movement of the camera itself by pressing on the shutter release button. Get a black cable release (or paint it dull black) and loosely attach it to some part of the camera body to keep it from swinging around.

Almost every 35mm camera comes with a split-image rangefinder screen. This type of screen does not work well at all when doing any kind of close-up work since most of the time a large part of your subject will be blacked out in the viewfinder. Other types of screens are available for most cameras, and it would be much better to replace the split-image type with one of the clear matte screens.

Tripods are usually indispensable in insect photography, but when photographing butterflies in the field, you will almost surely have to hand-hold the camera. Normally, by the time you set up a tripod and make the adjustments, a feeding butterfly will have moved to an undesired pose, flown to another plant, or flown away, period. However, carry along a tripod for those times when you find a chrysalis or a caterpillar.

Practice

One of the best things you can possibly do to ensure good pictures of butterflies is to *practice* before ever going into the field or garden. Collect a dead butterfly or cut a butterfly shape from stiff, colored paper or a picture from an old magazine. Either glue or wire it to a stick or a dried flower and start working with your empty camera. Do this with different sizes of butterflies, different colors, and both with wings open and with wings closed. Working outside, place the butterfly against different backgrounds such as tree bark, grasses, flowers, earth, and rocks. You can also do this exercise in your house during inclement weather, using a potted plant and different textures for backgrounds. Constantly check the depth of field preview button on the camera to see exactly what you would be getting on the film. Use different lenses and the lenses with various extension tubes until you know instantly which combination gives you what magnification.

Practice until you automatically know which way the lens turns to bring the subject in focus. Work the f-stop ring until you do not have to think about the direction to turn to give you more or less depth of field. If you are using some sort of close-up attachment, place the butterfly in a steady position, look at the background (with the butterfly in focus), then measure the distance with a ruler from subject to background. If you are using just a long lens, look on the distance scale marked on the lens. Learn to develop a feel for subject-to-background distance and the amount of sharpness (or blurriness) of the background at various f-stops. I know of nothing better than such exercises to improve your photo taking.

In the Field

Photographing active butterflies in the field requires some physical stamina and expertise. It also demands patience and the ability and agility to move slowly and to remain in odd, uncomfortable positions for several minutes at a time. Butterflies are endowed with a well-developed sense of self-preservation, and any sudden movement will send them fluttering out of range, so sneak up on the wary insects with all the stealth of a predator. Make all your movements with fluidity and slow deliberation in order not to betray your presence. This requires rigid self-discipline and concentration. Especially watch where you step (or crawl) when approaching a butterfly, for you may inadvertently move a branch of the plant the butterfly is resting on. Any movement of the resting or feeding place— or even of a branch of a nearby plant—which is faster than the present wind movement will usually cause the butterfly to take flight. Also, take care that your shadow does not fall across a basking or feeding butterfly, for this will either send it off in fright or at least cause it to close its wings.

Once you have slowly worked your way near a subject that is close to the ground, you should ever so slowly sink down until one knee is on the ground and the other knee is bent toward your chin. The bent knee offers an excellent support or "flexible tripod": You can either rest your arms on top of the knee or clasp the knee between the elbows, whichever puts the film plane parallel with the wings of the butterfly and helps in steadying the camera.

Now that you are at least in partial position, you must quickly decide on the portion of the butterfly's body you want in focus along with its eyes. As the human eye is always drawn to a creature's eyes in a photograph, concentrate first on getting the eyes of your butterfly in sharp focus. Then you can begin to move the camera a few millimeters one way or another to get the wings and body in focus, also. But do not take too long in moving the camera about. The more time you spend squinting through the viewfinder, the more your eyes will tire and become unable to focus properly, and your back and arm muscles will begin to tremble so that you can no longer hold the camera steady. It is far better to focus on the eyes, move the camera a time or two for maximum wing coverage, hold your breath, and gently press the cable release. If the butterfly does not fly away, then try for even better shots with more of the butterfly in focus.

Spending time watching the butterfly's actions is often beneficial. Some species, such as the small Yellows, Blues, Hairstreaks, and some Skippers, take off when disturbed, fly back and forth or round and round, then return and alight in exactly the same spot as before. In some instances, do not move in pursuit but remain perfectly still, and chances are you will get your shot after all. There are some species which allow a fairly close approach. Others, once disturbed, take off never to be seen again. Ever. It is good to know something of the habits of each species in order to save time waiting for one not likely to return.

Within each species there are "personalities" which show exceptions to the general species behavior. With persistence (or luck), you can occasionally find a butterfly, belonging to a group generally noted for their flightiness, which will sit for a long period of time, letting you get shot after shot after shot. At such times you almost wish it *would* leave.

318

Buckeye

One easy method—and one I often use if I spot something special and it appears as if I might get only one or two shots—is to quickly pick an object close by about the same size as the butterfly I am stalking. I then focus the camera on the object to include approximately the amount of butterfly and background I want in the photograph, add extension tubes if needed, adjust the speed and f-stop I want, then slowly approach the insect with everything preset. Some literature suggests that you start shooting when still far away from the insect, then continue to move forward, refocusing and shooting. In my opinion this is a terrible waste of time, film, and money. Spend the time on *slow* movements getting closer to your subject. You will avoid moving your hands in constant refocusing and cocking the shutter, for one of the things you do not want to do when photographing butterflies is to move any more than absolutely necessary. This applies especially to your camera and hands, being the closest things to the subject.

Also, before approaching a butterfly, note its general outline, always keeping in mind what you intend to do with your photo, and choose the desired format, whether vertical or horizonal. Since it is normally easier to hold a camera in the horizonal position, it is easy to forget that some things lend themselves more satisfactorily to a vertical format—butterflies newly emerged with downward hanging wings or when resting with wings closed, for example.

Background often helps decide the format. If the background is cluttered or distracting, then having more of the butterfly in the frame eliminates more of the background. In this case, use vertical format if the insect's wings are closed, horizontal if the wings are spread.

319

Often the background can enhance the coloring of the butterfly, the shape of its wings, or some other detail. If the background happens to be grass or leaves, throw it out of focus for a wonderful textured and mottled effect. If the butterfly is on a flower and there are other flowers in the background, these can be thrown out of focus by using a larger f-stop (opening the lens) and will become beautiful spots of blurred coloring with no distracting detail.

Since butterflies can see colors exceptionally well, the clothing you wear while photographing is extremely important. This is a time to see and not be seen, so bright clothing is best left for other occasions. Drab greens, browns, and khaki work best, thereby allowing you to blend in with the surroundings.

Your clothing should be loose fitting enough to allow for extra maneuverability, but nothing should remain loose, such as shirt-tails or unbuttoned sleeves, to flap about in the wind. Keep bandannas or photo equipment in pockets or bags and not loose to move or rattle. Hats are sometimes useful in helping shade and disrupt the face outline. They also help cut the glare from glasses and prevent sunburn and sunstroke. Avoid floppy brims, however, whose movement may scare the butterfly away. Knee pads, the type worn by athletes and which can be purchased at a sporting goods store, are most welcome when kneeling or crawling about on rocks or among stickers.

A small camera bag belted about your waist is very handy for carrying extension tubes, extra lenses, and film. Keep a couple of small cotton rags, washcloths, or bandannas in the bag for cleaning glasses and cameras—*never* the lens—and wiping a sweaty brow. It is often handy to have a small case which can be opened and closed quickly and easily and fitted with an assortment of small tools. Include a pair of small scissors for clipping twigs and grass blades, tweezers for removing debris, and an assortment of small artist's brushes for removing spider webs, dust, and so on. You really appreciate these tools when photographing eggs, larvae, and pupae.

Butterflies are easily spooked by anything bright or flashing. Leave at home all shiny jewelry such as watches, rings, or dangling earrings. It is worth the extra time to cover the silver-colored metal parts of your camera and flash with electrician's tape. This can be removed easily after a photo session, if desired. If purchasing a new camera, consider a black model, though it will be slightly more expensive. If the flash bracket is of shiny metal, paint it matte black. Everything you can possibly do to eliminate brightness, flashing, and movement is that much more to your advantage.

Do not leave the lens cap dangling from the lens. If you normally use this type of cap, remove it completely before venturing forth in pursuit of butterflies, or pursue is all you are likely to do. Use a regular, unattached cap for this work, easing it into your pocket after removal from the lens.

Whatever you do, don't spray yourself with insect repellent before heading out to photograph butterflies. Butterflies *are* insects, so they are very sensitive to the smell of this stuff. One whiff of Deepwoods Off, and the butterflies will head for unpolluted areas, not to be seen again while you are around.

At any time of the year, one of the best times of the day for photographing butterflies is early in the morning. At this time they are very hungry and allow a closer approach while nectaring. It is also the time when they are more likely to be basking. In the spring and fall months, especially, they spend much time in the cool mornings with wings spread wide, bringing their body temperature up to optimal operating levels. Late afternoons are also excellent during the summer, for then they have a tendency to "cool down," their feeding motions becoming much slower. It is at such times you can get the easiest and most spectacular shots.

For the best color rendition from your film, choose early morning, late afternoon, or brightly overcast days for your butterfly photography. During these periods the light is much softer and the shadows are less harsh or nonexistent.

Gardening Tips for Easier Butterfly Photography

If photos are one of your objectives when planting your garden to attract butterflies, then remember when laying out the flower beds to leave a walk space around some of the insects' favorite plants. This walk space could be either bare ground, native grasses, or leaf litter. These give plenty of room for moving with the butterfly and a background which appears natural if included in the photo. The flower beds can be edged with a walkway of brick, gravel, or hay, offering a convenient kneeling place on damp or dewy mornings without getting your clothes wet or dirty. On the other hand, bricks and gravel can be unappealing in a photo if you are trying for the pure, naturalistic approach for your photos.

In border plantings there are advantages to three different types of arrangements:

🦋 Plants spaced close together in a narrow border, giving a lot of flowers and good opportunities for photos by walking in front of the border. Long portions of the border should be composed of all the same species and color of flowers so that the background in the photo is not a clash of colors or shapes. This of course is how the butterflies also like the plants to be.

🦋 Narrow borders in an open lawn space, preferably running north and south, which provide space to walk on both sides, and with the east side receiving morning sun and the west side the afternoon sun. This eliminates some of the problems with deep shadows.

🦋 Plants spaced widely apart in a border or bed, leaving stepping space between in order to maneuver between the plants without demolishing the adjacent plants and the chance for future photos.

Keep the area around the butterflies' best-liked plants free of garden litter or unsightly debris. There is nothing more frustrating than to see a perfect butterfly specimen with wings calmly stretched out in the sun, only to find when you look through the viewfinder that a water hose, plastic plant container, or plant markers are causing ugly and distracting blobs in the background.

If you find that you usually photograph in the early morning, make it a habit to patrol the beds the evening before, removing seed pods, dead leaves, unsightly

321

grass clumps, or whatever. At this time, view every flower as a potential shot with a butterfly perched on it and clean up the area accordingly.

Before starting your photo session, place a few branches of greenery to hide such things as plastic cups of sugar water and piles of fermenting fruit. Also, use the f-stop, controlling the depth of field to throw the background out of focus if an object cannot be moved, covered up, or otherwise gotten rid of.

If you have a new garden with small perennials, then plant tall annuals, such as Mexican Sunflower, Hollyhocks, Sunflowers, Cosmos, Dill, or Fennel, behind them for an attractive background.

Consider wooden fences in your garden: They're more attractive in general than wire and afford a more natural background. If you have wire fences, try covering them by planting with perennial or annual vines which grow well in your area. Or again, plant in the staggered height method, tall plants at the back and lower growing plants in front. Inexpensive reed fencing can be attached to an existing wire fence, making an excellent natural-colored background. Any vines you allow to grow on the reed fence should be the annual sort, however, as the reed does not normally last but two to five years.

If there is no way to keep a wire fence out of an otherwise perfectly wonderful shot, then choose an angle where the sun does not reflect off the wire, select a large f-stop for a shallow depth of field, and throw the wire out of focus. Check the depth of field button often to be sure when the wire becomes sufficiently blurred.

If there is a particular plant or group of plants, such as Lantana, Thoroughwort, Mist-flower, Verbena, Flame Acanthus, or Mexican Sunflower, in the border, it is possible to set up a blind and wait for butterflies to come to you. While this lets you rest more comfortably, it greatly restricts the butterfly poses obtainable. The ability to move around, get the wings of the butterfly in a flatter plane, or move for better lighting is greatly reduced from a blind. However, you can achieve more shots from the blind due to your concealment, not frightening the insects.

If you include larval food plants in your garden plantings, you can take photos of the entire life cycle, from egg to adult. Close and frequent observations can sometimes net some unusual or especially interesting shots not usually obtainable on ordinary, casual walks or hikes. Since the food plant a caterpillar is chomping on is in your own garden, you can feel free to clip a branch and move it to a more desirable photographing position if needed—making sure, of course, that you replace the critter onto a living plant once you are done photographing it.

If you find a chrysalis and watch it closely, you can record photos of the emerging adult butterfly. Again, you can clip the branch of the plant with the attached chrysalis, snip away interfering background foliage, and place the branch in a more photogenic position. After emerging, the butterfly remains clinging to the chrysalis case or a nearby leaf or branch for quite some time, resting and letting its wings become completely dry. During this period, you may obtain excellent photos of the perfect specimen if you do not move the branch, causing the butterfly to take flight.

You will find photographing butterflies well worth the practice and effort. To capture permanently such flickering beauty will probably become quite addictive!

Following is a basic list of equipment with which you can take beautiful butterfly photographs:

> 35mm single-lens reflex camera
> 105mm or 200mm macro lens
> Extension tubes (automatic)
> Film of your choice (ISO 64 or 100)
> Cable release (black)
> Small powered flash (optional)
> Flash bracket (optional)
> Tripod (optional)

Sources for Special Photo Equipment

> Blacklock Photo Equipment, Inc.
> P.O. Box 560
> Moose Lake, Minnesota 55767

> Leonard Rue Enterprises
> RD 3, Box 31
> Blairstown, New Jersey 07825

> Lepp and Associates
> P.O. Box 6240
> Los Osos, California 93412

U.S.D.A. Hardiness Zone Map

−40° TO −30° F.	−30° TO −20° F.	−20° TO −10° F.	−10° TO 0° F.	0° TO 10° F.	10° TO 20° F.	20° TO 30° F.	30° TO 40° F.
3	4	5	6	7	8	9	10

APPROXIMATE RANGE OF AVERAGE ANNUAL MINIMUM TEMPERATURES

Regions of Texas

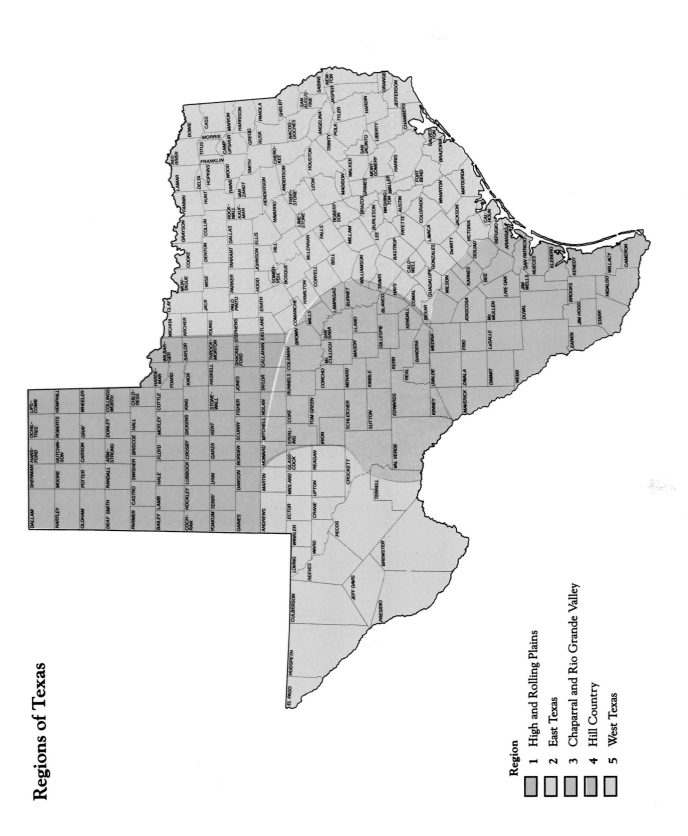

Region

1 High and Rolling Plains
2 East Texas
3 Chaparral and Rio Grande Valley
4 Hill Country
5 West Texas

Special South Florida Butterflies

The following is a list of butterflies and their food plants which appear mostly in the extreme southern portion of Florida—a special area for butterflies in much the same way South Texas attracts exotic butterflies. In fact, some of these species also occur in the Rio Grande Valley area of Texas. The same methods of attracting butterflies and obtaining food plants given for the South Texas garden can be applied here.

Butterfly	Food Plant
Atala (*Eumaeus atala*)	Coontie (*Zamia pumila*)
Crescentspot, Cuban (*Anthanassa frisia*)	Shrimp Plant (*Beloperone guttata*)
Dagger-wing, Ruddy (*Marpesia petreus*)	Banyan Tree, Wild (*Ficus citrifolia*) Fig, Short-leaf (*Ficus brevifolia*) Fig, Common (*Ficus carica*)
Duskywing, Florida (*Ephyriades brunnea*)	Byrsonima, Key (*Byrsonima lucida*) Cherry, Barbados (*Malpighia glabra*)
Hairstreak, Acis (*Strymon acis*)	Croton, Wild (*Croton linearis*)
Hairstreak, Angelic (*Electrostrymon angelia*)	Brazilian Pepper (*Schinus terebinthifolius*)
Hairstreak, Azia (*Tmolus azia*)	Tamarind, Wild (*Lysiloma bahamensis*)
Hairstreak, Columella (*Strymon columella*)	Indian-mallow (*Abutilon permolle*) Suriana (*Suriana maritima*)
Hairstreak, Martial (*Strymon martialis*)	Trema, Florida (*Trema micrantha*)
Hairstreak, Silver-banded (*Chlorostrymon simaethis*)	Balloon-vine, Common (*Cardiospermum halicacabum*)
Leafwing, Florida (*Anaea floridalis*)	Croton, Wild (*Croton linearis*)
Malachite (*Siproeta stelenes*)	Yerba Papagayo (*Blechum brownei*) Ruellia (*Ruellia coccinea*)
Monk (*Asbolis capucinus*)	Palm, Coconut (*Cocos nucifera*) Palm, Date (*Phoenix dactylifera*) Palm, Everglades (*Acoelorrhaphe wrightii*) Palmetto, Cabbage (*Sabal palmetto*)
Queen, Tropic (*Danaus eresimus*)	White Vine (*Sarcostemma clausa*)
Skipper, Hammock (*Polygonus leo*)	Dogwood, Jamaican (*Piscidia piscipula*) Karum Tree (*Pongamia pinnata*)
Skipper, Mangrove (*Phocides pigmalion*)	Mangrove, Red (*Rhizophora mangle*)
Skipper, Palmetto (*Euphyes arpa*)	Palmetto, Saw (*Serenoa repens*)
Skipper, Three-spotted (*Cymaenes tripunctus*)	Grass, Guinea (*Panicum maximum*)
Sulphur, Orange-barred (*Phoebis philea*)	Senna, Coffee (*Senna pendula*) Poinciana, Royal (*Poinciana pulcherima*)
Sulphur, Statira (*Aphrissa statira*)	Dalbergia (*Dalbergia exastophyllum*)
Swallowtail, Bahama (*Heraclides andraemon*)	Lime (*Citrus aurantifolia*) Orange, Sour (*Citrus aurantium*) Rue, Common (*Ruta graveolens*) Zanthoxylum (*Zanthoxylum* spp.)

Swallowtail, Queen (*Heraclides androgeus*)

Swallowtail, Schaus's (*Heraclides aristodemus*)

White, Florida (*Appias drusilla*)
Yellow, Mimosa (*Pyrisitia nise*)

Orange, Sweet (*Citrus sinensis*)
Zanthoxylum, Big (*Zanthoxylum elephantiasis*)
Torchwood (*Amyris elemifera*)
Prickly Ash, Lime (*Zanthoxylum fagara*)
Plum, Guinea (*Capparis lateriflora*)
Mimosa (*Mimosa pudica*)

Seed and Plant Sources
(Other Than Texas)

Some of these nurseries have mail order, others do not, so write to them for information first. Companies who advertise that they collect plants from the wild are not listed here. There are many other nurseries in each state not listed here. Contact local sources for these nurseries.

Andre Viette Farm and Nursery
Route 1, Box 16
Fisherville, Virginia 22939

Bullbay Creek Farm
Route 2, Box 381
Tallahassee, Florida 32301

W. Atlee Burpee & Co.
300 Park Avenue
Warminster, Pennsylvania 18991

Cedar Lane Farms
3790 Sandy Creek Road
Madison, Georgia 30650

The Country Garden
Route 2
Crivitz, Wisconsin 54114
(*seeds, perennials, and bulbs of some of the
hard-to-find plants*)

Bill Dodd's Rare Plants
P.O. Drawer 377
Semmes, Alabama 36575

Dry Country Plants
Las Cruces, New Mexico 88001

Dutch Gardens, Inc.
P.O. Box 400
Montvale, New Jersey 07645

H.G. Hastings Co.
P.O. Box 4274M
Atlanta, Georgia 30302

Joseph Harris Company, Inc.
Moreton Farm
Rochester, New York 14624

Holbrook Farm and Nursery
Route 2, Box 223-B
Fletcher, North Carolina 28732

Homochitto Outdoors
P.O. Box 630
Meadville, Mississippi 39653

Izard Ozark Natives
P.O. Box 454
Mountain View, Arkansas 72560

J.W. Jung Seed
Randolph, Wisconsin 53957

Louisiana Nature and Science Center
11000 Lake Forest Boulevard
New Orleans, Louisiana 70127-2816

Mid-Atlantic Wildflowers
S/R Box 226
Gloucester Point, Virginia 23062

Native Gardens
Route 1, Box 494
Fisher Lane
Greenback, Tennessee 37742

Natural Gardens
113 Jasper Lane
Oak Ridge, Tennessee 37830

Niche Gardens
Route 1, Box 290
Chapel Hill, North Carolina 27514

Oak Hill Farm
204 Pressley Street
Clover, South Carolina 29710

Park Seed Company
P.O. Box 46
Greenwood, South Carolina 29648-0046

Passiflora Wildflowers
Route 1, Box 190A
Germantown, North Carolina 27019

Plants of the Southwest
1570 Pacheco Street
Santa Fe, New Mexico 87501
(seed only)

Prairie Basse Native Plants
Route 2, Box 491F
Carencro, Louisiana 70520

Salter Tree Farm
Route 2, Box 1332
Madison, Florida 32340

Seed Savers Exchange
P.O. Box 70
Decorah, Iowa 52101

Southwestern Native Seeds
Box 50503
Tucson, Arizona 85703

Stokes Seeds, Inc.
737 Main Street, Box 548
Buffalo, New York 14240

Sunlight Gardens, Inc.
Route 3, Box 286TX
Loudon, Tennessee 37774

Thompson & Morgan, Inc.
P.O. Box 1308
Jackson, New Jersey 08527

Transplant Nursery
Parkertown Road
Lavonia, Georgia 30553

Virginia Natives
Wildside, P.O. Box 18
Hume, Virginia 22639

Wayside Gardens
Hodges, South Carolina 29695-0001

We-Du Nurseries
Route 5, Box 724
Marion, North Carolina 28752

Wildland and Native Seeds Foundation
2402 Hoffman Drive NE
Albuquerque, New Mexico 87110

Woodlanders, Inc.
1128 Colleton Avenue
Aiken, South Carolina 29801
(offers yellow-flowered Asclepias)

Seed and Plant Sources in Texas

As with the aforementioned nurseries, write to the following to find out whether they sell by mail or not. Most of them do not. This is only a sample listing of Texas sources. For more lengthy lists of both seed and plant sources, write for the publication Texas Native Tree and Plant Directory in care of Ron Hagquist, Marketing Division, Texas Department of Agriculture, P.O. Box 12847, Austin, Texas 78711, or to the National Wildlife Research Center, P.O. Box 1011, 2600 FM Road 973 North, Austin, Texas 78725-9990.

Alexander's Bluebonnet Seed
8917 Sam Carter Drive
Austin, Texas 78736

Armand Bayou Nature Center
8600 Bay Area Boulevard
P.O. Box 58828
Houston, Texas 77258

Bamert Seed Company
Route 3, Box 1120
Muleshoe, Texas 79347

Barton Springs Nursery
428 Sterzing Street
Austin, Texas 78704

Callahan's General Store
501 Bastrop Highway
Austin, Texas 78741

The Dallas Nature Center
(formerly Greenhills Environmental Center)
7575 Wheatland Road
Dallas, Texas 75249

Days of Thyme and Roses
Route 3, Box 134C
Montgomery, Texas 77356

Fort Worth Nature Center
P.O. Box 11694
Fort Worth, Texas 76109

Gone Native
Route 4, 2001 Broken Hills East
Midland, Texas 79701

Green Horizons
218 Quinlan, Suite 571
Kerrville, Texas 78028

The Groundskeeper
  Landscape & Garden Center
10201 Research Boulevard
Austin, Texas 78759

Gunsight Mountain Ranch & Nursery
P.O. Box 86
Tarply, Texas 78883

Heep's Nursery
Route 3, Palm Drive
Harlingen, Texas 78550

Hilltop Herb Farm
P.O. Box 1734
Cleveland, Texas 77327

Horizon Seeds, Inc.
P.O. Box 886 (7 miles east on Highway 60)
Herford, Texas 79045

Houston Daylily Gardens, Inc.
P.O. Box 7008, Department MN
The Woodlands, Texas 77380
(catalog $2.00)

Dr. Thad M. Howard
16201 San Pedro Avenue
San Antonio, Texas 78232
(bulbs only)

J'Don Seeds International
P.O. Box 10998-533
Austin, Texas 78766

Lilypons Water Gardens
839S FM 1489
Brookshire, Texas 77423

The Lowery Nursery
2323 Sleepy Hollow Road
Conroe, Texas 77385

Meanwhile Farm
Box 240
Wimberley, Texas 78676

Native American Seed
94 Jeter Road
Argyle, Texas 76226

Native Design Nursery
16318 Bandera Highway
Helotes, Texas 78023

Native Plant Project
P.O. Box 1433
Edinburg, Texas 78540
(gathers and distributes native seed)

Native Son Plant Nursery
507 Lockhart Drive
Austin, Texas 78704

Neiman Environments Nursery
Route 1, Box 48
Flower Mound, Texas 75028

Oak Hill Native Plant Nursery
792 Oakdale Drive Sunset Valley West
Austin, Texas 78745

Prairie Restoration
6508 Welch
Fort Worth, Texas 76133

Scherz Landscape Company
2225 Knickerbocker Road
San Angelo, Texas 76904

Sharp Brothers Seed Company
4378 Canyon Drive
Amarillo, Texas 79109

329

Texas Natives
910 Glen Oak
Austin, Texas 78745

Wildseed, Inc.
16819 Barker Springs
Suite 218
Houston, Texas 77084
(*seed now available in small packets at many
nurseries*)

Yucca Do Nursery
at Peckerwood Gardens
P.O. Box 655
Waller, Texas 77484

Butterfly Organizations, Societies, and Publications

American Entomological Society
1900 Race Street
Philadelphia, Pennsylvania 19013

The Butterfly Club of America
736 Main Avenue
Suite 200, Box 2257
Durango, Colorado 81302

Butterfly Lovers International
210 Columbus Avenue
San Francisco, California 94133

Entomological Society of America
4603 Calvert Road
College Park, Maryland 20740
Publishes: *The Bulletin of the Entomological
Society of America, Annals*, and *Journal of
Economic Entomology*, and *Environmental
Entomology*

The Entomological Society of Canada
1320 Carling Avenue
Ottawa, Canada KIZ 7K9
Publishes: *The Canadian Entomologist*

The Lepidoptera Research Foundation
c/o Santa Barbara Museum of Natural History
2559 Puesta del Sol Road
Santa Barbara, California 93105
Publishes: *The Journal of Research on the
Lepidoptera*

The Lepidopterists' Society
900 Exposition Boulevard
Los Angeles, California 90007
Publishes: *Journal of the Lepidopterists' Society*
and *News of the Lepidopterists' Society*

The Monarch Project
10 Southwest Ash Street
Portland, Oregon 97204

National Council of State Garden Clubs, Inc.
Preservation of Butterflies
4401 Magnolia Avenue
Missouri Botanical Garden
St. Louis, Missouri 63110
(*a special committee on the conservation,
preservation, and attracting of butterflies*)

Southern Lepidopterists' Society
c/o Richard Gillmore, Editor
35 South Devon Avenue
Winter Springs, Florida 32708
Publishes: *Southern Lepidopterists' News* and
Southern Lepidopterists' Bulletin

Texas Organization for Endangered Species
P.O. Box 12773
Austin, Texas 78711-2773

The Xerces Society
10 Southwest Ash Street
Portland, Oregon 97204
Publishes: *Wings* (newsletter) and *Atala*
(journal)

Young Entomologists' Society
c/o Department of Entomology
Michigan State University
East Lansing, Michigan 48824
Publishes: *Y.E.S. Quarterly*

Butterfly Events and Gardens

Austin Area Butterfly Count
(*annual Fourth of July North American Butterfly Count sponsored by The Xerces Society*)
contact Dr. Chris Durden, Coordinator, at 512-471-1075 or 512-477-3226

The Butterfly Trail
(*built for Zilker Botanical Gardens by the Texas Botanical Society*)
Austin Area Garden Council
2220 Barton Springs Road
Zilker Park
Austin, Texas 78746

Butterfly World
Tradewinds Park South
3600 West Sample Road
Coconut Creek, Florida 33073

Day Butterfly Center
Callaway Gardens
Pine Mountain, Georgia 31822

Plant Organizations, Societies, and Publications

Acadiana Native Plant Society
637 Girard Park Drive
Lafayette, Louisiana 70503

Alabama Wildflower Society
Route 2, Box 115
Northport, Alabama 35476

Arkansas Native Plant Society
c/o Department of Forest Resources
University of Arkansas at Monticello
P.O. Box 3468
Monticello, Arkansas 71655

Callaway Gardens
U.S. Highway 27
Pine Mountain, Georgia 31822

Corpus Christi Botanical Society
P.O. Box 8113
Corpus Christi, Texas 78412

El Paso Native Plant Society
c/o James F. George
6804 Tolvea
El Paso, Texas 79912

Florida Native Plant Society
Suncoast Chapter
Seffner, Florida 33584

Florida Native Plant Society
1133 West Morse Boulevard
Suite 201
Winter Park, Florida 32789

Friends of the Fort Worth Nature Center and Refuge
P.O. Box 11694
Fort Worth, Texas 76109

Garden Club of Georgia, Inc.
325 South Lumpkin Street
Athens, Georgia 30612

Houston Arboretum and Botanical Society
4501 Woodway Drive
Houston, Texas 77024

Louisiana Native Plant Society
Route 1, Box 151
Saline, Louisiana 71070
(*membership $5.00 annually, publishes newsletter*)

Mississippi Native Plant Society
Travis Salley
202 North Andrews Avenue
Cleveland, Mississippi 38732

National Council of State Garden Clubs
4401 Magnolia Avenue
St. Louis, Missouri 63110

National Wildflower Research Center
2600 FM Road 973 North
Austin, Texas 78725-9990

Native Plant Project
P.O. Box 1433
Edinburg, Texas 78540
Publishes: *Sabal* (monthly newsletter)

331

Native Plant Society of Texas
1204 South Trinity Street
Decatur, Texas 76234
(*membership $15.00 annually, regional chapters, publishes newsletter, has seed exchanges, and plant sales*)

Native Prairies Association of Texas
The Program Committee
Texas Woman's University
P.O. Box 22675
Denton, Texas 76204

North Carolina Wildflower Preservation
  Society
Totten Garden Center, 457-A
North Carolina Botanical Garden
University of North Carolina at Chapel Hill
Chapel Hill, North Carolina 27514

Oklahoma Native Plant Society
2435 South Peoria Avenue
Tulsa, Oklahoma 74114

Outdoor Nature Club
4141 South Braeswood #101
Houston, Texas 77025
(*owns Little Thicket Nature Preserve; many field trips throughout Texas*)

Tennessee Native Plant Society
Department of Botany
University of Tennessee
Knoxville, Tennessee 37996-1100

Texas Garden Clubs, Inc.
3111 Botanic Garden Road
Fort Worth, Texas 76107

Texas Organization for Endangered Species
P.O. Box 12773
Austin, Texas 78711-2773

The Wildflower Society
c/o Goldsmith Civic Garden Center
750 Cherry Road
Memphis, Tennessee 38119-4699

Xeriscape Garden Club
7200 North Mopac
Suite 450
Austin, Texas 78731

Gardening Magazines and Newsletters

Flower and Garden Magazine
4251 Pennsylvania Avenue
Kansas City, Missouri 64111

Fine Gardening
The Taunton Press
63 South Main Street
Box 355
Newton, Connecticut 06470

Gardens & More
P.O. Box 864
McKinney, Texas 75069

Growing From Seed
Thompson & Morgan
P.O. Box 1308
Jackson, New Jersey 08527

Horticulture
Walnut Street
P.O. Box 53880
Boulder, Colorado 80321-3880

Rodale's Organic Gardening
Emmaus, Pennsylvania 18099-0003

Texas Gardener
P.O. Box 9005
Waco, Texas 76714

Southern Living
Box 523
Birmingham, Alabama 35201

Wildflower
2600 FM Road 973 North
Austin, Texas 78725-9990

Gardening Supplies

Gardener's Eden
P.O. Box 7307
San Francisco, California 94120-7307

Gardener's Marketplace
Story Communications, Inc.
Schoolhouse Road
Pownal, Vermont 95261

Gardener's Supply
128 Intervale Road
Burlington, Vermont 05401

International Irrigation Systems
209 Main Street
Box 358
Amherst, Ohio 44001

Natural Gardening Research Center
Highway 48
P.O. Box 149
Sunman, Indiana 47041
(*information and supplies for biological control
of insects*)

Park Seed
P.O. Box 46
Cokesbury Road
Greenwood, South Carolina 29648-0046

Smith & Hawken
25 Corte Madera
Mill Valley, California 94941

Wayside Gardens
Hodges, South Carolina 29695-0001

Habitat Preservation

Heard Natural Science Museum
Route 6, Box 22
McKinney, Texas 75069

Native Prairies Association of Texas
The Program Committee
Texas Woman's University
P.O. Box 22675
Denton, Texas 76204

Natural Areas Preservation Association
4144 Cochran Chapel Road
Dallas, Texas 75209

Texas Committee on Natural Resources
Suite 3B
5518 Dyer
Dallas, Texas 75206

Texas Nature Conservancy
503 B East Sixth Street
Austin, Texas 78701

Texas Natural Heritage Program
General Land Office
Stephen F. Austin Building
1700 Congress Avenue
Austin, Texas 78767

Texas Organization for Endangered Species
P.O. Box 12773
Austin, Texas 78711-2773

Further Information

Arkansas Highway Department
Environmental Division
P.O. Box 2261
Little Rock, Arkansas 72203

Armand Bayou Nature Center
P.O. Box 58828
Houston, Texas 77258

City of Austin Environmental and
    Conservation Service Department
Xeriscape Program
206 East Ninth Street
Austin, Texas 78701

Florida State Maintenance Office
Department of Transportation
605 Suwannee Street
Mail Station 52
Tallahassee, Florida 32399-0450

333

Georgia Department of Transportation
#2 Capitol Square
Atlanta, Georgia 30334

Louisiana Project Wildflower
P.O. Box 3648
Lafayette, Louisiana 70502
318-233-7404

Mercer Arboretum
22306 Aldine-Westfield Road
Humble, Texas 77338

Mississippi State Highway Department
Public Affairs Division
P.O. Box 1850
Jackson, Mississippi 39215

National Wildflower Research Center
2600 FM Road North
P.O. Box 1011
Austin, Texas 78725-9990

Native Plant Project
P.O. Box 1433
Edinburg, Texas 78539

Native Plant Society of Texas
Texas Woman's University
P.O. Box 23836
Denton, Texas 76024

Oklahoma Department of Transportation
Roadside Wildflower Program
200 NE 21st Street
Oklahoma City, Oklahoma 73105

Roadside Environmental Unit
P.O. Box 25201
Raleigh, North Carolina 27611

Rodale's Organic Gardening
Resources for Organic Pest Control
Rodale Press, Inc.
Emmaus, Pennsylvania 18049
(*an important publication containing sources for
natural pest control supplies, pest control
guidelines, and so on*)

San Antonio Botanical Center
555 Funston Place
San Antonio, Texas 78209

Soil Conservation Society of America
7515 Northeast Ankeny Road
Ankeny, Iowa 50021
(*Sources of Native Seeds and Plants, $3.00 per
copy*)

Soil Conservation Service, USDA
Grant Building Room 403
611 East Sixth Street
Austin, Texas 78737

South Carolina Department of Highways and
Public Transportation
Public Affairs
P.O. Box 191
Columbia, South Carolina 29202
(*the department is increasing its roadside
plantings of wildflowers*)

South Texas Plant Materials Center
Caesar Kleberg Wildlife Research Institute
Texas A & I University
P.O. Box 218
Kingsville, Texas 78363

Tennessee Tourist Department
320 Sixth Avenue North
5th Floor
Nashville, Tennessee 37243
615-741-2158

Texas Agricultural Extension Service
Attention: Extension Horticulturist
Texas A & M University
College Station, Texas 77843

Texas A & M University
Department of Horticulture
Texas A & M University
College Station, Texas 77840

Texas Association of Nurserymen, Inc.
512 East Riverside Drive, Suite 207
Austin, Texas 78704

Texas Botanical Garden Society
P.O. Box 5642
Austin, Texas 78763
(*a butterfly trail established and a butterfly
house in preparation*)

Texas Department of Agriculture
P.O. Box 12847
Austin, Texas 78711
(*Texas Native Plant Directory*, an important
  source for nursery plants)

Texas Department of Highways
Landscape Division
Eleventh and Brazos
Austin, Texas 78701

The Texas Zoo
Victoria Riverside Park
P.O. Box 69
Victoria, Texas 77901

Travis County Extension Service
1600 B. Smith Road
Austin, Texas 78721

US Government Printing Office
Superintendent of Documents
710 North Capitol Street
Washington, DC 20402
ask for free government pamphlets on:
  PL National Parks
  PL 41 Insects
  PL 43 Forestry
  PL 44 Plants
  PL 46 Soils and Fertilizers
  PL 88 Ecology
  Home Garden Brochure

Wild Basin Wilderness Preserve
P.O. Box 13455
Austin, Texas 78711

Wildflower Hotline
Marcia Coale
McKinney, Texas
214-542-1947

Bibliography

Butterflies and Insects

Barth, Friedrich G. *Insects and Flowers.* Princeton, New Jersey: Princeton University Press, 1985.

Brewer, Jo. *Wings in the Meadow.* New York: Houghton Mifflin, 1967.

Brewer, Jo and Kjell Bloch Sandved. *Butterflies.* New York: Harry N. Abrams, 1976.

Brewer, Jo and Dave Winter. *Butterflies and Moths.* New York: Prentice Hall Press, 1986.

Christensen, James R. *A Field Guide to Butterflies of the Pacific Northwest.* Moscow, Idaho: The University Press of Idaho, 1981.

Daccordi, Mauro, Paolo Triberti, and Adriano Zanetti. *Guide to Butterflies and Moths.* New York: Simon and Schuster, 1987.

Devan, P.G. "Floral Coloration, Its Colorimetric Analysis and Significance in Anthecology." *The Pollination of Flowers by Insect.* New York: Academic Press, 1978.

Dornfeld, Ernest J. *The Butterflies of Oregon.* Forest Grove, Oregon: Timber Press, 1980.

Douglas, Mathew M. *The Lives of Butterflies.* Ann Arbor, Michigan: The University of Michigan Press, 1987.

Ehrlich, P. and A. Ehrlich. *How to Know the Butterflies.* Dubuque, Iowa: William C. Brown, 1961.

Emmel, Thomas C. *Butterflies—Their World, Their Life Cycle, Their Behavior.* New York: Alfred A. Knopf, 1975.

Faegri, K. and L. van der Pijl. *The Principles of Pollination Ecology.* New York: Pergamon Press, 1971.

Feltwell, John. *The Natural History of Butterflies.* New York: Facts on File, 1986.

Ferris, Clifford D. and F. Martin Brown. *Butterflies of the Rocky Mountain States.* Norman, Oklahoma: University of Oklahoma Press, 1981.

Field, William D. "A Manual of the Butterflies and Skippers of Kansas." *Bulletin of the University of Kansas* 39/10 (1938): 3-328. 1975.

Forey, Pamela and Cecilia Fitzsimons. *An Instant Guide to Butterflies.* New York: Bonanza Books, 1987.

Freeman, H.A. "The Distribution and Flower Preferences of the Theclinae of Texas." *Field and Lab* 18: 65–72. 1950.

Freeman, H.A. "Ecological and Systematic Study of the Hesperioidea of Texas." Dallas, Texas: *Southern Methodist University Studies* No. 6: 1-67. 1951.

Friedlander, Timothy Paul. *A Taxonomic Revision of Asterocampa Rober 1916 (Insecta, Lepidoptera, Nymphalidae).* Ph.D. Dissertation. Texas A & M University. 1985.

Gerberg, Eugene J. and Ross H. Arnette, Jr. *Florida Butterflies.* Baltimore, Maryland: Natural Science Publications, 1989.

Goodden, Robert. *The Wonderful World of Butterflies and Moths.* London: The Hamlyn Publishing Group Limited, 1977.

Goodden, Robert. *Butterflies.* Secaucus, New Jersey: Chartwell Books, 1988.

Harris, Lucien, Jr. *Butterflies of Georgia.* Norman, Oklahoma: University of Oklahoma Press, 1972.

The Hive and the Honey Bee. Hamilton, Illinois: Dadant & Sons, 1975.

Holland, W.J. *The Butterfly Book.* Garden City, New York: Doubleday, Doran & Company, 1931.

Howe, William H. *The Butterflies of North America.* New York: Doubleday, 1975.

Kimball, Charles P. *The Lepidoptera of Florida.* Gainesville, Florida: State of Florida Department of Agriculture, Division of Plant Industry, 1965.

Klots, Alexander B. *A Field Guide to the Butterflies of North America, East of the Great Plains*. Boston: Houghton Mifflin, 1951.

Knuth, Paul. *Handbook of Flower Pollination*. Volumes I, II, III. Oxford: Clarendon Press, 1906.

Kulman, H.M. "Butterfly Production Management." *Insect Ecology*. St. Paul, Minnesota: University of Minnesota Agricultural Experiment Station Technical Bulletin, 1977.

Lovell, John H. *The Flower and the Bee: Plant Life and Pollination*. New York: Charles Scribner's Sons, 1918.

Martin, E.C., E. Oertel, N.P. Nye, et al. *Beekeeping in the United States*. Washington, D.C.: U.S.D.A. Agriculture Handbook No. 335 (revised), 1980.

Miller, Lee D. and F. Martin Brown. *A Catalogue/Checklist of the Butterflies of America North of Mexico*. The Lepidopterists' Society, Memoir No. 2. Sarasota, Florida: Serbin Printing, 1981.

Mitchell, Robert T. and Herbert S. Zim. *Butterflies and Moths*. New York: Golden Press, 1964.

Opler, Paul A. and George O. Krizek. *Butterflies East of the Great Plains*. Baltimore: The Johns Hopkins University Press, 1984.

Orsak, L.J. *Butterfly Production Management in California with Emphasis on Native Plants: One Form of Urban Wildlife Enhancement*. Sacramento, California: California Native Plant Society, 1982.

Parenti, Umberto. *The World of Butterflies and Moths*. New York: G.P. Putnam's Sons, 1978.

Philbrick, Helen and John Philbrick. *The Bug Book*. Pownal, Vermont: Story Communications, 1974.

Pyle, Robert M. *The Audubon Society Field Guide to North American Butterflies*. New York: Alfred A. Knopf, 1981.

Pyle, Robert M. *The Audubon Society Handbook for Butterfly Watchers*. New York: Charles Scribner's Sons, 1984.

Richard, J. and Joan E. Heitzman. *Butterflies and Moths of Missouri*. Jefferson City, Missouri: Missouri Department of Conservation, 1987.

Saunders, Aretas A. *Butterflies of the Allegany State Park*. Albany, New York: The University of the State of New York, 1932.

Shields, Oakley. "Flower Visitation Records for Butterflies." *The Pan-Pacific Entomologist* 48: 189-203. 1972.

Shull, Ernest M. *The Butterflies of Indiana*. Bloomington, Indiana: Indiana University Press, 1987.

Smart, Paul. *The Illustrated Encyclopedia of the Butterfly World*. New York: Chartwell Books, 1984.

Tilden, J.W. and Arthur C. Smith. *A Field Guide To Western Butterflies*. Boston: Houghton Mifflin Company, 1986.

Tyler, Hamilton A. *The Swallowtail Butterflies of North America*. California: Naturegraph Publishers, 1975.

Van-Wright, Richard I. and Phillip R. Ackery, eds. "The Biology of Butterflies." *Symposium of the Royal Entomological Society Series*. London: Academic Press, 1984.

Watson, Allen. *Butterflies*. London: Kingfisher Books Limited, 1981.

Watson, Allen and Paul E.S. Whalley. *The Dictionary of Butterflies and Moths*. New York: McGraw-Hill Book Company, 1975.

Whalley, Paul. *Butterfly Watching*. London: Severn House Publishers Limited, 1980.

Also consulted were many articles from *Journal of Research on the Lepidoptera*, *News of the Lepidopterists' Society*, *Bulletin of Southern California Academy of Science*, and *Psyche*, and especially the works of Roy O. Kendall and Dr. Raymond Neck.

Gardening

Adams, W.D. "Propagation of Annual Plant Ornamentals." *Proceedings of the Texas Turfgrass Conference* 28: 85-89. College Station, Texas: Texas A & M University, Texas Turfgrass Association, 1974.

Allen, Oliver E. *Shade Gardens*. Alexandria, Virginia: Time-Life Books, 1979.

Bailey, L.H. and Ethel Zoe Bailey. *Hortus Second*. New York: The Macmillan Company, 1941.

Bailey, L.H. and Ethel Zoe Bailey. *Hortus Third*. Revised and expanded by the staff of the Liberty Hyde Bailey Hortorium. New York: Macmillan Company, 1976.

Beckett, Kenneth A., David Carr and David Stevens. *The Contained Garden*. New York: Viking Press, 1982.

Brooklyn Botanic Garden. *Gardening with Wildflowers*. Handbook No. 38. Brooklyn: Brooklyn Botanic Garden, 1979.

Brooklyn Botanic Garden. *Propagation*. Handbook No. 24. Brooklyn: Brooklyn Botanic Garden, 1982.

Bruce, Hal. *How to Grow Wildflowers and Wild Shrubs and Trees in Your Own Garden*. New York: Alfred A. Knopf, 1976.

Campbell, Stu. *The Mulch Book*. Charlotte, Vermont: Garden Way, 1974.

Crockett, James Underwood. *Crockett's Flower Garden*. New York: Little, Brown and Company, 1981.

Crockett, James Underwood, E. Oliver Allen and the editors of Time-Life Books. *Wildflower Gardening*. Alexandria, Virginia: Time-Life Books, 1977.

Curtis, Will C. *Propagation of Wild Flowers*. Farmingham, Maine: New England Wild Flower Society, 1978.

Dormon, Caroline. *Natives Preferred*. Baton Rouge, Louisiana: Claitor's Publishing Division, 1965.

Easey, Ben. *Practical Organic Gardening*. London: Faber and Faber, 1976.

Editors of Sunset Books and Sunset Magazine. *Garden Color, Annuals and Perennials*. Menlo Park, California: Lane Publishing, 1981.

Editors of Sunset Books and Sunset Magazine. *Gardening in Containers*. Menlo Park, California: Lane Publishing, 1970.

Editors of Sunset Books and Sunset Magazine. *New Western Garden Book*. Menlo Park, California: Lane Publishing, 1986.

Everett, Thomas H. and Roy Hay, eds. *Illustrated Guide to Gardening*. Pleasantville, New York: Reader's Digest, 1983.

Foster, Catherine Osgood. *Organic Flower Gardening*. Emmaus, Pennsylvania: Rodale Press, 1975.

Free, Montague. *Plant Propagation in Pictures*. Garden City, New York: Doubleday and Company, 1957.

Golueke, Clarence G. *Composting: A Study of the Process and Its Principles*. Emmaus, Pennsylvania: Rodale Press, 1972.

Gregg, Evelyn. *Bio-Dynamic Sprays*. Stroudsburg, Pennsylvania: Bio-Dynamic Farming and Gardening Association.

Gregg, Richard. *Companion Plants and How to Use Them*. Old Greenwich, Connecticut: Devon-Adair, 1966.

Gupton, Oscar and Fred Swope. *Wildflowers of the Shenandoah Valley and Blue Ridge Mountains*. Charlottesville, Virginia: University Press of Virginia, 1982.

Haring, Elda. *The Complete Book of Growing Plants from Seed*. Grandview, Missouri: University Books, 1967.

Hartmann, Hudson T. and Dale E. Kester. *Plant Propagation, Principles and Practices*. Englewood Cliffs, New Jersey: Prentice-Hall, 1959.

Heger, M. "Propagating Perennial Plants." *Minnesota Horticulture* 105(7): 194-195. 1977.

Hill, Madelene, Gwen Barclay and Jean Hardy. *Southern Herb Growing*. Fredericksburg, Texas: Shearer Publishing, 1987.

Kramer, Jack. *Hanging Gardens*. Piscataway, New Jersey: New Century Publishers, 1982.

Kramer, Jack. *The Natural Way to Pest-Free Gardening*. New York: Scribner's, 1972.

Martin, Laura. *The Wildflower Meadow Book, A Gardener's Guide*. Charlotte, North Carolina: East Woods Press, 1986.

Newman, L.H. *Create a Butterfly Garden*. London: Billing and Sons, 1967.

Nokes, Jill. *How to Grow Native Plants of Texas and the Southwest*. Austin, Texas: Texas Monthly Press, 1986.

Odenwald, Neil and James Turner. *Identification, Selection, and Use of Southern Plants for Landscape Design*. Baton Rouge, Louisiana: Claitor's Publishing Division, 1987.

Organic Gardening and Farming Magazine. *The Complete Book of Composting.* Emmaus, Pennsylvania: Rodale Press, 1971.

Organic Gardening and Farming Magazine. *The Organic Way to Plant Protection.* Emmaus, Pennsylvania: Rodale Press, 1966.

Ortho Books. *Landscaping with Wildflowers and Native Plants.* San Francisco: Ortho Books, 1984.

Phillips, Harry R. *Growing and Propagating Wild Flowers.* Chapel Hill, North Carolina: University of North Carolina Press, 1985.

Phillips, Judith. *Southwestern Landscaping with Native Plants.* Santa Fe, New Mexico: Museum of New Mexico Press, 1987.

Proctor, John and Susan Proctor. *Color in Plants and Flowers.* New York: Everest House, 1978.

Reilly, Ann. *Park's Success with Seeds.* Greenwood, South Carolina: Park Seed Co., 1978.

Ricker, P.L. "The Seeds of Wildflowers." In USDA *Yearbook of Agriculture: Seeds.* Washington, D.C.: U.S. Government Printing Office, 1961.

Rodale, J.I., ed. *Getting the Bugs out of Organic Gardening.* Emmaus, Pennsylvania: Rodale Press, 1973.

Rodale, J.I., ed. *The Organic Way to Mulching.* Emmaus, Pennsylvania: Rodale Press, 1972.

Smyser, Carol A. *Nature's Design.* Emmaus, Pennsylvania: Rodale Press, 1982.

Sperry, Neil. *Neil Sperry's Complete Guide to Texas Gardening.* Dallas, Texas: Taylor Publishing Company, 1982.

Sperry, Neil. *Neil Sperry's Complete Guide to Texas Gardening.* Second edition (revised). Dallas, Texas: Taylor Publishing Company, 1991.

Sullivan, Gene A. and Richard H. Daley. *Directory to Resources on Wildflower Propagation.* National Council of State Garden Clubs. St. Louis, Missouri: Missouri Botanical Garden, 1981.

Taylor, Kathryn S. and Stephen F. Hamblin. *Handbook of Wild Flower Cultivation.* New York: Macmillan Company, 1963.

Tekulsky, Mathew. *The Butterfly Garden.* Boston: The Harvard Common Press, 1985.

Tenebaum, Frances. *Gardening with Wild Flowers.* New York: Charles Scribner and Sons, 1973.

Terrell, Mrs. Arthur P., ed. *A Garden Book for Houston and the Gulf Coast.* River Oaks Garden Club. Houston, Texas: Pacesetter Press, 1975.

Wasowski, Sally and Julie E. Ryan. *Landscaping with Native Texas Plants.* Austin, Texas: Texas Monthly Press, 1985.

Wasowski, Sally with Andy Wasowski. *Native Texas Plants: Landscaping Region by Region.* Austin, Texas: Texas Monthly Press, 1988.

Webster, Bob. *The South Texas Garden Book.* San Antonio, Texas: Corona Publishing Company, 1980.

Welch, William C. *Perennial Garden Color.* Dallas, Texas: Taylor Publishing Company, 1989.

Wildseed. *A Grower's Guide to Wildflowers.* Houston, Texas: Wildseed, Inc., 1988.

Wilson, William H.W. *Landscaping with Wildflowers and Native Plants.* San Francisco, California: Ortho Books, 1984.

Wyman, Donald. *Wyman's Gardening Encyclopedia.* New York: Macmillan, 1971.

Yepsen, Roger B., Jr. *Organic Plant Protection.* Emmaus, Pennsylvania: Rodale Press, 1976.

Plant and Wildflower Guides

Abbott, Carroll. *How to Know and Grow Texas Wildflowers.* Kerrville, Texas: Green Horizons Press.

Ajilvsgi, Geyata. *Wild Flowers of the Big Thicket, East Texas, and Western Louisiana.* College Station, Texas: Texas A&M University Press, 1979.

Ajilvsgi, Geyata. *Wildflowers of Texas.* Fredericksburg, Texas: Shearer Publishing, 1984.

Arzeni, Charles B. and Terri M. Simon. *Plants of Mexico.* Charleston, Illinois: Eastern Illinois University, 1974.

Bell, C. Ritchie. *Florida Wild Flowers.* Chapel Hill, North Carolina: Laurel Hill Press, 1982.

Bragg, Louis H. and Robert L. Neill. *The Herbaceous Flowering Plants of the Buescher Division.* Smithville, Texas: The University of Texas System Cancer Center, 1979.

Brown, C.A. *Wildflowers of Louisiana and Adjoining States.* Baton Rouge, Louisiana: Louisiana State University Press, 1972.

Cliffe, Harry, ed. *A Plant List for Bexar County, Texas.* San Antonio, Texas: Native Plant Society of Texas, 1986.

Corell, D.S. and M.C. Johnston. *Manual of the Vascular Plants of Texas.* Renner, Texas: Texas Research Foundation, 1970.

Cox, Paul and Patty Leslie. *Texas Trees: A Friendly Guide.* San Antonio, Texas: Corona Publishing, 1988.

Dean, Blanche, Amy Mason and Joab Thomas. *Wildflowers of Alabama and Adjoining States.* University, Alabama: The University of Alabama Press, 1973.

Duncan, Wilbur and Leonard Foote. *Wildflowers of the Southeastern United States.* Athens, Georgia: The University of Georgia Press, 1975.

Enquist, Marshall. *Wildflowers of the Texas Hill Country.* Austin, Texas: Lone Star Botanical, 1987.

Fleetwood, Raymond J. *Plants of Santa Ana National Wildlife Refuge, Hidalgo County, Texas.* Alamo, Texas: United States Department of the Interior, Fish and Wildlife Service.

Gould, Frank W. *The Grasses of Texas.* College Station, Texas: Texas A&M University Press, 1975.

Gupton, Oscar and Fred Swope. *Wildflowers of the Shenandoah Valley and Blue Ridge Mountains.* Charlottesville, Virginia: University Press of Virginia, 1982.

Ham, Hal. *South Texas Wildflowers.* Kingsville, Texas: Conner Museum, Texas A&I University, 1984.

Hatch, Stephen L., Kancheepuram N. Gandhi and Larry E. Brown. *Checklist of the Vascular Plants of Texas.* College Station, Texas: Texas A&M University, The Texas Agricultural Experiment Station.

Howes, F.N. *Plants and Beekeeping.* London and Boston, Massachusetts: Faber and Faber, 1979.

Jones, Fred B. *Flora of the Texas Coastal Bend.* Sinton, Texas: Welder Wildlife Foundation, 1975.

Justice, William and C. Ritchie Bell. *Wild Flowers of North Carolina.* Chapel Hill: The University of North Carolina Press, 1983.

Kartesz, John T. and Rosemarie Kartesz. *A Synonymized Checklist of the Vascular Flora of the United States, Canada, and Greenland.* Chapel Hill, North Carolina: The University of North Carolina Press, 1980.

Loughmiller, Campbell and Lynn Loughmiller. *Texas Wildflowers.* Austin, Texas: University of Texas Press, 1984.

Lynch, Brother Daniel. *Native and Naturalized Woody Plants of Austin & the Hill Country.* Austin, Texas: Acorn Press, 1981.

Lynch, Brother Daniel. *Plants of Austin, Texas.* Austin, Texas: St. Edwards University, 1974.

Mahler, William F. *Keys to the Vascular Plants of the Black Gap Wildlife Management Area, Brewster County, Texas.* Dallas, Texas: Southern Methodist University, 1973.

Mahler, William F. *Flora of Taylor County, Texas.* Dallas, Texas: Southern Methodist University, 1973.

Mahler, William F. *Shinners' Manual of the North Central Texas Flora.* Dallas, Texas: Southern Methodist University Herbarium, 1984.

Mahler, William F. *Shinners' Manual of the North Central Texas Flora.* Fort Worth, Texas: Botanical Research Institute of Dallas, 1988.

Martin, William C. and Charles R. Hutchins. *Spring Wild Flowers of New Mexico.* Albuquerque, New Mexico: University of New Mexico Press, 1984.

Mason, Charles T., Jr., and Patricia B. Mason. *A Handbook of Mexican Roadside Flora.* Tucson, Arizona: University of Arizona Press, 1987.

McCoy, Doyle. *Roadside Trees and Shrubs of Oklahoma.* Norman, Oklahoma: University of Oklahoma Press, 1981.

McDougall, W.B. and Omer E. Sperry. *Plants of Big Bend National Park.* Washington, D.C.: U.S. Government Printing Office, 1951.

Meier, Leo and Jan Reid. *Texas Wildflowers.* Australia: Weldon Owen Publishing Limited, 1989.

National Wildflower Research Center. *Wildflower Handbook.* Austin, Texas: Texas Monthly Press, 1989.

Niering, William A. and Nancy C. Olmstead. *The Audubon Society Field Guide to North American Wildflowers—Eastern Region.* New York: Alfred A. Knopf, 1979.

Nixon, Elray. *Trees, Shrubs and Woody Vines of East Texas.* Nacogdoches, Texas: Bruce Lyndon Cunningham Productions, 1985.

Parker, Lucile. *Mississippi Wildflowers.* Gretna, Louisiana: Pelican Publishing Company, 1981.

Parks, H.B. *Valuable Plants Native to Texas.* Bulletin No. 551. College Station, Texas: Texas Agricultural Experiment Station, 1937.

Pellett, Frank C. *American Honey Plants.* Hamilton, Illinois: American Bee Journal, 1930.

Pesman, Walter M. *Flora Mexicana.* Globe, Arizona: Dale S. King, 1962.

Peterson, Charles D. and Larry E. Brown. *Vascular Flora of the Little Thicket Nature Sanctuary, San Jacinto County, Texas.* Houston, Texas: Brunswick Press Inc., 1983.

Powell, A.M. *Trees and Shrubs of Trans-Pecos Texas.* Big Bend National Park, Texas: Big Bend Natural History Association, 1988.

Radford, Albert, Harry Ahles and C. Ritchie Bell. *Manual of the Vascular Flora of the Carolinas.* Chapel Hill, North Carolina: The University of North Carolina Press, 1983.

Rechenthin, C.A. *Native Flowers of Texas.* Temple, Texas: U.S. Department of Agriculture, Soil Conservation Service, 1972.

Rickett, H.W. *Wild Flowers of the United States: Vol. 2, The Southeastern States.* New York: McGraw-Hill, 1967.

Rickett, H.W. *Wild Flowers of the United States: Vol. 3, Texas.* New York: McGraw-Hill, 1969.

Rose, Francis L. and Russell W. Strandtmann. *Wildflowers of the Llano Estacado.* Dallas, Texas: Taylor Publishing Company, 1986.

Sanborn, C.E. *Texas Honey Plants.* College Station, Texas: Texas Agricultural Experiment Station, Bulletin No. 102, 1908.

Simpson, Benny J. *A Field Guide to Texas Trees.* Austin, Texas: Texas Monthly Press, 1988.

Smith, Arlo. *A Guide to Wildflowers of the Mid-South.* Memphis, Tennessee: Memphis State University Press, 1979.

Spellenberg, Richard. *The Audubon Society Field Guide to North American Wildflowers—Western Region.* New York: Alfred A. Knopf, 1979.

Stanley, Paul C. *Trees and Shrubs of Mexico.* Washington, D.C.: Contributions, U.S. National Herbarium, U.S. Government Printing Office, 1920-1926.

Steffek, Edwin F. *The New Wild Flowers and How to Grow Them.* Portland, Oregon: Timber Press, 1983.

Stevens, William Chase. *Kansas Wild Flowers.* Lawrence, Kansas: University of Kansas Press, 1948.

Stupka, Arthur. *Trees, Shrubs, and Woody Vines of Great Smoky Mountains National Park.* Knoxville, Tennessee: The University of Tennessee Press, 1964.

Taylor, R. John and Constance E.S. Taylor. *An Annotated List of the Ferns, Fern Allies, Gymnosperms, and Flowering Plants of Oklahoma.* Durant, Oklahoma: Southeastern Oklahoma State University, 1991.

Texas Department of Agriculture. *Texas Native Tree and Plant Directory.* Austin, Texas, 1986.

Thomas, R. Dale and Charles M. Allen. "A Preliminary Checklist of the Dictoyledons of Louisiana." *Contributions of the Herbarium of Northeast Louisiana University.* Number 3. Monroe, Louisiana: Northeast Louisiana University, Department of Biology, 1982.

Tondera, Bonnie, Laura French and Michael Gibson. *Wildflowers of North Alabama.* Huntsville, Alabama: Desk-Top Publishing, 1987.

United States Department of Agriculture. *Common Weeds of the United States.* New York: Dover, 1971.

United States Department of Agriculture. *Seeds of Woody Plants in the United States.* Forest Service, U.S. Department of Agriculture, Agriculture Handbook No. 450. Washington, D.C.: U.S. Government Printing Office, 1974.

Vines, Robert A. *Trees, Shrubs and Woody Vines of the Southwest.* Austin, Texas: University of Texas Press, 1974.

Warnock, Barton H. *Wildflowers of the Big Bend Country, Texas.* Alpine, Texas: Sul Ross State University, 1970.

Warnock, Barton H. *Wildflowers of the Guadalupe Mountains and the Sand Dune Country, Texas.* Alpine, Texas: Sul Ross State University, 1974.

Warnock, Barton H. *Wildflowers of the Davis Mountains and Marathon Basin, Texas.* Alpine, Texas: Sul Ross State University, 1977.

Whitehouse, Eula. *Common Fall Flowers of the Coastal Bend of Texas.* Sinton, Texas: Rob and Bessie Welder Wildlife Foundation, 1962.

Wills, M.M. and H.S. Irwin. *Roadside Flowers of Texas.* Austin, Texas: University of Texas Press, 1961.

Photography

Angel, Heather. *Photographing Nature: Insects.* Hertfordshire, England: Fountain Press, 1975.

Bauer, Erwin and Peggy Bauer. *Photographing Wild Texas.* Austin, Texas: University of Texas Press, 1985.

Blacklock, Craig and Nadine Blacklock. *Photographing Wildflowers.* Minneapolis, Minnesota: Voyageur Press, 1987.

Miller, George Oxford. *Texas Photo Safaris.* Austin, Texas: Texas Monthly Press, 1986.

O'Toole, Christopher and Ken Preston-Mafham. *Insects in Camera.* Oxford: Oxford University Press, 1985.

Shaw, John. *The Nature Photographer's Complete Guide to Professional Field Techniques.* New York: American Photographic Book Publishing, 1984.

Shaw, John. *Closeups in Nature.* New York: American Photographic Book Publishing, 1987.

Outdoor Photography
Werner & Werner Corp.
162 Ventura Boulevard
Suite 201
Encino, California 01436
(*This is the best magazine on nature photography and it frequently has articles on photographing insects, including butterflies.*)

Index